Cognitive Approaches to Reading

Edited by

JOHN R. BEECH and ANN M. COLLEY

Department of Psychology, University of Leicester

JOHN WILEY & SONS

Chichester · New York · Brisbane · Toronto · Singapore

Library of Congress Catologing-in-Publication Data:

Cognitive approaches to reading.
  Includes indexes.
  1. Reading, Psychology of. I. Beech, John R.
II. Colley, Ann M.
BF456.R2C56   1987   153.6   87−8182
ISBN 0 471 91169 0

British Library Cataloguing in Publication Data:

Cognitive approaches to reading.
  1. Reading, Psychology of
  I. Beech, John R. II. Colley, Ann M.
  428.4′01′9   BF456.R2
  ISBN 0 471 91169 0

Typeset by Woodfield Graphics, Fontwell, Arundel, West Sussex.
Printed and bound in Great Britain by Biddles Ltd, Guildford, Surrey.

List of Contributors

John R. Beech: *Department of Psychology, University of Leicester, Leicester LE1 7RH, England*

Peter Bryant: *Department of Experimental Psychology, University of Oxford, South Parks Road, Oxford OX1 3UD, England*

Ann M. Colley: *Department of Psychology, University of Leicester, Leicester LE1 7RH, England*

Meredyth Daneman: *Department of Psychology, University of Toronto, Erindale College, Mississauga, Ontario L5L 1C6, Canada*

Usha Goswami: *Department of Experimental Psychology, University of Oxford, OX1 3UD, England*

Charles Hulme: *Department of Psychology, University of York, Heslington, York YO1 5DD, England*

Alan Kennedy: *Department of Psychology, University of Dundee, Dundee DD1 4HN, Scotland*

John C. Marshall: *Neuropsychology Unit, Neuroscience Group, The Radcliffe Infirmary, Woodstock Road, Oxford OX2 6HE, England*

Don C. Mitchell: *Department of Psychology, University of Exeter, Washington Singer Laboratories, Exeter EX4 4QG, England*

Philip H.K. Seymour: *Department of Psychology, University of Dundee, Dundee DD1 4HN, Scotland*

Christine M. Temple: *Department of Psychology, Royal Holloway and Bedford New College, University of London, Egham Hill, Egham, Surrey TW20 0EX, England and Neuropsychology Unit, Radcliffe Infirmary, Oxford, England*

Andrew W. Young: *Department of Psychology, University of Lancaster, Lancaster LA1 4YF, England*

Contents

Introduction

JOHN R. BEECH and ANN M. COLLEY

Over the last decade or so experimental and theoretical work in cognitive psychology has expanded rapidly. This discipline, which is concerned with all cognitive processes such as memory, thought, attention, reading, and so on, has perhaps been the fastest growing area within psychology, to the extent that other areas within psychology are now applying some of these techniques and theoretical approaches. The rapid growth of cognitive psychology is reflected in its increasing contribution to the study of reading. Laboratory-based investigations into the component processes of reading such as word recognition, syntactic analysis and memory have been paralleled by more applied investigations into the development of reading skill, disorders of reading and the effects of cerebral injury on reading. Many recent theoretical developments have evolved from the integration of information from these two lines of enquiry. The present volume is an attempt to give an up-to-date account of the major contributions of cognitive psychology towards the understanding of the reading process. Some current theoretical approaches stress the importance of interactions between component processes. The authors in this volume give such interactions due consideration although they do not focus explicitly on them.

John Marshall's chapter begins the book by examining written language from a cultural and biological viewpoint. He notes that spoken language is pervasive among all normal children across all cultures but that the prevalence of literacy is both historically brief and elitist. He makes many more comparisons: for instance, a contrast between spoken and written language is that one seems to be acquired almost effortlessly whereas the other requires explicit instruction in a systematic manner. This leads him to the conclusion that spoken language develops within the ambit of a module (that is, a semi-independently operating subsystem) which develops mainly biologically. By contrast, acquiring the skills of reading and writing requires much more effort and is mastered via purposeful and integrated teaching from adults.

Marshall goes on to discuss the use of sign language to make the point that development in the deaf, neurologically and psychologically, is analogous to the development of spoken language in normal children. Therefore, in accounting for the biological artificiality of written language, the fact that it requires the use of the visual modality cannot be invoked as an explanation in itself for the difference between written and spoken language. Marshall goes on to hint that our approach towards teaching children to read may have precipitated the 'artificiality' of acquiring written language. Given some rare instances in which children have developed oral language in conjunction with an expanding sight vocabulary, he wonders whether this could lead to the same effortless acquisition of written language for all children as is the case for spoken language.

The discussion turns to the work on the acquired dyslexias and dysgraphias. These are reading and writing disorders appearing in some previously fluent readers due to illness or accident. Accounts of these have depended on the notion of separate modules with particular functions; in particular, three routes (i.e. 'phonic', 'direct' and 'lexical') are suggested for each of the reading and writing systems. The evidence from the acquired dyslexias and dysgraphias suggests selective damage to these modules and there is also evidence for some variation in their development. Similarly, the demands of different types of orthographies place different kinds of demands on the use of these modules. In the case of developmental dyslexia, could impairments in a specific module affect development of the remaining components? Marshall gives this issue due consideration.

Marshall also makes the point that information-processing accounts of reading and writing have concentrated mainly on the analysis of words, rather than the processing of sentences or text. This level of processing, he believes, is nearly always implied by pathological performance. Philip Seymour, in the second chapter, deals with the processes involved in the recognition of words.

One view that has been held about word recognition processes is that the letters constituting a word are converted to a phonological code and that this code is used to access the meaning of the word. One criticism of this view is that English orthography is too irregular for this to be feasible. Another is that phonological dyslexics are unable to read pseudo-words even though they are able to read real words fluently, demonstrating fluent reading (or lexical access) in the absence of a capability of translating letters to sounds. Seymour concludes that the initial level of analysis for the normal reader must be morphemic, representing the entire word or at least the word's stem and affixes. In the case of normal readers reading non-words, this would require the ability to translate letters into 'phonologically significant segments'. The evidence is not clear whether this implies the operation of distinctive systems or one system operating on units which vary in size and complexity.

Seymour describes experiments involving the presentation of words which are normal, zigzagged or vertical. These format distortions should affect visual processing but not semantic or phonological coding. The evidence indicated that the distorted words were normalized in some manner before being recognized by adult readers. By contrast, beginning readers varied in the extent to which they were affected by these format distortions (Seymour and Elder, 1986), suggesting coding of the features of individual letters and word length rather than by means of letter identity and location. The format distortion effect is also discussed in relation to specific types of reading impairment. In the case of normal readers identifying non-words in a task in which a decision has to be made whether a word is a real word (called the 'lexical decision task'), it seems that if there are no vowels present the decision to reject is made quite quickly; however, the presence of vowels in the non-word leads to a process of checking the legality of the initial consonants before proceeding to the terminal clusters.

A major component of word recognition is the 'recognition interface', which contains a large number of units representing the words in an individual's sight vocabulary. This level of analysis is supposed to be affected by such factors as the frequency of occurrence of a word in written language and the duration of time from the last occasion when the word was read (the 'repetition effect'). Word length and format distortion, by contrast, are considered to be factors affecting the initial visual analysis of the word. However, present evidence suggests that word frequency has an effect on the retrieval of a phonological code during the course of output, whereas the repetition effect seems to be affecting the visual analysis stage, with the proviso that this depends on the definition of the operations under the control of this stage. Seymour goes on to outline his model based on these and other conclusions.

The next few chapters in the book are concerned with higher levels of processing of text. Meredyth Daneman's chapter focuses on the role of the temporary storage of information during the reading and analysis of text. As in previous chapters, we have to invoke the concept of subsystems, this time in order to conceptualize the operation of working memory (Baddeley, 1981, 1983). These subsystems consist of a central executive, an articulatory loop and a visuo-spatial scratch pad. These last two are subsidiary slave systems for the maintenance of phonological and visuo-spatial information, respectively, while the central executive processes and stores information. This kind of model acknowledges a relationship between the ability to store information temporarily and the demands imposed by processing related information. Thus an individual who is inefficient in executing certain processing operations will have a reduced capacity for holding important information temporarily. To test this notion, Daneman and Carpenter (1980) gave subjects sets of sentences to read aloud which became increasingly long. In addition, they had to remember the final word in each set. A reasonable correlation was found between reading comprehension of the sentences and memory span for these final words. Further research related this measure of memory span to the ability to reference a pronoun, indicating that readers with a large span were also able to keep the referential concept active for a longer duration. Daneman also discusses other relationships with reading memory span and other factors associated with processing and integrating text.

She reviews research on the articulatory loop. During reading, a subcomponent of the articulatory loop is the articulatory control process. This functions as a letter-to-sound transformer and also as a maintainer of this generated phonological information by the use of subvocal rehearsal. However, evidence suggests that the articulatory loop is not used in normal adult reading but may be used by fluent readers to assist with increased textual complexity. Furthermore, Daneman believes that it plays an important role for the beginning reader and that a deficiency in the articulatory loop is a major factor in producing reading disability.

Further research is described by Daneman which examines three new measures of working memory (verbal, math and spatial span) and their relationship with reading and vocabulary. The criterion tasks were verbal and it was found that the verbal working memory measure was most closely related, the math measure less so and the spatial measure not at all. This finding rules out the notion of a central processor, whereby these various working memory measures would have all successfully predicted reading skill. Instead it is argued that there are two separate processors, one for verbal-symbolic information (which also involves reading) and the other for spatial information. Daneman has also found that eliminating the memory component in the three working memory tasks makes no difference to the association with reading and vocabulary and concludes, perhaps somewhat ruefully, that research should focus more on memory processes rather than storage in the future.

Don Mitchell's chapter focuses on syntactic analysis. He starts by reviewing theories of parsing and outlines the major areas of controversy, which he then considers in the light of the empirical evidence. One issue that is raised by consideration of the various approaches to parsing is whether parsing is deterministic in the sense of being committed to a single hypothesis about the structure of a particular phrase. Most theorists do not believe so and would prefer a non-deterministic views of the process, whereby an initial hypothesis is abandoned if unsatisfactory and the material is then reanalysed. Mitchell presents evidence to support this view. His conclusions lead him to propose that there must be at least two stages of parsing and that in the second the initial interpretation is evaluated and rejected if incorrect.

He next examines the influence on parsing of semantic/pragmatic information and of detailed lexical information, and where in the parsing process they exert their influence. Rayner, Carlson and Frazier (1983) used eye-monitoring techniques which enabled them to observe how long subjects spent fixating upon different parts of sentences. They demonstrated that subjects dwelt longer on parts of sentences where ambiguities occurred, not during initial fixations (or first-pass eye movements) but during subsequent refixations (or second-pass eye movements). This indicates that semantic/pragmatic factors come into play during second-stage parsing. Mitchell argues that lexical factors in all probability also have their influence in this stage.

The final part of Mitchell's chapter consists of an attempt to put together a psychologically realistic model of parsing which incorporates two stages. The director formulates the original hypothesis while the monitor detects information inconsistent with this hypothesis and accesses lexical and pragmatic/semantic information in doing so. Two neurological syndromes, conduction aphasia and Broca's aphasia, are examined within the framework of this model and are found to lend some tentative support to Mitchell's notion of two stages.

Word recognition, temporary storage of information in working memory and syntactic analysis all contribute to the achievement of comprehension. In the fifth chapter, Ann Colley considers the higher-order text level processes which allow the construction of an internal representation of written material. The reader must have relevant background knowledge in order to understand text. The use of such knowledge in the production of inferences to 'fill in' detail not explicit in text is illustrated. She goes on to outline how background knowledge is stored and accessed and discusses the use of schema theory as a framework for the comprehension process. A major problem with schema theory is that it is so vaguely described that it barely provides a descriptive framework, and is certainly not a theory in any true sense. Recent work in artificial intelligence such as that of Schank (1982) is starting to provide a fuller description of schematic knowledge structures.

One issue which has resulted in extensive debate concerns the possible role of knowledge of the form and conventions of text in the comprehension process. Most of the research in this area has used narrative text, and story grammars have been proposed by a number of investigators to provide a syntactic analysis of story structure and a framework for comprehension. Colley reviews the criticisms which have been levelled against this approach, and concludes that there is no evidence that knowledge of the form of text is used during comprehension. This could, however, be due to the lack of research using textual forms other than stories.

In order for comprehension to succeed, the text itself must be coherent. In the next section an examination is made of the different factors which contribute to this coherence on both a global and local level. There is evidence that coherence requirements may vary with type of text, and one gap in our knowledge concerns the nature of this relationship and its role in the comprehension process. In the final section of her chapter, Colley discusses how a representation of text might be constructed. This discussion focuses on the framework proposed by van Dijk and Kintsch (1983) who suggest, in common with Johnson-Laird (1983), that both a linguistic representation of the text itself and a cognitive model of the information it portrays are constructed during comprehension.

In Chapter 6, Andrew Young examines cerebral hemisphere differences in reading skills. He draws evidence from case studies with neurological patients and from divided visual field studies with normal subjects. Problems with methodology and interpretation are rife in this area. In common with other language disorders, impairments in reading occur mainly after left hemisphere injury, although right hemisphere injury can result in some general problems with language comprehension. Commissurotomy (split-brain) and hemispherectomy (removal of a cerebral hemisphere) operations allow the opportunity to look at the two hemispheres independently, although there are problems of interpretation with these. After early left hemispherectomy, much language function recovers. The resulting language abilities do not, however, necessarily reflect the normal abilities of the right hemisphere since there may have been some reorganization of function pre- or postoperatively. There is also the possibility of subcortical left hemisphere structures continuing to function or of some concomitant damage to the right hemisphere reducing its function also. Young manages to draw some general conclusions concerning the language abilities of the right hemisphere from the large and confusing literature on neurological patients. Under certain circumstances it seems that it can support a reasonable level of language ability, that right hemisphere reading ability is poor in relation to its speech comprehension, and that reading based on the right hemisphere is not just simply worse than normal but is also different.

In normal subjects, a common finding is that there is a right visual field (left hemisphere) superiority for the tachistoscopic presentation of words in right-handed people. This is true for both naming and lexical-decision tasks. A number of different studies and techniques have tried to isolate which of the necessary constituent abilities is responsible for this finding. Evidence from these is compatible with clinical findings. Both cerebral hemispheres seem able to identify letters but the left hemisphere is more sensitive to orthographic structure. Research has pointed to possible differences in lexical access between the two hemispheres which have led investigators to ask whether they have separate lexicons. Results from studies of word-class effects and priming experiments are suggestive of a right hemisphere lexicon, but are not consistent. Young concludes that, in normal right-handed people, the cerebral mechanisms for reading depend upon the left hemisphere. The role of the right hemisphere in normal reading is not clear, but it can support language abilities when the left hemisphere is injured or removed in childhood.

The analysis of eye movements during reading has made some dramatic recent advances, according to Alan Kennedy in Chapter 7. For instance, present technology enables an experimenter to display text on a computer screen in such a manner that what is displayed is contingent on precisely where the subject fixates on the screen, enabling the investigation of the time and location of the decision-making process. Kennedy distinguishes between first-pass and second-pass eye movements. During the first encounter with text, the subject is aware of the lengths of words as the eye tends to fixate slightly to the left of the centre of a word in between saccades. Control of these saccades seems to be fairly precise and is influenced by physical aspects of the text, such as location, as well as by its meaning and syntax. An intriguing question concerns the integration of the successive 'snapshots' of textual information. To all intents and purposes the saccadic movement breaks the visual input, to give an impression of a succession of windows containing text; but how is this information integrated? Kennedy discounts the explanation which suggests that visual features extracted during one fixation are matched to features extracted during the next, a spatial computation then helping to generate an internal model of the contents of the page. He discounts this model on the evidence that changing visual features by altering the case of individual letters during a saccade is neither noticed by the subject nor affects performance. However, this would not discount a model in which letter identification is processed during first-pass fixations before undergoing the generation of an internal model of the layout of the page.

Second-pass eye movements are produced by saccades in the reverse direction due to either a small correction as a result of target location movement or to higher-order processing of the text. It would seem that the accuracy of landing in the appropriate position after a second-pass saccade is not affected by the extent of the saccade, at least within the range of 10–70 character positions (Kennedy and Murray, 1986), suggesting accurate memory for the location of previously presented words.

Kennedy proposes a spatial coding hypothesis to account for the second-pass saccade, suggesting that location of text is stored so that it may be retrieved at a later point in order to deal with an ambiguity. From this view, a reinspection assists a reconstruction of the meaning of the text and it reduces demands on working memory by retaining lower-order textual information via physical location. Kennedy reports recent unpublished work carried out in collaboration with Wayne Murray, pertinent to this hypothesis, which examined eye movements of poor readers aged 10–11 years and of reading age and chronological age controls matched for non-verbal IQ. They found marked differences in eye movements between the normal readers and the controls of the same age. This might simply be due to differences in reading experience; however, this makes their finding that the younger reading age controls behaved more like the good readers than the poor readers all the more interesting. Kennedy concludes that there is the possibility that an inability to code by location may be a cause of reading failure.

The next three chapters in the book examine reading development and reading disorders. In the first of these John Beech makes an examination of early reading development. After describing the prerequisites (or the relative lack of them) necessary to begin reading and the various main teaching methods, an outline is given of the processes involved in learning the meaning of printed words. This involves 'discrimination net guessing', initially by discriminating a region of difference between two similar words. With increasing knowledge of different word patterns, there is an expanding database for each word storing such information as word length and the relative positions of pertinent characters as well as information about common combinations between letters. A useful adjunct to the development of a reading vocabulary is the development of the skill of translating graphemes into their corresponding phonemes, if only as a device for decoding words that cannot be retrieved lexically. However, it seems that the fluent reader need not have such a mechanism, as in the case of the phonological dyslexic who is a fluent reader but who has difficulty in reading non-words (Campbell and Butterworth, 1985).

In view of the following chapter by Bryant and Goswami, only a brief examination is made of the relationship between reading development and the level of ability in processing phonemes. Phonemic-processing ability enables words to be decoded into individual sounds and this should lead to an ability to decode printed words into their individual sounds. A review of the role of contextual knowledge in the development of reading skills is then given, followed by an elaboration of the model of LaBerge and Samuels (1974), which has been very influential as a theoretical framework for reading development. One problem with this model is the lack of consideration of how embryonic modules performing certain specialized functions might develop. To this end, Beech proposes that two distinctive forms of processing might develop some common processes, at least in the early phase of reading development. These systems would consist of a system for grapheme–phoneme translation and another for lexical analysis. The common processing would take place particularly for the initial visual analysis of the letters constituting a word. The disparity between the modes emerges at the phonological stage. Letter-to-sound conversion, by its nature, would generate sequences of phonological representations, whereas the phonological representation elicited from reading vocabulary, as it comes from a semantic representation, could be retrieved and generated from the oral lexicon. How such modules might develop and co-function is discussed further. A consideration is also given to reading by means of analogy. Certain implications are drawn from the use of such a strategy, for instance the aforementioned expanding database for each word might also accrue information concerning words with analogous orthographic sequences and pronunciation. Finally, it is proposed that the development of particular processes may not occur in a set sequence, as is often proposed, but may depend on the teaching environment or simply the proclivity of the individual child.

As discussed earlier, an awareness that words are composed of individual sounds should be an important aspect of decoding print. In Chapter 9, Peter Bryant and Usha Goswami assess the evidence for such a connection, initially making the explicit hypothesis that a problem in phonological awareness causes or partially causes a problem in reading. A direct test would be to train children in phonological awareness and monitor the consequent effect on reading. They critically examine studies which have done this, but note that only two of them trained phonological awareness *per se* and used a realistic reading measure. These suggest only a weak connection.

The authors discuss the problem of establishing causality to support their hypothesis. A first step to establishing a causal connection is to produce a correlation between the salient variables controlling for other variables such as IQ. However, a correlation would not constitute sufficient evidence for causality in itself. A survey of the literature establishes an association across a variety of paradigms. To establish a causal relationship it is necessary to carry out experiments which usually require much more investment of effort. These involve training the subjects, as previously described, or undergoing a longitudinal examination. The longitudinal study might find a connection between a preschool variable and later reading performance; however, both variables might be influenced by some third variable or other variables to produce the obtained correlation. By contrast, a training study, if successful, should establish a causal connection. However, one has to be careful to train the precise skill that is intended and, furthermore, to ensure that the training is carried out at the appropriate time and is of sufficient quality and duration. A third way is to make a comparison between poor readers and younger children of the same reading age. The authors argue that finding an impairment in a particular skill in poor readers relative to the reading age controls would demonstrate a substantial disadvantage, considering that their mental age is actually superior; whereas, a lack of difference between the two groups might indicate 'no genuine deficit' in the poor readers. However, an alternative view to that of the authors would suggest that a lack of difference means that the poor readers are demonstrating a maturational lag in reading and related processes but not in other intellectual functions (Beech and Harding, 1984).

In the closing sections of their chapter, Bryant and Goswami examine individual differences in reading style. They are cautious about examining such differences merely in terms of reading 'phonologically' or 'visually' and develop a case for analogical reading as well, particularly in young children. They link together the development of analogical relationships between words with associated phonological relationships, particularly via the use of rhyming, discussing the recent experimental work of Goswami to support this conclusion. They conclude that getting to know the form of the connections between these processes should enable the creation of the right form of training experiment.

Charles Hulme's chapter takes a broad view of the problems confronting children who are retarded in reading but not impaired in IQ, hearing and eyesight and without any abnormal problems with their environment. The retarded reader, therefore, has a reading standard which is clearly incommensurate with overall ability. After examining various methods for looking at the cause-and-effect relationship between reading and other variables, Hulme reviews the possible candidates, starting with visual problems. He notes that there is a relationship between poor readers and abnormal eye movements but rejects the notion of a deficit in eye-movement control preventing reading development. Recent work on the connection between ocular dominance and reading, which has received much publicity, is critically examined and it is concluded that if such a relationship were to exist, it would do so only for a small minority. Hulme examines other work claiming connections between various visual phenomena and reading problems, but again concludes it is a long way from establishing causality.

Possible links between short-term memory and reading problems are assessed; in particular, when decoding graphemes to phonemes, some evidence suggests that a problem in retaining the phonological code could lead to difficulties in pronouncing the whole word. There is recent evidence that memory difficulties precede reading difficulties in two recent studies, but another study has failed to find such an effect. An examination is then made of the evidence for a causal relationship between phonological skills and reading and although this is stronger than in other areas, a definite causal connection still needs to be made.

Hulme believes that given the complexity of the skill of reading, a variety of types of impairment might lead to reading problems, which in turn suggests that subtypes of reading problems might be identified. The subgroups commonly suggested correspond to the problems in phonic skills and to the inability to recognize the visual appearance of a word.

Suggestions are made as to the expected differences between such subgroups. Finally, Hulme proposes that children with problems in phonological processing ought to be given remedial training on the relevant tasks, perhaps including phonics training. The use of such multisensory techniques as tracing is advocated as well.

The final chapter reviews evidence from the alexias, already discussed briefly by Marshall. Christine Temple begins by describing deep dyslexia, a reading disorder in which patients seems no longer capable of translating graphemes to their corresponding sounds, as indicated, for example, by their inability to read non-words. This suggests that they rely entirely on their reading lexicon, or sight vocabulary, in order to read. She reviews various hypotheses put forward to account for the intricacies of the syndrome, but concludes that its complicated nature has made it less tractable to clear analysis than the other dyslexias.

Surface dyslexics have greater difficulty reading words with irregular spelling patterns than regularly spelled words. The errors they make when reading irregular words can produce a more rule-like pronunciation or, occasionally, an inappropriate pronunciation of one or more graphemes. They can confuse homophones, in that, although they may be able to read both forms correctly (e.g. *read–reed*), they have problems providing definitions of each form. Temple suggests that they are overly dependent upon phonological reading to account for this effect. Two early accounts of the syndrome suggested either the use of grapheme–phoneme conversion and/or a reliance on reading based on analogy with real words. But more recently there has been the suggestion that the unit of analysis, whether it is graphemic or phonemic or both, is more variable. It is also noted that there is sufficient variability in the symptoms of surface dyslexics to suggest that surface dyslexia is a group of different syndromes.

Phonological dyslexia is the third reading disorder which is discussed in detail. As in deep dyslexia, the phonological dyslexic has problems in reading non-words, but to a lesser degree. However, although there are indications of some impairments in semantic processing in deep dyslexics, this does not seem to arise in phonological dyslexia. Contrasting interpretations of these and other characteristics of phonological dyslexia are analysed. Finally, Temple suggests that an assumption made by neuropsychologists studying the acquired dyslexias is that the reading system consists of modules; if one is damaged, this might lead to some kind of local modification without involving the complete system.

Although the chapters in this book represent different areas of study of normal and abnormal reading, there are some areas of overlap and some themes which are common to several chapters. Undoubtedly the kinds of theories put forward are a reflection of the current state of theorizing in cognitive psychology. For instance, the concept of modularity has recurred several times in a variety of different guises. Related to this, several chapters have contrasted some kind of phonological route for reading with a lexical route. Some chapters have argued for different modules for these two contrasting routes and some have argued for the predominance of one module over another either when the readers concerned are acquired or when they are developmental dyslexics. This is not the only viewpoint to be found in the literature, for instance Marcel (1980) and others have argued for a unitary system. In Marcel's case, individual letters are processed serially and are then segmented by a parser and the resulting chunks related to lexical entries. Temple gives a more complete description of his theory.

When investigators were faced initially with the very practical problems of reading disability, they put forward relatively straightforward explanations. Subsequent laboratory experimentation and/or the discovery of further case studies has, however, served to complicate matters, or lead to the rejection of these initial hypotheses. We are now much more aware of the complexity of the reading process and its disorders. Currently there is a danger that our knowledge about reading could be building up unsystematically and without direction. One way forward might be to construct simulation programmes of our models in order to apply a more fine-grained analysis of the kinds of processes and structures which we propose. Such an approach would be very much within the ethos of cognitive psychology.

REFERENCES

Baddeley, A.D. (1981). The concept of working memory: A review of its current state and probable development. *Cognition*, **10**, 17-23.

Baddeley, A.D. (1983). Working memory. *Philosophical Transactions of the Royal Society, London*, **302**, 311-324.

Beech, J.R., and Harding, L.M. (1984). Phonemic processing and the poor reader from the developmental lag point of view. *Reading Research Quarterly*, **19**, 357-366.

Campbell, R., and Butterworth, B. (1985). Phonological dyslexia and dysgraphia in a highly literate subject: a developmental case and associated deficits of phonemic awareness. *Quarterly Journal of Experimental Psychology*, **37A**, 435-475.

Daneman, M., and Carpenter, P.A. (1980). Individual differences in working memory and reading. *Journal of Verbal Learning and Verbal Behavior*, **19**, 450-466.

van Dijk, T.A., and Kintsch, W. (1983). *Strategies of Discourse Comprehension.* New York: Academic Press.

Johnson-Laird, P.N. (1983). *Mental Models.* Cambridge: Cambridge University Press.

Kennedy, A., and Murray, W.S. (1986). On the necessity of eye movements for reading. Paper presented to International Conference on Cognitive Approaches to Reading, Leicester, April.

LaBerge, D., and Samuels, S.J. (1974). Toward a theory of automatic information processing in reading. *Cognitive Psychology*, **6**, 293-323.

Marcel, T. (1980). Surface dyslexia and beginning reading: A revised hypothesis of the pronunciation of print and its impairments. In M. Coltheart, K.E. Patterson and J.C. Marshall (Eds.) *Deep Dyslexia.* London: Routledge & Kegan Paul.

Rayner, K., Carlson, M., and Frazier, L. (1983). The interaction of syntax and semantics during sentence processing: Eye movements in the analysis of semantically biassed sentences. *Journal of Verbal Learning and Verbal Behavior*, **22**, 358-374.

Schank, R.C. (1982). *Dynamic Memory*. New York: Cambridge University Press.

Seymour, P.H.K., and Elder, L. (1986). Beginning reading without phonology. *Cognitive Neuropsychology*, **1**, 43-82.

Cognitive approaches to reading
Edited by J. R. Beech and A. M. Colley
© 1987 John Wiley & Sons Ltd

CHAPTER 1

The Cultural and Biological Context of Written Languages: Their acquisition, deployment and breakdown

JOHN C. MARSHALL

Neuropsychology Unit, The Radcliffe Infirmary, Oxford

INTRODUCTION

Language in *visible* form is usually regarded as a cultural invention, and opposed in that respect to auditory-vocal language, an aspect of our biological heritage. The evidence that supports such a distinction between speech and written language is extensive and, superficially at least, quite compelling.

All normal children in all extant cultures acquire the ability to speak and to understand speech. As far as we know, there are no extinct human societies that did not likewise have a fully developed language. By contrast, the vast majority of children and adults, past and present, are illiterate. The history of *mass* literacy in the Western world is extremely brief, and over considerable areas of the globe literacy is even now the prerogative of a small, privileged class. In 1945 Herbert Hoover declared that the liquidation of illiteracy was one of the five or six major tasks for the postwar world. It still is.

The overinflated claims of students of 'motherese' notwithstanding (see Newport, Gleitman and Gleitman, 1977; Bard and Anderson, 1983, for critiques), children acquire their native auditory–vocal language in the absence of anything that could rationally be regarded as 'teaching' or 'training'. The acquisition of reading and writing skills, *per contra*, is held to require intensive schooling. 'Instruction' must be scheduled into the timetable, and, when that instruction is perceived as insufficiently rigorous, irate letters to *The Times* complain that 'the permissive society', 'Marxist social workers', 'pop music' and 'child-centred teachers' have all conspired to produce a disastrous lowering of standards 'since I was at school'. Within the teaching profession (and the research disciplines upon which pedagogy draws), controversy rages (more or less continuously) about the 'best' way to teach reading and writing. 'Phonics' versus 'look-and-say' is always good for an argument, and enterprising educational publishers are always on the lookout for yet another 'reading instruction programme' (especially when it is supported by 'the latest scientific research').

Language development in the auditory–vocal mode typically exhibits a characteristic pace and sequencing from a very early age, with control over many of the 'core' aspects of syntax and lexicon acquired by the age of five or six. Learning to read and write usually begins after the child has mastered the basic structure of his or her auditory–vocal language. The concept of 'reading readiness' (i.e. a developmental 'age' below which the child is judged incapable of benefitting from instruction in reading) has no analogue in the acquisition of oral language; we do not systematically withhold speech from children until we believe them capable of comprehending and producing the adult forms thereof. According to some psychologists, the child is incapable of learning to read and write not only until he or she can use the spoken language for everyday communication, but also until the child can reflect 'metalinguistically' upon the phonological structure of that language.

The pace and sequence of oral language development is remarkably cons-tant across languages (and cultures), despite considerable variation in child-rearing practices and the culturally permitted forms of adult–child communication. By contrast, once the child is 'ready to learn', the pace and sequence of the child's control over reading and writing skills is held to depend upon the nature, timing and extent of the specific instructional programme to which he or she is subjected. 'Word-attack' is purportedly facilitated by phonological analysis, 'decoding' by instruction in letter–sound correspondences and 'comprehension' by close attention to 'context'.

In the oral mode, there are no 'primitive' or protolanguages such that one language is, as a whole, less expressive, less complex and hence easier for the child to acquire. This claim is not falsified by the undoubted existence of complexity variations in subcomponents of oral languages (trade-offs between, say, word order and morphology) such that, in the course of acquisition, particular subsystems within and between languages reach their final adult state at different (average) ages (see Slobin, 1982). Neither is the claim jeopardized by the fact that, in the historical development of an oral language, vocabulary will expand to meet the requirements of a complex industrial society; biblical and rabbinic Hebrew may have had no word for 'air-conditioning', but the language of Isaac Luria was not thereby more primitive than that of David Ben-Gurion. In the visual mode, however, there are purported forerunners of 'real writing' (Gelb, 1963): descriptive–representational devices, such as warning signs, and identifying–mnemonic devices, such as potters' marks. There is also a tendency on the part of some scholars to think of word-syllabic writing systems (from Sumerian to Hittite) as more 'primitive' than syllabic systems (from Elamite to Japanese), which are in turn more primitive than the Greek alphabet, which developed out of Phoenician syllabary *c.* 900 BCE. What better example could there be of 'cultural evolution' than the unique emergence of the alphabet among the (very clever) Greeks and the subsequent 'conquest of the world' (as Gelb, 1963, writes) by variations upon that alphabet.

'Pidgins' are auxiliary communication systems that come into being 'when speakers of several mutually unintelligible languages are in close contact' (Bickerton, 1984); by definition, a pidgin 'has no native speakers' (Bickerton, 1984). Insofar as pidgins can be thought of as 'primitive' oral languages, the crucial biological fact is that children exposed to such 'degenerate' input rapidly import (from within themselves) many core features of 'fully-fledged' language without environmental models for those features (Sankoff and Laberge, 1973). A new, more complex creole (with native speakers) is thereby created. With respect to reading and writing, children exposed to 'primitive' Chinese, 'ideographic' writing or Japanese (Kana) syllabic writing do not of their own accord convert these systems into 'advanced' alphabetic writing. The only way for the normal child to acquire English orthography is to be exposed to ('taught') English orthography; only a 'cultural genius' could invent an alphabet, the principles of which are then transmitted by skilled pedagogy to the less able (in a fashion analogous to the diffusion of knowledge of Newtonian physics).

Proposals to 'reform' an oral language are never taken seriously, despite the best efforts of learned Frenchmen to ban *'le snack-bar'* or the analogous English purists' opposition to such insidious 'Americanisms' as 'gotten'. Proposals to reform written language, from George Bernard Shaw's simplification of English spelling to the romanization of Chinese, are taken (fairly) seriously, although Peking's adoption of *pinyin* is still far from complete.

Environmental deprivation, consequent, for example, upon blindness, may have surprisingly little effect, quantitative or qualitative, upon the acquisition of oral language. With respect to the development of word meanings, even the use of 'sight' terms by the blind child can be conceptually quite normal (Landau and Gleitman, 1985); the child's innate capacity for extracting meaning from auditory–vocal language will override a severely impoverished perceptual environment when that impoverishment is visual. But environmental deprivation, consequent, for example, upon deafness, seems to have very dramatic deleterious effects upon the child's acquisition of reading and writing skills (Conrad, 1979). The child's capacity to extract meaning from written language thus appears to be dependent upon (even parasitic upon) the *prior* acquisition of auditory–vocal language and perhaps, as noted earlier, upon the child's ability to make explicit meta-linguistic judgments about the morphological, syllabic and phonemic structure of the oral language.

We are thus led to view auditory–vocal language as under the control of an endogenously determined module (Fodor, 1983; Liberman and Mattingly, 1985) and to regard 'the growth of language as analogous to the development of a bodily organ' (Chomsky, 1976). In this domain,

> . . . a central part of what we call 'learning' is actually better understood as the growth of cognitive structures along an internally directed course under the triggering and partially shaping effect of the environment. In the case of human language, there evidently is a shaping effect: people speak different languages which reflect differences in their verbal environment. But it remains to be seen in what respects the system that develops is actually shaped by experience, or rather reflects intrinsic processes and structures triggered by experience. (Chomsky, 1980).

Thus far, the biological approach to auditory-vocal language seems to be justified. Specific, language-committed brain mechanisms are triggered by linguistic experience; and where, in a very small proportion of children, normal language growth fails to occur, there is usually good evidence of central nervous system pathology (Marshall, 1980; Curtiss, 1985) that implicates language-committed cortex in the perisylvian region of the left hemisphere or the auditory pathways to that area.

By contrast, the story that scholars have frequently told about the development of reading and writing skills is very different. Here the stress is upon an 'unnatural' set of cultural attainments, command over which can be obtained only by laborious, explicit teaching. Despite instruction that is adequate for a majority of children to achieve literacy (with time and effort), a substantial proportion of children (15 per cent or more on some estimates) never achieve the fluent command of visual language that is necessary to participate fully in a technological society. The acquisition of literacy is thus seen to rest upon a fragile collection of different, more basic skills, which must be taught, brought together and integrated by trained adult intervention.

I have perhaps exaggerated, but not I think caricatured, arguments for the equation of auditory-vocal language with biology and written language with culture and pedagogy. But to what extent is it really possible to uphold such a strict dichotomy?

VISUAL LANGUAGE—A (BRIEF) DIGRESSION

Thus far, I have (by intent) failed to differentiate explicitly between visual language and written language. Yet the distinction is important, for there is no evidence that the biological status of visual language *per se* is any 'weaker' than that of auditory–vocal language. If, with Geschwind (1985), we 'define *reading* as the ability to extract meaning from *any* type of visual representation of language', proponents of the view that the natural ontogenetic development of language is uniquely tied to the aural–oral mode are faced with an immediate counterexample.

Deaf communities throughout the world have developed highly sophisticated sign languages. These communication systems have all the formal complexity and expressive power of spoken language; they serve everyday conversation, intellectual argumentation, wit and poetry no less effectively than do spoken English or Arabic (Klima and Bellugi, 1975). The formal structure of sign languages is, of course, specifically adapted to their mode of physical realization. American Sign Language (ASL), for example, fully exploits the potentialities of three dimensions of space and one of time. In particular, sign languages employ many more layers of simultaneously occurring features (instantiated physically by hand configuration, position and nested movements through space) than are possible in the essentially sequential realization of spoken language (Bellugi, 1980). The simultaneous coding of grammatical contrasts in a natural sign language leads to the following result: although the mean duration of individual ASL signs is double that of spoken English words, the production rate for sentences (propositions) is essentially equivalent in the two modes (Bellugi, 1980). This situation stands in striking contrast to that found with artificial sign systems, such as signed English. In signed English, each sign is realized in one-to-one *temporal* correspondence with the morphemes of spoken English. The consequence is that proposition rate in signed English is half that of spoken English, and deaf users of the system complain that it is difficult to comprehend 'the message content as a whole' (Bellugi, 1980); the system is too close to the edge of processing and (visual) memory capacity for comfortable communication. Signed English is thus a morpheme-based visual analogue of spoken English in which, as in an aural language, the signals are not preserved in the physical medium. Signed English is structurally similar to (ordinary) written English, with the chief difference that the latter is preserved in an 'external memory' that allows repeated consultation of the message. Little is known about the acquisition and deployment of signed English as a native language (but see Fuller, Newcombe and Ounsted, 1983), although what limited information is available suggests that it may be a biologically 'unnatural' system for many of the same reasons that written languages are so judged.

When we turn back to highly evolved sign languages, however, the situation is quite different. The sign languages that have been passed down through the generations from deaf parents to their deaf (and often hearing) children appear to have *all* the basic psychobiological properties of spoken languages. Children exposed to a sign language from birth acquire that language with no more explicit 'teaching' than is involved in acquisition of a spoken language. Sign language development exhibits the same kind of endogenously driven pacing and sequencing found in spoken language development; within the constraints imposed by its intrinsic grammar, 'simplifications' and overgeneralizations in ASL acquisition parallel those in spoken language acquisition. In so far as there are differences in rate of acquisition, sign languages (as first languages) appear to be acquired somewhat faster than spoken languages (Bellugi, 1987; Petitto, 1983). There is even evidence, albeit limited, from the study of the deaf children of hearing parents that children can develop their own, quite complex, sign languages with minimal input from any environmental models (Goldin-Meadow, 1979).

Evidence from the acquired aphasias in native signers demonstrates that the neuronal substrate for sign language is left-hemisphere based to at least the same extent as is spoken language. Subject again to the grammatical constraints imposed by the visual modality, the sign language aphasias seem to parallel the forms of breakdown seen in the aphasias of spoken languages. To a first approximation at least, the taxonomy of ASL aphasias maps onto the taxonomy of aphasic impairment of spoken language even at the level of lesion sites within the left hemisphere (Poizner, Klima and Bellugi, 1987). In short, study of ASL—language in a visuo-spatial modality—provides no evidence to make one doubt that 'different domain-specific cognitive representations are computed by the two halves of the adult brain, irrespective of the physical form whereby those representations are made manifest' (Marshall, 1986). If written language is indeed biologically 'unnatural' the reason is not to be sought in the constraints of the visual modality *per se,* although it *may* be found in the nature of the mapping between (abstract) grammatical structure and mode of physical expression.

We can now return to the purported dichotomy between the relative 'naturalness' of spoken and written languages.

IS WRITTEN LANGUAGE REALLY 'UNNATURAL'?

The argument that writing has a cultural history but speech a biological history rests in part upon the claim that writing has developed over far too short a time span to allow for genetic and epigenetic changes in the human population specific to a biological capacity for writing *per se.* It is within such a context that scholars stress the emergence (or rather invention) of 'true' writing systems in *c.* 900 BCE (the alphabet) or *c.* 3500 BCE (Proto-Sumerian pictographic). This latter 'origin' may be pushed back by some 5000 years if we take into account the evidence of Schmandt-Besserat (1981). Her work suggests that clay tokens of different geometric shapes and sometimes bearing incised and punched markings were used (in the Middle East) to represent numeral systems and specific commodities as early as 8500 BCE. This system was then modified around 3500 BCE when clay envelopes were developed to hold the tokens. At this point, 'check marks on the surface of the clay envelope, or *bulla*, which repeated for convenience the number and kind of tokens inside, proved so effective that soon tablets with check marks supplanted the old system of *bullae* and tokens' (Schmandt-Besserat, 1977). Tokens impressed upon clay tablets and representing units of grain metrology, land measure and animal numeration were then employed from Palestine to Saudi Arabia and Iran by some 5000 years ago.

Schmandt-Besserat's earliest date for a protowriting system (8500 BCE) is still very recent if one believes that *Homo sapiens* (or even *Homo erectus*) was endowed with a fully functional 'modern' vocal language 100 000–400 000 years ago. The history of written language is not quite so brief (comparatively) if the 'calendric' notational systems that date from the beginning of the last Ice Age (*c.* 28 000 BCE) are taken as cognitive prototypes for visual language (Marshak, 1985).

Given how little we know about the long-range development of vocal language, 'evolutionary' arguments about the relative naturalness of spoken and written language would seem to bear little weight. Children who are not exposed to a spoken language do not spontaneously invent one. Why should we be so surprised that so few people in illiterate societies invent a written language (Basso and Anderson, 1973)? And, one might remember, prior to the invention of the tape recorder, our only *direct* evidence for any human group having possessed a spoken language comes from their *written* records!

One might also bear in mind the problem of the half-empty glass, which is simultaneously half full. Concentration on the fact that some 10–15 per cent of children fail to acquire the reading skills that are required by complex Western (or 'Westernized') societies should not cause us to lose sight of the fact that 85 or 90 per cent of normal children do develop good competence in reading and writing. With adequate exposure and sufficient motivation, the vast majority of contemporary children (and presumably all previous generations thereof) can achieve the feat of literacy. The competence is acquired furthermore irrespective of whether they are presented with the very different orthographies of French or English, Arabic or Hebrew, Korean or Navajo, Serbo-Croatian or Japanese.

To what extent is good teaching a prerequisite of literacy? One would hesitate to deny the value of decent teaching in any domain. Nonetheless, the fact remains that some children achieve a good understanding of written language before formal schooling (Clark, 1976) and many have mastered the basic skills of literacy after only a year or two of instruction (and do so despite the swings in educational fashion about how reading 'must' be taught). We could perhaps learn more by studying the precocious reader than by our current overemphasis on the problems of the retarded reader (Clark, 1976). We already know that some children do (to some extent) 'invent' an orthography for themselves. There are, for example, many well-documented examples of children who, given only letters and letter names, go on to devise very sophisticated means of representing visually the structure of their spoken language (Bissex, 1980; Read, 1971). With minimal instruction in reading or writing, Glenda Bissex's son Paul (at age five) typed for her:

EFUKANOPNKAZIWILGEVUAKANOPENR

and read it aloud as 'If you can open cans, I will give you a can opener'. When she gently pointed out to him that many writers put spaces between words, he proceeded to type:

EFU WAUTH KLOZ I WEL GEVUA WAUTHEN-MATHEN

('If you wash clothes I will give you a washing machine'). Paul's spelling may not be standard, but the question of 'cracking the code' seems not to have been problematic.

However much reading and writing skills may depend upon an 'inbuilt' biology, exposure to a particular system and understanding of the relationship of its particular orthographic structure to the spoken language is a prerequisite for acquisition of literacy. How else is the child going to 'learn' that, in his or her culture, the orthography is based on the morpheme (Chinese), the syllable (Japanese *Kana*) or the phoneme (Italian)? The very question, however, presupposes that the child will *first* acquire the spoken language and then map onto the written language those aspects of linguistic form that are represented more or less explicitly in the orthography. Prevailing wisdom says that a child could not acquire written Swedish or Japanese *de novo* as it were. Yet we do not actually know whether the claim is true. For obvious reasons, no-one has ever performed a variant of Psammetichos' isolation experiment but with access to print in appropriate contexts. Nonetheless, there is evidence that some children can acquire reading and writing skills at a very early age, more or less simultaneously with their acquisition of oral language (Söderbergh, 1971, 1976; Steinberg and Steinberg, 1975). Should we regard such children as bizarre geniuses? Or should we try to learn from their success how to create conditions under which the majority of children can learn to read and write as easily as they learn to speak?

In particular, could there be a 'natural' sequence to the acquisition of literacy that the child attempts to follow (albeit not necessarily consciously) irrespective of the ordering of the instructional routines imposed by parent or teacher? Recent data and theory (Frith, 1985; Seymour and Elder, 1986) on the acquisition of literacy in English do seem to suggest a developmental progression from 'logographic' to 'alphabetic' skills that, in part, matches the historical (cultural) 'evolution' of orthographies (see also Rozin and Gleitman, 1977). The precise extent to which the sequence is 'fixed' and the points at which it is labile (i.e. under the control of instructional variables) are not known. The limited information available does, however, imply some degree of endogenous determination. Certainly, current research can in no way be taken to suggest that written language is dangerously close to the biological boundary of what the human brain is incapable of comprehending and manipulating.

How, then, should we envisage the nature of the system that underlies reading and writing skill?

THE NEUROPSYCHOLOGICAL ANALYSIS OF READING AND WRITING

Much of the driving force behind recent analyses of reading and writing skills has come from investigations of acquired impairment consequent upon brain damage sustained in adult life by previously fully literate individuals. Similar analyses of developmental disorders of written language acquisition have also been undertaken (Marshall, 1984).

Current practice in the study of the acquired dyslexias and dysgraphias (Marshall and Newcombe, 1973) is to define patterns of breakdown with reference to information-processing models of fluent adult reading, writing and spelling skills. Converging evidence from normal subjects (in experiments that often involve latency measures) and from the detailed patterns of breakdown in single-case studies of patients with relatively focal brain damage can then be used to further refine and extend the model (Patterson, Marshall and Coltheart, 1985). Such information-processing accounts of reading, writing and spelling have been primarily concerned with *lexical* access, storage and retrieval (Marshall and Newcombe, 1981) rather than with sentence and text processing. Concentration upon core lexical processes is justified by the observation that this level is (almost) always implicated in pathological performance, with higher-level deficits arising as a consequence of word-level impairment.

Current theories of reading and writing skills postulate a highly *modular* functional architecture. Three functionally and anatomically distinct 'routes' are implicated in reading: (a) a 'phonic' route that assigns a (segmented) phonological representation to sublexical graphemic units prior to semantic access; (b) a 'direct' route that assigns a pronunciation to *words* in the subject's sight vocabulary; (c) a 'lexical' route that assigns a semantic representation to sight vocabulary prior to phonological access. Three similar quasi-independent routes are postulated for writing. These routes are in turn independent of their reading analogues. That is, all the computational mechanisms involved are specialized, single-purpose, one-way devices (see Marshall, 1987).

Models of this nature are supported by observations of brain-damaged patients who show relative preservation of one route with severe impairment of other components of the system (Marshall, 1986b). Some of the most striking patterns of preserved and impaired performance have, for convenience, been given shorthand 'syndrome' labels for quick and easy clinical communication (Newcombe and Marshall, 1981). Thus 'surface dyslexia', for example, refers to a pattern of performance in which 'regular' words (and non-words) are read more accurately than 'irregular' words, and where, in the latter case, errors can (often) be interpreted as a 'regularization' of an exceptional correspondence between print and sound (*pint* read with a short *i* as in *hint*). Other syndrome labels in circulation include: 'deep dyslexia' (Coltheart, Patterson and Marshall, 1980); 'phonological dyslexia' (Patterson, 1982); 'visual' or 'word-form dyslexia' (Newcombe and Marshall, 1984; Warrington and Shallice, 1980); 'direct dyslexia' (Newcombe and Marshall, 1981). It must, however, be borne in mind that these labels and their dysgraphic counterparts have no intrinsic theoretical significance; they are merely short codes that refer to clusters of symptoms the interpretation of which is given by the functional model.

Modular systems of the type proposed clearly allow substantial scope for *normal* variation in qualitative and quantitative performance within a community exposed to a particular orthography. Likewise, different orthographies—orthographies that *explicitly* represent different linguistic levels with greater or lesser regularity—will vary in the demands they place upon different parts of the overall architecture (Marshall and Newcombe, 1981). Systematic comparisons of normal and dyslexic reading in, say, Serbo-Croatian, Italian, Japanese *Kana*, French, and Japanese *Kanji* will accordingly make it possible to specify which of the mappings that the orthography *in principle* makes available are actually utilized under different conditions (see Marshall, 1976; Paradis, Hagiwara and Hildebrandt, 1985).

In (normal) adults exposed to English orthography there are well-documented differences in the relative weightings that subjects give to lexical and extralexical strategies in reading. These 'Chinese' versus 'Phoenician' contrasts can be quite dramatic, with, for example, superior reading by sight vocabulary in the context of grossly underdeveloped 'Phoenician' skills (Baron and Strawson, 1976).

Such normal (adult) variation in the efficiency of the different reading and writing routes in conjunction with the extreme fractionations between and within routes seen after acquired brain damage leads one to inquire whether similar variability can be found in children. One pertinent theoretical question is thus whether the acquisition of literacy, and the developmental disorders of reading and writing, can be interpreted over the *same* functional architecture that is implicated in adult performance.

The question cannot be answered by *fiat*. That is, one should not argue that developing systems must have a qualitatively different structure from the end-point of their development. Neither should one argue that pathologies of a developing system *must* fractionate into different clusters of impaired and preserved performance from those seen when the mature system is subject to focal damage. It is an entirely empirical issue whether or not the qualitative nature of the variation in normal adult reading is comparable with that found in children learning to read (normally). It is likewise an empirical issue whether or not the varieties of developmental dyslexia can be interpreted as consequent upon the selective failure of a particular (adult) component (or components) to develop appropriately, with relatively intact, normal functioning of the remaining components (Marshall, 1984).

The evidence from children who are acquiring the skills of literacy within normal limits for age shows qualitative and (perhaps) quantitative variability in the deployment of the three primary reading routes that is equivalent to that seen in (normal) adults (Baron, 1979; Bryant and Impey, 1986; Treiman, 1984). Likewise, variations in symptomatology between children with developmental dyslexia seem to match the variations seen in the acquired dyslexias (Marshall, 1985). These basic facts are not in dispute, although their interpretation is (Ellis, 1985).

Marshall (1984) interprets the data as consistent with a 'preformist' account of the development of the reading (and writing) systems, an account in which the underlying modules come into play at different points in time but in the same form that they take in the adult system. The basis of the claim (which cannot yet be fully evaluated) is this: there is as yet no evidence that the *normal* development of reading skill changes in a 'stagewise' (metamorphic) manner such that the nature of the reading mechanisms employed in stage n is qualitatively changed by the addition of further mechanisms at stage n + 1. The pattern rather seems to be one of simple addition with relatively minor (and highly constrained) interaction between components. Likewise, there is (as yet) no evidence that developmental failure distorts the functional architecture of the reading system in ways that cannot be accounted for by selective impairment of particular (adult) components. If qualitative distortion were the case, we would not find the subtypes of developmental dyslexia mapping so directly onto the varieties of acquired dyslexia (see, for example, Coltheart *et al.*, 1983; Cossu and Marshall, 1985, 1986; Prior and McCorriston, 1983; Siegel, 1985; Temple and Marshall, 1983). The position taken in Marshall (1985) is that normal reading and the acquired and developmental dyslexias are all interpretable over a common functional architecture. Much confusion in developmental studies has arisen from mistaking change *within* a common architecture (either in the form of normal growth or recovery from disorder) with change *of* architecture.

The status of these similarities between the acquired and developmental dyslexias has been attacked on yet other grounds by Bryant and Impey (1986). In essence, they argue that failure of a particular (adult) component to develop cannot *explain* the problems of a dyslexic child when analogous 'failure' (as assessed by standard psycholinguistic diagnostics) can be found in chronologically younger children who nonetheless read at grade level. The counterargument, however, is simple, and shows how the strategy of matching children on reading age rather than chronological age can be misleading.

In order to read English (or French) at an adult level, one must acquire an adequate sight vocabulary (simply because of the notorious presence of highly 'irregular' words). Campbell and Butterworth (1985) have shown, in a very detailed single-case study, that it is *possible* to acquire a very extensive sight vocabulary without having command over any relevant 'phonic' skills. One would guess, however, that this achievement is only possible for people who have ('innately') really superior lexical recognition skills in the visual modality; for 'merely' normal children one need not doubt but that effective phonological recoding skills are of great benefit in the acquisition of mature reading.

When one observes a 'normal' child with chronological age (CA) and reading age (RA) at, say, ten years, whose pattern of reading performance is similar to that of a (chronologically older) child with 'phonological dyslexia' (i.e. with an underdeveloped 'phonic' route), one of three developmental courses will ensue:

1.   By virtue of superior lexical skill (Campbell and Butterworth, 1985), the child will acquire adult levels of reading skill despite the grossly impaired 'phonic route'.
2.   The phonic route will mature late (i.e. after age ten), and the child will likewise become a normal adult reader.
3.   The child will later be diagnosed as suffering from developmental phonological dyslexia. That is, a discrepancy between CA and RA *will* show up when the child is, say, sixteen (CA). The explanation will involve failure of the phonic route uncompensated by a highly superior ability to acquire sight vocabulary.

Now consider the other horn of the argument. A phonic route (even one of grossly above-average efficiency) will not suffice to acquire adequate adult reading of English (or French); the reason again is the presence of large numbers of irregularly written words. Thus when one observes a normal child (chronological and reading age ten years, say) who reads predominantly by the phonic route (and has a poorly developed sight vocabulary), there are only *two* developmental possibilities:

1. The 'lexical route' will mature late (i.e. after age ten), and the child will become a normal adult reader.
2. The child will later become a developmental surface dyslexic. That is, a discrepancy between CA and RA *will* show up when the child is, say, sixteen years (CA). The explanation will involve failure of the 'lexical route' which, by virtue (or vice) of English orthography, cannot in point of logic be fully compensated even by a highly superior phonic route.

The data put forward by Bryant and Impey (1986) are fully consistent with the description and interpretation of developmental dyslexias given in Marshall (1984). It is, of course, true that the *description* 'failure of component X to develop' does not provide an *explanation* of why that component failed to develop. The description does, however, suggest which areas of psychological functioning one should look to when a child manifests a particular pattern of impaired and preserved performance. Likewise, the existence of behavioural parallels between the acquired and developmental dyslexias does not in itself imply a common type or locus of neuronal malfunctioning. It does, however, suggest that, at one level of explanation, it would be worthwhile to look for demonstrable cytoarchitectonic anomalies of neuronal development in children with specific learning deficits. Recent work (Galaburda and Kemper, 1979; Galaburda *et al.*, 1985) has, of course, begun to reveal precisely such developmental anomalies of cell migration in the brains of (some) dyslexic children. Modern linkage analysis is beginning to produce evidence that may reveal the genetic basis for (some of) these abnormalities; one form of specific reading disability (autosomal dominant) has been traced to a gene locus on chromosome 15 (Smith *et al.*, 1983a, b).

CONCLUSIONS

Geschwind (1985) has noted that efficient acquisition of language skills may presuppose two necessary conditions. The first is the intact functioning of an appropriate neurological substrate; the second is 'the condition of being placed in an environment where communication with one's peers is impossible unless one acquires the language'. The context in which reading and writing skills are acquired rarely (if ever) meets the second condition.

Nonetheless, although reading and writing are typically 'taught' in the formal setting of a classroom, and although the emergence of mature skill is no doubt influenced by teacher–child interaction, the basic prerequisites are grounded in human biology. Studies of the 'social' context of reading *qua* cultural invention, transmitted by teaching, should not cause us to lose sight of the biological foundations of visual language. If functional information-processing analyses of the phenotypes of reading impairment can be integrated with secure knowledge of their genotypic structure, we may yet come to understand what those biological foundations are.

REFERENCES

Bard, E.G., and Anderson, A.H. (1983). The unintelligibility of speech to children. *Journal of Child Language*, **10**, 265-292.

Baron, J. (1979). Orthographic and word specific mechanisms in children's reading of words. *Child Development*, **50**, 60-72.

Baron, J., and Strawson, C. (1976). Use of orthographic and word-specific knowledge in reading words aloud. *Journal of Experimental Psychology: Human Perception and Performance*, **2**, 386-393.

Basso, K.H., and Anderson, N. (1973). A Western Apache writing system: The symbols of Silas John. *Science*, **180**, 1013-1022.

Bellugi, U. (1980). Clues from the similarities between signed and spoken language. In U. Bellugi and M. Studdert-Kennedy (Eds.) *Signed and Spoken Language: Biological Constraints on Linguistic Form*. Weinheim: Verlag Chemie.

Bellugi, U. (1987). The acquisition of a spatial language. In F. Kessel (Ed.) *The Development of Language and Language Researchers: Essays in Honor of Roger Brown*. Hillsdale, N.J.: Erlbaum.

Bickerton, D. (1984). The language bioprogram hypothesis. *The Behavioral and Brain Sciences*, **7**, 173-221.

Bissex, G.L. (1980). *GNYS AT WRK: A Child Learns to Write and Read*. Cambridge, Mass.: Harvard University Press.

Bryant, P.E., and Impey, L. (1986). The similarities between normal readers and developmental and acquired dyslexics. *Cognition*, **24**, 121–137.

Campbell, R., and Butterworth, B. (1985). Phonological dyslexia and dysgraphia in a highly literate subject: A developmental case with associated deficits of phonemic processing and awareness. *Quarterly Journal of Experimental Psychology*, **37A**, 435-475.

Chomsky, N. (1976). *Reflections on Language*. London: Temple Smith.

Chomsky, N. (1980). *Rules and Representations*. New York: Columbia University Press.

Clark, M.M. (1976). *Young Fluent Readers*. London: Heinemann.

Coltheart, M., Masterson, J., Byng, S., Prior, M., and Riddoch, J. (1983). Surface dyslexia. *Quarterly Journal of Experimental Psychology*, **35A**, 469-695.

Coltheart, M., Patterson, K.E., and Marshall, J.C. (Eds.) (1980). *Deep Dyslexia*. London: Routledge & Kegan Paul.

Conrad, R. (1979). *The Deaf School Child: Language and Cognitive Function*. London: Harper and Row.

Cossu, G., and Marshall, J.C. (1985). Dissociation between reading and writing in two Italian children: Dyslexia without dysgraphia? *Neuropsychologia*, **23**, 697-700.

Cossu, G., and Marshall, J.C. (1986). Theoretical implications of the hyperlexia syndrome: Two new Italian cases. *Cortex*, **22**, 579–589.

Curtiss, S. (1985). The development of human cerebral lateralization. In D.F. Benson and E. Zaidel (Eds.) *The Dual Brain*. New York: Guilford Press.

Ellis, A.W. (1985). The cognitive neuropsychology of developmental (and acquired) dyslexia: A critical survey. *Cognitive Neuropsychology*, **2**, 169-205.

Fodor, J.A. (1983). *The Modularity of Mind*. Cambridge, Mass.: MIT Press.

Frith, U. (1985). Beneath the surface of developmental dyslexia. In K.E. Patterson, J.C. Marshall and M. Coltheart (Eds.) *Surface Dyslexia*. London: Erlbaum.

Fuller, P., Newcombe, F., and Ounsted, C. (1983). Language development in a child unable to recognize or produce speech sounds. *Archives of Neurology,* **40,** 165-168.

Galaburda, A.M., and Kemper, T.L. (1979). Cytoarchitectonic abnormalities in developmental dyslexia: A case study. *Annals of Neurology,* **6,** 94-100.

Galaburda, A.M., Sherman, G.F., Rosen, G.D., Aboitiz, F., and Geschwind, N. (1985). Developmental dyslexia: Four consecutive patients with cortical anomalies. *Annals of Neurology,* **18,** 222-233.

Gelb, I.J. (1963). *A Study of Writing.* Chicago: Chicago University Press.

Geschwind, N. (1985). Biological foundations of reading. In F.H. Duffy and N. Geschwind (Eds.) *Dyslexia: A Neuroscientific Approach to Clinical Evaluation.* Boston: Little, Brown and Company.

Goldin-Meadow, S. (1979). Structure in a manual communication system developed without a conventional language model: Language without a helping hand. In H. and H.A. Whitaker (Eds.) *Studies in Neurolinguistics,* Vol. 4. New York: Academic Press.

Klima, E.S., and Bellugi, U. (1975). Wit and poetry in American Sign Language. *Sign Language Studies,* **8,** 204-223.

Landau, B., and Gleitman, L.R. (1985). *Language and Experience: Evidence from the Blind Child.* Cambridge, Mass.: Harvard University Press.

Liberman, A.M., and Mattingly, I.G. (1985). The motor theory of speech perception revisited. *Cognition,* **21,** 1-36.

Marshack, A. (1985). *Hierarchical Evolution of the Human Capacity: The Paleolithic Evidence.* New York: American Museum of Natural History.

Marshall, J.C. (1976). Neuropsychological aspects of orthographic representation. In R.J. Wales and E. Walker (Eds.) *New Approaches to Language Mechanisms.* Amsterdam: North-Holland.

Marshall, J.C. (1980). On the biology of language acquisition. In D. Caplan (Ed.) *Biological Studies of Mental Processes.* Cambridge, Mass.: MIT Press.

Marshall, J.C. (1984). Toward a rational taxonomy of the developmental dyslexias. In R.N. Malatesha and H.A. Whitaker (Eds.) *Dyslexia: A Global Issue.* The Hague: Nijhoff.

Marshall, J.C. (1985). On some relationships between acquired and developmental dyslexias. In F.H. Duffy and N. Geschwind (Eds.) *Dyslexia: A Neuroscientific Approach to Clinical Evaluation.* Boston: Little, Brown and Company.

Marshall, J.C. (1986). Signs of language in the brain. *Nature,* **322,** 307-308.

Marshall, J.C. (1987). Routes and representations in the processing of written language. In E. Keller and M. Gopnik (Eds.) *Motor and Sensory Processes in Language.* Hillsdale, N.J.: Erlbaum.

Marshall, J.C., and Newcombe, F. (1973). Patterns of paralexia. *Journal of Psycholinguistic Research,* **2,** 175-199.

Marshall, J.C., and Newcombe, F. (1981). Lexical access: A perspective from pathology. *Cognition,* **10,** 209-214.

Newcombe, F., and Marshall, J.C. (1981). On psycholinguistic classifications of the acquired dyslexias. *Bulletin of the Orton Society,* **31,** 29-46.

Newcombe, F., and Marshall, J.C. (1984). Varieties of acquired dyslexia: A linguistic approach. *Seminars in Neurology,* **4,** 181-195.

Newport, E.L., Gleitman, H., and Gleitman, L.R. (1977). Mother, I'd rather do it myself: Some effects and non-effects of maternal speech style. In C.E. Snow and C.A. Ferguson (Eds.) *Talking to Children: Language Input and Acquisition.* Cambridge: Cambridge University Press.

Paradis, M., Hagiwara, H., and Hildebrandt, N. (1985). *Neurolinguistic Aspects of the Japanese Writing System.* New York: Academic Press.

Patterson, K.E. (1982). The relation between reading and phonological coding: Further neuropsychological observations. In A.W. Ellis (Ed.) *Normality and Pathology in Cognitive Functions.* London: Academic Press.

Patterson, K.E., Marshall, J.C., and Coltheart, M. (Eds.) (1985). *Surface Dyslexia.* London: Erlbaum.

Pettito, L. (1983). From gesture to symbol: The relationship between form and meaning in the acquisition of personal pronouns in American Sign Language. PhD dissertation, Harvard University.

Poizner, H., Klima, E.S., and Bellugi, U. (1987). *What the Hands Reveal about the Brain.* Cambridge, Mass.: MIT Press.

Prior, M., and McCorriston, M. (1983). Acquired and developmental spelling dyslexia. *Brain and Language,* **20,** 263-285.

Read, C. (1971). Pre-school children's knowledge of English phonology. *Harvard Educational Review,* **41,** 1-34.

Rozin, P., and Gleitman, L.R. (1977). The structure and acquisition of reading II: The reading process and the acquisition of the alphabetic principle. In A.S. Reber and D.L. Scarborough (Eds.) *Toward a Psychology of Reading.* Hillsdale, N.J.: Erlbaum.

Sankoff, G., and Laberge, S. (1973). On the acquisition of native speakers by a language. *Kivung,* **6,** 32-47.

Schmandt-Besserat, S. (1977). The invention of writing. *Discovery,* **1,** 4-7.

Schmandt-Besserat, S. (1981). Decipherment of the earliest tablets. *Science,* **211,** 283-285.

Seymour, P.H.K., and Elder, L. (1986). Beginning reading without phonology. *Cognitive Neuropsychology,* **3,** 1-36.

Siegel, L.S. (1985). Deep dyslexia in childhood? *Brain and Language,* **26,** 16-27.

Slobin, D. (1982). Universal and particular in the acquisition of language. In E. Wanner and L.R. Gleitman (Eds.) *Language Acquisition: The State of the Art.* Cambridge: Cambridge University Press.

Smith, S.D., Kimberling, W.J., Pennington, B.F., and Lubs, H.A. (1983a). Specific reading disability: Identification of an inherited form through linkage analysis. *Science,* **219,** 1345-1347.

Smith, S.D., Pennington, B.F., Kimberling, W.J., and Lubs, H.A. (1983b). A genetic analysis of specific reading disability. In C. Ludlow (Ed.) *Genetic Aspects of Speech and Language Disorders.* New York: Academic Press.

Söderbergh, R. (1971). *Reading in Early Childhood: A Linguistic Study of a Preschool Child's Gradual Acquisition of Reading Ability.* Stockholm: Almqvist and Wiksell.

Söderbergh, R. (1976). Learning to read between two and five: Some observations on normal hearing and deaf children. In C. Rameh (Ed.) *Semantics: Theory and Application.* Washington, DC: Georgetown University Press.

Steinberg, D.D., and Steinberg, M.T. (1975). Reading before speaking. *Visible Language,* **9,** 197-224.

Temple, C.M., and Marshall, J.C. (1983). A case study of developmental phonological dyslexia. *British Journal of Psychology,* **74,** 517-533.

Treiman, R. (1984). Individual differences among children in reading and spelling styles. *Journal of Experimental Child Psychology,* **37,** 463-477.

Warrington, E.K., and Shallice, T. (1980). Word-form dyslexia. *Brain,* **103,** 99-112.

Cognitive approaches to reading
Edited by J. R. Beech and A. M. Colley
© 1987 John Wiley & Sons Ltd

CHAPTER 2

Word Recognition Processes.
An analysis based on
format distortion effects

P. H. K. SEYMOUR

Department of Psychology, University of Dundee

INTRODUCTION

We know that the characteristics of the words we read must initially be represented in a *visual* format of some kind. This input is recognized as an occurrence of a specific lexical or morphemic identity (or set of such identities). Once this has happened it becomes possible to access other types of information, especially speech forms and representations of meaning. Hence, the processing system of an accomplished reader might be thought to contain domain-specific coding systems (visual, semantic, phonological) together with interface structures which mediate transformations between codes. This mediation logically involves a *pattern recognition* function (for identification of codes in one system) combined with a retrieval or *addressing* function (for activation of equivalent codes in another system) (Seymour, 1979). In this discussion I shall refer to the system which mediates between visual and higher-level codes in reading as the *word recognition interface*.

During the last hundred years or so there have been extensive efforts to investigate word recognition processes experimentally (see Henderson, 1982, for a comprehensive and incisive review). This enterprise has involved the imposition, on readers of varying competence, of tasks which are considered *a priori* to engage the resources of the word recognition system (usually vocal report or lexical, semantic or same-different decision). The tasks are combined with variations in linguistic or procedural factors which are expected to exert effects which can be assigned a theoretically useful interpretation. I shall not attempt a comprehensive review of this research here but will instead describe some studies which have been conducted in the cognitive laboratory at Dundee and use this discussion as a vehicle for highlighting issues of theory and method.

MORPHEMIC VERSUS PHONOLOGICAL PROCESSING

One question concerns the *modality* of the code employed by the word recognition process. A traditional view has been that word recognition is, in its earliest developments, an auditory process, and that there is mileage in the proposal that reading of an alphabetic or syllabic script might involve a conversion to an auditory code prior to recognition. This proposal entails the intervention of an operation of letter–sound conversion (grapheme–phoneme translation) at a *pre*-lexical level (i.e. before contact with the recognition interface). Much recent discussion has been directed towards demonstrations that this is not a viable possibility for a written language such as English in which the relationship between letter groups and pronunciation is inconsistent and subject to higher-level influences (Coltheart, 1978, 1980; Henderson, 1982). Further, the existence of a condition known as phonological dyslexia, in which word reading is efficient although new words and pronounceable non-words cannot be read, is now well documented for both acquired and developmental cases (Beauvois and Dérouesné, 1979; Patterson, 1982; Temple and Marshall, 1983; Seymour and MacGregor, 1984). It is also true that young children can develop a substantial word recognition vocabulary in the absence of an ability for grapheme–phoneme translation (Seymour and Elder, 1986).

Lexicality effects

The contrast between word and non-word stimuli defines a factor of *lexicality*. The lexicality effect (efficient word reading combined with inefficient non-word reading) is taken to imply: (1) that a functional distinction can be made between morpheme recognition and grapheme–phoneme translation; and (2) that the translation process cannot be a general and necessary prerequisite for access to the word recognition interface (Ellis, 1984). The second conclusion implies that the code used to access the word recognition interface is not a speech representation. Given the data on phonological dyslexia it follows that the elements of the code must be of *morphemic* significance, representing either whole words or smaller segments (word stems and affixes). This proposal is sometimes taken to imply that the word recognition interface is specialized for the identification of meaningful visual segments. If this view is taken, the explanation of a reader's ability to pronounce new words or nonsense words seems to require some other process by which *phonologically* significant segments can be recognized. These could be grapheme clusters which correspond to vowel and consonant phonemes (called 'spelling patterns' by Gibson *et al.*, 1962), or somewhat larger segments, including whole syllables or demisyllables (combinations of a vowel with a preceding or following consonant group) (Shallice and McCarthy, 1985).

If this notion of *sublexical* correspondences is not accepted, it becomes necessary to assume that pronunciations for new words or non-words can be generated through the mediation of the morphemically specialized system. Such a proposal has been argued by Marcel (1980), Glushko (1979), Henderson, (1982) and others. The assumption is made that new words are classified as being similar to particular known words and that pronunciation is derived by a process of lexical pooling in the phonological system. The theory predicts that non-word pronunciation will be determined by the pronunciations of orthographically similar entries in the word recognition system. Thus, the non-word *dalk* should be categorized as similar to 'walk', 'talk' and 'chalk', and should always be pronounced 'dawk' (/dɔːk/). However, an analysis of responses to non-words having consistently irregular lexical environments of this type carried out at Dundee by Maccabe (1984) did not support this prediction. On average, such items were given a lexicalized pronunciation on only about 50 per cent of occasions (the actual rates varied from one structure to another), and were pronounced according to simple correspondences (i.e. /dælk/) the remainder of the time. This result seems sufficient to reject the lexical pooling model as a generally applicable account of the manner in which new words or non-words are read aloud. It is also inconsistent with a standard two-route model of the kind described by Coltheart (1978). In this theory it is assumed that non-words are always read by a grapheme–phoneme translation procedure which is functionally distinct from the morpheme recognition process. If this view was correct, *dalk* should always be read as /dælk/.

These arguments suggest the availability of systems which recognize both morphemic structures and phonological structures. Shallice has suggested that both types of structure might be accommodated in single phonological channel. This entails a redefinition of the word recognition interface to include a capability for identification of sublexical structures (Shallice, 1981; Shallice and McCarthy, 1985; Shallice and Warrington, 1980). Alternatively, it could be argued that the phonological segments are recognized by a different process, but one which deals with syllabic and demisyllabic segments in addition to simple grapheme–phoneme correspondences (Patterson and Morton, 1985). Such a system might contain the abstract letter–sound associations $a \rightarrow$ /æ/, $l \rightarrow$ /l/, $k \rightarrow$ /k/ and *-alk* $\rightarrow$ /ɔːk/, and might make use of the larger structure on a proportion of occasions.

Shallice's scheme appears to run into problems in accounting for the results from cases of acquired phonological dyslexia. When discussing the contrasting disorder, acquired surface dyslexia, in which morpheme recognition is damaged although sublexical processing may be preserved (Marshall and Newcombe, 1973; Coltheart *et al.*, 1983; Shallice, Warrington and McCarthy, 1983), Shallice has argued that neurological degradation may affect the larger morphemic or syllabic structures first and the more elementary grapheme–phoneme correspondences later. In order to accommodate phonological dyslexia it would seem necessary to assume either that the degradation process can operate in the reverse direction, affecting elementary correspondences before the higher-level ones, or that there is some other procedure, located perhaps in the semantic system, which can be used for word reading. The latter view, implying a duplication of morphemic pathways, is close to the 'dual lexicon' position discussed by Seymour and MacGregor (1984). This assumes the availability of a primitive 'logographic lexicon', possibly interfaced most directly with the semantic system, operating in conjunction with a more sophisticated 'orthographic lexicon', in which morphemic locations are addressed by a code which is defined in terms of phonological significant vowel and consonant spelling patterns.

In phonological dyslexia the difference between word and non-word reading may be dramatic, affecting either accuracy or reaction time, or both (Seymour, 1986; Seymour and MacGregor, 1984). In individual cases, the distributions of vocal reaction times to words and non-words often have radically different appearances, with responses to words being clustered within a range up to 1000–1500 ms, while responses to non-words include very few fast times and may be scattered over a range up to 5000 ms and beyond. The lack of overlap in the distributions strongly suggests that quite different processes are involved.

Conclusion

The study of lexicality effects (contrasts between word and non-word reading) has been undertaken with the aim of distinguishing between two modes of processing—recognition of morphemes or whole words versus recognition of phonologically significant (vocalic, consonantal or syllabic) grapheme clusters. There is clear evidence that it is possible for individuals to deal relatively efficiently with morphemes despite the presence of a severe inefficiency in using submorphemic phonological correspondences. It seems that this distinction between units of differing size and significance should be modelled in an account of the recognition interface, although it is not clear whether functionally separate recognition systems are implied or whether a single system with a capability for recognition of units of differing size and significance is to be preferred.

FORMAT DISTORTION EFFECTS

The preceding discussion suggests that the graphemic units referred to the interface structure(s) must vary in size, perhaps from single graphemes up to whole words. The isolation of these units has been thought to require the involvement of a process of graphemic segmentation or *parsing*. Shallice has proposed that this might involve a filter mechanism within the visual processor which either blocks or passes elements from the letter array (Shallice, 1981). An assumption of his model is that the code on which the parsing process operates consists of abstract (case- and font-independent) letter identities which are coded according to their horizontal left-to-right position.

In order to investigate processing at this graphemic level we require experiments which examine factors which exert an effect on the visual (as opposed to semantic or phonological) processing system. I have attempted to do this at Dundee using a technique of *format distortion*. The basic procedure is to present word or non-word stimuli for vocalization or decision in both normal and distorted formats, viz:

```
                                    V
                                    E
                                    R
                  Z G  A            T
  NORMAL          I Z  G            I
                                    C
                                    A
                                    L
```

and to examine the effects of the distortion on accuracy and latency. In experiments reported by Seymour and May (1981), zigzag and vertical distortions of this type were presented to adult readers in a lexical-decision task and in a vocalization task. The lists contained 180 items, half words and half non-words. The word sets varied in frequency (high or low) and in length (three, five or seven letters). The non-word sets included legal and illegal items (lexical decisions) or pseudo-homophones and non-homophones (vocalization). Items from each subset were randomly assigned to one of three formats (normal, zigzag, vertical).

Format × length interactions

The format variation had no consistent effects on accuracy. However, there was a large effect on reaction time, which is illustrated for the lexical-decision task in Figure 2.1. The results for words make it clear that distortion delayed the response time and that this effect interacted with word length. The effect

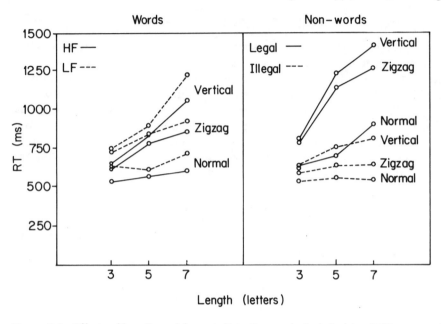

Figure 2.1   Effects of length and format distortion on lexical decision RT by normal adult readers for words of high and low frequency and for legal and illegal non-words. From Seymour and May (1981).

of length was relatively slight for normal formats but increased to about 60 ms per letter for the zigzag format and to about 120 ms per letter for the vertical format. This pattern was duplicated in the two tasks and was equivalent for both high- and low-frequency words. However, the frequency effect interacted with tasks, being larger for lexical decisions than for vocalization with mean differences in reaction time of 92 ms and 34 ms respectively.

These results suggest the necessity for a *normalization* procedure of some kind prior to recognition of distorted arrays. Although ordered horizontal and vertical positions might be considered equivalent at an abstract level, it seems that the recognition interface is tuned to accept inputs which incorporate horizontal, left-to-right spatial descriptions. One possibility is that normalization involves the removal of inappropriate descriptions and their replacement by equivalent left—right statements. The faster processing of the zigzag arrays might then be explained on the grounds that these arrays already contain horizontal position codes.

Some cases of developmental dyslexia demonstrate a difficulty in carrying out this normalization process. One of the subjects described by Seymour and MacGregor (1984) was considered to exhibit a visual analytic dyslexia which was characterized by slow responses in matching tasks and very slow resolution of the vertical distortion. Vertical words were read with a processing time per letter of 400–500 ms, although the length effects on reading of normally formatted words were slight and similar to those found in competent readers. This effect can be interpreted as an indication of an impairment of the *analytic* function of the visual processor. It seems possible that parsing into small elements (single graphemes) is not normally required for word recognition (which depends on larger morpheme- or word-sized arrays). Hence, an impairment of letter-by-letter parsing becomes evident only when the subject is forced to resort to this process in order to resolve the vertical distortion or to make comparisons of detail between letter arrays (see Seymour, 1986, for other cases).

The interaction between distortion and length is not invariably obtained. For example, Seymour and Elder (1986) applied a format distortion experiment in the course of a study of the first year of reading development. Words which were familiar to the children were presented in lower case letters in the normal and zigzag or vertical formats. It was assumed that if this early form of word recognition (which was referred to as logographic recognition) was dependent on identification of word shapes or *gestalts*, then the zigzag and vertical distortions should effectively abolish reading. In practice, the children varied greatly in the impact of distortion on reading accuracy and some of them succeeded in reading a large percentage of the distortions. A measure of vocal reaction time was taken and was related to word length (see Seymour and Elder, 1986, Figure 1). The data did not show the length × distortion interaction which is characteristic of adult reading. There was a time cost attributable to the distortions, but it was equivalent across a length variation of 3–6 letters. It was concluded that the children recognized the words by identifying salient features (letter shapes, overall length) which were not destroyed by the distortions.

It seems possible that a result of this type is characteristic of a primitive form of word recognition (logographic recognition) which is not dependent on the availability of a code specifying letter identities and their spatial locations. A process of this kind might survive in adult reading as a procedure for handwriting recognition (where, as pointed out by Newcombe and Marshall, 1980, identification of individual letters may create difficulties) and as a basis for semantic access under marginal viewing conditions. A study by Webb (1984) provides some support for this view of handwriting recognition. Adult subjects made lexical decisions in response to typewritten and handwritten words and non-words. There was a delay of response to handwritten stimuli, but this was not associated with an increase in processing time per letter, implying that illegibility of handwriting is not a distortion which is normalized by a sequential recoding procedure.

There are a number of other instances of toleration of distortions in cases of non-phonological reading. Saffran and Marin (1977) discussed a case of deep dyslexia (see Chapter 11 in this volume) who successfully read words despite distortion by case alteration, vertical presentation, zigzag arrangement of letters and interpolation of plus signs between letters. Beauvois and Dérouesné (1979) demonstrated successful reading of handwritten words of poor legibility in a case of severe phonological dyslexia (although words written from right to left could not be read). Unfortunately, these investigations did not include measurements of reaction time, and we cannot therefore know whether there was a time cost associated with the processing of the distortions, or whether there was an interaction with word length. However, in investigations of developmental phonological dyslexia where these measurements have been undertaken, I have found that a proportion of subjects appear able to read the distortions without resort to serial processing, especially in lexical and semantic decision tasks (Seymour, 1986; Seymour and MacGregor, 1984). The effect also varies within groups of normal readers, being negligible for some individuals.

Non-phonological reading is not invariably associated with efficient processing of distortions. Howard (1986) has described a deep dyslexic patient whose reading accuracy was significantly impaired. Some of the beginning readers in Seymour and Elder's (1986) study failed on a substantial number of distorted words.

The results reported by Seymour and MacGregor (1984) and by Seymour (1986) reveal a third pattern of response to distorted displays. Some dyslexic cases show a large effect of length on speed of reading normally formatted words. Reading appears to involve a serial process, with a rate of 200 ms per letter or more which contrasts dramatically with the normal rate of 20 ms per letter or less. This serial function may be restricted to vocalization or may occur for semantic and lexical decision tasks as well. Since these subjects already read serially, they do not have to switch to this mode when confronted with the distortions. Hence, the data show a strong effect of word length but no length × distortion interaction.

Interactions with lexicality and legality

Figure 2.1 also gives the results from Seymour and May's (1981) study for rejection of non-word stimuli in the lexical decision task. The items consisted of legal (pronounceable) non-words and illegal (vowel-less) non-words. Two points can be made from the data. First, legal non-words produce a distortion × length interaction which is similar in form to that observed for words. However, the magnitude of the effect is greater for the non-words than for the words (the processing rates were: 56 ms per letter for normal presentation, 119 ms per letter for the zigzag presentation and 153 ms per letter for the vertical presentation). This lexicality × format × length interaction is consistent with the notion that non-word recognition requires parsing of the letter array into smaller segments than does word recognition. It may be that non-word recognition depends on the isolation of sublexical segments (vowel, consonant and syllabic groupings) and that these must be individually normalized, thus increasing the impact of distortion. The results for vocalization of non-words were very similar.

The second aspect of the results concerns the processing of the illegal non-words. It can be seen from Figure 2.1 that the length × format effect was very much reduced for the illegal arrays, with no length effect for normal presentation and effects of only 15 ms per letter and 28 ms per letter for the zigzag and vertical presentations. These results suggest that a test for orthographic legality was applied early in processing and used as a basis for a decision to bypass the normalization operation. Distortion imposed some cost on the efficiency of this test, but one that was relatively small.

In order to clarify the basis of the legality test a second experiment was run in which two types of illegal non-word were compared. The items either contained or did not contain a vowel and included an illegal consonant sequence located at the beginning or at the end, viz:

	Illegal beginning	Illegal end
Vowel	TFELK	BLEBX
No vowel	TFMLK	BLMBX

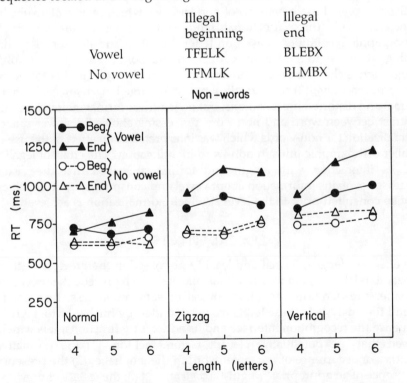

Figure 2.2 Effects of length and format on negative lexical decision RT to non-words varying in presence or absence of a vowel and position of a consonant illegality. From Seymour and May (1981).

The results of this study are displayed in Figure 2.2. It seems clear that the absence of a vowel was the critical feature allowing rapid rejection of non-words and a minimization of the length × format effects. When a vowel was present the reaction time was slower and there were effects of the position of the illegality, and of the format and length variations. Thus, two levels of legality testing seem to be implicated: (1) a test for presence of a vowel; and (2) tests of consonant legality which are applied to initial clusters before terminal clusters.

Conclusion

The format distortion effect, together with its interaction with word length, suggests that word recognition in competent readers is often based on a standardized horizontal spatial code. Arrays conforming to this structure can be handled by an approximation to a parallel process but non-standard inputs have to be normalized by a time-consuming serial process. The individual analyses revealed three patterns of performance which may, tentatively, be associated with three functional modes of the visual processor: (1) orthographic recognition, based on letter identities and horizontal spatial coding, gives rise to the length × format interaction; (2) direct logographic recognition is characterized by an absence of length effects and of format × length interactions; (3) serial reading produces large length effects for both normal and distorted presentations, but no length × format interaction. The contrast between word and non-word processing showed a slower rate of normalization for non-words which was interpreted as an effect of the use of smaller orthographic units in non-word identification. The effect of legality and its interaction with length and format suggested that the visual processor contains information about vowel and consonant structure which may be consulted prior to the level at which normalization is achieved.

LEXICAL EFFECTS

The effects of length, format and legality discussed in the previous section appear to relate to operations of visual analysis which precede the processes of pattern recognition and phonological or semantic access. In order to extend the analysis to these levels we need to identify further factors which influence the recognition interface and its addressing functions. It is widely agreed that the potentially relevant factors include: (1) the normative *frequency* of occurrence of the target word in the language; (2) the presence or absence of an appropriate linguistic *context*; and (3) the *recency* of previous encounters with the word. Numerous studies have established that accuracy of report and speed of reaction are facilitated for familiar words (frequency effect), for words in context (association effect) or for recently processed words (repetition effect) (Henderson, 1982; Mitchell, 1982; Seymour, 1979). In the remainder of this chapter I will consider two of these factors (frequency and repetition), largely from the standpoint of their localization relative to the recognition interface.

Frequency effect

The interpretation of the effect of word frequency is central to many models of word recognition. It is generally considered that the recognition interface contains a number of units (pattern recognizers), each corresponding to a word in a person's reading vocabulary. According to one view, the units are equivalent to one another, although organization is introduced in the manner of which they are stacked or ordered. Recognition involves a serial self-terminating procedure by which the input is checked against the stored elements with great rapidity until a match is detected (see Forster, 1976, and Rubenstein, Lewis and Rubenstein, 1971, for variants of this search theory). In accounts of this type the word-frequency effect is assumed to reflect the rank order in which the elements are arrayed for checking, although it is generally assumed that the scale of the search is reduced by examining only those elements which have a degree of orthographic correspondence with the input. The alternative model, formalized by Morton (1968, 1969), treats the recognition units as variables which internalize the properties which affect word recognition. It is assumed that the units, referred to as *logogens*, can be viewed as evidence counters having a resting level of activation and a threshold which defines the amount of evidence necessary before transmission to the higher-level phonological or semantic systems can occur. Morton proposed that the threshold might reflect general frequency of usage and recency of encounter, and that the resting level might be sensitive to contextual priming.

A problem for Morton's theory was posed by experiments examining the influence of stimulus *degradation* on performance in the lexical decision task. It has been shown that degradation combines *interactively* with the presence or absence of a context (Becker and Killion, 1977; Meyer, Schvaneveldt and Ruddy, 1972) and with repetition (Besner and Swan, 1982), but *additively* with variations in word frequency (Stanners, Jastrzembski and Westbrook, 1975). This additive outcome also occurs when frequency is paired with the length × format interaction discussed earlier (Seymour and May, 1981). The interactive result can be interpreted either (1) as an effect of reductions in the *rate* of accumulation of evidence in the logogens under conditions of degradation (this assumes that context, repetition and degradation are all influences on the interface), or (2) as an indication that context and repetition are influences on the visual analysis stage which is selectively affected by degradation.

In discussing the implications of these results for the logogen model it is necessary to take account of the revision of the theory proposed by Morton (1980a). On the basis of demonstrations that prior occurrence of a visual word facilitated subsequent tachistoscopic recognition (a 'repetition effect') whereas prior naming of the word in response to a picture or definition did not do so, Morton argued that a distinction should be made between an *input* logogen system concerned with recognition and an *output* logogen system concerned with speech production. (The input logogen is equivalent to what has been referred to as the word recognition interface in the present chapter.) It is critical to the reasoning underlying the logogen revision that the repetition effect should be localized within the word recognition interface, since otherwise it would not be possible to argue that the occurrence or non-occurrence of repetition effects could be treated as evidence forcing the division of the lexical systems into separate modality-specific components concerned with distinct input and output functions. Hence, if repetition is an effect on the interface, and if degradation enlarges the effect (Besner and Swan's repetition × degradation interaction), then we must assume that the interaction is characteristic of influences on the interface and that a variable which does not produce the interaction is not an influence on the interface. Since frequency and degradation combine additively rather than interactively, we conclude that a frequency variation is *not* a property of the interface. This is the position taken by Morton (1980a). He concluded that frequency was probably a property of the cognitive system. His suggestion was that lexical decisions depend on retrieval of semantic information and that high-frequency words facilitate this process on account of the richness of their associations, or some other factor. The effect of these arguments is to remove the necessity to postulate that word recognition units have thresholds which vary according to frequency of usage, or, alternatively, that the elements contained in the interface are rank ordered by frequency.

Further problems are posed by the relationship between the frequency effect and different lexical processing *tasks*. In the description of Seymour and May's (1981) study, I noted that there were frequency effects on both lexical decisions and word vocalization but that the effect was significantly larger for lexical decisions. This finding has also been reported by Balota and Chumbley (1984). In addition, these authors examined the effects of frequency on a semantic categorization task (decisions as to whether or not words were members of a specified category). They found no frequency effects in this task, thus confirming a result earlier reported by Wilkins (1971). These findings are damaging to the proposals: (1) that frequency is an influence on the recognition interface; or (2) that the frequency effect observed in lexical-decision tasks arises in the cognitive (semantic) system. If the effect was a property of the interface it should be observable across all tasks which involve word recognition. If it was a property of the semantic system it should be observable in a task which involves semantic processing.

A recent study by Rycroft (1986) at Dundee reinforces these conclusions. In one condition of her study subjects read aloud lists of fourteen high- or low-frequency words. There was a large effect of frequency on reading speed, indicating that frequency has a major effect on some part of the process of phonological retrieval. The same word lists were employed in two search tasks, which were modelled on the procedures of Neisser and Beller (1965). In a *visual search* task subjects scanned the lists looking for a specific word. In the *semantic search* task they scanned the lists looking for a synonym of the target. Target frequency, list frequency and target position were systematically varied. Measures of search rate indicated that the semantic search was slower than the visual search but that neither task was sensitive to either target frequency or list frequency. These results suggest that frequency is not an influence on visual or semantic processing, but that it does affect speed of phonological retrieval (the 'output logogen' in Morton and Patterson's (1980) theory).

One other possibility is that semantic access relies on a different procedure from phonological access. The arguments presented earlier suggested that semantic access might be achieved by a process of logographic recognition. If phonological access depended on a process of *orthographic* (letter-based) recognition which was sensitive to frequency while semantic access involved a *logographic* process which was not, a role for frequency in the analysis of orthographic word recognition might be retained, although the differential size of the effect in lexical decisions and vocalization and the different patterns of interaction or additivity with stimulus quality would still require explanation.

Another possibility is that lexical decisions depend on consultation of phonological codes in the output logogen whereas semantic decisions do not. However, this would not explain why the frequency effect should be larger for lexical decisions than for vocalization. To accommodate this result it seems necessary to entertain the possibility that lexical decisions are made on the basis of some other (non-semantic, non-phonological) code. A candidate for this role might be a store of orthographic representations used in spelling production. In the schemes proposed by Morton (1980b) and Seymour and MacGregor (1984), spelling knowledge is represented in a distinct system which is accessible from visual input. If lexical decisions depended on access to this system, and if the frequency effect on spelling retrieval was larger than the effect on phonological retrieval, the discrepancy in sizes of the frequency effect between vocalization and lexical decision could be explained.

Repetition effect

A word which as been recently encountered can be more readily perceived in a tachistoscope (Murrell and Morton, 1974) and more rapidly classified in a lexical-decision task (Scarborough, Cortese and Scarborough, 1977). I have already noted that this effect has been assigned a critical role in the revision of the structure of the logogen system. If two inputs are presented, I1 and I2, and I2 gives evidence of facilitation relative to I1 or some other control, then it is concluded that I1 and I2 affected the same logogen unit. If I2 is not facilitated, then it is concluded that I1 and I2 affected different logogen units. Observations of this type have been used to support the conclusions: (1) that input and output functions involve distinct logogen systems; (2) that there are distinct visual and auditory input systems; (3) that, within the visual modality, word recognition is distinct from picture recognition; and (4) that logogens are abstract units which tolerate changes of form (print vs hand-writing, upper vs lower case) and which operate on morphemic structures as well as whole words (Clarke and Morton, 1983; Murrell and Morton, 1974; Warren and Morton, 1982).

Allport and Funnell (1981) have pointed out that it is critical to this chain of argument that repetition should be a property of the logogen units and not of the sensory analysis processes which precede reference to the inter-face. Two lines of evidence have been considered to support Morton's position. One of these is the occurrence of a repetition × quality interaction (Besner and Swan, 1982) which can be interpreted as an effect of differences in rate of recruitment of information by logogen units which have differing threshold settings. The other is the observation that long-term repetition effects (i.e. those which survive over a number of trials in an experiment, or over an interval of up to an hour or so) are more readily demonstrated for word stimuli than for non-word stimuli (Scarborough, Cortese and Scar-borough, 1977). This latter view is, of course, dependent on the proposal that logogen systems are specialized for *morpheme* recognition. If, as proposed in Shallice's (1981) model, the system also contained recognition units for sublexical components, and if these were sensitive to repetition, then the restriction of the effect to words would no longer be a necessary require-ment. In practice, it seems that long-term non-word repetition effects may be observed and that the critical factor is the duration of the interval between the lexical-decision response and the occurrence of the next stimulus (Monsell, 1985). On the question of the interaction with quality, the effect is ambiguous between the interpretation that degradation affects the logogen count rate and the possibility that repetition modifies the visual analysis process.

Further investigation of the effects of format distortions may be helpful in this context. The arguments already presented suggested that the zigzag and vertical distortions force the occurrence of a serial *normalization* procedure at the parsing level of the visual processor prior to the reference to the interface. If it could be shown that repetition modified the speed of the normalization process, then this would carry a strong implication that the effects were located prior to the interface. This possibility was tested in the experiments reported by Seymour and May (1981). In one study, adult subjects made lexical decisions about five-letter words and non-words which were repeated at intervals of 8, 16 or 32 trials. The words varied in frequency and the non-words in legality. They were presented in one of the three formats (normal, zigzag, vertical) using the same format for both presentations. A summary of the reaction time results appears in Figures 2.3 and 2.4. The data illustrate a stable repetition effect for both words and legal non-words extending over a period of up to 32 intervening trials. It is clear that the effect is greatly enlarged by the introduction of the distortions. Hence, there is a strong repetition × distortion interaction. The effect is larger for low-frequency words than for high-frequency words, and occurs for words and non-words alike, provided the non-words form legal sequences.

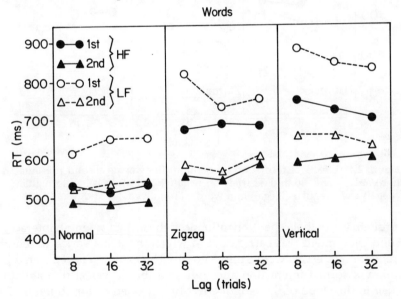

Figure 2.3 Efffects of format and repetition (first versus second presentation) at lags of 8, 16 and 32 trials on positive lexical decisions to words of high and low frequency. From Seymour and May (1981).

Illegal non-words do not produce a repetition effect. According to the arguments presented earlier, illegal non-words can be rejected prior to entry to the parsing and normalization phase. The absence of a repetition effect for these items implies that repetition does not influence the preliminary processes of formation of letter identities and the tests for a vowel and legal consonant sequence. It seems that the main effect is at the parsing stage, although the interaction of repetition with frequency (also reported by Scarborough, Cortese and Scarborough, 1977) suggests that there may also be an effect located beyond the interface in the phonological (or orthographic) processor.

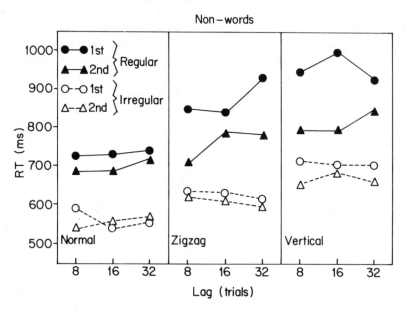

Figure 2.4 Effects of format and repetition (first versus second presentation) at lags of 8, 16 and 32 trials on negative lexical decisions to regular (legal) and irregular (illegal) non-words. From Seymour and May (1981).

In order to verify that repetition influenced the format × length interaction a second experiment was carried out in which the items varied in length. The repetition intervals were 8 and 25 trials. The experiment replicated the repetition × format interaction and indicated that it was attributable to a *reduction* in the slope of the length effect for repeated distorted items. The effect shifted from 57 to 19 ms per letter for zigzag displays and from 83 to 44 ms per letter for vertical displays. Comparable results were obtained in a vocalization task. For non-words the slope values were slightly larger, but the same reduction in processing time per letter was evident on the repeat trials. This result makes it clear that the saving produced by repetition arises because the speed of the normalization process is increased if the item (whether a word or a non-word) has recently been analysed.

In these two experiments, the items were presented in the same formats at both occurrences. For this reason, it is unclear whether the enhancement of the repetition effect for distorted items reflects merely the fact that the item has previously been presented or the fact that it has been presented in an unusual format. It might be argued that an unusual format at first presentation would increase the repetition effect on account of the additional processing applied during the normalization phase. This possibility can be tested by decoupling the formats of the first and second presentations. An additional experiment was run which made it possible to examine the reaction times for words and non-words in the three formats when the format of the preceding occurrence was also systematically varied. The items were five-letter words and non-words, repeated at lags of 8 or 25 trials, representing all possible combinations of first and second presentation format, excluding repetitions of the same format. If the format of the first presentation was important, we would expect to find that the repetition effect on a zigzag or vertical item was greater following earlier presentation of a distorted item than following earlier presentation of a normal item. This effect did not occur. Responses to zigzag items were reduced from 853 ms to 689 ms following a normal presentation and to 717 ms following a vertical presentation. Responses to vertical items were reduced from 992 ms to 781 ms after a normal presentation and to 778 ms after a zigzag presentation. These repetition effects remained significantly larger than the effects observed for normal presentations which had been preceded by a zigzag or vertical presentation. Thus, it seems that the repetition × format interaction is dependent on the format of the *second* presentation rather than on the format of the first presentation. In order to verify this effect a further experiment was run in which word and non-word length was varied and all nine possible format repetition contingencies were tested (i.e. including same format repeats). This experiment confirmed the previous finding by showing: (1) that the size of the repetition effect depended on the format of the second presentation, and (2) that there was no advantage for same format repeats over different format repeats. An analysis of length effects again indicated that the reduction due to repetition was attributable to a faster processing rate per letter.

Conclusion

The discussion in this section has been directed mainly towards an analysis of the effects of combining factors traditionally associated with the recognition interface (frequency and repetition) with the factors of length and format which are associated with the stage of visual analysis. The results clearly confirm that frequency and repetition cannot both be logogen-level effects. Frequency is independent of the length × format interaction whereas repetition modifies the size of the interaction by reducing processing time per letter during normalization of distorted displays.

The possibility that frequency might be a logogen effect appeared to be discounted by its variability across different word recognition tasks. The most likely conclusion was that it affected the retrieval of phonological codes. Thus, frequency effects appear to belong to the analysis of the *output* logogen system and to fall within the domain of models of name retrieval (Brown and McNeil, 1966; Oldfield, 1966).

The primary location of the repetition effect seems to be beyond the stage of preliminary orthographic analysis but within the domain of visual processing, either at the level of the interface or at the level of construction of a code which is acceptable to the interface. The issue here is whether parsing operations, including the normalization of distortions, are considered to be part of the function of the interface (i.e. under the control of the logogens) or whether they are viewed as an independent set of processes which generate codes which are passed to the interface for recognition and classification. If the latter view is taken, repetition would be best viewed as an effect on a visual analysis stage preceding recognition, and thus as a *pre-logogen effect. A conclusion of this kind would, of course, be damaging to Morton's proposal that the presence or absence of repetition effects might be used as a tool for division of the lexicon into functionally independent logogen systems.

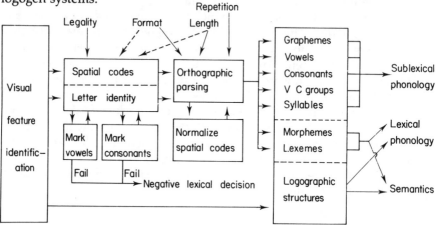

Figure 2.5   Schematic information-processing model of word recognition functions suggested by the analysis of the format distortion effects.

DISCUSSION

In this chapter I have taken the view that the study of word recognition involves the identification of the *factors* which are plausible influences on the process and a clarification of the logic for assigning theoretical *interpretations* to observed effects and interactions. The analysis has been based on the idea that word identification is a multistage process which can be discussed in terms of: (1) coding of visual properties of the input; (2) categorization of familiar graphemic structures in a word recognition interface; and (3) accessing higher-level codes in the semantic and phonological systems.

Some conclusions from the research can be captured in the form of a processing diagram (see Figure 2.5). This model, which elaborates the proposals of Seymour and MacGregor (1984), assumes that preliminary visual processing results in the formation of a visual feature code and of an abstract graphemic code. These are referred to a word recognition interface which is subdivided into a number of domains (depending on the type of unit to be recognized) and which mediates access to the phonological and semantic systems.

Logographic recognition

It is proposed that a direct pathway exists by which featural descriptions of words may be referred to a discriminatory system without the mediation of a letter code. The recognition system is labelled 'logographic structures' in the diagram and is equivalent to the 'logographic lexicon' discussed by Seymour and Elder (1986) in their analysis of early prephonological reading. Discrimination is based on *features* rather than word outlines or gestalts and is in this sense an analytic process even though some global characteristics, such as length, may be considered. In the diagram I have assumed that logographic recognition is sufficient for access to semantics or to lexical phonology (word forms contained in a speech production or output logogen system). Logographic recognition is characterized by an absence of word length effects and by a capacity to resolve distortions without the intervention of a serial normalization process. It is further assumed that a logographic lexicon cannot recognize new words or non-words unless these are established by identification of the equivalent phonological or semantic codes and by appropriate refinement of the dimensions of discrimination.

Orthographic recognition

In the account of reading acquisition proposed by Seymour and MacGregor (1984), development involves a movement away from a reliance on logographic recognition towards the establishment of an orthographically based system. In the model in Figure 2.5 this entails an expansion of the capabilities of the recognition interface together with the establishment of procedures for letter identification and parsing.

Letter identification and spatial coding

A first stage is the assignment of identities to the individual graphemes and the coding of their spatial arrangement on the display. The identity codes may be *abstract* in that they are assigned irrespective of variations in case or font. The spatial code is more specific and refers to relative locations within a two-dimensional coordinate system, using concepts such as (left of), (right of), (above), (below). It is probable that the identity and spatial codes can be assigned in parallel and that this stage is not subject to length effects. Variations in the legibility of individual graphemes (e.g. in cursive handwriting) should affect the speed of establishing the identity code.

Vowel and consonant marking

A further assumption is that the preliminary stage of letter identification involves a discrimination between vowels and consonants. The lexical decision data suggest that failure to find a vowel provides the basis for an early negative response and that processing at this level is largely unaffected by distortion or length variations. It is possible, therefore, that the vowel detection operation is carried out in parallel and without reference to the spatial codes. In the diagram I have suggested that the marking of consonant groups also takes place at this level. This could be viewed as an examination of the letter groups surrounding the vowels, possibly with reference to stored statistical information about English orthography (e.g. lists of permissible consonant sequences for different initial, medial or terminal positions). *Orthographic legality* is the principal influence on this processing stage but there may be some subsidiary effects of length and format (indicated by dashed arrows in the diagram). For orthographically legal arrays the output from the stage will consist of a set of spatially coded letter identities which have been grouped into vowel and consonant subsets.

Orthographic parsing

The *orthographic parsing* component in Figure 2.5 is concerned with the selection of sets of letter identities and their transfer to the recognition interface. A principal conclusion from the Seymour and May (1981) study is that this process delivers standard (horizontal, left-to-right) spatial structures to the interface. These may consist of the entire letter array or of smaller groups of vowels or consonants taken in isolation or in combination. If the spatial format is standard transfer may be in parallel for the elements within a group, although the groups themselves may be handled serially or in cascade. Thus, orthographic recognition of whole words need not involve a length effect, although an effect would be evident if there was a significant

use of smaller orthographic segments (the assumed basis of length ×
lexicality interactions). Arrays incorporating a non-standard spatial structure
must be *normalized* by the parser. I have assumed that this involves letter-by-
letter handling of the group to be transferred and the insertion of the
appropriate horizontal codes. It is this normalization process which
generates the substantial format × length interaction which occurs in the
data of normal readers and which has been taken as an index of orthographic
recognition.

The recognition interface

In Figure 2.5 I have represented the interface as a system which is conceptually divisible into domains defined according to: (1) the type of *input*
(logographic features or orthographic identities); and (2) the status of the
unit which is recognized (morphemic or phonological). Within the
orthographic domains, recognition of morphemes or lexical units gives
access to stored vocabulary in an output logogen (lexical phonology) or to
semantics, whereas recognition of smaller units gives access to vowel,
consonant and syllabic entities (sublexical phonology).

It is clearly desirable that some variables should be identified which are
direct influences on the interface, since it is through the study of the effects
of such variables that the properties of the word recognition system can be
determined. However, the review of research suggests that this objective is
difficult to accomplish.

Lexicality

The primary argument for the morpheme/phonological division within the
interface is provided by the reader's capability to identify both words and
non-words and by the dissociation of these processes in dyslexia. These
lexicality effects thus influence the manner in which the interface is conceptualized. The effects on processing (i.e. faster reading of words than of
non-words) can be assigned to the parsing stage, where non-words may
produce larger length effects than words, but may also be attributable to
postinterface differences in accessing or assembling lexical and sublexical
phonology.

Word frequency

There has been a strong presumption that morphemic and lexical
recognition units vary in accessibility according to their familiarity. As was
noted in the discussion, a serious objection to this view is posed by the
demonstrations that frequency effects vary markedly across lexical-

processing tasks, all of which appear, on the face of it, to involve the media-tion of the interface. This objection is not fatal within a dual lexicon framework since the logographic and orthographic lexicons might differ in their sensitivity to frequency and might have differing degrees of involve-ment in the performance of the various tasks. The other main line of evidence concerns the additivity of the frequency and format effects. This outcome is consistent with a role for frequency in the recognition interface provided that the interface is independent of the operations of the parser. However, as was noted in the earlier discussion, such a conclusion is not compatible with the proposal that repetition is an influence on the interface.

Repetition

The interactions of repetition with format and length make it clear that repetition has a major influence on orthographic parsing. If an item has recently been encountered the speed of the serial normalization operation is increased. An implication is that the visual processor retains information about aspects of orthographically regular arrays, whether words or non-words, which can be used in spatial recoding, and that the capacity of this store is in excess of thirty items. In a model in which frequency is represented as a property of the interface, the repetition effect must be located in an independent parsing operation which refers selected codes to the recognition units. This interpretation undermines the validity of the repetition effect as an index of distinctions between logogen systems. Morton's position can be preserved by treating frequency as a postinterface (output logogen) effect and by representing the parsing operations as a set of programmes which are driven by the recognition units, i.e. by assuming that parsing and recognition are not independent functions.

CONCLUSIONS

The introduction of a powerful variable, format distortion, combined with the length factor, provides a useful technique for highlighting aspects of the word recognition process. The manipulation combines in distinctive ways with standard variables such as legality, repetition and word frequency, and these outcomes can be assigned a processing interpretation of the kind summarized in Figure 2.5. Nonetheless, ambiguities remain regarding the internal structure of the recognition interface and the exact role of the impor-tant variables of repetition and word frequency.

REFERENCES

Allport, D.A., and Funnell, E. (1981). Components of the mental lexicon. *Philosophical Transactions of the Royal Society of London*, **B295**, 397-410.

Balota, D.A., and Chumbley, J.I. (1984). Are lexical decisions a good measure of lexical access? The role of word frequency in the neglected decision stage. *Journal of Experimental Psychology: Human Perception and Performance*, **10**, 340-357.

Beauvois, M.-F., and Dérouesné, J. (1979). Phonological dyslexia: three dissociations. *Journal of Neurology, Neurosurgery and Psychiatry*, **42**, 115-125.

Becker, C.A., and Killion, T.H. (1977). Interaction of visual and cognitive effects in word recognition. *Journal of Experimental Psychology: Human Perception and Performance*, **3**, 389-401.

Besner, D., and Swan, M. (1982). Models of lexical access in visual word recognition. *Quarterly Journal of Experimental Psychology*, **34A**, 313-325.

Brown, R., and McNeil, D. (1966). The 'tip of the tongue' phenomenon. *Journal of Verbal Learning and Verbal Behavior*, **5**, 325-337.

Clarke, R., and Morton, J. (1983). Cross-modality facilitation in tachistoscopic word recognition. *Quarterly Journal of Experimental Psychology*, **35A**, 79-96.

Coltheart, M. (1978). Lexical access in simple reading tasks. In G. Underwood (Ed.) *Strategies of Information Processing*. London: Academic Press.

Coltheart, M. (1980). Reading, phonological recoding, and deep dyslexia. In M. Coltheart, K. Patterson and J.C. Marshall (Eds.) *Deep Dyslexia*. London: Routledge & Kegan Paul.

Coltheart, M., Masterson, J., Byng, S., Prior, M., and Riddoch, J. (1983). Surface dyslexia. *Quarterly Journal of Experimental Psychology*, **35A**, 469-495.

Ellis, A.W. (1984). *Reading, Writing and Dyslexia*. London: Erlbaum.

Forster, K. (1976). Accessing the mental lexicon. In R.J. Wales and E. Walker (Eds.) *New Approaches to Language Mechanisms*. Amsterdam: North-Holland.

Gibson, E.J., Pick, A., Osser, H., and Hammond, M. (1962). The role of grapheme–phoneme correspondence in the perception of words. *American Journal of Psychology*, **75**, 554-570.

Glushko, R.J. (1979). The organisation and activation of orthographic knowledge in reading aloud. *Journal of Experimental Psychology: Human Perception and Performance*, **5**, 674-691.

Henderson, L. (1982). *Orthography and Word Recognition in Reading*. London: Academic Press.

Howard, D. (1986). Reading without letters? In M. Coltheart, R. Job and G. Sartori (Eds.) *The Cognitive Neuropsychology of Language*. London: Erlbaum.

Maccabe, D. (1984). Phonography: data and speculation. Paper presented at meeting of the Experimental Psychology Society, London.

Marcel, A.J. (1980). Surface dyslexia and beginning reading: A revised hypothesis of the pronunciation of print and its impairments. In M. Coltheart, K. Patterson and J.C. Marshall (Eds.) *Deep Dyslexia*. London: Routledge & Kegan Paul.

Marshall, J.C., and Newcombe, F. (1973). Patterns of paralexia: A psycholinguistic approach. *Journal of Psycholinguistic Research*, **2**, 175-199.

Meyer, D.E., Schvaneveldt, R.W., and Ruddy, M.G. (1972). Activation of lexical memory. Paper presented at meeting of the Psychonomic Society, St Louis.

Mitchell, D.C. (1982). *The Process of Reading*. Chichester: Wiley.

Monsell, S. (1985). Repetition and the lexicon. In A.W. Ellis (Ed.) *Progress in the Psychology of Language*, Vol. 2. London: Erlbaum.

Morton, J. (1968). Grammar and computation in language behaviour. Progress Report No. 6, Center for Research in Language and Language Behaviour, University of Michigan, May 1968.

Morton, J. (1969). Interaction of information in word recognition. *Psychological Review*, **76**, 165-178.

Morton, J. (1980a). Disintegrating the lexicon: An information processing approach. Paper presented at CNRS Conference at L'Abbeye de Royaumont, June 1980.
Morton, J. (1980b). The logogen model and orthographic structure. In U. Frith (Ed.) *Cognitive Processes in Spelling*. London: Academic Press.
Morton, J., and Patterson, K.E. (1980). A new attempt at an interpretation, or, an attempt at a new interpretation. In M. Coltheart, K.E. Patterson and J.C. Marshall (Eds.) *Deep Dyslexia* London: Routledge & Kegan Paul.
Murrell, G.A., and Morton, J. (1974). Word recognition and morphemic structure. *Journal of Experimental Psychology*, **102**, 963-968.
Neisser, U., and Beller, H.K. (1965). Searching through word lists. *British Journal of Psychology*, **56**, 349-358.
Newcombe, F., and Marshall, J.C. (1980). Transcoding and lexical stabilisation in deep dyslexia. In M. Coltheart, K. Patterson and J.C. Marshall (Eds.) *Deep Dyslexia*. London: Routledge & Kegan Paul.
Oldfield, R.C. (1966). Things, words and the brain. *Quarterly Journal of Psychology*, **18**, 3-16.
Patterson, K.E. (1982). The relation between reading and phonological coding: Further neuropsychological observations. In A.W. Ellis (Ed.) *Normality and Pathology in Cognitive Functions*. London: Academic Press.
Patterson, K.E., and Morton, J. (1985). From orthography to phonology: An attempt at an old interpretation. In K.E. Patterson, J.C. Marshall and M. Coltheart (Eds.) *Surface Dyslexia: Neuropsychological and Cognitive Studies of Phonological Reading*. London: Erlbaum.
Rubenstein, H., Lewis, S.S., and Rubenstein, M.A. (1971). Evidence for phonemic recoding in visual word recognition. *Journal of Verbal Learning and Verbal Behavior*, **10**, 645-657.
Rycroft, B. (1986). The influence of word frequency and sequential context on visual search tasks, semantic search tasks and pronunciation tasks. Unpublished MA thesis, University of Dundee, 1986.
Saffran, E., and Marin, O.S.M. (1977). Reading without phonology: Evidence from aphasia. *Quarterly Journal of Experimental Psychology*, **29**, 515-525.
Scarborough, D.L., Cortese, C., and Scarborough, H.S. (1977). Frequency and repetition effects in lexical memory. *Journal of Experimental Psychology: Human Perception and Performance*, **3**, 1-17.
Seymour, P.H.K. (1979). *Human Visual Cognition: A Study in Experimental Cognitive Psychology*. West Drayton: Collier Macmillan.
Seymour, P.H.K. (1986). *Cognitive Analysis of Dyslexia*. London: Routledge & Kegan Paul.
Seymour, P.H.K., and Elder, L. (1986). Beginning reading without phonology. *Cognitive Neuropsychology*, **3**, 1-36.
Seymour, P.H.K., and MacGregor, C.J. (1984). Developmental dyslexia: A cognitive experimental analysis of phonological, morphemic and visual impairments. *Cognitive Neuropsychology*, **1**, 43-82.
Seymour, P.H.K., and May, G.P. (1981). Locus of format effects in word recognition. Paper presented at meeting of the Experimental Psychology Society, Oxford, July 1981.
Shallice, T. (1981). Neurological impairments of cognitive processes. *British Medical Bulletin*, **37**, 187-192.
Shallice, T., and McCarthy, R. (1985). Phonological reading: From patterns of impairment to possible procedures. In K.E. Patterson, J.C. Marshall and M. Coltheart

(Eds.) *Surface Dyslexia: Neuropsychological and Cognitive Studies of Phonological Reading*. London: Erlbaum.

Shallice, T., and Warrington, E.K. (1980). Single and multiple component central dyslexic syndromes. In M. Coltheart, K. Patterson and J.C. Marshall (Eds.) *Deep Dyslexia*. London: Routledge & Kegan Paul.

Shallice, T., Warrington, E.K., and McCarthy, R. (1983). Reading without semantics. *Quarterly Journal of Experimental Psychology*, **35A**, 111-138.

Stanners, R.F., Jastrzembski, J.E., and Westbrook, A. (1975). Frequency and visual quality in a word–nonword classification task. *Journal of Verbal Learning and Verbal Behavior*, **14**, 259-264.

Temple, C.M., and Marshall, J.C. (1983). A case study of developmental phonological dyslexia. *British Journal of Psychology*, **74**, 517-533.

Warren, C.E.J., and Morton, J. (1982). The effects of priming on picture recognition. *British Journal of Psychology*, **73**, 117-130.

Webb, A. (1984). The effects of handwriting and print in a lexical decision task. Unpublished MA thesis, University of Dundee, 1984.

Wilkins, A.J. (1971). Conjoint frequency, category size, and categorisation time. *Journal of Verbal Learning and Verbal Behavior*, **10**, 382-385.

CHAPTER 3

Reading and Working Memory

MEREDYTH DANEMAN

Erindale College, University of Toronto

INTRODUCTION

Reading is a form of problem solving; the reader has to solve the problem of what successively encountered words, phrases and sentences in a written text mean.

My very simple definition for a very complex task serves to spotlight two pivotal properties of the reading process. One is that reading is sequential and integrative. The second is that reading is problem solving.

Contrary to what advertisements for commercial speed-reading courses would have us believe, the reader cannot apprehend a whole page of text in one go. There are in fact profound perceptual and cognitive limitations on the systems. The perceptual limitations are an empirical fact; the cognitive ones a logical necessity. Due to sophisticated eye-tracking technology and considerable experimental ingenuity, we know that the reader's perceptual span is restricted to a very small window around the point of fixation (McConkie and Rayner, 1975; Rayner, 1975, 1978). The kind of detailed information needed to make semantic decisions can only be picked up at most six printed characters in advance of the point at which the reader is fixating (Rayner, 1975). As a consequence, the reader proceeds through the text from left to right, fixating almost every word at least once (Carpenter and Daneman, 1981; Just and Carpenter, 1980). The virtual word-by-word character of the reading process must impose enormous cognitive or storage demands on the reader. After all, reading involves much more than recognizing and comprehending a stream of isolated words. As my definition suggests, a major component of skilled reading is the ability to compute the semantic and syntactic relationships among the successive words, phrases and sentences, thereby constructing a coherent and meaningful representation of the text. Integrating each new word with previously processed information means that the reader must have access to the results of earlier processes. Otherwise, how could he or she resolve the apparent inconsistency in the following passage? *Tim opened the magazine. Then he carefully removed the bullets it contained* (Daneman and Carpenter, 1983). Or how could he or she compute the referent for *he* in this sentence? *Although he spoke softly, yesterday's speaker could hear the little boy's question* (Just and Carpenter, 1980). If recently processed information could not be stored at least temporarily, the reader would be continually backtracking to reread parts or even whole sentences and passages. In other words, one consequence of its sequential and integrative nature is that skilled reading depends on the temporary storage of information while new information is being processed.

Temporary storage during information processing is not unique to reading; it is an essential feature of other forms of problem solving too. To calculate the solution to $911 - 13 + 48$, the mathematics problem solver must have access to the results of consecutive stages of processing. Of course the unskilled problem solver could resort to external storage aids such as fingers or pen and paper. However, skilled mathematics problem solvers will likely keep track of preliminary results mentally. To solve the problem of which of a series of irregular geometric shapes can be placed together to produce a hexagon, the spatial problem solver will also be at a distinct advantage if he or she can keep track of the results of each intermediate manipulation in memory. As my simple definition reminds us, reading shares some of the features of general problem solving. Hence, we could and should look to general information-processing theory for clues to the mechanisms underlying reading and individual differences in reading ability.

Recent models of reading have indeed appealed to information-processing theory to account for the way in which information might be represented in a state highly accessible to the ongoing reading processes. They have appealed to the information-processing construct of *working memory* to account for temporary storage during reading and the information-processing construct of *working memory capacity* to account for individual differences in temporary storage during reading. This chapter examines the role of working memory in reading. The first part of the chapter reviews the theoretical arguments and empirical evidence that have been offered in support of working memory's role in reading performance. The second part of the chapter provides evidence from recent work that seriously questions the usefulness of invoking the construct of working memory capacity, particularly from the standpoint of explaining and measuring individual differences in reading skill.

THE CASE FOR WORKING MEMORY

Working memory: its function

In essence, working memory is viewed as a limited-capacity system responsible for the temporary storage and processing of information in the performance of complex cognitive tasks. It was proposed as an alternative to existing short-term memory models because of concerns with the ecological relevance of the short-term memory construct. Prototypical short-term memory models (e.g. Atkinson and Shiffrin, 1968, 1971; Posner and Rossman, 1965; Waugh and Norman, 1965) assumed that short-term memory plays a crucial role in the performance of ecologically relevant complex cognitive tasks such as verbal comprehension, mathematical and spatial reasoning, tasks which for their solution require that individuals temporarily store information and then operate on it. However, the earlier work was concerned with understanding the memory system *per se*, and researchers concentrated on inventing short-term memory tasks and paradigms (e.g. memory span, probe digit span) and exploring the properties of these tasks, rather than searching for empirical evidence for short-term memory's functional role in non-memory tasks. As soon as efforts were made to test the intuitively appealing notion that temporary storage is crucial for performing complex information-processing tasks (e.g. Baddeley and Hitch, 1974), it became evident that the existing models of short-term memory were inadequate. Short-term memory theory was replaced by working memory theory (Baddeley, 1981, 1983; Baddeley and Hitch, 1974) and short-term memory measures by working memory measures (Daneman and Carpenter, 1980, 1983; Daneman and Green, 1986). The popularity of the working memory approach has been as much a function of its perceived relevance to a wide range of non-memory information-processing tasks, such as reading, as it is to understanding the memory system itself.

Working memory: its structure

Working memory has been conceptualized as an alliance of separate but interacting temporary storage subsystems, at least three in its current form (Baddeley, 1981, 1983). The core of the system is the central executive component; it is the centre responsible for processing information and temporarily storing the products of its processes. It is assumed to have a limited amount of capacity for which its processing and storage functions compete (Baddeley and Hitch, 1974). However, the central executive is able to discharge some of the storage responsibilities to the two auxiliary slave systems it controls. These are the articulatory loop, which is specialized for maintaining verbal material by subvocal rote rehearsal (Baddeley, Eldridge and Lewis, 1981; Baddeley and Hitch, 1974; Baddeley, Lewis and Vallar, 1984), and the visuo-spatial scratch pad, which is specialized for maintaining visuo-spatial information in a similar fashion (Baddeley *et al.*, 1975; Baddeley and Lieberman, 1980).

Either the central executive with its general processing and storage functions or the articulatory loop with its subvocal rote rehearsal processes or both could play an important functional role in reading.[1] This chapter discusses each possibility in turn, although the emphasis will be on the all-important central executive.

The central executive

My interest in the central executive stemmed from my hunch that it might resolve a puzzling inconsistency in the literature on reading, an inconsistency between logic and theory on the one hand and empirical evidence on the other.

Logic seemed to demand, and theory to assume, the importance of temporary storage during the ongoing reading processes. As mentioned in the introduction, linguistic analyses of even the simplest of sentences seem to require for comprehension the temporary storage of information while new information is being processed. Given that temporary storage capacity is limited (Atkinson and Shiffrin, 1971; Broadbent, 1975), and given that individuals differ from one another in their temporary storage capacity (Hunt, Lunneborg and Lewis, 1975), then on logical grounds we should expect that individuals with small temporary storage capacities should have comprehension deficits relative to individuals with larger capacities (Kintsch and Vipond, 1979). These assumptions are made explicit in Kintsch and van Dijk's (1978) theory of reading comprehension. According to Kintsch's theory, readers process text in cycles, working with at most several propositions or meaning units at a time. Because propositions in one cycle are frequently related to propositions in a previous cycle, readers must integrate the related propositions if they are to establish a coherent representation for

---

[1] One might think that the visuo-spatial scratch pad could also play a role in reading since reading does, after all, employ a visual medium. However, the visuo-spatial store is assumed to hold information in a non-verbal (non-symbolic) code. Hence its major role is in imagery mnemonics (Baddeley and Lieberman, 1980). Studies that have purported to show differences among good and poor readers in their visuo-spatial short-term memory capacities have not controlled for the fact that subjects tend to recode visuo-spatial stimuli verbally; as a result, these studies have not taken into account the possibility that verbal coding or verbal storage differences were responsible for the observed differences in performance on the visuo-spatial short-term memory task (Cummings and Faw, 1976; Goyen and Lyle, 1973). When the effects of verbal coding are eliminated or controlled, differences between good and poor readers tend not to be found (Ellis and Miles, 1978; Jorm, 1983).

the text. Integration is more easily accomplished if the earlier relevant propositions are still active in working memory; otherwise a more difficult and time-consuming reinstatement search of long-term memory must be attempted. In Kintsch's model, there are two parameters, maximum input size (n) and short-term memory carryover capacity (s), that determine how many propositions the reader can carry over in working memory from one processing cycle to the next. The value of n depends on how familiar a reader is with a given text. The value of s depends on the reader's personal temporary storage capacity. In theories of reading such as Kintsch's, individual differences in temporary storage capacity can greatly affect the readability of a text and the qualitative outcome of the comprehension processes.

Contrary to logic and theory, however, existing evidence suggested that temporary storage capacity did not differentiate good from poor readers. Studies using the standard digit span test or a probe digit span test found no systematic differences between good and poor readers (Guyer and Friedman, 1975; Hunt, Frost and Lunneborg, 1973; Hunt, Lunneborg and Lewis, 1975; Perfetti and Goldman, 1976). Studies using letter strings or similar sounding words as measures of short-term storage and as predictors of reading comprehension were only slightly more successful (Farnham-Diggory and Gregg, 1975; Rizzo, 1939; Valtin, 1973). The main conclusion from a fairly large body of research was that, with the exception of severely retarded or brain-damaged individuals, poor readers did not have a deficit in short-term storage capacity. Thus the facts contradicted the theory.

Prompted by Baddeley and Hitch's (1974) conception of a dynamic central executive, Daneman and Carpenter (1980) proposed that the inconsistency between theory and fact was more apparent than real. Baddeley and Hitch's (1974) reconceptualization of short-term memory as a working memory with processing as well as temporary storage functions suggested the need for a reconceptualization of the theory, not the theory that temporary storage plays a role in reading but the theory of temporary storage *per se*. According to the working memory theory that replaced short-term memory theory, temporary storage capacity should be defined in *functional* rather than *structural* terms. It is not that individuals differ in structural temporary storage capacity, that is in the number of 'slots' for passively storing items or chunks of information, as traditional short-term memory theory (e.g. Broadbent, 1975; Miller, 1956) would have us believe. Rather, they differ in functional storage capacity, that is in the amount of capacity that is effectively left over for temporary storage once the requirements for the computational or processing aspects of the task have been met (Perfetti and Lesgold, 1977). In other words, individual differences reside in the trade-off between the processing and storage functions, with the major source of individual differences residing in the processing component, in the efficiency with which individuals can execute the processes to which the central executive is being applied. However, inefficient processes will amount to a smaller functional storage capacity, because any individual who required more capacity to execute the processes would have less residual capacity for temporarily storing intermediate products of the processes. Of course, the reconceptualization of temporary storage as functional rather than structural necessitates a revision of the measures of temporary storage so that they tax processes and storage conjointly rather than simply storage as the traditional digit span, letter span and word span tests do. According to Daneman and Carpenter (1980), the secret to the apparent inconsistency between theory and data was that the theory was wrong, and consequently the measures based on this theory were invalid and the data collected with such measures irrelevant.

As an alternative to digit span and word span tests which taxed storage predominantly, Daneman and Carpenter (1980) devised the reading span test which taxed sentence comprehension processes while simultaneously imposing a storage task. Subjects had to read aloud increasingly longer sets of unrelated sentences and then recall the last word of each sentence in the set. According to our theory, individuals less efficient at processing sentences would be able to maintain fewer sentence-final words. Hence, a measure of the number of sentence-final words recalled would be a measure of the functional storage capacity of the central executive or, put another way, an indirect measure of the efficiency with which it could execute the sentence comprehension processes.

And the inconsistency was indeed resolved. Reading span predicted reading comprehension performance in cases where traditional digit span and word span tests had failed (Daneman and Carpenter, 1980). Individuals with reading spans of only two or three sentence-final words performed more poorly than individuals with reading spans of four or five sentence-final words on a global test of reading comprehension and also more specific tests of integration. The findings were subsequently replicated across a fairly wide range of ages and comprehension tasks (Baddeley *et al.*, 1985; Daneman and Blennerhassett, 1984; Daneman and Carpenter, 1983; Daneman and Green, 1986; Masson and Miller, 1983). The correlations between reading span and reading comprehension were quite impressive. They ranged between 0.42 and 0.90, and with a modal correlation of 0.55 tended to be well above the 0.30 barrier that typically plagues individual-differences researchers (Hunt, 1980).

The capacity of the central executive seemed to play a particularly important role in the processes that integrate successive ideas in a text. The reading span measure correlated very highly with tasks that required readers to retrieve information mentioned earlier in the passage and relate it to the information they were currently reading. Some examples are provided below.

One process requiring integration is computing the antecedent referent for a pronoun. We assessed this by interrogating readers about a pronoun mentioned in the last sentence of a passage just read. So for example, one passage about famous men and their wives ended in the following manner.

And then there's the poet Milton, author of *Paradise Lost*, and his wife. It's hard to believe that Mary had nothing to do with Milton's career. After being married for a while, Milton wrote a pamphlet in favor of divorce. She is best known for this insignificant and deprecating fact.

The pronoun question at the end was 'Who is best known for this insignificant and deprecating fact?' Readers would have to know that *she* referred back to Mary Milton and not to Napoleon's wife Josephine, or Socrates' wife Xanthippe, both of whom had been mentioned earlier in the passage. Readers with small spans were less accurate than readers with large spans at computing pronominal reference (Daneman and Carpenter, 1980). Moreover, readers with small spans were less likely to compute a pronoun's referent when six or seven sentences intervened between pronoun and referent. By contrast, large span readers could always compute the referent even at these longer distances. Our theory was that the process of associating a pronoun with its referent noun is easier if the referent noun is still active in working memory and the duration that a piece of information remains active will vary as a function of the individual's working memory capacity. A writer uses a pronoun rather than a noun when he or she assumes that the referential concept is active or 'foregrounded' (Chafe, 1972). Chafe suggested that the foregrounding is attenuated after two sentence boundaries, although he admitted that this criterion is arbitrary and that he was unable to formalize the upper limit. Our working memory analysis suggested that the boundary might vary for different readers, with large span readers able to keep a concept foregrounded for a longer period of time.

Monitoring and revising one's comprehension errors is another skill that involves the integration of successive ideas in a text. We examined these integration skills by assessing the reader's ability to detect and recover from apparent inconsistencies, as in: *The violinist stepped onto the podium and turned majestically to face the audience. He took a bow that was very gracefully propped on the music stand.* Most readers initially interpret the ambiguous word *bow* as 'a bend at the waist' because this is the meaning more strongly primed by the preceding sentence. However, 'bend at the waist' is inconsistent with the subsequent disambiguating phrase *propped on the music stand*, and a resolution of the inconsistency requires a reinterpretation of *bow* to mean 'violin part'. When probed after reading such passages, readers with small spans were less accurate than readers with large spans in answering questions like 'What did the violinist take?' (Daneman and Carpenter, 1983). Small span readers would frequently say 'He bowed to the audience', indicating that they had not resolved the inconsistency. By contrast, large span readers would more often say, 'He took a violin bow off the music stand', indicating that they had detected the inconsistency and recovered the correct interpretation. Our theory was that recovery of the correct interpretation was harder for small span readers because they were less likely to have in working memory some representation of the orthographic properties of the misinterpreted word. Since the orthographic information *bow* is the only property shared by the two meanings 'bend at the waist' and 'violin part', without it small span readers would be lacking a useful retrieval route to the alternative meaning. Readers with small spans may have devoted so much capacity to the processes of reading that they were less likely to have accessible in working memory a verbatim representation of the earlier phrase containing the ambiguous word.

Recovery from an inconsistency also depends on whether the verbatim wording has been purged from working memory by an intervening sentence boundary. We demonstrated this by contrasting the following two versions of the *bow* passage: (1) *He took a bow that was very gracefully propped on the music stand*. (2) *He took a bow. It was very gracefully propped on the music stand*. In case (2) a sentence boundary intervened between the ambiguous word and the disambiguating phrase. Readers with small spans were less able to integrate information across a sentence boundary. By contrast, readers with large spans answered as many questions correctly when a sentence boundary intervened as when it did not (Daneman and Carpenter, 1983). These results we explained in terms of the accessibility of the earlier read verbatim wording. A sentence boundary causes a marked decline in verbatim memory for recently comprehended text (Jarvella, 1971; Perfetti and Lesgold, 1977). Eye fixation and reading time studies have shown that readers pause at the end of sentences, possibly to do additional integration processes (Dee-Lucas *et al.*, 1982; Just and Carpenter, 1980; Mitchell and Green, 1978). These additional processes may stress the limits of working memory capacity and contribute to the purging of verbatim wording. Presumably, readers with small spans were more prone to losing the verbatim wording at sentence boundaries and this is why they were less able to recover from inconsistencies when the text required the integration of information across a sentence boundary.

The acquisition of new word meanings from context also requires sophisticated integration skills. These integration processes were examined by assessing the reader's ability to decipher the meaning of a previously unknown word such as *spaneria* based on its usage in the following context:

Cecilia, Tracy, and Sonja weren't the closest of friends. It would have seemed odd to anyone who knew these three to see them sitting at a table together at 'Mingles'. In fact these three girls rarely had any time to spare to talk to other women. They tended to view them as the 'enemy'. Yet, here they were on a Saturday night at 'Mingles'. They were disappointed to say the least. Usually these girls would have spent the evening dancing and having their drinks bought for them. They never had any difficulty in attracting a fair deal of attention. Their conversation tonight remained at a shallow level as each anxiously waited for things to pick up. Then they would go their own ways without the slightest regard for each other. Their present boredom was their own fault though. The deciding game of the Stanley Cup finals was on tonight. Had they remembered this earlier they could have anticipated the spaneria and shown up later. But as it was they had to carry on an awkward conversation while desperately waiting for the game to end.

Individuals with small reading spans were less able to piece together cues in the context and infer that *spaneria* means 'scarcity of men' (Daneman and Green, 1986). Our interpretation, familiar by now, was that the integration processes that are part and parcel of contextual comprehension are less easily accomplished if the earlier relevant cues are no longer accessible to working memory, to the central executive component of working memory if you will.

We were quite excited about the potential ramifications and implications of our learning-from-context research. Although we had only examined the way individuals use context to construct word meanings from scratch, we believed the theory had broader applicability. After all, we do not only use context to comprehend unknown word meanings; we also use it to enrich our comprehension of partially known meanings. Our previous understanding of *anthropomorphize* may have just sufficed to pass a multiple-choice vocabulary recognition test. But think how much the partial understanding could be enhanced each time we encountered *anthropomorphize* showcased adroitly in contexts such as the following:

And as everybody in an automated office knows, people end up anthropomorphizing the computer. There is talk of 'putting the computer to bed', of 'feeding' it programs. There are computer terminals named Chuck, Muffy, and John Travolta now processing insurance claims. (Greenman, 1983, p. 62)

We argued that individuals with large reading spans should be able to capitalize on multiple and variable contexts to acquire, expand and hone their knowledge of word meanings. In addition, we maintained that the results of our learning-from-context study had important implications for theories of verbal intelligence. As Jensen (1980) and Sternberg and Powell (1983) have pointed out, the ability to infer meaning from context is an important component of vocabulary acquisition and the net products of this ability are reflected in the extent of an individual's vocabulary knowledge. Indeed, Sternberg has argued that learning from context may be the mechanism underlying the high intercorrelations among tests as diverse in content and form as those tapping vocabulary knowledge, reading comprehension and verbal intelligence. However, if learning from context is to play an explanatory role in a theory of verbal intelligence, it must be supplemented with a theory of why individual differences in the ability to learn from context exist. We contended that our research had begun such a quest by identifying, measuring and testing one source of individual differences in learning from context—the processing and storage capacity of the central executive (Daneman and Green, 1986).

In summary, the new working memory framework generated considerable optimism among researchers interested in accounting for why some readers are better than others. The initial research suggested that individual differences in the functional temporary storage capacity of the central processor would be responsible for individual differences in the quality of reading comprehension performance. As a measure of functional storage capacity, reading span was able to predict skill at a variety of comprehension processes. The complete list of such processes was in principle very large.

The articulatory loop

Whereas my work has focused on the central executive, Baddeley's has focused on the articulatory loop. It is not that Baddeley underestimates or minimizes the importance of the central executive in reading. On the contrary, he recognizes that the central executive is the crux of the system and that sceptics have 'justifiably criticized the working memory approach to reading on the grounds that it attributes many of the crucial components of the reading process to the central executive, while leaving no detailed specification as to how they are performed' (Baddeley, 1979, p. 368). However, Baddeley has argued that the central executive is the most difficult to conceptualize and investigate (Baddeley, 1981, 1983), and since his pioneering research with Hitch on the central executive (Baddeley and Hitch, 1974) he has allocated relatively little attention to it. Instead, he has adopted the strategy of focusing first on the more tractable subsidiary slave systems, particularly the articulatory loop (Baddeley, 1978, 1979; Baddeley, Eldridge and Lewis, 1981; Baddeley, Lewis and Vallar, 1984).

In its most recent version (Baddeley, Vallar and Wilson, in press) the articulatory loop consists of two subcomponents: a phonological input store and an articulatory control process. With auditory presentations, the information is registered directly in the phonological store. With visual presentations, as in reading, the information is first transformed by the articulatory control process into a phonological code before it can be registered in the store. The articulatory control process can also refresh the memory trace in the phonological store through the process of subvocal rehearsal. The concept of an articulatory loop has proved very useful for linking together a large body of laboratory data on the speech-like characteristics of short-term memory span. (See Baddeley, Lewis and Vallar,

1984, for a discussion of the various phenomena accounted for by the articulatory loop, phenomena such as the phonological similarity effect, the word length effect and the articulatory suppression effects.) But can the concept of an articulatory loop be usefully applied to ecologically relevant and complex cognitive tasks such as reading?

Given that the articulatory loop is responsible for the phonological functions of working memory, asking whether it plays a role in reading is tantamount to asking whether subvocalization plays a role in reading. The latter question is, of course, old (see Huey, 1908) and the literature voluminous (Baddeley, 1979; Baddeley, Eldridge and Lewis, 1981; Baron, 1976; Conrad, 1972; Jorm, 1983; Kleiman, 1975; Levy, 1977, 1978; Liberman *et al.*, 1977). Because the answer seems to differ as a function of the reader's fluency, I will first consider the evidence for subvocalization in fluent reading and then the evidence in non-fluent or beginning reading.

Most of the studies have investigated the role of phonological recoding in fluent reading by means of the articulatory suppression technique, in which subjects are presumably prevented from subvocalizing by having to articulate repeatedly an irrelevant word such as 'the' or a series of irrelevant words such as 'one, two, three' concurrently with reading. Although the evidence is far from consistent, on the whole it has suggested that, for fluent readers, phonological recoding is not obligatory and hence the articulatory loop is not essential for the comprehension of simple sentences. So for example, articulatory suppression will not impair comprehension of the sentence *Before take-off, the air hostess demonstrated the safety procedures and checked every passenger's seat belt* if the task is simply to choose the appropriate paraphrase from the following alternatives: (1) *Before departure, the air hostess went through the safety procedures and checked every passenger's seat belt*; and (2) *Before take-off, the air hostess demonstrated the safety procedures but didn't check every passenger's seat belt* (cf Levy, 1978). However, the articulatory loop may play a role when the task is made tricky by making comprehension of and/or memory for the sentence depend on the strict maintenance of word order or verbatim surface information. Say, for example, comprehension were tested by presenting the subject with a sentence either identical in form to the originally read sentence *Before take-off, the air hostess demonstrated the safety procedures and checked every passenger's seat belt*, or with a minor change in word order as in *Before take-off, the air hostess checked every passenger's seat belt and demonstrated the safety procedures*, or a minor change in wording as in *Before take-off, the air stewardess demonstrated the safety procedures and checked every passenger's seat belt*. The subject's task in each case would be to detect whether the sentence had or had not changed. In such examples, performance would likely be impaired if utilization of the articulatory loop were prevented by articulatory suppression. In the word order reversal example, the sentence is semantically identical and phonologically very similar to the original. If a distinction is to be made, word order information would be crucial. The articulatory loop with its subvocal rehearsal process appears particularly well adapted to maintaining specific word order (Baddeley, 1979; Levy, 1977). In the lexical substitution example, the sentence is semantically very similar to the original. If a distinction is to made, the phonological difference between *air hostess* and *air stewardess* becomes crucial. The articulatory loop with its phonological format would be useful for retaining the phonological information (Baddeley, 1979). Because normal fluent reading seems to depend very little on the retention of the kinds of surface features of words and word order that the above two examples demand, it is unlikely that the articulatory loop plays a major role in everyday fluent reading.

Although the articulatory loop may not be necessary for fluent reading, it may play a more important role in learning to read. Skilled adult readers may be able to access lexical entries for familiar words directly from the graphemic information (Coltheart, 1978). However, even for adults, phonological recoding would be necessary for identifying unfamiliar or new words. For children who are learning to read, many of the words will be unfamiliar, so phonological recoding will be particularly important in lexical access and comprehension. Liberman *et al.* (1977) have shown that beginning readers have difficulty in analysing a word into its component phonemes and syllables and then blending them together again to identify the word. According to Baddeley (1978), the articulatory loop should play an important role in learning to read by allowing 'the reader to store the phonemic representations of each letter read, until sufficient representations have been accumulated to blend into a syllable, which then can itself be stored' (p. 149) until the next syllable can be decoded, and so on. The fact that beginning readers make more errors on word-final than word-initial consonants (Liberman *et al.*, 1977) is consistent with Baddeley's view that the process depends on available temporary storage capacity and the child uses up more and more of the capacity as he or she progresses through the word. In an earlier version of the articulatory loop than the one I described here (see Baddeley, 1979), the decoding, blending and word-finding processes would be carried out by the central executive, with the articulatory loop simply serving the support role of storing and accumulating the decoded sounds, leaving the central executive with more capacity to devote to decoding, blending and word-finding. In the updated version of the articulatory loop described here (see also Baddeley, Vallar and Wilson, in press), the articulatory control process of the articulatory loop has the capacity to convert print to phonology itself. Hence, the entire burden of phonological recoding would rest on the articulatory loop.

The strongest case for the importance of the articulatory loop in learning to read has come from the study of children who experience severe difficulties in learning to read. Developmentally retarded readers appear to have deficits in the utilization and/or operation of the articulatory loop. Because the subcomponents of the articulatory loop interact, it is often difficult to localize any deficit precisely; however, the deficits appear to occur in all components of the system. Developmentally retarded readers rehearse less (Torgesen and Goldman, 1977) and perform more poorly on verbal tasks requiring the short-term retention of order information (Bakker, 1972), suggesting deficient utilization or operation of the articulatory rehearsal process. They are less able to generate pronunciations for unfamiliar or nonsense words (Jorm, 1981; Snowling, 1980), suggesting deficient utilization or operation of the phonological recoding function of the articulatory control process. They are less susceptible to phonological confusions in short-term memory (Mann, Liberman and Shankweiler, 1980), suggesting deficient utilization of a phonological form of storage. And finally, because some severely dyslexic children have such small digit spans (Miles and Wheeler, 1974), a result of poor temporary retention of item information not just order information (Hulme, 1981), it is possible that they may even have basic structural deficiencies in the phonological input store. Given that the articulatory loop is controlled by the central executive, any of the above deficits in articulatory loop functioning may of course be due to deficiencies in the controlling functions of the central executive itself.

Because dyslexic children appear to have deficits in their utilization of the articulatory loop, one could infer that impaired functioning of the articulatory loop constitutes the major stumbling block to their learning to read, thereby implying that the articulatory loop plays an important role in normal reading acquisition. This has been the reasoning of a number of researchers and theoreticians (Baddeley, 1979; Campbell and Butterworth, 1985; Jorm, 1983).

Taken as a whole, the research has suggested that the articulatory loop figures more prominently when reading is non-fluent.

THE CASE AGAINST WORKING MEMORY

The central executive

My case against the concept of a central executive in reading stems from my attempts to answer two interesting questions arising from the previously described research that used reading span as a measure of central executive capacity. The questions were: (a) Is reading comprehension limited by the capacity of a general working memory system or a specific language-based system? and (b) What is the nature of the trade-off between the processing and storage functions of the central executive during reading? In the sections to follow I will describe the rationale for asking these questions, the research done to answer them, and the reasons why the answers have impelled me to rethink the usefulness of invoking the construct of a central executive to explain and measure individual differences in reading skill.

The rationale: general versus language-specific processor

The research with reading span raised the question of whether comprehension is limited by the capacity of a general and central working memory system or by one specialized for the language processes. A legitimate concern about the reading span test is that it is too much like reading comprehension itself. Indeed, I have argued elsewhere that reading span may be a successful predictor of reading comprehension precisely because it captures many of the processing requirements of sentence comprehension and consequently has an excellent probability of tapping those aspects of working memory important to comprehension (Daneman, 1982, 1984). But, by the same token, the complexity of the reading span processes makes interpretation of the correlation difficult (Baddeley *et al.*, 1985), and the specificity of the reading span processes may leave us with the rather trivial conclusion that all we have shown is that sentence comprehension (reading span) is correlated with paragraph comprehension (reading and listening comprehension tests).

To go beyond the trivial interpretation and explore further the relationship between working memory capacity and reading comprehension, Daneman and Tardif (in press) pitted a verbal working memory span measure against two non-verbal measures, one that tapped mathematical processes and the other spatial processes. Strong evidence for a general working memory system, for a central executive in fact, would be a situation in which the non-verbal working memory span measures predicted reading comprehension skill as well as did the verbal working memory span measure. Strong evidence against a general and central processor and in favour of a language-specific one would be a situation in which only the verbal working memory span measure was correlated with reading skill.

The rationale: process versus memory

The reading span test did not allow us to examine in a direct fashion the way in which the processing and storage components of the central executive interact. Although Daneman and Carpenter (1980) talked about a 'trade-off between processing and storage' (p. 45), we had a particular kind of trade-off in mind. As mentioned earlier, we assumed that the processes interfere with the storage rather than *vice versa*, that processing efficiency not storage is the real locus of individual differences in central executive capacity. Hence, although the reading span test yielded a measure of memory, that is, 'number of sentence-final words recalled', it was really an indirect measure of the efficiency with which individuals could execute the sentence comprehension processes. It follows from this that another way of measuring individual differences in central working memory capacity would have been simply to measure processing efficiency directly. However, the reading span test did not allow for a direct measure of the efficiency or accuracy of the processes.[2] Hence, we could not rule out alternative models such as one in which storage interferes predominantly with processing or one in which interference is bidirectional.

In order to investigate the dynamic interplay between processing and storage functions and the relative weights of these in predicting individual differences in information-processing abilities such as reading, our new measures of working memory were devised in such a way as to allow us to evaluate separately the processes and the memory for these processes. The next section describes three new measures of working memory: verbal span, math span and spatial span (Daneman and Tardif, in press).

The research

Subjects were administered the verbal, math and spatial span measures at three successive sessions. Their performance on these tasks was correlated with performance on standardized tests of reading ability and vocabulary knowledge.

For *verbal span*, each trial consisted of a card containing a series of four separate words such as *tea dot pot ion*. This was dubbed the 'boxcar' task because in a few cases two of the separate words could be linked together to form a new word like *box* and *car* form a new word *boxcar*. In fact, on each card two boxcar words could be created without changing the order of the four given words. In the above example, they are *teapot* and *potion*. In one of the two, here *teapot*, there is a syllable boundary where the two smaller words are linked (*tea-pot*). In the other, *potion*, there is no syllable boundary at the link; that is, the word is not *pot-ion*, but *po-tion*. The rule in each case was to find the boxcar word that did not have a syllable boundary between the two smaller words; in the above example it would be *potion*. In the example *heat line her age*, the two boxcar words are *heather* and *lineage*. The correct response is *heather* (syllabified as *heath-er*) not *lineage* (syllabified as *lin-e-age*) because the former has no boundary between the *t* of *heat* and the *h* of *her* whereas the latter still has a boundary between the *e* of *line* and the *a* of *age*. Table 3.1 contains additional examples from the verbal span task. Subjects

---

[1] We could have measured reading times for the sentences. However, like Sternberg (1985), we prefer power to speed measures of skilled performance, and in the case of the reading span test reading the sentences quickly would not necessarily be the most efficient strategy for performing well on the task.

saw one card at a time and their task was to say aloud as quickly and accurately as possible the boxcar word that conformed to the rule. As soon as they made their response, they were presented with the next card in the set and so on to the end of the set, at which time they had to recall the correct boxcar word from each card in the set. The correct memory response for the set in Table 3.1 would be *donate, sinewed, father.* Set size varied from two to four cards. With five examples at each set size, subjects saw 45 cards in all. The task allowed us to obtain a measure of subjects' accuracy at the verbal processes by determining whether or not they responded with the appropriate boxcar word for each of the 45 trials. The task also allowed us to obtain a measure of their memory for the products of the processes by determining how many of the appropriate boxcar words they could recall at the end of each set. And finally, we could eliminate the major memory requirement entirely by having subjects perform the same boxcar verbal processes on a set of 45 new exemplars, but this time without the requirement of having to store their responses to each trial and recall them at the end of the set. The number of processes correct out of 45 provided a memory-free verbal process measure to be contrasted with the memory-loaded one.

Table 3.1 Sample of a three-card set from the verbal span test and a three-card set from the math span test.

Card					Correct response
Verbal span					
	1. par	shot	don	ate	donate
	2. gang	sine	wed	lock	sinewed
	3. ear	fat	her	nest	father
Math span					
	1. 13	6	63		663
	2. 7	35	72		735
	3. 4	69	2		42

For *math span,* each card contained a series of three numbers such as *9 26 72.* Again a boxcar process was required. Subjects had to shunt together two of the three numbers (without changing their order, adding, or applying any arithmetical operation) so that the resulting larger number was divisible by 3. The correct response in this case would be *972* (formed by joining *9* and *72*) because *972* is divisible by 3. Table 3.1 contains additional examples of math span trials. For each card, subjects had to say as quickly and accurately as possible the number that conformed to the rule, and at the end of the set of two, three or four cards they had to recall aloud the correct numbers from each card in the set. The correct memory response for the set in Table 3.1

would be *663, 735, 42*. As in verbal span, both accuracy of the math processes and memory for the products of them could be measured. Also, a memory-free math process score was obtained by having subjects perform the math processes on a new set of 45 cards without the requirement of recalling their responses at the end of a set.

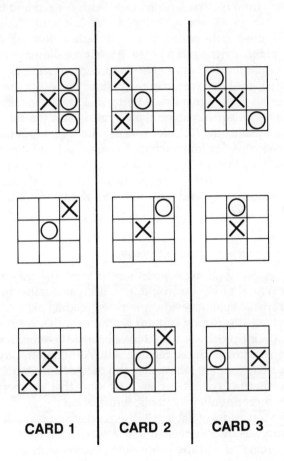

CARD 1   **CARD 2**   **CARD 3**

Figure 3.1 Sample of a three-card set from the spatial span test.

For *spatial span*, each card depicted a two-dimensional representation of a three-dimensional tic-tac-toe game. The card was divided into a top, middle and bottom panel, each containing a 3 × 3 cell grid which subjects were to imagine as the top, middle and bottom platforms on a three-dimensional tic-tac-toe board. Some of the cells were occupied by red and blue tokens representing the pieces of the two players in the game. Embedded in this configuration of tokens was a winning sequence, that is, three tokens of the same colour that formed a straight line in conformity with the rules of three-dimensional tic-tac-toe (a line that was horizontal, vertical or diagonal in a two-dimensional or three-dimensional plane). The subject's task in each case was to locate the winning line. Figure 3.1 illustrates a set of three consecutive cards from the spatial span task, with the red and blue tokens represented as Os and Xs, respectively. On the first card, depicted at the extreme left of Figure 3.1, the winning line is a two-dimensional vertical row of Os in the top plane. On the second card, it is a three-dimensional diagonal row of Xs, beginning in the bottom left-hand corner of the top plane and ending in the top right-hand corner of the bottom plane. On the third card, the winning line is a three-dimensional horizontal row of Xs forming a stair-way through the middle row. Subjects saw one card at a time and identified the winning line by touching the three tokens with their index finger. At the end of a set of two, three or four such cards, subjects had to recall the loca-tions of each winning line in the set by pointing to the correct positions on an actual three-dimensional Plexiglas tic-tac-toe gameboard. For the memory-free version, they did not have to recall the locations from successive trials in a set.

The answer: general versus language-specific processor

As suggested previously, strong support for the view that reading depends on a general or central processor would have been a situation in which the math span and spatial span measures predicted reading skill as well as did the verbal span measure. Strong support for the view that reading depends on a language-specific processor would have been a situation in which only the verbal span measure predicted reading skill. Although the actual results fell between the two extremes, I think they still provide considerable support for a language-specific system, or at least one that is specialized for manipulating and representing symbolic information.

As seen in the top panel of Table 3.2, the predictive power of a working memory measure was directly related to the surface similarity between its processing requirements and the processing requirements of the criterion task(s). Because the criterion tasks were verbal, verbal span (either its process or its memory component) was the best predictor. Verbal span was highly correlated with reading comprehension, vocabulary and overall verbal ability, with correlations ranging from 0.56 to 0.62. Math span, which likely shares some of the symbol-manipulating processes of verbal span, also tended to be significantly correlated with verbal ability. However, given that math span taps additional and unique quantitative processes, it was not as good a predictor as verbal span. The correlations between math span and the verbal ability tests ranged from 0.26 to 0.51. Moreover, none of the

Table 3.2 Correlations among variables

	Reading comprehension	Vocabulary knowledge	Verbal ability
Working memory			
Verbal span			
processes	0.58***	0.55***	0.62***
memory	0.55***	0.56***	0.61***
Math span			
processes	0.26	0.34*	0.33*
memory	0.49**	0.44**	0.51**
Spatial span			
processes	−0.13	0.12	−0.01
memory	−0.06	−0.11	−0.09
Memory-free processes			
Verbal processes	0.56***	0.56***	0.62***
Math processes	0.38*	0.35*	0.40*
Spatial processes	0.05	0.12	0.09
Task novelty			
High (session 1)	−0.06	0.16	0.06
Moderate (session 2)	0.46**	0.45**	0.50**
Low (session 3)	0.33*	0.24	0.31

* $p < 0.05$.
** $p < 0.01$.
*** $p < 0.001$.
Note: Data are from Daneman and Tardif (in press). Verbal ability scores reflect a combination of the reading comprehension and vocabulary knowledge scores.

correlations between math span and the verbal ability tests was significant when the effects of verbal span were partialled out first. By contrast, verbal span remained significantly correlated with all verbal ability tests when the effects of math span were removed statistically. And finally, spatial span, which appears to have the least overlap in processes with the verbal and mathematical tasks, did not correlate significantly with verbal span, math span or any of the verbal ability tests. Indeed, all correlations involving spatial span and the verbal ability tests were virtually zero.

Of course, the finding that verbal span was the best predictor of reading comprehension is open to two interpretations. One is that reading relies on a language-specific system rather than a general working memory system. The second is that math span and spatial span were not good measures of working memory capacity. An argument can be made against the second interpretation on the basis of the findings of a larger study (see Daneman, 1986) in which the same subjects were given a wide range of mathematical and spatial ability tests in addition to the reading and vocabulary ability tests reported here. The findings of the larger study showed a high degree of domain specificity; math span was the best predictor of mathematical ability and spatial span was the best predictor of spatial ability. Hence, all three span measures seemed to be equally good at tapping task-specific skills. With the second interpretation ruled out, it seems reasonable to interpret the results for the reading portion as showing that reading is limited by a system specialized for representing and processing verbal or symbolic information only.

The Daneman and Tardif (in press) results are consistent with two recent individual-differences studies showing a high degree of processing specificity in working memory (Baddeley *et al.*, 1985; Daneman and Green, 1986).

Daneman and Green (1986) contrasted the original reading span test with a speaking span variant which required subjects to generate sentences for increasingly longer sets of unrelated words rather than comprehend sentences containing the words. While the two span measures were themselves correlated, speaking span was the better predictor of a contextual vocabulary production task and reading span was the better predictor of a contextual vocabulary comprehension task. Because the two span tests imposed identical storage requirements, namely storing increasingly longer sets of unrelated words, Daneman and Green argued that their differential predictor power reflected their rather different processing requirements— verbal production processes in the case of speaking span and verbal comprehension ones in the case of reading span. Daneman and Green argued against a single central processor with a unitary capacity, but in keeping with functional notions of working memory, we argued for a general and central processor whose storage capacity will depend on how efficient the individual is at the specific processes demanded by the task to which it is being applied. Of course the Daneman and Green (1986) study only involved a contrast between two verbal measures of working memory capacity. On the basis of the more recent Daneman and Tardif (in press) study which extended the analysis to mathematical and spatial measures of capacity, we believe the concept of a general or central processor needs revision.

Baddeley *et al.* (1985) pitted reading span against counting span, a nonverbal working measure used by Case, Kurland and Goldberg (1982), in order to determine which was the better predictor of reading comprehension. The two span measures were moderately correlated with one another, and again, reading span, the measure with the processing requirements most resembling the criterion task, was the better predictor of the two, with counting span contributing nothing to the correlation after the effects of reading span were partialled out. Despite this pattern of results, Baddeley *et al.* (1985) were reluctant to abandon the notion of a single central processor.

Their general argument against positing a separate language-specific processor for reading comprehension was that 'other investigations into working memory have not indicated the need for separate central processors' (Baddeley *et al.*, 1985, p. 130). Their specific argument was that the counting span test, a measure designed to tax the processing capacities of children, may not have been sufficiently taxing to provide an appropriate measure of working memory for adults (cf also Daneman and Carpenter, 1980, for a similar argument). Baddeley *et al.* (1985) chose to defer their decision on the issue of 'a general and central limitation in information processing' until 'the development of a wider range of measures of working memory capacity' (p. 130).

We think we now have a wider range of measures of working memory capacity and that the picture suggests the need for abandoning the notion of a 'general and central limitation on information processing', a 'central executive' (Baddeley, 1981, 1983) if you will. At very least we may have to posit two separate processors, one for representing and manipulating verbal-symbolic information and a second for representing and manipulating spatial information. It is the verbal-symbolic processor that would be directly involved in reading, the topic of this chapter.

However, this view of a language-specific processor for reading will need further qualification in light of the results discussed in the next section on the interaction between processing and storage functions.

The answer: process versus memory

So far I have hardly differentiated between the process and the memory components of the span measures, except to point out that the verbal process and verbal memory components were both highly correlated with reading comprehension. Indeed, the correlations were very similar, 0.58 for verbal processes and 0.55 for verbal memory. The near equivalence of the processing capacity and memory capacity measures (see also Daneman, 1986) is entirely compatible with the theory of individual differences in central working memory capacity espoused earlier. According to the theory, temporary storage capacity is contingent upon processing efficiency. Consequently, performance on the processing and memory components should be positively correlated and both should be related to the same complex information-processing tasks. However, it was our next manipulation that seriously calls into question the necessity for invoking the concept of temporary storage in accounting for individual differences in reading.

One way to investigate how important the memory component is, and in fact whether memory interferes at all with processing, is to eliminate the major memory requirements of the span task altogether. This, you will remember, was done by having subjects perform memory-free versions of the verbal, mathematical and spatial processes. The middle panel of Table 3.2 shows how the memory-free process scores correlated with reading and verbal ability. A comparison of the predictive power of the two process measures, the one with the additional memory load (top panel) and the one without the additional memory load (middle panel), shows an almost identical pattern of results. In other words, presence or absence of a memory component during processing did not influence the predictive power of the measure. The only factor that seemed to be important in determining whether a particular task would or would not predict reading skill was the domain of the processes that task tapped. For the task to predict reading skill, the processes had to be symbolic, that is, involve the manipulation of words (verbal processes) and, to a lesser extent, numbers (math processes). The additional memory requirement during process execution was dispensable. Of course there are theoretical problems with making a distinction between process and storage (cf also Baddeley and Hitch, 1974), and eliminating the requirement to store the final product of a process does not eliminate all memory requirements from the task, because each stage in the execution of that process will likely generate intermediate products to be stored. However, to the extent that we have shown that elimination of the major memory load did not affect the predictive power of the measure, there seems little reason to use measures of temporary storage for *assessing* individual differences in reading comprehension.

But what about invoking the concept of temporary storage for *understanding* individual differences in verbal comprehension abilities? Here, the answer is not so clear. From a theoretical standpoint, the concept of temporary storage in comprehension is very attractive. As discussed earlier, linguistic analyses of text seem to demand that information be retained temporarily while new information is being processed. Our data do not demand that we relinquish the concept of temporary storage. Indeed, they corroborate earlier arguments that the amount of storage capacity an individual will have is a direct function of how efficient that individual is at the computational aspects of the task, and consequently, like the computational aspects, functional storage capacity will also be related to the skill with which the processor can do its work.

However, because the data now show that for matters of measurement it is not mandatory to tax the memory component, and thereby suggest that memory does not influence or interfere with processing efficiency in any relevant way, one might argue that working memory as an individual-differences construct is unnecessary theoretical baggage. But of greater concern than this, I think that the individual-differences construct of working memory may stunt theoretical advancement. If the 'memory' is simply a by-product of the 'processes', it is the processes themselves and what leads to skilled execution of the processes that should be receiving the lion's share of our attention.

The articulatory loop

The perspicacious reader may have noticed that my criterion for what constituted positive evidence for working memory's role in reading was not consistent across the sections on the central executive and the articulatory loop. In both cases, the positive evidence was largely based on showing that individual differences in the capacity of the working memory system in question could account for individual differences in reading; however, the kind of individual differences differed. In the central executive section, I required my measure of working memory to differentiate between good and poor readers in a normal population of adults or children. Indeed, replacement of the old short-term memory with the newer working memory framework was largely based on the fact that the old measures of short-term memory such as digit span and word span could not differentiate between good and poor readers unless the poor readers were extremely poor, that is, labelled as retarded or developmentally dyslexic. A measure such as reading span was preferred because it could predict differences in reading comprehension skills even in a fairly circumscribed population of university students (Daneman and Carpenter, 1980). By contrast, in the articulatory loop section I accepted, as support for the articulatory loop's role in learning to read, evidence based on a comparison between normal and developmentally retarded readers (e.g. Jorm, 1983), readers who for the most part are just those few individuals who *do* show deficiencies in digit span. Hence, my criterion was more lax in the defence of the articulatory loop. Of course, in the articulatory loop section I was simply reflecting the prevailing opinion in a literature to which I have not myself contributed. Now that it is time to present my own case against the articulatory loop, I will challenge two aspects to the approach. Unlike my case against the central executive, this one is not based on any new empirical evidence.

My first point is that we should be aware of problems associated with extreme-groups designs. I am not proposing a wholesale dismissal of approaches that use clinical populations to infer normal functioning. Indeed such approaches can be very useful and informative. However, we should always be alert to the dangers of including very wide ranges of abilities in our sample. If we use very wide ranges of reading abilities, it will make even the weakest predictors of reading ability look extremely powerful (cf also Sternberg, 1985). If people low enough in reading ability were included in the sample, even the ability to use a knife and fork would be correlated with reading ability. One safeguard against this is to limit one's study to populations of individuals whose retardation is specific to reading rather than to populations of individuals whose reading disorders occur in the context of low intelligence and low overall academic performance (e.g. Jorm, 1983). Nevertheless, if differences in the articulatory loop can only be witnessed with extreme-groups designs, this suggests that, at best, the articulatory loop plays a minor or back-up role in reading.

My second point in the case against the articulatory loop has to do with the fact that articulatory loop research is still very much tied to the use of traditional measures of immediate memory such as digit span. I see an irony here. Those who have abandoned short-term memory in favour of working memory and concentrated their research efforts exclusively on the articulatory loop subsystem have in fact been studying, with few exceptions, the very same system they abandoned. And just as the original concept of a short-term verbal memory was criticized for its lack of relevance to ecologically interesting complex cognitive tasks, so too might the articulatory loop be.

My gut feeling is that the major usefulness of the articulatory loop will be in explaining the speech-like parameters of experimenter-invented short-term memory tasks such as memory span (e.g. Baddeley, Lewis and Vallar, 1984; Ellis and Hennelley, 1980). As for ecologically relevant tasks, the articulatory loop will probably be most relevant for *speech* comprehension (Baddeley, Vallar and Wilson, in press). Of course, as long as we are talking about the updated model (Baddeley, Vallar and Wilson, in press) which gives the articulatory loop the ability to execute grapheme-to-phoneme recoding rules, the system must play some role in reading. However, give it the ability to execute some more symbol-manipulating processes and we will have created the kind of language-specific processor argued for in the previous section on the central executive, thereby eliminating the need for two separate systems. In any case, if, as advocated here, we turn our attention to the processes that contribute to individual differences in reading rather than to the process-contingent memories, the distinction between a processor and an auxiliary articulatory loop will become irrelevant.

CONCLUDING REMARKS

This chapter began with the premise that reading should be studied within the context of general information processing or cognitive theory, and then explored the relevance of one information processing construct, namely working memory capacity, in accounting for individual differences in reading ability. Recent empirical findings were presented which challenged the notion that a single central working memory system is responsible for reading and all information processing. Rather the evidence invited a domain-specific notion of control, with reading being under the control of a system specialized for manipulating verbal or symbolic information only. In addition, the evidence cast doubt on the usefulness of pursuing the concept of temporary storage in reading given that it was totally dispensable in the measurement of individual differences in reading ability. Naturally temporary storage could still play a role in the theory of reading, even if redundant in matters of measurement. However, the recommendation was for a shift in theoretical and empirical focus from storage to process.

This emphasis on process over storage is certainly not a first. Indeed, history has a habit of repeating itself. In 1978 Baddeley published a paper entitled 'The trouble with levels' in which he attacked Craik and Lockhart's (1972) widely accepted levels-of-processing framework for studying memory. Baddeley (1978) argued that levels-of-processing, in its effort to counteract the inflexible multistore approach to memory by emphasizing processes over storage, had become too concerned with searching for 'broad general principles' (p. 140). Baddeley (1978) advocated 'a return to the detailed analysis of specific subcomponents of human memory' (p. 148) as a more fruitful 'way of separating out and analyzing more deeply the complex underlying processes' (p. 150). He presented his working memory approach not as a direct replacement for levels-of-processing because it is concerned for the most part with different issues, but as an illustration of his preferred approach to memory. And now, after less than a decade of working memory research, I find myself repeating history so to speak, having written a paper that could easily be entitled 'The trouble with working memory' in which my conclusion, albeit in the context of working memory, sounds very Craik and Lockhartish. My conclusion is that we should be concentrating on the 'work' rather than the 'memory' of working memory, that the memory is simply a by-product of the skill with which the work is done. Some wit once protested that it is not really history that repeats itself but historians that repeat each other. However, I am by no means advocating a return to the search for general encoding processes or principles. Indeed, I would urge that we focus on much more specific processes in our investigation of ways to measure and understand reading skills.

What are the processes that are good predictors of reading comprehension? What are the processes that underlie these reading comprehension skills? Has this latest research (e.g. Daneman, 1986; Daneman and Tardif, in press) provided any leads?

With respect to predictive validity, I think the research has fared quite well. We have identified one process, the boxcar verbal process, which is a very good predictor of performance on tests of reading and vocabulary ability. However, predictive validity is not enough. It would be nice to have construct validity too. In other words, we ought to be able to characterize what aspects of the process are important so that we could predict what other classes of processes would be good predictors of verbal intelligence too.

With respect to construct validity, one could argue that our research has explained nothing, that our argument has been circular. What we have done is identify a new task that is correlated with complex verbal functioning because it too is saturated with 'verbal' processes. We then want to use this task to explain individual differences in verbal functioning. However, had we known about this boxcar process beforehand, we might have included it in our battery of criterion tasks as a marker of verbal intellectual functioning, not an explanation of it. The only way to escape circularity is to show that our predictor task is derived independently of the criterion ones, according to some theoretical construct (Detterman, 1982). As long as our processes were couched in the context of working memory theory, we were safe. Now, stripped of the working memory construct, we are threatened with circularity, one could argue.

I think that a certain amount of circularity is inevitable as long as domain specificity of the process is the critical ingredient in predicting performance on complex information-processing tasks such as reading. However, there is a possibility of avoiding the circularity, at least partially. Although I do not wish to retract my position on the general principle of task specificity, there may be a second important principle in individual-differences measurement and theory, and one which does not rely on domain specificity of processes. This is the principle of 'degree of novelty', which is most clearly articulated in Sternberg's (1985) new triarchic theory of intelligence and for which the current research provides some preliminary support.

Sternberg (1985) has argued that tasks or processes best tap intelligent performance when they are novel in a person's experience, that is, when they require some problem-solving in learning or executing. Tasks can be novel to learn or execute or both. Sternberg suggests that the optimal degree of novelty for intelligence testing is an intermediate one where the task is novel either in terms of comprehending how best to do it or in terms of actually executing it, but not both.

Daneman and Tardif (in press) had the ideal set-up to observe possible changes in the predictive power of tasks as a function of where they are on the experiential continuum. Our three working memory span tasks, verbal, mathematical and spatial, shared a lot of structural features but at the same time differed in the exact nature of the processes they tapped. Moreover, the tasks were given to subjects at three successive sessions, with order of presentation counterbalanced across subjects. When I recalculated process span scores according to session of administration (1, 2 or 3) rather than process domain of the task (verbal, math, spatial) and correlated session scores with our tests of reading and vocabulary, the pattern was very clear. As seen in the bottom panel of Table 3.2, performance at session 1 was uncorrelated with reading and vocabulary skills; performance at session 2 was highly correlated, with correlations ranging from 0.45 to 0.50; performance at session 3 was marginally correlated with reading comprehension only. The fact that session 2 was the best predictor is consistent with the theory that the best measures of intellectual functioning involve some but not excessive novelty. I would argue that at session 1 the task was too novel because it posed novelty in terms of comprehending how to do it and in terms of actually doing it. By session 2, however, only the execution was novel. Subjects would have acquired some understanding of the genre of task and were left with having to master the specific parameters of the new process.

In summary, these results suggest that degree of novelty may be an important theoretical construct in abilities measurement, and optimal degree of novelty may even sometimes compensate for lack of domain specificity of the process in predicting individual differences in a given task. Just how novelty and domain specificity complement or trade off each other is an interesting question for future individual-differences research.

ACKNOWLEDGMENT

The research reported in this chapter was supported in part by Grant A2690 from the Natural Sciences and Engineering Research Council of Canada.

Thanks are extended to Murray Stainton and Twila Tardif for their help in conducting some of the research.

REFERENCES

Atkinson, R.C., and Shiffrin, R.M. (1968). Human memory: A proposed system and its control processes. In K.W. Spence and J.T. Spence (Eds.) *The Psychology of Learning and Motivation: Advances in Research and Theory*, Vol. 2. New York: Academic Press.

Atkinson, R.C., and Shiffrin, R.M. (1971). The control of short-term memory. *Scientific American*, **225**, 82-90.

Baddeley, A.D. (1978). The trouble with levels: A reexamination of Craik and Lockhart's framework for memory research. *Psychological Review*, **85**, 139-152.

Baddeley, A.D. (1979). Working memory and reading. In P.A. Kolers, M.E. Wrolstad and H. Bouma (Eds.) *Processing of Visible Language*. New York: Plenum.

Baddeley, A.D. (1981). The concept of working memory: A view of its current state and probable future development. *Cognition*, **10**, 17-23.

Baddeley, A.D. (1983). Working memory. *Philosophical Transactions of the Royal Society, London*, **302**, 311-324.

Baddeley, A.D., Eldridge, M., and Lewis, V.J. (1981). The role of subvocalization in reading. *Quarterly Journal of Psychology*, **33A**, 439-454.

Baddeley, A.D., Grant, S., Wight, E., and Thomson, N. (1975). Imagery and visual working memory. In P.M.A. Rabbitt and S. Dornic (Eds.) *Attention and Performance V*. London: Academic Press.

Baddeley, A.D., and Hitch, G.J. (1974). Working memory. In G.A. Bower (Ed.) *The Psychology of Learning and Motivation*, Vol. 8. New York: Academic Press.

Baddeley, A.D., Lewis, V., and Vallar, G. (1984). Exploring the articulatory loop. *Quarterly Journal of Experimental Psychology*, **36A**, 233-252.

Baddeley, A.D., and Lieberman, K. (1980). Spatial working memory. In R. Nickerson (Ed.) *Attention and Performance VIII*. Hillsdale, N.J.: Erlbaum.

Baddeley, A.D., Logie, R., Nimmo-Smith, I., and Brereton, N. (1985). Components of fluent reading. *Journal of Memory and Language*, **24**, 119-131.

Baddeley, A.D., Vallar, G., and Wilson, B. (in press). Comprehension and the articulatory loop: Some neuropsychological evidence. In M. Coltheart (Ed.) *Attention and Performance XII*, London: Erlbaum.

Bakker, D.J. (1972). *Temporal Order in Disturbed Reading*. Rotterdam: Rotterdam University Press.

Baron, J. (1976). Mechanisms for pronouncing printed words: Use and acquisition. In D. LaBerge and S.J. Samuels (Eds.) *Basic Processes in Reading*. Hillsdale, N.J.: Erlbaum.

Broadbent, D.E. (1975). The magical number seven after fifteen years. In A. Kennedy and A. Wilkes (Eds.) *Studies in Long-Term Memory*. New York: Wiley.

Campbell, R., and Butterworth, B. (1985). Phonological dyslexia and dysgraphia in a highly literate subject: A developmental case with associated deficits of phonemic processing and awareness. *Quarterly Journal of Experimental Psychology, 37A*, 435-475.

Carpenter, P.A., and Daneman, M. (1981). Lexical retrieval and error recovery in reading: A model based on eye fixations. *Journal of Verbal Learning and Verbal Behavior, 20*, 137-160.

Case, R., Kurland, D.M., and Goldberg, J. (1982). Operational efficiency and the growth of short-term memory span. *Journal of Experimental Child Psychology, 33*, 386-404.

Chafe, W.L. (1972). Discourse structure and human knowledge. In R.O. Freedle and J.B. Carroll (Eds.) *Language Comprehension and the Acquisition of Knowledge*. Washington, DC: Winston.

Coltheart, M. (1978). Lexical access in simple reading tasks. In G. Underwood (Ed.) *Strategies of Information Processing*. London: Academic Press.

Conrad, R. (1972). The developmental role of subvocalizing in short-term memory. *Journal of Verbal Learning and Verbal Behavior, 11*, 521-533.

Craik, F.I.M., and Lockhart, R.S. (1972). Levels of processing: A framework for memory research. *Journal of Verbal Learning and Verbal Behavior, 11*, 671-684.

Cummings, E.M., and Faw, T.T. (1976). Short-term memory and equivalence judgments in normal and retarded readers. *Child Development, 47*, 286-289.

Daneman, M. (1982). The measurement of reading comprehension: How not to trade construct validity for predictive power. *Intelligence, 6*, 331-345.

Daneman, M. (1984). Why some readers are better than others: A process and storage account. In R.J. Sternberg (Ed.) *Advances in the Theory of Intelligence*, Vol. 2. Hillsdale, N.J.: Erlbaum.

Daneman, M. (1986). Taking the memory out of working memory. Unpublished manuscript, University of Toronto.

Daneman, M., and Blennerhassett, A. (1984). How to assess the listening comprehension skills of prereaders. *Journal of Educational Psychology, 76*, 1372-1381.

Daneman, M., and Carpenter, P.A. (1980). Individual differences in working memory and reading. *Journal of Verbal Learning and Verbal Behavior, 19*, 450-466.

Daneman, M., and Carpenter, P.A. (1983). Individual differences in integrating information between and within sentences. *Journal of Experimental Psychology: Learning, Memory, and Cognition, 9*, 561-583.

Daneman, M., and Green, I. (1986). Individual differences in comprehending and producing words in context. *Journal of Memory and Language, 25*, 1-18.

Daneman, M., and Tardif, T. (in press). Working memory and reading skill reexamined. In M. Coltheart (Ed.) *Attention and Performance XII*, London: Erlbaum.

Dee-Lucas, D., Just, M.A., Carpenter, P.A., and Daneman, M. (1982). What eye fixations tell us about the time course of text integration. In R. Groner and P. Fraisse (Eds.) *Cognition and Eye Movements*. Amsterdam: North-Holland.

Detterman, D.K. (1982). Does 'g' exist? *Intelligence*, 6, 99-108.

Ellis, N.C., and Hennelley, R.A. (1980). A bilingual word-length effect: Implications for intelligence testing and the relative ease of mental calculation in Welsh and English. *British Journal of Psychology*, 71, 43-52.

Ellis, N.C., and Miles, T.R. (1978). Visual information processing in dyslexic children. In M.M. Gruneberg, P.E. Morris and R.N. Sykes (Eds.) *Practical Aspects of Memory*. London: Academic Press.

Farnham-Diggory, S., and Gregg, L.W. (1975). Short-term memory function in young readers. *Journal of Experimental Child Psychology*, 19, 279-298.

Goyen, J.D., and Lyle, J.G. (1973). Short-term memory and visual discrimination in retarded readers. *Perceptual and Motor Skills*, 36, 403-408.

Greenman, R. (1983). *Words in Action*. New York: Times Books.

Guyer, B.L., and Friedman, M.P. (1975). Hemispheric processing and cognitive styles in learning-disabled and normal children. *Child Development*, 46, 658-668.

Huey, E.B. (1908). *The Psychology and Pedagogy of Reading*. New York: Macmillan. Reprinted, Cambridge, MA: MIT Press, 1968.

Hulme, C. (1981). *Reading Retardation and Multi-Sensory Teaching*. London: Routledge & Kegan Paul.

Hunt, E. (1980). Intelligence as an information-processing concept. *British Journal of Psychology*, 71, 449-474.

Hunt, E., Frost, N., and Lunneborg, C. (1973). Individual differences in cognition: A new approach to intelligence. In G.H. Bower (Ed.) *The Psychology of Learning and Motivation: Advances in Research and Theory*, Vol. 7. New York: Academic Press.

Hunt, E., Lunneborg, C., and Lewis, J. (1975). What does it mean to be high-verbal? *Cognitive Psychology*, 7, 194-227.

Jarvella, R.J. (1971). Syntactic processing of learned speech. *Journal of Verbal Learning and Verbal Behavior*, 10, 409-416.

Jensen, A.R. (1980). *Bias in Mental Testing*. New York: Free Press.

Jorm, A.F. (1981). Children with reading and spelling retardation: Functioning of whole-word and correspondence-rule mechanisms. *Journal of Child Psychology and Psychiatry*, 22, 171-178.

Jorm, A.F. (1983). Specific reading retardation and working memory: A review. *British Journal of Psychology*, 74, 311-342.

Just, M.A., and Carpenter, P.A. (1980). A theory of reading: From eye-fixations to comprehension. *Psychological Review*, 87, 329-354.

Kintsch, W., and van Dijk, T.A. (1978). Toward a model of text comprehension and production. *Psychological Review*, 85, 363-394.

Kintsch, W., and Vipond, D. (1979). Reading comprehension and readability in educational practice and psychological theory. In L.G. Nilsson (Ed.) *Perspectives on Memory Research*. Hillsdale, N.J.: Erlbaum.

Kleiman, G.M. (1975). Speech recoding in reading. *Journal of Verbal Learning and Verbal Behavior*, 24, 323-339.

Levy, B.A. (1977). Reading: Speech and meaning processes. *Journal of Verbal Learning and Verbal Behavior*, 16, 623-638.

Levy, B.A. (1978). Speech analysis during sentence processing: Reading versus listening. *Visible Language*, 12, 81-101.

Liberman, I.Y., Shankweiler, D., Liberman, A.M., Fowler, C., and Fischer, F.W. (1977). Phonetic segmentation and recoding in the beginning reader. In A.S. Reber and D.L. Scarborough (Eds.) *Towards a Psychology of Reading: The Proceedings of the CUNY Conference*. Hillsdale, N.J.: Erlbaum.

Mann, V.A., Liberman, I.Y., and Shankweiler, D. (1980). Children's memory for sentences and word strings in relation to reading ability. *Memory & Cognition*, **8**, 329-335.

Masson, M., and Miller, J.A. (1983). Working memory and individual differences in comprehension and memory of text. *Journal of Educational Psychology*, **75**, 314-318.

McConkie, G.W., and Rayner, K. (1975). The span of the effective stimulus during a fixation in reading. *Perception and Psychophysics*, **17**, 578-586.

Miles, T.R. and Wheeler, T.J. (1974). Toward a new theory of dyslexia. *Dyslexia Review*, **11**, 9-11.

Miller, G.A. (1956). The magical number seven, plus or minus two: Some limits on our capacity for processing information. *Psychological Review*, **63**, 81-97.

Mitchell, D.C., and Green, D.W. (1978). The effects of context and content on immediate processing in reading. *Quarterly Journal of Experimental Psychology*, **30**, 609-636.

Perfetti, C.D., and Goldman, S.R. (1976). Discourse memory and reading comprehension skill. *Journal of Verbal Learning and Verbal Behavior*, **14**, 33-42.

Perfetti, C.D., and Lesgold, A.M. (1977). Discourse comprehension and individual differences. In P. Carpenter and M. Just (Eds.) *Processes in Comprehension*. Hillsdale, N.J.: Erlbaum.

Posner, M.I. and Rossman, E. (1965). Effects of size and location of informational transforms upon short-term retention. *Journal of Experimental Psychology*, **70**, 496-505.

Rayner, K. (1975). The perceptual span and peripheral cues in reading. *Cognitive Psychology*, **7**, 65-81.

Rayner, K. (1978). Eye movements in reading and information processing. *Psychological Bulletin*, **85**, 618-660.

Rizzo, N.D. (1939). Studies in visual and auditory memory span with specific reference to reading disability. *Journal of Experimental Education*, **8**, 208-244.

Snowling, M.J. (1980). The development of grapheme–phoneme correspondence in normal and dyslexic readers. *Journal of Experimental Child Psychology*, **29**, 294-305.

Sternberg, R.J. (1985). *Beyond IQ: A Triarchic Theory of Human Intelligence*. Cambridge: Cambridge University Press.

Sternberg, R.J., and Powell, J.S. (1983). Comprehending verbal comprehension. *American Psychologist*, **38**, 878-893.

Torgesen, J.K., and Goldman, T. (1977). Verbal rehearsal and short-term memory in reading-disabled children. *Child Development*, **48**, 56-60.

Valtin, R. (1973). Reports of research on dyslexia in children. Paper presented at International Reading Association, Denver (ERIC Document Reproduction Service No. EO 079713).

Waugh, N.C., and Norman, D.A. (1965). Primary memory. *Psychological Review*, **72**, 89-104.

Cognitive approaches to reading
Edited by J. R. Beech and A. M. Colley
© 1987 John Wiley & Sons Ltd

CHAPTER 4

Reading and Syntactic Analysis

DON C. MITCHELL

Department of Psychology, University of Exeter

ROLE OF SYNTACTIC ANALYSIS IN READING

Reading for meaning depends upon a variety of different forms of information processing, most of which are examined at some point or another in this volume. The present chapter is concerned with processes that start with ordered strings of words and use the information to compute the syntactic structure of successive sentences in the text. The raw materials for these procedures include the end-products of the word recognition processes considered by Seymour in Chapter 2 and the output forms the basis for the more general textual processes discussed by Colley in Chapter 5. I hope to show that syntactic analysis of this kind is a prerequisite for successful comprehension and then to give some indication how it might be carried out. But first it is useful to pause and ask exactly what it entails.

In simple terms, comprehension depends on two kinds of structural decision. First, it is necessary to assign appropriate syntactic labels to various strings of words in the sentence (e.g. noun phrase, verb phrase, relative clause, etc.). Second, it is essential to specify the relationships between the different linguistic objects by linking them up in a sensible manner. Thus, in sentence (1), below, the strings 'the aggressive lecturer' and 'a student' have to be *labelled* as NPs and 'who was sleeping' has to be identified as a relative clause, while the adjective 'aggressive' has to be *linked* or attached to the noun 'lecturer' and the relative clause to the 'student', etc.

(1) The aggressive lecturer, ignoring conventional etiquette, prodded a student who was sleeping.

Clearly if these decisions are incorrect, or if they are not made at all, then the material will be difficult or impossible to understand. They also play an important part in determining the intonation patterns employed when people read aloud.

From this it can be seen that syntactic processing is an important subcomponent of reading and should be included in any comprehensive theoretical account of the reading process. The motives for studying parsing are not exclusively theoretical, however. There are also *practical* reasons for giving careful consideration to the process. Evidence from componential analyses of reading achievement suggests that individual differences in higher-level syntactic and semantic skills make a significant contribution to overall reading competence and it also seems that this effect is independent of differences associated with variations in word reading skills (see Hunt, 1986). It therefore seems likely that difficulties at the syntactic level might be implicated in certain forms of reading backwardness.

The present chapter will use psycholinguistic evidence to piece together what is currently known about syntactic processing. The first part of the chapter will concentrate on the performance of fluent readers and later we will consider some recent work on parsing in disabled readers, particularly agrammatic aphasics. To set up a framework, we now consider some of the more influential theories of parsing.

FORMAL AND INFORMAL THEORIES OF PARSING

Over the last fifteen years or so, researchers have put forward numerous proposals concerning the ways in which sentences might be analysed into their structural components. In some cases the intention has been to outline and elaborate on the principles and procedures which might be used in any efficient parsing system (human or artificial). In others the main aim has been to develop a viable artificial parser and implement it on a machine. Thirdly, there are theories that are concerned not so much with the *principles* of parsing as with how *people* tackle the process. This last group is the most relevant to the study of reading, but it is useful to consider some of the more general theories because they introduce themes, concepts and issues which help to clarify what is involved in parsing. In the remainder of this section I shall briefly describe several different approaches to parsing, keeping roughly to the chronological order in which they were proposed. After that I shall draw out some of the recurrent questions and issues raised in these accounts. In the next section I shall review some of the recent literature on these topics and consider which of the various theoretical positions can be sustained in the light of empirical work. Finally, on the basis of this evidence I shall go on to present an outline of what a psychologically valid parser should look like.

Heuristic strategies

In the late sixties and early seventies Fodor, Bever and Garrett (e.g. 1974, for a review) expounded a view of parsing which is based on the idea that people use heuristic strategies to determine the syntactic structure of sentences. Heuristic strategies are simple rules that can be applied to the input and used directly to compute the probable structure of each clause or sentence as it appears. One example was a rule-of-thumb which they dubbed the *canonical-sentence strategy*. This comes into operation when the text contains the sequence of constituents *NP–V–NP*. The strategy is simply to assign the labels *subject, main verb* and *object* to the three constituents respectively. It turns out that this strategy will often produce the correct analysis of the sentence because in the vast majority of sentences of this form the *S–V–O* pattern is the standard or canonical structure. In a second strategy (the *lexical analysis strategy*), Fodor *et al.* proposed that the parser uses detailed lexical information about certain words to generate hypotheses about the overall structure of the clause and, perhaps more importantly, to constrain the range and number of hypotheses to be considered in the subsequent analysis of the sentence. Other strategies dealt with processing at clause boundaries and the use of surface structure cues. Although these proposals do not amount to a general theory of parsing (as the authors themselves admit, see p. 361 of their book), it seems likely that simple rules-of-thumb like these may play an important role in the process of parsing sentences. At the very least, the proposal was influential in setting the scene for more comprehensive accounts to follow.

ATNs and cascaded ATNs

One of the most popular types of parsing theory is that based on a formalism known as augmented transition networks (ATNs: Woods, 1970; Stevens and Rumelhart, 1975; Wanner, 1980; see Mitchell, 1982, pp. 87–99 for a simplified account). An ATN can be regarded as a highly organized set of rules for building and linking linguistic structures. Each rule tests for the presence of certain features in the input and carries out a particular action or operation whenever the relevant features are found. An important characteristic of ATNs is that the rules are syntactically *context-dependent*. In other words, they are only applied at very specific points in the sentence—i.e. when the parser is in the correct state or configuration. ATNs have a simple and appealing way of expressing this context-dependency. Every state or configuration that the parser can potentially assume is represented by a circle labelled with an appropriate mnemonic tag (e.g. Si, NPi, RCi, etc.). In each state, the rules that can legitimately be applied are represented by a series of labelled *arcs*, leaving the circle standing for the state in question. Each arc ends in a new destination state corresponding to the configuration of the parser *after* the rule has been applied. Where several different rules might be implemented, the ATN specifies the order in which the different options should be attempted. By convention, the rule examined first is the one represented by the arc immediately to the right of the twelve o'clock position on the state circle, followed by the next arc in the clockwise direction, and so on.

In the simplest cases an arc is traversed (and the rule therefore applied) if the current word has a given property. In other cases much more complicated conditions have to be satisfied before the rule can be implemented. For instance, a commonly employed condition is that the next N words have to be successfully run through an entirely separate ATN structure (i.e. a 'subroutine') before the corresponding arc can be traversed.

Using this kind of formalism, a sentence can be parsed by allowing control to pass from a distinctive 'initial' state to an 'end' state, via a series of intermediate steps. At any point in the analysis, possible continuations are considered (tested) one at a time according to a prespecified order of priorities. The parser checks through the alternatives until it finds one in which the conditions are satisfied. It then builds the substructure associated with the arc and passes control on to the next state. The process continues in this way either until the final state is reached (in which case the sentence has been successfully parsed) or until it reaches a state from which no further progress is possible (indicating that one of the earlier choices must have been mistaken). The parser deals with deadlocks of this kind by using some kind of *backtracking* procedure to unravel recent choices, destroy the associated structures and return to a state in which it is possible to test a previously unexplored network of arcs.

ATN parsers differ from one another in a variety of ways, such as the range of different states postulated, the order of priorities assigned to different arcs (rules), the nature of the information which can be tested or examined before allowing a rule to be applied and the nature of the backtracking procedures employed following deadlock. Of these, the major differences probably lie in the specification of the kind of information that can be used as a condition for traversing an arc. While all models include at least some arcs which test words for their part of speech (e.g. N, V, etc.) some also use semantic information either to guide the immediate choice of an option (e.g. Miller and Johnson-Laird, 1976) or to test the acceptability of some recently built structure (e.g. Winograd, 1972; Bobrow and Webber, 1980). In this latter case, conventional syntactic analysis and semantic checking are interleaved with one another in an arrangement which is sometimes referred to as 'cascaded ATNs' (Woods, 1980). We will return to these alternatives later.

Anderson's ACT parser

For all their strengths as artificial parsers, ATNs have properties which make them seem unrealistic as models of *human* parsing. Anderson (1976, Section 11.2) has drawn attention to a number of these features. Perhaps the most important are (1) their techniques for error recovery and (2) their strict dependence on the options available in the current state. On the first issue, the basic problem is that typical backtracking procedures depend upon keeping track both of the options already tried and those which still remain available. Anderson (1976) has argued that a system operating in this way would call for storage facilities beyond those traditionally assumed to be available to average readers. The second feature (i.e. state dependence) has the unfortunate consequence that ATNs are unable to make any progress at all in processing phrases like 'the large cuddly puppy' in example (2) (taken from Anderson, 1976, p. 473).

(2)   Daddy bought a very the large cuddly puppy.

Since misplaced phrases of this kind are not totally uninterpretable there must be ways of analysing material which is not predicted in the present state of the parser.

These, and other, considerations have led Anderson (Anderson, 1976; Anderson, Kline and Lewis, 1977) to put forward an alternative to the ATN model. This is based upon Anderson's ACT system for modelling cognitive processes. Like those in ATNs, the primitives in the ACT system are condition–action rules, or *productions* to use the accepted jargon. However, Anderson's system differs from ATNs both in the *content* of the rules and in the *circumstances* in which they can be activated. Thus, to avoid some of the problems associated with backtracking, the parser incorporates a set of productions which allow it to look one or two words beyond the current position before deciding which label to assign to the word under examination. This *lookahead* facility distinguishes the ACT model from ATNs, which are obliged to make their preliminary decisions on the basis of the current word alone. The ACT system also has access to detailed information about content words (over and above part of speech). The result is that the flow of control in the parsing system can change depending on the precise words that appear in the text. For example, the parser goes through a different set of operations when the word 'gives' in a sentence frame is replaced by the word 'receives' (Anderson, 1976, pp. 464–465; see also Anderson, Kline and Lewis, 1977, p. 291). The changes in rule content are not restricted to those associated with the *condition* part of the rule. ACT also introduces new types of *action*. For example, there is a production which marks a noun phrase as *contradictory* if there is a number mismatch (e.g. 'a large balls').

Turning next to the regime for *activating* productions, the major changes are that the ACT system can allow more than one rule to be activated at the same time (see Anderson, Kline and Lewis, 1977, p. 288) and that the system included procedures which can self-activate when their initial words are encountered in the input. The first feature helps the system to cope with ambiguity while the second frees it to do something about misplaced phrases like that in example (2).

The Frazier and Rayner model of parsing

This is set out in more general terms than the preceding models. However, it has a number of features which are worth noting. The first is that, like ATNs, it 'copes with temporary ambiguity of natural language by initially pursuing just a single analysis of the sentence' (Frazier and Rayner, 1982, p. 170). Since this occasionally leads to mistakes there must be procedures for backtracking (again like ATNs). However, Frazier and Rayner suggest that this is not accomplished by unravelling the earlier decisions in any routine or automatic fashion. Instead they argue that the 'parser will use whatever information indicates that its actual analysis is inappropriate to attempt to diagnose the source of its error' (Frazier and Rayner, 1982, p. 182).

The entire system consists of two relatively independent subprocessors: the *syntactic processor*, which builds structures by using general parsing principles (e.g. late closure, minimal attachment, etc., see Frazier, 1983, pp. 224–225), and the *thematic processor*, which independently examines the range of alternative structures which the words of the sentence could potentially enter and submits the most plausible of these to be considered by the syntactic processor. If the two sets of structural decisions are incompatible with one another, then the syntactic processor takes this as an indication that it might be able to improve on its first choice, and in response to this it sets about backtracking and reanalysing the material. A final feature of the system is that detailed lexical information if assumed to influence some aspect of the parsing process (Clifton, Frazier and Connine, 1984).

Deterministic parsers

Marcus (1980) has argued that parsers can be made more efficient if they avoid the extensive backtracking and revision which characterize systems like ATNs. To do this they must operate in such a way 'that once a parse node is created it cannot be destroyed; that once a node is labeled with a given grammatical feature, that feature cannot be removed; and that once one node is attached to another node as its daughter, that attachment cannot be broken' (Marcus, 1980, p. 12). He referred to devices of this kind as *deterministic parsers* and provided a detailed description of one such system—a program called PARSIFAL.

It is worth commenting on several features of this theory. The first is that, like Anderson's ACT model, it makes use of a *lookahead* facility. Indeed, as Marcus (1980, p.16) points out, *any* deterministic parser is obliged to use lookahead, because otherwise it would be incapable of making the correct structural decision when it encountered locally ambiguous phrases like 'the boys' in sentences (3a) and (3b).

(3a) Have the boys take the exam today.
(3b) Have the boys taken the exam today?

In the particular case of PARSIFAL the parser has facilities which enable it to scan up to three constituents ahead before making its structural decisions about the current constituent.

Moving on to slightly less central features of the theory, PARSIFAL, like both of the preceding models, is capable of using lexical 'expectations' to guide the parser in dealing with sentences like (4a) and (4b) (taken from Marcus, 1980, p. 15).

(4a) I wanted John to make Sue feel better.
(4b) I called John to make Sue feel better.

The program is also able to make use of semantic information in selecting its structures. However, the mechanisms for doing this are rather different from those suggested elsewhere. Instead of working out the semantic acceptability of individual structures generated by the parser, PARSIFAL proceeds by computing the *comparative* acceptability of all different options and feeds this information directly into the preliminary decision-making mechanism (Marcus, 1980, Chapter 10). Finally, the theory proposes that the complete parsing system is made up of two distinct subprocesses. First, there is the basic deterministic component described above. If this fails to analyse the sentence, a second 'higher level "conscious" grammatical problem solving component comes into play' (Marcus, 1980, p. 204).

Word-expert and lexical-functional parsers

Like several of the systems already described, these systems use detailed lexical information to guide the parsing process. However, in both *word-expert systems* (e.g. Small and Rieger, 1982) and *lexical-functional* parsers (e.g. Ford, Bresnan and Kaplan, 1982) the information recovered from the lexicon is the *major* determinant of the initial course of processing. The present account of this approach will concentrate on the Ford *et al*. theory.

Central to this framework is the observation that verbs can enter into a variety of different structural relationships with other constituents of the sentence. For example, a word like 'wanted' can occur with a direct object alone, as in (5a). Alternatively, it can occur with a complement structure, as in (5b).

(5a) The woman wanted the dress.
(5b) The woman wanted the dress to remain on the rack.
(5c) The woman wanted the dress on the rack.

Ford *et al*. proposed that the various possible lexical forms of the verb are recovered from the lexicon when the word is recognized. After this, one (but only one) of the forms is used to guide the subsequent analysis of the sentence. (Precisely *which* one is determined by the relative priorities or 'strengths' of the alternative forms in the lexical representation.) Having settled upon a particular form, the parser hypothesizes the syntactic structure associated with that form and proceeds to try to interpret the following material in terms of the postulated structure. Thus, in example (5c) above, if it starts by assuming the lexical form for 'wanted' is the one in which the verb appears with the direct object alone (as in 5a), then it will go on to interpret the phrase 'on the rack' as a relative. However, if it initially uses the complement form (as in 5b), then (5c) will also be analysed as a complement.

There are many other aspects of the theory, but for the moment the important features are first that the parser initially commits itself to a single analysis (and backtracks if this turns out to be wrong), and second that the order in which the alternative structural hypotheses are considered is determined, whenever possible, not by the structure or properties of the parser itself but by detailed information recovered from the lexicon (e.g. lexical forms, their relative strengths, etc.).

'Connectionist' parsers

The final approach to parsing we will consider is based on 'massively parallel' or 'connectionist' processing systems. An outline of such a parser has been described by Waltz and Pollack (1985). As with other parallel distributed processing (PDP) systems (e.g. Rumelhart and McClelland, 1982), the processor consists of a set of tokens connected to one another by excitatory or inhibitory links. The tokens stand for the various different linguistic objects that might be present in the sentence (e.g. particular words and word senses at the lexical level and constituents such as NP, VP or PP at the syntactic level). When the system is in its initial state all units are set to some prespecified resting level. The analytic parsing process is then started off by activating the tokens for each of the words in the test sentence (i.e. the 'input' words). These then activate the tokens representing all the constituents that can incorporate the individual words and these, in turn, activate the units for higher-level structures. At the same time constituents that are mutually incompatible inhibit one another. After considerable activity the system eventually settles down to a stable state in which all the competing sources of inhibition and activation are in a state of equilibrium. The syntactic tokens still active at this point are taken to represent the correct parsing of the sentence.

As a potential parsing device, this model has a number of interesting properties. First, while the activation of different constituents might initially occur in parallel, inhibitory processes ensure that one or other of the competing tokens is quickly suppressed where there are mutually inconsistent potential structures. In other words, the system will tend to behave rather like an ATN and commit itself initially to one particular analysis. Secondly, it is not easy to classify the system as deterministic or nondeterministic in the sense used by Marcus (1980) (see above). This is because units are capable of being activated over a continuous range of values, and hence there is no particular value at which a structure can be said to be 'built' or subsequently 'destroyed'. The issue could probably be addressed within the framework by introducing activation thresholds into the system, but elaborations of this kind do not seem to play a part in the current version of the model.

Turning to another recurrent issue, according to the model, the parsing outcome *can* be influenced by semantic and pragmatic factors (see Waltz and Pollack, 1985, pp. 62–65). These effects are introduced in exactly the same way as others—by the interactions of particular sets of units. Thus if a linguistic object (or a combination of such objects) is implausible for any reason then its token is inhibited by some other token in the system. These semantic/pragmatic interactions have exactly the same status as any other interactions within the system and so effects of this kind are not viewed as a separate stage of processing. Indeed, the entire architecture is uniform and undifferentiated, with no clear division into processing subcomponents.

Themes, issues and empirical questions

As can be seen from the recurring themes in the theories outlined above, much of the recent debate has revolved about a relatively small number of different issues. Some of the debating points which have emerged are as follows:

1. Is human parsing deterministic or not? Marcus (1980) clearly favours the deterministic position. However, all of the other theorists specifically propose that the parser can initially commit itself to one particular analysis and then abandon this preliminary hypothesis and

reanalyse the material if the first guess turns out to be unsatisfactory. This will be referred to below as the *guess-and-backtrack* strategy. Moving beyond the hypothesis of strict determinism itself, there is some disagreement about whether there is any benefit at all to be gained by using lookahead. Anderson, along with Marcus, argues that there is, but other theorists are either silent on this issue or provide no mechanism for using lookahead (as in most conventional ATNs).

2.   Is parsing a unitary process or are there two or more different stages? Several investigators propose at least two stages (cf cascaded ATNs, Frazier and Rayner's syntactic and thematic processors, Marcus's deterministic and problem-solving parsing components). Others attribute the functions of these putative second processors to processing rules that are computationally identical to those responsible for all other aspects of the parsing process (e.g. additional productions within the same architectures—as in ACT—or additional nodes and links in a connectionist network).

3.   Is human parsing directed or influenced by detailed lexical information? Most of the theories outlined above make some provision for such influences and one or two make this issue a central feature of the model (e.g. heuristic strategies, lexical-functional parsers). Perhaps the only parsers which exclude the possibility of detailed lexical effects are the simplest ATNs.

4.   Is parsing influenced by semantic or pragmatic considerations and, if so, at what stage of processing does this occur? Again, all of the theories seem to accept that the eventual outcome of the parsing process can be influenced by semantic and pragmatic considerations. However, they differ quite markedly in their proposals about the precise mechanisms and procedures underlying these effects. Some suggest that semantic factors influence the initial (or sole) parsing process (e.g. Miller and Johnson-Laird, 1976; Anderson, 1976; Marcus, 1980; Ford, Bresnan and Kaplan, 1982; Waltz and Pollack, 1985). Others maintain that semantic and pragmatic factors are considered *after* the initial structural hypothesis has been set up (e.g. Winograd, 1972; Frazier and Rayner, 1982).

In the next section the empirical evidence relevant to each of these questions will be reviewed and the influence of punctuation and of the physical layout of text will be considered. While these last two factors have not played an important role in any of the theorizing to date, the experimental work suggests that they are quite important, and so there is a reasonable case for including them in the discussion along with the more fashionable issues outlined above.

EXPERIMENTAL WORK ON PARSING

Determinism versus non-determinism

As indicated earlier, determinism is not a feature which characterizes a wide variety of different parsing theories. However, it *has* been the subject of much heated debate within the linguistics literature (e.g. Marcus, 1980; Sampson, 1983; Berwick and Weinberg, 1984, 1985; Fodor, 1985) and so it is worth considering it in some detail here. It should be stressed that the aim is not to trace the intricacies of the linguistic arguments, but to examine the psycholinguistic evidence for and against determinism.

Several recent empirical studies can be used to throw light on the issue. Without exception, the results argue *against* the view that the human parser is totally deterministic. The data come primarily from studies in which people are required to read sentences containing strings of words that are structurally ambiguous at some point during a strict left-to-right analysis. For example, in a sentence which starts like (6a) below, the second noun phrase 'his parents' could either be the object of the verb 'visited' or else it could be the subject of a new clause, as in (6b).

(6a) After the young Londoner had visited his parents. . .

(6b) After the young Londoner had visited his parents prepared to celebrate their anniversary.

In (6b) the ambiguous segment is followed by a string of words which effectively resolves the temporary ambiguity. With this continuation, the noun phrase must be interpreted as the subject of the main clause rather than as the object of the verb in the preposed clause.

To develop the argument against determinism we have to examine how a totally deterministic parser would cope with sentences of this kind. Let us consider the process in stages. First, the parser would detect the potential ambiguity in attaching the critical noun phrase to the developing structure. Before committing itself to either of these structures, it would attempt to adjudicate between the two possibilities by using its 'lookahead' facility to examine the words and phrases that turn up later in the sentence. This exercise would establish that the 'subject' interpretation of the noun phrase is, in fact, the correct one. The parser would then construct this interpretation and proceed to analyse the rest of the sentence without further hitches. In other words, a completely deterministic parser would *always* make the correct decision first time and would never pause to reconsider its commitment at any later stage in the analysis.

However, this is not what *people* seem to do when they read sentences of this kind. Rather, fluent readers tend to commit themselves prematurely to one of the alternative interpretations and read on, apparently assuming that they have made the correct choice. If they are mistaken, they soon encounter material which is difficult to reconcile with the existing structures and when this happens they tend to dwell for extended periods on the new words. (The reason for this is presumably that they are trying to reinterpret the earlier material and reconcile it with the phrases that follow.) The tendency to pause markedly on material following ambiguous segments has been shown both with eye-monitoring techniques (e.g. Frazier and Rayner, 1982) and with a variety of different linguistic structures using subject-paced reading tasks (e.g. Mitchell, 1986; Mitchell and Holmes, 1985; Zagar and Mitchell, 1986).

It seems reasonably clear that at least some of these effects occur because subjects initially misinterpret the structure of the ambiguous segment. When surface structure cues are introduced to indicate which structure is correct, the pause is eliminated. For example, Mitchell and Holmes (1985) and Mitchell (1986) showed that with sentences like (6b) above the insertion of a comma after the first verb eliminates the pause which otherwise occurs when people read the material following the ambiguous noun phrase. Presumably this happens because the comma marks the end of the preposed clause, resolving the ambiguity that occurs in the absence of punctuation. Since the structural interpretation which remains is the one that is compatible with the rest of the sentence, the reader is able to use the punctuation to avoid the need to reanalyse the sentence at a later stage.

Taken together, these findings seem to fit in most obviously with a non-deterministic view of parsing. However, Fodor (1985, footnote 16) has put forward an ingenious argument which makes it possible to interpret all of these effects within a deterministic framework. She points out that a 'determined determinist' could explain the pauses by arguing that they coincide with points at which the reader catches up with a backlog of computational work. Specifically, a deterministic parser might postpone all of its structural decisions while initially working through the ambiguous segment of the sentence, and then complete the necessary calculations as soon as it encounters material indicating which of the alternative hypotheses was correct. The additional processing load at this point would explain the pauses that are obtained in on-line reading studies. Moreover, there is a ready explanation for the punctuation effect described above. When the comma is inserted at the end of the preposed clause the following noun phrase is no longer structurally ambiguous, and so the parser would not be obliged to postpone any of its decisions and there would be no backlog of processing to deal with immediately after the noun phrase. Consequently there would be no reason to expect an unusually long pause at this point.

Clearly, then, the determinists have a viable account of the basic findings set out above. However, other aspects of the data reported by Mitchell (1986a) suggest that this hypothesis cannot be sustained. In addition to sentences like (6b) above there were others, like (7), in which the noun phrase was made unambiguous not by punctuation but by the fact that the selection restrictions of the preceding verb prevent it from taking the following noun phrase as a direct object.

(7)   Just as the guard shouted the intruder escaped through a window.

Now, if the parser behaves as Fodor's 'determined determinist' suggests it might, and postpones its decision about attaching the noun phrase ('the intruder') until it comes across the main verb ('escaped'), then the on-line reading data should show the conventional pause at this point. However, there was no such pause (relative to a control condition in which a comma was inserted after the first verb). Moreover, there was evidence that the structural decisions about the noun phrase were *not* postponed as hypothesized. In certain conditions the sentences were segmented in the subject-paced reading task so that the string of words *prior to* the main verb appeared in a display by themselves. On the hypothesis that the structural analysis of the second noun phrase is postponed throughout this display, there should be no sign that subjects noticed any anomaly in 'shouting an intruder'. However, contrary to this prediction, the results showed that they took longer to read displays of this kind than controls in which the noun phrase is fully ambiguous (e.g. when the word 'shouted' was replaced by the word 'shot' in this particular example). This seems to provide a clear indication that the noun phrase was being tested as a potential direct object *well before* the main verb was first encountered. Again the evidence argues against the 'modified' version of the deterministic hypothesis.

Taken as a whole, then, these results suggest that human parsing is not totally deterministic. However, this still leaves open the possibility that people are capable of avoiding some of the construction/destruction that characterizes the more extreme alternatives to determinism (e.g. 'guess-and-backtrack' parsing). In particular, it could well be that lookahead is of *some* use in guiding parsing, even if it is not capable of ruling out *all* inappropriate hypotheses. In fact, it turns out that even this more modest suggestion is not supported by the data. Mitchell (1986) found that garden-path effects occur even when the structural ambiguity can be resolved by looking at the word *immediately after* the ambiguous segment. In other words, people misinterpret sentences even when they could avoid doing so by using the most limited possible form of lookahead. Indeed, in this experiment subjects performed no better in this condition than when the 'disambiguating information' (i.e. the main verb) was not physically available for examination in the display during which the 'lookahead' facility is supposed to be employed.

To date, then, there is no empirical evidence that the human parser is immediately able to choose the 'correct' structural interpretation of constituents in ambiguous sentences. Of course, it *is* able to do this eventually (i.e. by the end of the sentence). So, while the structural guess may occasionally be wrong at first, the parser must be free to abandon this preliminary hypothesis and move on to consider alternative interpretations of the material. Since this sequence of operations involves first *constructing* a representation of the initial hypothesis and then *destroying* either this representation itself or its links with its linguistic context, it follows that human parsing must be non-deterministic.

Number of distinct phases of parsing

The conclusion that the human parser is non-deterministic has some fairly obvious implications for the structure of the parser. In parsers using a guess-and-backtrack strategy, the course of operations can be directed at two different points in the proceedings, (a) when the system settles upon its preliminary hypothesis or 'guess' and (b) when it decides to revise or abandon this option and move on to one of the other, initially less attractive, hypotheses. It follows that in a system of this kind the parser must be divided into two distinct processing stages—one in which a possible option is *proposed* and a second in which it is evaluated more fully and eventually *disposed of* if it is found to have shortcomings (for more on the rationale behind this distinction see Crain and Steedman, 1985). The processing requirements are different in the two cases. The first decision is used to *determine* the course of action and so, ideally, the choice should be made very quickly (to keep up with the information as it arrives). It may also be necessary for the system to make its commitment on the basis of incomplete evidence (either because the relevant material has not yet appeared or because time pressure prevents it from being fully processed). On occasion this will cause the system to make the wrong decision, but this need not have far-reaching consequences since these mistakes should be trapped in the second phase of processing. The second operation is mainly concerned with *evaluating* the output of the first—checking to see that it is compatible with the words that appear in the remainder of the sentence and making sure that it is consistent with any other information that may not have been available to the first processor. Desirable features of this operation are not so much that it should operate rapidly (although this would obviously be an advantage) but rather that it should be thorough and should detect any inadequacies in the working hypothesis at the earliest possible stage in the proceedings. Ideally, it should have access to a wide variety of sources of information which might influence decisions about the viability of a structural hypothesis (e.g. pragmatic, semantic and contextual information). It is not clear what happens when this device decides to terminate a line of analysis. It may be that it hands control to a third processor (a *backtracker*) which sets about working back and unravelling the sequence of preliminary decisions until it gets back to a point where some alternative set of structural hypotheses can be set in their place. Alternatively, it is possible that the linguistic objects constructed during the first phase are automatically purged if they are not ratified in the second stage. In this case it may be sufficient for the second (evaluating) process simply to return control to the first, merely adding some kind of tag to prevent this device from reanalysing the material in the same way on the second pass. Either way it seems clear that in guess-and-backtrack parsing there must be at *least* two different phases of parsing, and we shall concentrate on these two operations in the following discussion of experimental results.

Semantic and pragmatic effects in parsing

There is clear evidence that semantic and pragmatic factors can influence the process of parsing a sentence. For example, Rayner, Carlson and Frazier (1983) carried out an experiment in which a preliminary stage was to paraphrase sentences like (8a) and (8b).

(8a) The florist sent the flowers was very pleased.
(8b) The performer sent the flowers was very pleased.

In these sentences, the string of words 'sent the flowers' is structurally ambiguous since 'sent' could either be the main verb—in which case the first noun phrase is the agent (i.e. the 'sender')—or alternatively, the string 'sent the flowers' could be a reduced relative clause—in which case the first noun phrase would be the recipient (i.e. the person to whom the flowers were sent). Now, pragmatic considerations tell us that florists are more likely to be the *senders* and performers the *recipients* of flowers. This means that the pragmatic bias in (8a) acts against the correct (reduced relative) interpretation of the sentence while that in (8b) works in its favour.

Rayner, Carlson and Frazier (1983) found that their subjects provided correct paraphrases of 70 per cent of sentences of the second kind, but that this figure was reduced to only 50 per cent with sentences of the first kind. Since the errors were predominantly syntactic in nature, this provides a clear indication that pragmatic bias can play a role in the parsing process. (For further evidence pointing to the same conclusion see the review by Norris, 1987. Also, for comparable findings when the ambiguous material is presented in the auditory modality see Tyler and Marslen-Wilson, 1977.)

As it stands, these pragmatic effects could exert their influence either during the first stage of parsing (by helping the parser to select the correct option for immediate analysis) or during the second stage (by providing additional evidence on which to throw out mistaken hypotheses). Detailed measures of reading time suggest that the effect is associated predominantly with the second stage of parsing and that pragmatic factors have little or no influence on the initial choice of hypothesis. Specifically, Rayner, Carlson and Frazier (1983) used an eye-monitoring technique to determine how long subjects dwelt on different regions of the sentence as they first fixated on the material. The results showed that during this first pass the data were almost indistinguishable for the two types of sentence. In particular, neither the reading time per character nor the average fixation duration was shorter in sentences like (8b) in which pragmatic information might have been expected to help subjects to select the correct structural hypothesis. Thus, it seems that the pragmatic effects must come into play *after* the first pass and therefore presumably during the second phase of the parsing process.

Lexical guidance of parsing

There is now good evidence that detailed lexical information can guide the course of processing. Ford, Bresnan and Kaplan (1982) showed that subjects' interpretation of sentences like (5c) above changes according to the precise word occupying the verb slot. Thus, in that example, when the verb was 'wanted', 90 per cent of the subjects interpreted the final phrase as a relative, while this figure was reduced to only 30 per cent when the verb was replaced by the word 'positioned'. Subsequent studies by Clifton, Frazier and Connine (1984) and by Mitchell and Holmes (1985) established that these effects occur on-line, while the sentence is still being processed. Clifton *et al.* showed that the response latency in a secondary task was faster when the sentence continued predictably than when the completion was unexpected. Detailed lexical effects were revealed by the finding that this pattern of latencies could be reversed by replacing one verb with another in exactly the same sentence frame. Similar results were obtained by Mitchell and Holmes using a garden-path technique in a subject-paced reading task. In this study it was found that, with several different types of sentence, subjects showed a tendency to enter a garden path after misinterpreting the structural role of a critical phrase. However, this effect could be eliminated if one verb were replaced by another. For example, a proportion of the sentences were similar to (6b) above. In this case people tend to be garden-pathed because they initially interpret 'his parents' as if it were the direct object of 'visited'. As a result they have considerable difficulty in processing the words that follow the ambiguous noun phrase. However, when the word 'visited' is replaced by 'arrived' there is no comparable difficulty—presumably because the subjects opted for the correct interpretation of the phrases in the first place. Like the previous study, this shows that detailed information about the verb can influence on-line parsing decisions (for a more detailed review of this work see Mitchell and Zagar, 1986).

As in the earlier discussion of pragmatic effects, it is not clear whether these lexical influences occur during the first, second or during both stages of the parsing process. The theoretical framework offered by Ford, Bresnan and Kaplan (1982) locates the effect in the first phase. In particular, these authors suggest that the parser initially tries to interpret the input in terms of the structural hypothesis associated with the 'strongest' lexical form of the verb, and that it moves on to the alternatives only when this fails. The results reported by Clifton *et al.* provide some support for this view because they showed verb-guidance effects almost immediately after the verb. However, a recent experiment by Mitchell (1987) suggests that lexical effects may also have a major influence during the *second* phase of processing. As before, the study employed a subject-paced reading task and made use of materials like (6b). In this case the first display ended after the ambiguous noun phrase. It was found that the reading time for the intransitive version (e.g. with the verb 'arrived') was several hundred milliseconds longer than that in the corresponding transitive condition (as in (6b) above). This suggests that subjects were trying to interpret the critical noun phrase as the direct object of the preceding word even when this was impossible (because an intransitive verb clearly cannot take a direct object). If this is correct, then it follows that the verb cannot have had an overriding influence in guiding the parser's initial choice of structural hypothesis, in which case the effect it *did* have must have been during a later revision of the preliminary analysis.

To summarize, then, the evidence suggests that, particularly with verbs, detailed lexical information can be used to guide the parsing process and at least part of this effect occurs during the second (filtering) phase of the parsing procedure.

Punctuation and format effects

Day-to-day experience tells us that punctuation and the layout of the text can have a marked effect on the ease with which we can make sense of the material. However, there is a case for putting these phenomena on a firmer footing by subjecting them to empirical test. To do this, Mitchell (1986) used sentences with preposed clauses like (9) and examined the effect of inserting a comma at the end of the first clause.

(9) After the child had visited (,) the doctor / prescribed a course of injections.

The sentences were divided into two displays (marked by the oblique line) and the subjects had to read and understand them in a self-paced reading task. In line with studies which have already been described (e.g. Frazier and Rayner, 1982; Mitchell and Holmes, 1985), it was found that subjects were garden-pathed in the conditions without commas. That is, they took longer to read the second displays of sentences like (9) than to read the corresponding displays in control sentences where the potential ambiguity was avoided by replacing the optionally transitive verb (i.e. 'visited') by another which could not take the following noun phrase as a direct object (e.g. 'sneezed'). In the conditions *with* commas, however, this difference was eliminated. Apparently, in this case subjects showed no tendency to be garden-pathed by taking the second noun phrase ('the doctor') to be the object of the first verb. It seems, therefore, that the physical presence of the punctuation mark at the end of the clause must have caused the parser to override the biases that normally operate with word strings of this kind. Thus, the result provides clear empirical evidence that punctuation can influence the course of parsing.

Evidence for format or layout effects in parsing comes from a second study using a variety of sentence forms some of them similar to example (9) above. The sentences were partitioned in different ways. In some conditions the first display coincided with the preposed clause, while in others it took in the following noun phrase as well as the clause. The results, reported by Mitchell (1987), showed that the total reading time for the sentences varied according to the way in which they were segmented. For example, in sentences like (9) the total viewing time for the two displays was almost a second shorter when the division coincided with the clause boundary than when it was displaced to include the following noun phrase. This serves to emphasize that parsing is influenced by factors other than linguistic variables. Effects of this kind would have to be accounted for in a comprehensive model of the parsing process.

TOWARDS A PSYCHOLOGICALLY REALISTIC MODEL

The evidence summarized in the previous section places a number of constraints on psychological models of parsing. In this section I shall describe a framework which I have recently been developing (Mitchell, 1986, 1987) and go on to discuss how it can be used to account for the findings outlined above.

The model is represented diagrammatically in Figure 4.1 and uses conventions that were originally introduced to provide a general description of the process of reading (see Mitchell, 1982, pp. 141–142). Thus, circles represent processes or subprocesses and rectangles represent different forms of working or temporary memory. A double-headed arrow between a circle and a rectangle is used to indicate that the process represented by the circle may draw upon information in the specified memory in the course of carrying out its computations. (If there is no such connection or if the link is overprinted with a cross, this can be taken to imply that the process does not have access to the form of storage in question.) Finally, a bold, unidirectional arrow between a circle and a rectangle expresses the fact that some or all of the products of the process are deposited in the working memory indicated.

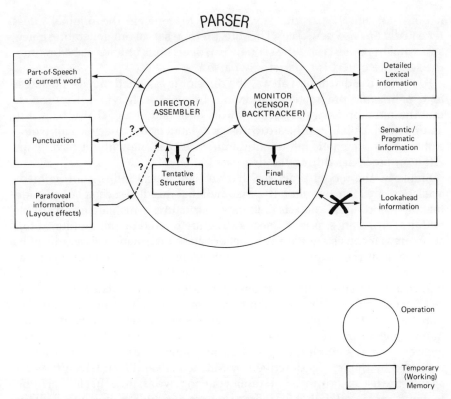

Figure 4.1   Outline of a psychologically realistic parser. See text for an explanation of the conventions used.

Following the discussion above, the parsing process (represented by the outer circle) is divided into two subprocesses—the *director* and the *monitor*. The director is responsible for assigning preliminary structures to individual words or strings of words as they are first read (i.e. for making the initial guess in the guess-and-backtrack parser). These tentative structures are placed in a working memory where they are made available to the second subprocess which monitors this output in the light of all the information available to it. If the preliminary structure is compatible with information from all other sources, it is first retained until the end of a clause and then transferred to a second store as a final structure. On the other hand, if the monitor detects some kind of anomaly or inconsistency (at a level beyond some preset 'anomaly threshold'), then the tentative structure is deleted (not shown in diagram) and the director is somehow wound back so that (1) it resumes the configuration it had when it first posited the just-rejected hypothesis (again, not represented in the present version of the diagram) and (2) its internal registers or housekeeping procedures are adjusted so that it does not simply use the environment to generate the original guess repeatedly on each new cycle. The director then sets about generating a new structural hypothesis and the sequence of operations unfolds as before until the sentence or text is satisfactorily parsed.

Following the discussion above, the director is assumed to have no access to semantic and pragmatic information. In contrast, however, we propose that the monitor *does* have access to this information and that it uses it to assess the plausibility of the structures generated by the director. This would explain how pragmatic information influences parsing without having any effect on processes during the first pass.

Similarly, the model proposes that detailed lexical information is made available only to the monitor. It is assumed that this device can use the information to curtail the analysis of tentative structures which are incompatible with it. For instance, it may reject a structure offered by the monitor if this structure is inconsistent with subcategorization information about one of its component verbs—explaining the results reported by Mitchell and Holmes (1985) and Mitchell (1986). By hypothesis, the director has no access to this information and therefore occasionally puts forward a structure which is, in fact, incompatible with detailed lexical information about the words incorporated into the structure. These mistakes are quickly trapped by the monitor, which then institutes changes to put the parser back on course. The recovery is not smooth enough to avoid reading difficulties, however, as indicated by the results described by Mitchell (1986, 1987). Given the case against the use of lookahead in human parsing, we assume that lexical information is restricted to that for words up to and including the one which the director is currently trying to process (i.e. assign a syntactic label). In other words, it is assumed that neither the director nor the monitor has access to comparable information about words, other than the current one, that have yet to be assigned a structural role.

Moving on to punctuation and format effects, it is most likely that these exert their main influence on the director. However, at this stage we cannot rule out the possibility that these factors also have some effect on the monitor. Presumably, the director treats punctuation marks rather like lexical items and uses the information, together with its own internal conventions, to generate appropriate structural hypotheses. The format effects require a somewhat more elaborate account and we are probably still some way from specifying these effects completely. A preliminary suggestion is that the director makes use of visual information within the right parafoveal field, and that it keeps the existing clause open if there is any printed information in the area immediately to the right of the word currently being analysed. On the other hand, if there is nothing there (e.g. at the end of a line), the initial evidence reported by Mitchell (1987) suggests that the present clause may be closed wherever this is possible. This account makes the obvious prediction that there will be processing difficulties in the following display if this strategy forces premature closure. However, the possibility has not yet been submitted to experimental test.

At this point it may be worth taking stock and summarizing the characteristics of the present model. To do this it is useful to compare the present description of parsing with those proposed in the theories outlined at the beginning of the chapter.

First, the current model differs from the Marcus and Anderson parsers in that it is non-deterministic and makes no use of lookahead in the course of its operations. It also differs from the proposals put forward by Waltz and Pollack and by Anderson in that it comprises two distinct phases of processing rather than a single undifferentiated mechanism. Thirdly, while it makes use of detailed lexical information to guide the parsing process, it differs from other parsers which do this in that it assumes that the evidence is used to *check* the options selected by a preliminary scheduling device rather than to *direct* the course of analysis in the first place.

Overall, the present proposal is most similar to the Frazier and Rayner model and to ATN models with interleaved semantic processing (e.g. Bobrow and Webber, 1980). The major difference from the former is that Rayner and Frazier proposed that the two different subcomponents of parsing share the same raw material (word strings), while in the current model the monitor's main source of input consists of the tentative structures made available by the director. In other words, the present description involves a degree of serial processing between the two subprocesses rather than parallel analysis from a shared data base. Turning to the ATN-based models, the only real difference between these and the current account is that here non-semantic (and particularly lexical) processing as well as *semantic* processing takes place during the interleaved phase of analysis.

Much of the foregoing discussion of the model amounts to little more than scene-setting. While it is important to know the kinds of factors that influence the different stages of processing, a more challenging question concerns the way in which the processors use the various classes of information to generate their structural products. With different strings of words, precisely what computations are carried out in the course of assembling the output? Unfortunately, most of the empirical work to date has not been precise enough to provide the detailed data required to tackle this question. Further refinement of the models must await the results of future research. However, there is one body of data that is worth examining in the light of our conclusions about the nature of parsing processes in 'normal' readers. This concerns the form of syntactic analysis used by people who show some kind of deficit in the use of grammatical information.

PARSING DIFFICULTIES IN NEUROPSYCHOLOGICAL PATIENTS

A common research strategy in recent work on cognitive psychology has been to test and refine theories of 'normal' performance by checking whether they provide a useful framework for understanding patterns of deficit in neurological patients (e.g. see Chapter 11 by Temple in this volume). For the present purposes the syndromes which are potentially most informative are the 'agrammatic' aphasias, particularly conduction aphasia and Broca's aphasia.

Conduction aphasia

The most obvious symptom of conduction aphasia is that the auditory span is very much lower than usual, sharply limiting the patient's ability to retain or reproduce unrelated speech-based codes. For our purposes the interesting observation is that the syndrome is sometimes (but not always) associated with comprehension loss. When there *is* a deficit of this kind, the difficulty may occasionally be attributed simply to the patient's inability to remember sentences verbatim. However, in certain cases it appears that there is likely to be more specific damage to the parser or to some other aspect of comprehension.

We start with a case in which the parsing component itself seems to be intact. The patient in question was studied by Vallar and Baddeley (1984). The interesting feature of this case was that the patient, PV, was perfectly capable of understanding *short* sentences up to nine words long, but had considerable difficulty when the sentence length was increased to thirteen or more words. The fact that at least some of the sentences were handled correctly suggests that the parsing subprocesses themselves were unimpaired. The difficulties might have arisen because PV was unable to retain the newly parsed constituents prior to report or, alternatively, it is possible that the working memory resources available to the parser are progressively reduced as the load imposed by verbatim retention is increased. In either case it is interesting to note that parsing can, in fact, be carried out successfully by patients with very limited spans. This suggests that the types of working memory employed in parsing may be rather different from the forms of storage that support phonological recall.

In other cases of conduction aphasia there *does* seem to be some breakdown in the parsing skills themselves. For example, Friedrich, Martin and Kemper (1985) describe a patient, EA, who had considerable difficulty in understanding passive sentences. Thus, when presented with a sentence like 'The car was hit by the ball', she showed a marked tendency to match it with a picture showing a car hitting a ball rather than the reverse. Since there was little sign of comparable problems with *active* sentences, the authors suggested that she was probably misapplying the canonical order heuristic in this task.

Other tasks showed that semantic and pragmatic information played a role in EA's comprehension. For example, in a task in which she was required to repeat sentences containing relative clauses, it was found that her performance was strongly influenced by reversibility and the plausibility of the material. In particular, she tended to make more mistakes on sentences that were reversible and improbable than on those that were not. This finding could well be interpreted as evidence that the damage to the parser is more or less restricted to the director, which therefore produces an output which is somewhat unreliable. The semantic and pragmatic effects are easily explained on this account because the (relatively intact) monitor should be able to improve performance with suitable materials by detecting and censoring any implausible structures. It would therefore be considerably more successful in avoiding errors which result in semantically unacceptable structures than those that are reasonably plausible.

Broca's aphasia

A similar pattern of results has been found in the comprehension performance of Broca's aphasics. Using a sentence/picture matching task, Caramazza and Zurif (1976) found that performance with reversible sentences was close to the chance level, but that this rose markedly (to about 90 per cent) when they were able to use lexical or pragmatic information to adjudicate between the alternative interpretations (e.g. with sentences like 'The apple that the boy is eating is red'). As before, the most obvious interpretation of the result is that the director is somehow impaired in these patients, and that the relatively high level of performance is achieved wherever possible by using the monitor in an unusually active and compensatory fashion. Thus, the monitor might consider (and reject) several successive proposals put forward by the director before eventually finding one pragmatically acceptable and letting it through as the final structure.

However, there is some suggestion that this account of the data may not be entirely satisfactory. After more detailed investigation of their grammatical capabilities, Linebarger, Schwartz and Saffran (1983) have reported that despite their comprehension difficulties, patients of this kind are surprisingly accurate in judging whether or not a string of words forms a grammatical sentence. As it stands, this finding is difficult to reconcile with the suggestion that the director is failing in its function of generating tentative structures. It clearly must be managing to produce *some* kind of a reliable output (to provide a satisfactory basis for the grammaticality judgment task). One possibility is that the monitor retains its capacity to work through the sentence, checking that the successive words are syntactically acceptable, but that it fails to *assemble* the structures that constitute the normal end-products of this process (or does so in an unreliable way). Successfully running such a 'routine' might enable the patients to report that the sentence is grammatical without providing enough information for them to determine its correct interpretation. (For other interpretations of this effect see further discussion by Zurif and Grodzinsky, 1983, and by Linebarger, Schwartz and Saffran, 1983.)

Whether the parsing difficulties of agrammatic patients originate in their failure to *construct* reliable representations or in difficulties they might have in *exploiting* or *interpreting* them, there is at least evidence that the problems do not show up uniformly in all sentence types. For example, active sentences are typically dealt with more successfully than passive ones are and, in an extensive study with a large sample of different types of agrammatic patient, Caplan, Baker and Dehaut (1985) have shown that there is a relatively stable ranking in the difficulties caused by nine different sentence structures. While it is too early to attempt to give a full account of these findings, it seems likely that they will provide a useful starting point not only for developing explanations of the specific deficits shown in various neuropsychological syndromes, but also for refining theories of normal parsing itself.

The patterns of performance with 'agrammatic' patients, then, seem to fit in reasonably well with the kind of theoretical framework which has been developed from work with 'normal' readers. In particular, it favours models with different processing stages for semantic and non-semantic influences and argues against models which assume that the parsing architecture is uniform and undifferentiated. Clearly, there is scope for clarification and refinement of these deficits. It is hoped that this will occur as the cognitive neuropsychologists begin to take account of the more recent empirical work on parsing.

CONCLUDING REMARKS

As this chapter shows, the framework for a reasonable theory of parsing is beginning to emerge. However, several areas of imprecision remain within this tentative model. To start with, we do not know much about the computations used to select and build preliminary structures, about the processes used to monitor these structures or, indeed, about the details of backtracking that occurs once a parsing hypothesis has been rejected. Also, much of the work has concentrated on fluent readers. While there has been some investigation of early syntactic acquisition, we do not know a great deal about how parsing develops over the period during which children typically learn to read. Again, the bulk of the empirical work has focused on the parsing of a single language (English), and it is not clear whether the conclusions reached earlier are characteristic of human parsing in general or whether it is more appropriate to regard them as tactics and techniques that have evolved to cope with the idiosyncratic features of just one language. Given all these gaps in our understanding and given the strong interdisciplinary interest in both theoretical and practical aspects of parsing, what does seem clear is that work on this topic will become increasingly active over the next few years.

REFERENCES

Anderson, J.R. (1976). *Language, Memory and Thought*. Hillsdale, N.J.: Erlbaum.

Anderson, J.R., Kline, P.J., and Lewis, C.H. (1977). A production system model of language processing. In M.A. Just and P.A. Carpenter (Eds.) *Cognitive Processes in Comprehension*. Hillsdale, N.J.: Erlbaum.

Berwick, R.C., and Weinberg, A.S. (1984). *The Grammatical basis of Linguistic Performance*. Cambridge, MA: MIT Press.

Berwick, R.C., and Weinberg, A.S. (1985). Deterministic parsing and linguistic explanation. AI Memo No. 836. Cambridge, MA: MIT Press.

Bobrow, R.J., and Webber, B.L. (1980). Knowledge representation for syntactic/semantic processing. In *Proceedings of the 1st Annual Conference for the American Association for Artificial Intelligence*. Stanford University, Stanford.

Caplan, D., Baker, C., and Dehaut, F. (1985). Syntactic determinants of sentence comprehension in aphasia. *Cognition*, **21**, 117-175.

Caramazza, A., and Zurif, E.B. (1976). Dissociation of algorithmic and heuristic processes in language comprehension. *Brain and Language*, **3**, 572-582.

Clifton, C., Frazier, L., and Connine, C. (1984). Lexical and syntactic expectations in sentence comprehension. *Journal of Verbal Learning and Verbal Behavior*, **23**, 696-708.

Crain, S., and Steedman, M. (1985). On not being led up the garden path: The use of context by the psychological syntax processor. In D.R. Dowty, L. Karttunen and A.M. Zwicky (Eds.) *Natural Language Parsing: Psychological, Computational and Theoretical Perspectives*. Cambridge: Cambridge University Press.

Fodor, J.D. (1985). Deterministic parsing and subjacency. *Language and Cognitive Processes*, **1**, 3-42.

Fodor, J.A., Bever, T.G., and Garrett, M.F. (1974). *The Psychology of Language: An Introduction to Linguistics and Generative Grammar*. New York: McGraw-Hill.

Ford, M., Bresnan, J.W., and Kaplan, R.M. (1982). A competence based theory of syntactic closure. In J.W. Bresnan (Ed.) *The Mental Representation of Grammatical Relations*. Cambridge: MIT Press.

Frazier, L. (1983). Processing sentence structure. In K. Rayner (Ed.) *Eye Movements in Reading: Perceptual and Language Processes*. New York: Academic Press.

Frazier, L., and Rayner, K. (1982). Making and correcting errors during sentence comprehension: Eye movements in the analysis of structurally ambiguous sentences. *Cognitive Psychology*, **14**, 178-210.

Friedrich, F.J., Martin, R., and Kemper, S.J. (1985). Consequences of a phonological coding deficit on sentence processing. *Cognitive Neuropsychology*, **2**, 385-412.

Hunt, E. (1986). The next word on verbal ability. Paper presented at the International Conference on Cognitive Approaches to Reading, Leicester, April 1986.

Linebarger, M.C., Schwartz, M.F., and Saffran, E.M. (1983). Sensitivity to grammatical structure in so-called agrammatic aphasics. *Cognition*, **13**, 361-392.

Marcus, M. (1980) *A Theory of Syntactic Recognition for Natural Languages.* Cambridge, Mass: MIT Press.

Miller, G.A., and Johnson-Laird, P.N. (1976). *Language and Perception.* Cambridge: Cambridge University Press.

Mitchell, D.C. (1982). *The Process of Reading: A Cognitive Analysis of Fluent Reading and Learning to Read.* Chichester: Wiley.

Mitchell, D.C. (1986). On-line parsing of structurally ambiguous sentences: Evidence against the use of lookahead. Submitted for publication.

Mitchell, D.C. (1987). Lexical guidance in human parsing: Locus and processing characteristics. In M. Coltheart (Ed.) *Attention and Performance XII: The Psychology of Reading.* Hillsdale, N.J.: Erlbaum.

Mitchell, D.C., and Holmes, V.M. (1985). The role of specific information about the verb in parsing sentences with local structural ambiguity. *Journal of Memory and Language,* **24**. 542-559.

Mitchell, D.C., and Zagar, D. (1986). Psycholinguistic work on parsing with lexical functional grammars. In N.E. Sharkey (Ed.) *Advances in Cognitive Science.* Chichester: Ellis Horwood.

Norris, D.G. (1987). Syntax, semantics and garden-paths. In A.W. Ellis (Ed.) *Progress in the Psychology of Language,* Vol. III. London: Erlbaum.

Rayner, K., Carlson, M., and Frazier, L. (1983). The interaction of syntax and semantics during sentence processing: Eye movements in the analysis of semantically biased sentences. *Journal of Verbal Learning and Verbal Behavior,* **22**, 358-374.

Rumelhart, D.E., and McClelland, J.L. (1982). An interactive model of context effects in letter perception. Part 2. *Psychological Review,* **89**, 60-94.

Sampson, G.R. (1983). Deterministic parsing. In M.King (Ed.) *Parsing Natural Language.* London: Academic Press.

Small, S., and Rieger, C. (1982). Parsing and comprehending with word experts. In W.G. Lenhert and M.H. Ringle (Eds.) *Strategies for Natural Language Processing.* Hillsdale, N.J.: Erlbaum.

Stevens, A.L., and Rumelhart, D.E. (1975). Errors in reading: Analysis using an augmented transition network model of grammar. In D.A. Norman and D.E. Rumelhart (Eds.) *Explorations in Cognition.* San Francisco: W.H. Freeman.

Tyler, L.K., and Marslen-Wilson, W.M. (1977). The on-line effects of semantic context on syntactic processing. *Journal of Verbal Learning and Verbal Behavior,* **16**, 683–692.

Vallar, G., and Baddeley, A.D. (1984). Phonological short-term store, phonological processing and sentence comprehension: A neuropsychological case study. *Cognitive Neuropsychology,* **1**, 121-142.

Waltz, D.L., and Pollack, J.B. (1985). Massively parallel parsing: A strongly interactive model of natural language interpretation. *Cognitive Science,* **9**, 51-74.

Wanner, E. (1980). The ATN and the sausage machine: Which one is baloney? *Cognition,* **8**, 209-225.

Winograd, T. (1972). *Understanding Natural Language.* New York: Academic Press.

Woods, W.A. (1970). Transition network grammars for natural language analysis. *Communications of the ACM,* **13**, 591-606.

Woods, W.A. (1980). Cascaded ATNs. *Journal of the Association for Computational Linguistics,* **6**, 1-12.

Zagar, D., and Mitchell, D.C. (1986). Characteristics of lexical guiding effects in parsing. Submitted for publication.

Zurif, E., and Grodzinsky, Y. (1983). Sensitivity to grammatical structures in agrammatic aphasics: A reply to Linebarger, Schwartz and Saffran. *Cognition,* **15**, 207-213.

Cognitive approaches to reading
Edited by J. R. Beech and A. M. Colley
© 1987 John Wiley & Sons Ltd

CHAPTER 5

Text Comprehension

ANN M. COLLEY

Department of Psychology, University of Leicester

INTRODUCTION

The processing of information during comprehension occurs at several levels, from the recognition of individual words to the application of the reader's knowledge to interpret the text and make necessary inferences. Haberlandt and Graesser (1985) differentiate between word-level (encoding and lexical access), sentence-level (segmentation and interpretation) and text-level (topic identification, knowledge activation and intersentence integration) processes. Other chapters in this book deal with word-level and sentence-level processes. This chapter will focus on the higher-order or text-level processes which allow a meaningful interpretation of the content of text to be constructed.

Comprehension has been described as a constructive process (e.g. Bartlett, 1932; Spiro, 1980). Text is language written in context, with an intended message which may go beyond its linguistic representation. In order to understand it the reader must, in many instances, use information which is explicit *and* implicit. Inferences may be required to integrate parts of the text, and in order to make these the reader must have some background knowledge of the situation portrayed in the text. The reader's own goals, attitudes and understanding of the communicative intention of the author are factors which must also be taken into account. Graesser (1981) has outlined six basic knowledge domains which are involved in text comprehension: linguistic, rhetorical, causal, intentional, spatial and, lastly, roles, personalities and objects. The linguistic domain includes phonemic, lexical, syntactic, semantic and pragmatic knowledge. The rhetorical domain includes information about the form and conventions of different kinds of text, which can range from a technical description to a literary novel. Brewer (1980) has used a threefold classification of discourse kinds, i.e. descriptive, narrative, expository, and has argued that cognitive structures deal with these differently. The only discourse type to be extensively researched is narrative text, and the use of rhetorical knowledge in comprehension of this discourse form will be discussed in the next section of this chapter. The last four domains can be subsumed under the general heading of world knowledge, and the way in which such knowledge is stored and accessed during comprehension will also be discussed in the next section.

There are three possible outcomes from the comprehension process. First, the reader may construct an interpretation which matches that intended by the author. Secondly, the reader may construct a satisfactory interpretation of the text which differs from that intended by the author, in which case there may be ambiguity in the surface (semantic/syntactic) structure of the text or the text may be ambiguous in the pragmatic sense, i.e.. it may be perfectly plausible in more than one context. Thirdly, the reader may fail to construct an interpretation of the text. This again may be due to its surface structure or to the lack of appropriate knowledge (lexical or topic-related) on the part of the reader. Thus success in comprehension is dependent upon not only knowledge-based but also text-based factors and these will be discussed in the third section of this chapter. The process of comprehension will be discussed in the fourth section. Most of the issues raised in this chapter, although applied to reading, will probably apply also to the comprehension process during listening. Clearly reading and listening differ in their initial stages of information acquisition, but thereafter it is assumed that the manner in which they access higher-level processes is the same. Indeed, reading comprehension ability is strongly related to listening comprehension ability (Palmer *et al.*, 1985).

KNOWLEDGE-BASED FACTORS IN COMPREHENSION

Our ability to infer relationships and causality not explicitly stated is crucial to the comprehension of many extracts of text which we encounter. This was demonstrated by Bransford and Johnson (1973) using the following sentence:

> Bill is able to come to the party tonight because his car broke down. (p. 391)

A causal link between the two halves of this sentence is implied by the presence of 'because'. However, there is insufficient information stated in the sentence to allow the reader to make sense of this causal link without additional inferences. Most readers can make necessary inferences of the kind:

> Bill was originally going to leave town, but now he could not leave because his car broke down. Since he could not leave he could come to the party, since the party was in town. (p. 391)

They are able to do this because they have sufficient knowledge of the kind of circumstances which might link the two events stated in the sentence.

The necessity of appropriate background knowledge for comprehension is readily illustrated where text contains information from a specialized knowledge domain. Chiesi, Spilich and Voss (1979) compared two groups designated as experts (high knowledge—HK) or non-experts (low knowledge—LK) in terms of their knowledge about baseball, on acquisition of domain-related information. It was expected that both groups would have some basic knowledge of the goal structure of the game, but that HK individuals would have more knowledge about the outcomes of actions in terms of game states, and should be able to produce a unified interpretation of the successive actions in a game. This conceptual framework was supported in a series of experiments, and the authors discussed their results in terms of the selective mapping of game-related information onto a well-developed knowledge base for the HK individuals.

Background knowledge may also bias the interpretation of ambiguous text. R.C. Anderson *et al.* (1977) compared interpretations of two prose passages by two groups of subjects from different specialisms. One group consisted of music education students, the other consisted of physical education students from weightlifting classes. The first prose passage could describe a prison break (usual interpretation) or a wrestling bout. The second passage could describe an evening of card-playing (usual interpretation) or a rehearsal session of a woodwind ensemble. The background of the subjects influenced their interpretations of the passages. The weightlifting students gave the first passage the 'wrestling' interpretation more often than the music students, who gave the second passage the 'music' interpretation more often than the weightlifting students. Most of the subjects were completely unaware that there was an interpretation other than that to which they had become committed.

A further situation which emphasizes the importance of background information occurs when text is presented with an incomplete or novel context. Bransford and Johnson (1972; 1973) provided examples of both, and also demonstrated that in order to comprehend and recall text well, it is necessary to have information about an appropriate context *before* reading a passage. Their famous 'balloon' passage produced poorer recall and lower ratings for comprehension when the context (a picture) was only partial or was presented after subjects had read the text.

Topic-related information is necessary both for extracting information from text and for making the necessary inferences that make it coherent. I will next consider how this topic-related knowledge may be stored, accessed and used in encoding information.

Knowledge structures and comprehension

Our knowledge about the world is held in long-term memory in a form which is not a direct match to the input and which is abstracted from it. The schema has been proposed as a knowledge structure to store this abstracted information (e.g. Kintsch and van Dijk, 1978; Norman and Rumelhart, 1975; Rumelhart, 1980; Rumelhart and Ortony, 1977; Thorndyke, 1984). Related concepts are frames (Minsky, 1975), scripts (Schank and Abelson, 1977) and MOPs (memory organization packets: Schank, 1982). Definitions of a schema vary only slightly from author to author. Rumelhart (1980) describes a schema as a package of knowledge from a given domain which contains both the knowledge itself and rules about how that knowledge is to be used. Four general properties characteristic of most descriptions of schemata are given by Rumelhart and Ortony (1977). First, schemata are hierarchically organized in memory. Second, they vary in generality, with specific schemata at the base of the hierarchy and more general abstract schemata further up. Thus a general schema, e.g. microcomputer, may have more specific schemata, e.g. IBM PC, Apple MacIntosh, embedded under it at a lower level. Third, schemata contain knowledge rather than definitions, since a given property of a schema need not apply to all examples or *instantiations* of a schema category. Some examples may, however, be more typical of a schema category than others. Fourth, a schema has variables which are filled or instantiated when it is used. Properties specified by a schema are therefore only defined when the schema is used to encode or process information.

Schema theory not only accounts for storage of information but is also a procedural theory of knowledge acquisition. It is assumed that schemata are used to interpret incoming sensory information, retrieve information from memory and guide the sequence of processing. They embody a *prototype* which is a typical category member or event. When incomplete information concerning an event or object is given, more detail can be filled in using this prototype. Schemata can therefore be used to guide inferences. They can also be used to guide the encoding of incoming information by generating expectations for features that are normally present for a given category.

In attempting to comprehend text, the reader is building up an internal model of the message or story contained in the text. Relevant schemata are instantiated to determine their *goodness of fit* to the situation portrayed in the text. Misrepresentation may occur when schemata are incorrectly instantiated due to ambiguity in the text or incorrect inferences from a poorly developed schema. A further cause of misrepresentation comes from the misapplication of schemata due to emotional state or attitudes (Bower, 1978)—the 'hot cognitions' which are currently attracting so much research interest.

There is some consensus concerning the manner in which schemata guide the comprehension process. The process of schema utilization has both data-driven and conceptually-driven elements (Graesser, 1981; Norman and Rumelhart, 1975; Rumelhart, 1980). The initial part of the process is data-driven. Incoming information activates low-level schemata which then activate those higher-level schemata which on probabilistic grounds provide the best fit to the information. Subschemata are then activated by these higher-level schemata in order to determine goodness of fit. If a fit is found then the relevant schemata are applied in a conceptually-driven fashion to generate expectations for a search for predicted input. If no fit is found, then the activated higher-level schemata and their subschemata are rejected.

One form of schema which has been particularly well researched is the script (Schank and Abelson, 1977). A script is a specialized form of schematic representation, invoked to explain how we encode events. It is therefore of particular relevance to the comprehension of narrative discourse either in a newspaper description of an event or a story. Schank and Abelson's well-worn example is the restaurant script, which contains a prototypical sequence for entering a restaurant, ordering and eating a meal. There is evidence for the use of script-like structures in comprehension and memory by both children (e.g. McCartney and Nelson, 1981; Nelson, 1979) and adults (e.g. Anderson, Spiro and Anderson, 1978; Bellezza and Bower, 1981, 1982; Bower, Black and Turner, 1979; Galambos and Rips, 1982). There are however a number of problems with the original conceptualization of the script which are discussed by Schank (1982). One of the most important of these is the finding that information from similar scripts causes recognition confusions in memory (Bower, Black and Turner, 1979), indicating that information is stored in a structure which may be shared by several scripts. Schank discusses the implications of this for memory structures, and presents a revision of his original notion which copes with this and additionally emphasizes the dynamic nature of memory. He recognizes the necessity for the existence of both specific structures such as scripts, based directly upon experience, and more general structures containing more abstract information. The former take advantage of the repeated occurrence of similar events, while the latter allow generalization across situations and therefore learning. Schank proposes that scripts are standardizations of more general structures and may be constructed on demand from general structures. This proposal is supported by recent empirical findings (Abbott, Black and Smith, 1985). One type of more general structure is the *scene*, which contains a general description of a setting and activities in pursuit of a goal related to that setting. The restaurant script presented by Schank (1982) is shown in Figure 5.1. It consists of a sequence of scenes and deviations which have occurred within scenes. Failed expectations or deviations from a script are stored and used to interpret similar new experiences. When sufficient similar deviations are encountered a new structure may be created, or the original memory structure may be found to be inadequate and may be abandoned. Schank's work is founded in artificial intelligence. However, there is also empirical evidence that actions irrelevant to an instantiated script are remembered well in both laboratory and natural situations (Graesser *et al.*, 1980; Nakamura *et al.*, 1985), which has led to the proposal of a schema copy + tag model (Graesser *et al.*, 1980; Graesser, 1981), whereby irrelevant actions are tagged to an instantiated script.

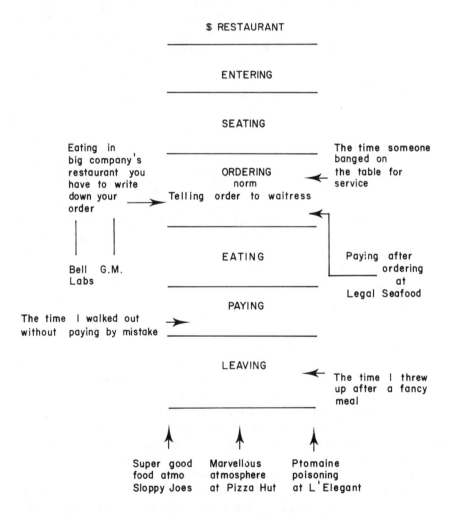

Figure 5.1   The restaurant script. From Schank (1982), (*Reproduced by permission of Cambridge University Press*).

In Schank's theory, scenes are organized by MOPs, which he defines as follows:

A MOP consists of a set of scenes directed towards the achievement of a goal. A MOP always has one major scene whose goal is the essence or purpose of the events organized by the MOP. (p. 97).

He describes three major kinds of MOP. Physical MOPs organize scenes containing information about physical appearance and physical actions. Societal MOPs are concerned with social settings involving social interaction. Personal MOPs are idiosyncratic and include personal scenes together with either physical or societal scenes. Episodes may contain all three kinds of MOP, since they may have physical, societal and personal aspects. Schank's theory is similar to other descriptions of schematic representation with respect to its use of successive abstractions. For example, meta-MOPs organize MOPs. They describe abstract scenes and can thus be used as a template for the construction of MOPs. For example, a meta-MOP for a trip could define a series of abstract scenes as follows:

mm–TRIP = PLAN + GET RESOURCES + MAKE ARRANGEMENTS + PREPARATORY TRAVEL + PREPARATIONS + PRIMARY TRAVEL + ARRIVAL + DO.

which could be used to construct a MOP for a trip by aeroplane as follows:

M–AIRPLANE = PLAN + GET MONEY + CALL AIRLINE + GET TICKETS + DRIVE TO AIRPORT + CHECK IN + WAITING AREA + BOARDING + FLYING + DEPLANING etc.

Universal scenes, organized by universal MOPs, are context-free abstractions from generalized scenes, which in turn have specific scenes attached to them.

Findings which support Schank's theory have recently been obtained by Reiser, Black and Abelson (1985), who examined retrieval of autobiographical memories using activities (sequences of goal-directed actions, or MOPs in Schank's theory) and actions (actions common to many activities, or generalized scenes in Schank's theory). Retrieval was facilitated when an activity was specified, which led them to conclude that activities are more important in retrieval because they are the structures which provide the context for storage in the first place.

Alba and Hasher (1983) have provided a detailed and critical evaluation of schema theory. The reader is referred to their paper for a full exposition of their arguments and the empirical evidence cited in support of them. Their major conclusion is that memory representation contains more detail (both lexical and syntactic) than is suggested by schema theory. The semantic abstracted aspect of information may be more readily accessible than its surface representation in many circumstances due to task demands, particularly since semantic content is usually the goal of processing. Schema theory copes well with distortions in memory (although Alba and Hasher argue that these are not very common) but cannot readily account for the accurate recognition memory for material presented only once which has been found by some investigators (e.g. Bates *et al.*, 1980; Kintsch and Bates, 1977). Alba and Hasher conclude that there is no coherent alternative to account for research findings which do not fit neatly into the framework provided by schema theory. They do point out, however, that the format of storage suggested by Kintsch and van Dijk (1978) for the representation of discourse may provide a suitable basis for such a theory. This assumes that a detailed representation is successively abstracted in a hierarchical propositional structure, and that memory representations are available for both surface structure and abstracted information.

van Dijk and Kintsch (1983) have extended their theoretical framework and this will be discussed in some detail later in this chapter. However, for the purpose of this discussion it is important to note that van Dijk and Kintsch (1983) acknowledge that the knowledge invoked during the comprehension process is organized in schemata, i.e.. packages which can function as units and which vary in abstractness. Verbatim surface representations may be present under certain circumstances, for instance style and rhetorical devices are valuable in understanding the communicative and interactional intent of language and are present in surface structure. A schematic framework does, however, seem to be the best candidate for the representation of knowledge that will be reapplied. A hierarchical propositional structure may well be constructed during comprehension in order that successive semantic abstractions may be made, but it is not necessarily the case that this sort of structure will be useful in storing knowledge about the world which must be reapplied and modified with further experience. Much of the detailed information contained in such a representation will be redundant in such circumstances, and it is not clear how modification of such a structure and thus learning could proceed. Schema theory and Schank's theory in particular have a strong emphasis on such issues. The question of the extent to which surface detail persists in memory is an important one, however, and deserves more systematic exploration than it has received hitherto.

An alternative to schema theory has been proposed by Morton, Hammersley and Bekerian (1985). They describe a naturalistic phenomenon whereby it is often possible to recall many attributes of an individual (e.g. physical appearance, occupation, address, etc.) except his or her name. Their model of memory proposes that memory consists of individual unconnected units or *records* with a form of access key or *heading,* the contents of which cannot be retrieved. Access to a record necessitates the matching of a *description* to its heading. Morton *et al.* suggest that their model accounts for the access problem they have illustrated. The name of the individual who is the subject of the attempt at recollection is contained in the heading which cannot be accessed. A sufficiently good description can nevertheless be formulated to access the record containing information about that individual. The name of the individual can eventually be retrieved because it is contained in a record elsewhere, which is searched in a conscious attempt to retrieve it. A description does not have to be a complete match for a heading. This raises questions of minimum requirements for matching that would preclude false searches in similarly described but irrelevant records, and indeed of the form of headings themselves, to which Morton *et al.* give only partial consideration.

The problem of access need not be a serious one for schema theory. The phenomenon described by Morton *et al.* usually concerns individuals who are not well known to us but who are at best acquaintances. We simply may not have developed a Bill Smith schema, but information about Bill Smith may be contained in a variety of packages. The inability to fit a name to a set of attributes, then, may be due to idiosyncracies of storage and we may be searching in the wrong location in memory. It would be unjust to discuss the theory of Morton *et al.* without pointing out that it does provide a good explanation of other phenomena in memory which are associated with access, such as differences between recall and recognition. It also assumes that information contained in records can be in a variety of formats, so detailed as well as abstracted information could be stored. However, it is not clear from the description of the theory how information is abstracted, and if learning is to occur one has to assume that new records must be stored, since old records cannot be modified, which hardly seems parsimonious.

Questions raised by critics of schema theory concerning the amount of detail contained in memory representations have still to be satisfactorily accounted for within a unified framework. A further problem, raised by critics and exponents of schema theory alike, is that it is not sufficiently precisely stated to be tested and falsified. Nevertheless, it is clear from the large body of research in this area, drawn both from empirical studies of memory and comprehension and from artificial intelligence, that the notion of schematic representation still has much to offer as a description of the way in which we store and integrate domain-related knowledge. It is not surprising therefore that it forms a fundamental part of descriptions of the comprehension process (e.g. van Dijk and Kintsch, 1983; Graesser, 1981; Rumelhart, 1977).

So far I have said little about the way in which our goals and attitudes are brought to bear on the comprehension process. The main reason for the omission is that we know virtually nothing about this. A broad statement could be made to the effect that our goals and attitudes may influence the selection of the schemata used to encode information during comprehension. However, given the status of our current knowledge of schema use, and indeed of the structure of schemata, such a statement has little explanatory power!

In this section I have discussed how knowledge of the topic of text may be used during comprehension and represented in memory, but what of knowledge of the conventions of the text itself? The use of rhetorical knowledge of textual form during comprehension has been the focus of some controversy in recent years, which I will now briefly describe.

Knowledge structures for textual form

One specialized form of knowledge which can be applied in text comprehension is rhetorical knowledge concerning the form of different kinds of discourse. Different discourse types have their own form and conventions, which we learn through experience with them. Research in this area has concentrated on knowledge of the form and conventions of narrative discourse. It has been suggested by a number of investigators (e.g. Mandler and Johnson, 1977; Rumelhart, 1975, 1977; Stein and Glenn, 1979; Thorndyke, 1977) that structural information concerning the organization and interrelation of different parts of a story can be summarized in a *story grammar* which contains a set of rules which can generate a story. The units of story analysis are propositions, and these are structured in a hierarchy according to the rules of the grammar. The exact nature of this grammar varies from investigator to investigator. Rewrite rules specify the order in which parts of the story occur. The following are examples of the first rewrite rules from several of these grammars:

Rumelhart (1975), STORY → SETTING + EPISODE(S).
Thorndyke (1977), STORY → SETTING + THEME + PLOT + RESOLUTION.
Mandler and Johnson (1977), STORY → SETTING + EVENT STRUCTURE.

To give an example of the use of these first rewrite rules, in Mandler and Johnson's dog story in Table 5.1, phrases 1–3 constitute the setting and phrases 4–11 constitute the event structure. The complete rewrite rules for a story (see Table 5.2) specify its structure in some detail and allow the representation of its events in hierarchical form.

Goal-directed episodes are common to most story grammars. In Thorndyke's grammar, episodes are contained in the plot. In Mandler and Johnson's grammar, the event structure orders the episodes. For all of these grammars, the setting, i.e.. the location, time and introduction of characters, precedes the episodes which contain the story events. The components

Table 5.1 The dog story. From Mandler and Johnson (1977) (*Reproduced by permission of Academic Press*).

---

1 It happened that a dog had got a piece of meat
2 and was carrying it home in his mouth.
3 Now on his way home he had to cross a plank lying across a stream.
4 As he crossed he looked down
5 and saw his own shadow reflected in the water beneath.
6 Thinking it was another dog with another piece of meat,
7 he made up his mind to have that also.
8 So he made a snap at the shadow,
9 but as he opened his mouth the piece of meat fell out,
10 dropped into the water,
11 and was never seen again.

Table 5.2 The complete rewrite rules for a story. From Mandler and Johnson (1977) (*Reproduced by permission of Academic Press*).

FABLE → STORY AND MORAL

STORY → SETTING AND EVENT STRUCTURE

SETTING → $\begin{matrix} \text{STATE (AND EVENT)} \\ \text{EVENT} \end{matrix}$

STATE → STATE ((AND STATE)^n)

EVENT → EVENT(($\begin{matrix} \text{AND} \\ \text{THEN} \\ \text{CAUSE} \end{matrix}$ EVENT)^n)((AND STATE)^n)

EVENT STRUCTURE → EPISODE((THEN EPISODE)^n)

EPISODE → BEGINNING CAUSE DEVELOPMENT CAUSE ENDING

BEGINNING → $\begin{matrix} \text{EVENT} \\ \text{EPISODE} \end{matrix}$

DEVELOPMENT → $\begin{matrix} \text{SIMPLE REACTION CAUSE ACTION} \\ \text{COMPLEX REACTION CAUSE GOAL PATH} \end{matrix}$

SIMPLE REACTION → INTERNAL EVENT((CAUSE INTERNAL EVENT)^n)

ACTION → EVENT

COMPLEX REACTION → SIMPLE REACTION CAUSE GOAL

GOAL → INTERNAL STATE

GOAL PATH → $\begin{matrix} \text{ATTEMPT CAUSE OUTCOME} \\ \text{GOAL PATH (CAUSE GOAL PATH)}^n \end{matrix}$

ATTEMPT → EVENT

OUTCOME → $\begin{matrix} \text{EVENT} \\ \text{EPISODE} \end{matrix}$

ENDING → $\begin{matrix} \text{EVENT (AND EMPHASIS)} \\ \text{EMPHASIS} \\ \text{EPISODE} \end{matrix}$

EMPHASIS → STATE

---

given to episodes vary from author to author. For example, according to Rumelhart (1977) an episode contains four variables—P, E, G and O:

Episode about protagonist P:
(1)   EVENT E CAUSES P TO DESIRE GOAL G.
(2)   P TRIES TO GET G UNTIL OUTCOME O OCCURS.

According to Thorndyke (1977):

EPISODE → SUBGOAL + ATTEMPT + OUTCOME.

According to Mandler and Johnson (1977):

EPISODE → BEGINNING CAUSE DEVELOPMENT CAUSE ENDING.

All of these rules for generating episodes describe a subgoal, an attempt to achieve it and the outcome of the attempt.

Story grammars were not only devised to provide a syntactic analysis of story structure and thereby distinguish between stories and other discourse forms, but were also proposed as models of structures for comprehension. They have subsequently been evaluated and found to be inadequate both for their syntactic role and as components of the comprehension system (Black and Wilensky, 1979; Garnham, 1983; Johnson-Laird, 1983). Their limitations as linguistic devices are outlined by Black and Wilensky, whose arguments are appraised and extended by Garnham and by Johnson-Laird. Relevant to their potential role in the comprehension process is the observation that many events which comprise a story may be related only via inferences. In order to make these inferences the reader must use general knowledge about the relationships between events, and hence must establish a semantic structure between events. This removes the necessity of applying a story grammar, since its role is assumed to be the establishment of a semantic structure via the use of syntactic rules. Black and Wilensky suggest that a more fruitful approach is to concentrate on the knowledge required to understand different text genres and the structures used to store and process it.

This alternative view of story comprehension is that schemata corresponding to structural components of stories organize information (Black and Bower, 1980; Black, 1984). Two such schemata are discussed by Black (1984). Stories contain goal-based episodes which in turn contain goals, and the subgoals which must be achieved in order to achieve these. One schema is therefore an episode schema. There is evidence that episodes show independence in memory (Mandler, 1978; Black, Turner and Bower, 1979), and that stories in which the order of events is rearranged are recalled with events in the conventional order (Mandler and Johnson, 1977). A second schema is the plot unit schema, which contains goals and outcomes within a theme. For example, the passage:

Paul wanted to date Susan, but she was going out with Ken. Paul asked Ken to stop seeing her, but Ken just laughed at him. Susan stopped seeing Ken when Paul told her that Ken was also going out with her worst enemy. (Black, 1984, p. 251)

contains four plot units: competition (Paul and Ken want to date Susan), denial of request (Ken refusing to stop dating Susan), fleeting success (Ken dates Susan, but not for long) and retaliation (Paul tells on Ken). There is evidence that plot units are used in writing stories and in grouping stories into categories (Reiser, Black and Lehnert, 1985), and that networks of plot units predict the content of story summaries (Lehnert, 1981).

The emphasis of this approach is on content rather than structure, although in practice it is very difficult to separate content from structure in stories. The cognitive units proposed relate to goals and actions, and hence may apply to action in general rather than exclusively to narrative stories. This view is similar to that expressed by Garnham (1983, in press) in his criticisms of the story grammar approach.

van Dijk and Kintsch (1983) argue for the necessity of both specific structures for conventional text forms, or *superstructures*, and more general structures. General structures for processing information relating to action are necessary because, first, since stories are about action, understanding stories requires understanding of action. Second, if we have structures to deal with action, then it is unparsimonious to have in addition further structures which deal with action in discourse. Superstructures for text form are necessary because stories have semantic and pragmatic constraints which are distinct from other forms of action discourse (e.g. police reports). They also focus on interesting rather than more mundane events, whereas much action is mundane. Finally, action discourse may omit details of action and may present events in an order different to that in which they normally occur. Action and its description in story form may then require the adoption of different conventions for comprehension. But does this necessarily mean that superstructures for story form are required? A significant proportion of what we learn about action is acquired indirectly, e.g. via hearsay or from media reports. The rhetorical conventions that apply to these sources of information and the amount of detail present may vary, but presumably the information they provide is used to update knowledge structures for action which are then in turn used in the comprehension process. It is not obvious why knowledge of rhetorical conventions would be a useful or necessary addition to this.

van Dijk and Kintsch argue that stories are problematic for the evaluation of the role of rhetorical structure in comprehension, due to the confounding of rhetorical form with content. They suggest that other forms of discourse would be more fruitfully examined in this context, and present an investigation using descriptive discourse which emphasizes the use of superstructures in comprehension (Kintsch and Yarbrough, 1982). van Dijk and Kintsch point out that descriptive text may contain a variety of forms such as illustration, argument, definition, classification and description of procedures. The investigation compared the comprehension of descriptive passages with 'good' and 'bad' rhetorical form (see Table 5.3). The reader is introduced to each form by cues in the text. The 'bad' text was constructed by reordering of sentences and deletion of rhetorical cues which would have destroyed coherence in the reordered version. Comprehension of the 'good' text was greatly superior to comprehension of the 'poor' text. Kintsch and van Dijk interpret this as indicative of the important role of rhetorical superstructures in the construction of a representation of descriptive text.

Interpretation of the Kintsch and Yarbrough study is not, however, that straightforward. The effect of the reordering of sentences in the 'poor' text in Table 5.3(b) is to make the context of the passage obscure in addition to destroying the form of the classification. It is clear in the 'good' passage that the subject of the passage is an examination of locomotor patterns in evolutionary terms. The first two sentences contain this information. The context for the second passage is far from clear. The importance of context was examined extensively by Bransford and Johnson (1973). In one of their experiments, a passage was presented describing the sequence of operations involved in washing clothes which lacked crucial information about context:

> The procedure is actually quite simple. First you arrange things into different groups. Of course, one pile may be sufficient depending on how much there is to do . . . (p. 400)

Comprehension and recall of the passage was poor. The role played by context in this passage is presumed to be one of determining which schemata containing general knowledge are likely to provide a good fit to the information in the passage. Where context is not available before the passage is read, these schemata cannot be found and hence comprehension of the passage is poor. In a similar manner, at the start of the passage in Table 5.3(b) part of the context is missing. It is obvious that the passage is about locomotion, but it is not obvious that evolutionary patterns of locomotion are being examined. Thus context is only partial and textual form is confounded with content. Lorch and Lorch (1985), in an investigation of recall of descriptive texts, found that recall of randomly ordered text was good when an introductory paragraph gave information about the topic structure of the text.

The argument that we have knowledge structures for textual form is, at first sight, a compelling one, simply because we are aware of different form conventions. There is as yet insufficient evidence for the use of such conventions in providing a framework for the encoding of text. Certain forms of discourse which focus on human action, e.g. stories, newspaper articles, have a form which is intimately linked to the actions they describe, so it

Table 5.3 A classification text in good (a) and poor (b) rhetorical form. From van Dijk and Kintsch (1983) (*Reproduced by permission of Academic Press*).

(a)
In order to obtain an understanding of how man has evolved it is often helpful to analyze him in relation to the other primates. One major way of seeing this relationship is by examining locomotor patterns.

The most developmentally constricted form of locomotion is called vertical clinging and leaping. All prosimians fall into this form. In this pattern the animal normally clings to the branch with its head above its limbs. In its predominant locomotive form the animal pushes off from the branch or tree with its hind limbs and springs or leaps to the next.

A developmentally more advanced form is quadrupedalism. As the name suggests all four limbs are involved in this pattern. Macaques and howler monkeys typify this form.

Next is ape locomotion which is characterized by arm swinging and/or occasional linked branch-to-branch swinging, climbing, and knuckle walking. The gibbon, orangutan, and chimpanzee locomotive patterns are characterized by this form.

Finally, we find bipedalism which is the characteristic locomotive form of man: Bipedalism includes standing, striding, and running. This form completes an adaptive developmental sequence which began sometime in the deep past with vertical clinging and leaping.

(b)
A developmentally rather advanced form is quadrupedalism. As the name suggests all four limbs are involved in this pattern. Macaques and howler monkeys typify this form.

It should be noted that bipedalism is the characteristic locomotive form of man: Bipedalism includes standing, striding, and running. This form completes an adaptive developmental sequence which began sometime in the deep past with vertical clinging and leaping.

In order to obtain an understanding of how man has evolved it is often helpful to analyze him in relation to the other primates. One major way of seeing this relationship is by examining locomotor patterns.

The most developmentally constricted form of locomotiion is called vertical clinging and leaping. All prosimians fall into this form. In this pattern the animal normally clings to the branch with its head above its limbs. In its predominant locomotive form the animal pushes off from the branch or tree with its hind limbs and springs or leaps to the next.

Ape locomotion is usually characterized by arm swinging and/or occasional linked branch-to-branch swinging, climbing, and knuckle walking. The gibbon, orangutan, and chimpanzee locomotive patterns are characterized by this form.

---

seems unnecessary to propose that textual form is used during the encoding of the information they contain. There are types of discourse which have much stricter conventions, e.g. scientific or technical reports, some poetic forms. The role of superstructures in the comprehension of these has yet to be investigated.

TEXT-BASED FACTORS IN COMPREHENSION

We need organized background knowledge in order to extract information from text, but in addition the text itself must be organized in such a way that information can be readily encoded. I will next consider textual factors that influence the ease with which a coherent representation of the content of text may be constructed.

Global coherence

In order to be comprehensible, text has to be *coherent*, that is, it must have a consistent theme and the events or arguments which comprise the theme must be organized logically within the text. It is quite possible, however, to maintain coherence in narrative text while manipulating the order or amount of information given, providing consistency of theme and spatial relationships is maintained. Rhetorical strategies allow an author to lead the reader to make certain hypotheses about causality or outcome which are updated or changed dramatically when further events are presented (e.g. in a mystery story or thriller). The reader may then satisfactorily comprehend sections of a text, but this can differ from the end-product of an entire passage or story. Brewer (1980) outlines four rhetorical strategies which are available to an author to manipulate moment-to-moment comprehension. These are: varying the order of events from the underlying order, selection of detail, varying the visibility of the narrator and varying the amount of information available to the narrator. Consistency of theme may be main-tained yet text may appear bizarre if it describes an implausible sequence of events. It may therefore be implausible yet coherent (Garnham, Oakhill and Johnson-Laird, 1982). Problems in comprehension in this case would result from the application of the reader's knowledge base rather than from the text itself.

Causal cohesion is of particular importance in the comprehension of stories, as Trabasso and his colleagues have shown (Trabasso and van den Broek, 1985; Trabasso, Secco and van den Broek, 1984; Trabasso and Sperry, 1985; Trabasso, Stein and Johnson, 1981). It is assumed that in forming a representation of narrative, the reader attempts to structure facts or events (given or inferred) in a causal network from which expectations of events can be generated. Within this network there are causal pathways, some of which continue through the story (causal chains) while others do not (dead-ends). By identifying which events belong to causal chains and which are dead-ends, the reader can edit the network for the purpose of storage and retrieval. Trabasso and Sperry (1985) looked at judgments of the importance of statements in folk tales and found that two properties predicted these judgments: the number of direct causal connections and whether or not a statement described an event which was part of a causal chain running through the story. Thus the centrality of statements to the theme of a story is determined by the causal relationships of the events they describe with other events.

Local coherence

On a more local sentence level, thematic and linguistic cohesion is necessary for text to be comprehensible.

Thematic cohesion

Thematic cohesion between sentences is crucial for successful representation of text. The form of this representation may vary according to discourse type. For most discourse types there must be logical continuity between sentences. For descriptive passages, spatial relationships must be maintained from one sentence to the next. For example, Black, Turner and Bower (1979) found that changing the point of view, i.e.. the perspective from which scenes are described, in sentences resulted in slower reading and lower ratings of comprehensibility than when point of view was consistent throughout.

Linguistic cohesion

Linguistic cohesion refers to the way in which linguistic conventions allow one part of a text to be linked to another at the sentence level. The most obvious form of linkage is by the use of conjunctions, e.g.

It is raining outside *and* I do not have a raincoat. *Therefore* I will stay inside until the rain stops.

Another way in which sentences can be linked is by co-referencing, where objects, events or persons are common to two or more sentences. One device for co-referencing is the anaphor, which is a term (pronoun or phrase) which has its meaning contained elsewhere in the text, e.g.

John typed his book chapter into his IBM PC. *He* pressed the wrong key and lost *it all*.

He and *it all* are anaphors referring to *John* and his *book chapter* respectively. These anaphoric references must be understood in order to integrate the two sentences.

Clark and Haviland (1977) describe a general strategy for co-referencing successively presented information in text. This is the *given−new strategy* (Clark, 1977; Clark and Haviland, 1977). Text contains information which either refers back to previously given information (given) or information which is new to the text (new). In order to integrate new information into the representation of the text which the reader is constructing, it is necessary to access the antecedent information referenced by the given information, e.g.

I went shopping yesterday. The walk did me good.

The walk is given because it refers back to the shopping expedition. *Did me good* is new information which must be integrated with the information in the first sentence. Given information can take the form of an anaphor or can be inferred from its antecedent information. Inferences play a major role in the given–new strategy. In order to understand the above example it is necessary to infer that the narrator went shopping on foot rather than by car. Such inferences are *authorized* (Clark, 1977), that is, the author intends the reader to draw them. Cohesion of a passage is reduced or lost where the given information and its antecedent are separated by intervening material, e.g.

I went shopping yesterday. The bookshop was very crowded. A new book on reading has just been published and lots of people were buying it. The walk did me good.

This sentence is less cohesive because of the distance between the given information *The walk* and its antecedent. Intervening material has the effect of *backgrounding* the antecedent. In order for the passage to be cohesive, the given information should be *foregrounded* (Lesgold, Roth and Curtis, 1979), i.e.. active in the mind of the reader. Lesgold *et al*. demonstrated that the acceptability of some sentence forms in text is a function of foregrounding or backgrounding of information. They give the following examples:

1.   I am trying to find a black dog. Yesterday that dog bit a little girl. She was scared but she wasn't really hurt.
2.   Yesterday a black dog bit a little girl. It got away and we are still trying to find it. She was scared but she wasn't really hurt. (p. 291)

The first example is immediately comprehensible. The given information in the third sentence is the anaphor *she*, for which the antecedent *a little girl* is adjacent. The second example is less cohesive. The antecedent in this case is backgrounded by the time the given information appears in the last sentence. Passages of this kind take longer to comprehend as the antecedent has to be reactivated in memory (Lesgold, Roth and Curtis, 1979).

If the information in new sentences can be readily integrated with that in previous sentences, text has *referential continuity*. To go back to example 2 above, referential continuity can be improved by replacing the pronoun *she* with the noun phrase *the little girl*:

Yesterday a black dog bit a little girl. It got away and we are still trying to find it. The little girl was scared but she wasn't really hurt.

Garnham, Oakhill and Johnson-Laird (1982) presented subjects with descriptive and narrative passages of the following types: unmodified, modified by presenting the sentences in random order and modified as before but with referential continuity restored. Subjects were required to recall the passages and rate their comprehensibility. The descriptive passages were affected little by modification. As the authors point out, such passages contain little co-referencing. However, comprehensibility and recall of the narrative passages were affected quite dramatically by modification, although restoration of referential continuity helped to obviate this effect.

Coherence of text is crucial for comprehension. Factors which contribute to this coherence vary according to discourse type. Causal cohesion and referential integration are crucial for the formation of a representation of narrative text. They are of lesser significance for descriptive text, where consistency of spatial relationships, a consistent spatial point of view and presentation of information in a manner which allows a representation to be built up in a consistent manner (Ehrlich and Johnson-Laird, 1982) are important. Different types of text have different coherence requirements, and strategies for establishing coherence will presumably vary with text type. We do not know whether or not knowledge of text type assists in the selection of these strategies.

A coherent text allows a representation to be built up in a consistent manner. The next section will examine how this representation is constructed.

CONSTRUCTING A REPRESENTATION OF TEXT

The notion that verbal material is broken down into propositions or 'units of meaning' is common to many theories of cognitive processing. There is evidence that in reading, sentences are broken down into underlying propositions (e.g. Ratcliffe and McKoon, 1978). These propositions then allow the construction of a model of the events or situation portrayed in the text—the 'situation model' of van Dijk and Kintsch (1983). This model can be constructed providing the reader has an appropriate knowledge base and that the text-based factors described in the previous section allow coherent information to be extracted from the text.

The use of schemata in the comprehension process has been described earlier in this chapter. van Dijk and Kintsch (1983) have incorporated similar notions into their account of the comprehension process, although they place greater emphasis on the problem-solving nature of comprehension. They see discourse-processing as a strategic process which takes into account not only the content of the discourse but also its intention or communicative context. Strategies are procedural knowledge about understanding discourse, and as is the case for other problem-solving procedures, these need to be learned and eventually automatized. As a strategic process, processing proceeds by using a working hypothesis about the correct structure and meaning of the portion of text under analysis. This working hypothesis may, after further processing, be demonstrated to be incorrect. Successive refinement is a feature of this and several other accounts of the comprehension process (e.g. Collins, Brown and Larkin, 1980; Rumelhart, 1980; Graesser, 1981). The working hypothesis is formed not only from cues derived from the text but also from the goals and knowledge of the individual processing the text. During the acquisition of reading skill some strategies are learned early, e.g. word and clause comprehension. Others, such as deriving the 'gist' of a story, are acquired later. Some forms of discourse, such as reading a scientific article or technical report, require specialized training.

The model involves not only creating a propositional representation of the text in memory—the *textbase*, which is limited to information in or implied by the text—but also updating relevant information activated in memory to aid comprehension and give context—the *situation model* in episodic memory. Both a linguistic representation of text and a cognitive model of the situation it portrays are necessary for a number of reasons, the most important of which concerns the use of a situation model in understanding the referents and coreferents in the surface structure of discourse. A full exposition of the arguments is given in van Dijk and Kintsch (1983, pp. 338–344) and Johnson-Laird (1983, pp. 377–399). The situation model is a cognitive model of the situation portrayed by the text and contains inferred material. Situation models allow learning since they integrate information from the text with existing knowledge. van Dijk and Kintsch assume that they are schematic in nature and may use scripts or result in their formation.

van Dijk and Kintsch's model does not present a complete representation format for knowledge, but assumes various forms of organization. The comprehension process initially involves the strategic formation of propositions on the basis of word meanings, activated from semantic memory, and syntactic analysis. Propositional strategies use a strategic unit, the propositional schema, for analysing surface structures for the construction of the textbase. This textbase contains detailed information about the meaning of the text. The 'gist' of a section of text is contained in its *macrostructure*. This is a hierarchical structure of macropropositions with greater condensing of text occurring at each higher level, which allows information from the text to be integrated into the situation model. Local coherence strategies allow meaningful connections to be made between different sentences in the construction of a macrostructure. These may require the use of knowledge from the situation model to link propositions. The textbase can be seen as the lowest levels of the macrostructure. The macrostructure derived by a reader for a particular text may differ from that intended by the author, since it is a function of the interaction of the reader and the text and each reader may have different background knowledge and goals.

Perrig and Kintsch (1985) obtained experimental results which supported the distinction between a linguistic representation of text and a situation model. They argued that recall of text would be based on the textbase, whereas the situation model would be used for making inferences about the information contained in the text and their results support this argument. They examined the ability of subjects to recall texts and judge the correctness of inferences concerning content. Two texts were used, which described the spatial layout of a small town. In one text the reader was taken on a route through the town (route version), while in the other the relative locations of parts of the town were described (survey version). In their first experiment, the route version of the text was more cohesive than the survey version and was better recalled. Perrig and Kintsch argue that cohesion is important for the construction of the textbase upon which recall is based. The subjects were unable to judge inferences based on either of the texts accurately or to draw accurate maps based on them, probably due to the length of the text and the complexity of the spatial layout described. Perrig and Kintsch interpreted this as indicative of a distinction between a textbase, from which subjects were able to recall text, and a situation model necessary for inferences, which subjects had been unable to construct. Their second experiment used shorter, simpler texts and an additional condition was employed in which subjects were given a map of the town. Again the route text was more cohesive than the survey text, and was better recalled. This suggests a surface representation but not necessarily a propositional one. Subjects were able to judge the correctness of inferences, but their accuracy was determined by the version of the text they had been given and the type of inferences they had to judge. Females who had received the route text were better at judging route inferences than survey inferences, while the reverse was true for those who had received the survey text. Males were better at judging the survey inferences irrespective of the form of the text. The issue raised by these results is that of the form of the representation in the situation model. For the females at least, the survey text presumably resulted in a spatial representation whereas the route text resulted in a linear procedural representation.

Perrig and Kintsch suggest that a situation model may use a propositional, spatial or linear (string) code (J.R. Anderson, 1983), while the macrostructure uses a propositional code. The type of discourse (i.e. descriptive, narrative, etc.) will have implications for the local coherence strategies which are used for referential integration in the creation of the macrostructure, as suggested by the findings of Garnham, Oakhill and Johnson-Laird (1982) described earlier. The world knowledge necessary to establish local coherence may be contained in the situation model in several forms. How then is this knowledge integrated with the macrostructure, which van Dijk and Kintsch assume is propositional in nature? A related question is, how can information contained in the macrostructure in propositional form be used to update related knowledge contained in the situation model? It is possible that the macrostructure may contain spatial and linear representations at levels above the surface representation. A causal chain of the kind discussed by Trabasso and his colleagues may be derived from the propositional representation of a story, and descriptive passages within the story may be represented in spatial form. The macrostructure may then be similar to the mixed hierarchies of Anderson's ACT system (Anderson, 1983), which contain different representation types. Strategies for establishing coherence may be a function of the form in which information is to be summarized in the macrostructure, and discourse type may play a significant role in determining the selection of such strategies. This is all highly speculative, but the issues raised deserve to be the focus of further debate and investigation.

CONCLUDING REMARKS

In the process of understanding text, information contained in it is integrated with the reader's knowledge about its topic area. A description of the comprehension process must therefore consider the nature of the memory structures from which knowledge is applied to text, and which will be used to store information derived from text. The weight of evidence favours schematic structures, and the recent theoretical work by Schank (1982) has outlined how such structures can cope with the processes of abstraction and learning necessary for a dynamic memory system. Schank's framework could also be applied to the application and generalization of information derived from the text in the form of the situation model of van Dijk and Kintsch (1983). It is not clear what role, if any, knowledge concerning the conventions of different discourse types plays in comprehension. Story grammars have largely been abandoned on both logical and empirical grounds and the schematic superstructures proposed by van Dijk and Kintsch lack empirical support, although many forms of discourse have still to be investigated.

Representation form has been largely neglected in descriptions of the comprehension process. Any comprehensive description of the macrostructure and the situation model, and any account of the process by which information from the macrostructure is incorporated into the situation model, must take this into account. Representation form also deserves to be explored in its relationship with coherence requirements. In different sections of this chapter coherence strategies have been discussed in their relationship with both discourse type and representation form, but the nature of this relationship has not as yet been examined.

The comprehension process itself as described by van Dijk and Kintsch is strategic in nature and has much in common with problem-solving processes of the kind described by Newell and Simon (1972) and J.R. Anderson (1982). This dynamic approach, which focuses on the strategic application of procedural knowledge in the comprehension process, may prove to be fruitful, particularly in the study of reading acquisition. As Garnham (in press) points out, interpretation of written material may, in many instances, vary with the goal of the reader. A dynamic strategic approach provides a framework for examining the individual differences which result from the purpose, competence and existing knowledge of different readers. Future research will doubtless add detail to the framework provided by van Dijk and Kintsch.

ACKNOWLEDGMENTS

I would like to thank John Beech and Alan Garnham for their helpful comments on an earlier draft of this chapter.

REFERENCES

Abbott, V., Black, J.B., and Smith, E.E. (1985). The representation of scripts in memory. *Journal of Memory and Language*, **24**, 179-199.

Alba, J.W., and Hasher, L. (1983). Is memory schematic? *Psychological Bulletin*, **93**, 203-231.

Anderson, J.R., (1982). Acquisition of cognitive skill. *Psychological Review*, **89**, 369-406.

Anderson, J.R. (1983). *The Architecture of Cognition*. Cambridge, Mass.: Harvard University Press.

Anderson, R.C., Reynolds, R.E., Schallert, D.L., and Goetz, E.T. (1977). Frameworks for understanding discourse. *American Educational Research Journal*, **14**, 367-381.

Anderson, R.C., Spiro, R.J., and Anderson, M.C. (1978). Schemata as scaffolding for the representation of information in connected discourse. *American Educational Research Journal*, **15**, 433-440.

Bartlett, F.C. (1932). *Remembering: A study in Experimental and Social Psychology*. Cambridge: Cambridge University Press.

Bates, E., Kintsch, W., Fletcher, C.R., and Giuliani, V. (1980). The role of pronominalization and ellipsis in texts: Some memory experiments. *Journal of Experimental Psychology: Human Learning and Memory*, **6**, 676-691.

Bellezza, F.S., and Bower, G.H. (1981). The representational and processing characteristics of scripts. *Bulletin of the Psychonomic Society*, **18**, 1-4.

Bellezza, F.S., and Bower, G.H. (1982). Remembering script-based text. *Poetics*, **11**, 1-23.

Black, J.B. (1984). Understanding and remembering stories. In J.R. Anderson and S.M. Kosslyn (Eds.) *Tutorials in Learning and Memory*. New York: W.H. Freeman.

Black, J.B., and Bower, G.H. (1980). Story understanding and problem solving. *Poetics*, **9**, 233-250.

Black, J.B., Turner, T.J., and Bower, G.H. (1979). Point of view in narrative comprehension, memory and production. *Journal of Verbal Learning and Verbal Behavior,* **18**, 187-198.

Black, J.B., and Wilensky, R. (1979). An evaluation of story grammars. *Cognitive Science,* **3**, 213-229.

Bower, G.H. (1978). Experiments on story comprehension and recall. *Discourse Processes,* **1**, 211-231.

Bower, G.H., Black, J.B., and Turner, T.J. (1979). Scripts in memory for text. *Cognitive Psychology,* **11**, 177-220.

Bransford, J.D., and Johnson, M.K. (1972). Contextual prerequisites for understanding: Some investigations of comprehension and recall. *Journal of Verbal Learning and Verbal Behavior,* **11**, 717-721.

Bransford, J.D., and Johnson, M.K. (1973). Consideration of some problems of comprehension. In W.G. Chase (Ed.) *Visual Information Processing.* New York: Academic Press.

Brewer, W.F. (1980). Literary theory, rhetoric and stylistics: Implications for psychology. In R.J. Spiro, B.C. Bruce and W.F. Brewer (Eds.) *Theoretical Issues in Reading Comprehension.* Hillsdale, N.J.: Erlbaum.

Chiesi, H., Spilich, G.J., and Voss, J.F. (1979). Acquisition of domain-related information in relation to high and low domain knowledge. *Journal of Verbal Learning and Verbal Behavior,* **18**, 257-273.

Clark, H.H. (1977). Inferences in comprehension. In D. LaBerge and S.J. Samuels (Eds.) *Basic Processes in Reading: Perception and Comprehension.* Hillsdale, N.J.: Erlbaum.

Clark, H.H., and Haviland, S.E. (1977). Comprehension and the Given–New Contract. In R.O. Freedle (Ed.) *Discourse Production and Comprehension.* Norwood, N.J.: Ablex.

Collins, A.M., Brown, J.S., and Larkin, K. (1981). Inference in text understanding. In R.J. Spiro, B.C. Bruce and W.F. Brewer (Eds.) *Theoretical Issues in Reading Comprehension.* Hillsdale, N.J.: Erlbaum.

van Dijk, T.A., and Kintsch, W. (1983). *Strategies of Discourse Comprehension.* New York: Academic Press.

Ehrlich, K., and Johnson-Laird, P.N. (1982). Spatial descriptions and referential continuity. *Journal of Verbal Learning and Verbal Behavior,* **21**, 296-306.

Galambos, J.A., and Rips, L.J. (1982). Memory for routines. *Journal of Verbal Learning and Verbal Behavior,* **21**, 260-281.

Garnham, A. (1983). What's wrong with story grammars. *Cognition,* **15**, 145-154.

Garnham, A. (in press). Understanding. In G. Claxton (Ed.) *New Directions in Cognition.* London: Routledge & Kegan Paul.

Garnham, A., Oakhill, J., and Johnson-Laird, P.N. (1982). Referential continuity and the coherence of discourse. *Cognition,* **11**, 29-46.

Graesser, A.C. (1981). *Prose Comprehension Beyond the Word.* New York: Springer.

Graesser, A.C., Woll, S.B., Kowalski, D.J., and Smith, D.A. (1980). Memory for typical and atypical actions in scripted activities. *Journal of Experimental Psychology: Human Learning and Memory,* **6**, 503-515.

Haberlandt, K.F., and Graesser, A.C. (1985). Component processes in text comprehension and some of their interactions. *Journal of Experimental Psychology: General,* **114**, 357-374.

Haviland, S.E., and Clark, H.H. (1974). What's new? Acquiring new information as a process in comprehension. *Journal of Verbal Learning and Verbal Behavior,* **13**, 512-521.

Johnson-Laird, P.N. (1983). *Mental Models*. Cambridge: Cambridge University Press.

Kintsch, W., and Bates, E. (1977). Recognition memory for statements from a classroom lecture. *Journal of Experimental Psychology: Human Learning and Memory*, 3, 150-159.

Kintsch, W., and van Dijk, T.A. (1978). Toward a model of text comprehension and production. *Psychological Review*, 85, 363-394.

Kintsch, W., and Yarbrough, J.C. (1982). The role of rhetorical structure in text comprehension. *Journal of Educational Psychology,*, 74, 828-834.

Lehnert, W.G. (1981). Plot units and narrative summarization. *Cognitive Science*, 5, 293-331.

Lesgold, A.M., Roth, S.F., and Curtis, M.E. (1979). Foregrounding effects in discourse comprehension. *Journal of Verbal Learning and Verbal Behavior*, 18, 291-308.

Lorch, R.F. Jr, and Lorch, E.P. (1985). Topic structure representation and text recall. *Journal of Educational Psychology*, 77, 137-148.

Mandler, J.M. (1978). A code in the node: The cue of a story schema in retrieval. *Discourse Processes*, 1, 14-35.

Mandler, J.M., and Johnson, N.S. (1977). Remembrance of things parsed: Story structure and recall. *Cognitive Psychology*, 9, 111-191.

McCartney, K.A., and Nelson, K. (1981). Children's use of scripts in story recall. *Discourse Processes*, 4, 59-70.

Minsky, M. (1975). A framework for the representation of knowledge. In P. Winston (Ed.) *The Psychology of Computer Vision*. New York: McGraw-Hill.

Morton, J., Hammersley, R.H., and Bekerian, D.A. (1985). Headed records: A model for memory and its failures. *Cognition*, 20, 1-23.

Nakamura, G.V., Graesser, A.C., Zimmerman, J.A., and Riha, J. (1985). Script processing in a natural situation. *Memory and Cognition*, 13, 140-144.

Nelson, K. (1979). How children represent their world in and out of language. In R.S. Siegler (Ed.) *Children's Thinking: What Develops?* Hillsdale, N.J.: Erlbaum.

Newell, A., and Simon, H.A. (1972). *Human Problem Solving*. Englewood Cliffs: Prentice-Hall.

Norman, D.A., and Rumelhart, D.E. (1975). Memory and knowledge. In D.A. Norman and D.E. Rumelhart (Eds.) *Explorations in Cognition*. San Francisco: Freeman.

Palmer, J., MacLeod, C.M., Hunt, E., and Davidson, J. (1985). Information processing correlates of reading. *Journal of Memory and Language*, 24, 59-88.

Perrig, W., and Kintsch, W. (1985). Propositional and situational representations of text. *Journal of Memory and Language*, 24, 503-518.

Ratcliffe, R., and McKoon, G. (1978). Priming in item recognition: Evidence for the propositional structure of sentences. *Journal of Verbal Learning and Verbal Behavior*, 17, 403-418.

Reiser, B.J., Black, J.B., and Abelson, R.P. (1985). Knowledge structures in the organization and retrieval of autobiographical memories. *Cognitive Psychology*, 17, 89-137.

Reiser, B.J., Black, J.B., and Lehnert, W.G. (1985). Thematic knowledge structures in the understanding and generation of narratives. *Discourse Processes*, 8, 357.

Rumelhart, D.E. (1975). Notes on a schema for stories. In D.G. Bobrow and A.M. Collins (Eds.) *Representation and Understanding*. New York: Academic Press.

Rumelhart, D.E. (1977). Understanding and summarizing brief stories. In D. LaBerge and S.J. Samuels (Eds.) *Basic Processes in Reading: Perception and Comprehension*. Hillsdale, N.J.: Erlbaum.

Rumelhart, D.E. (1980). Schemata: The building blocks of cognition. In R.J. Spiro, B.C. Bruce and W.F. Brewer (Eds.) *Theoretical Issues in Reading Comprehension.* Hillsdale, N.J.: Erlbaum.

Rumelhart, D.E., and Ortony, A. (1977). The representation of knowledge in memory. In R.C. Anderson, R.J. Spiro and W.E. Montague (Eds.) *Schooling and the Acquisition of Knowledge.* Hillsdale, N.J.: Erlbaum.

Schank, R.C. (1982). *Dynamic Memory.* New York: Cambridge University Press.

Schank, R.C., and Abelson, R. (1977). *Scripts, Plans, Goals and Understanding.* Hillsdale, N.J.: Erlbaum.

Spiro, R.J. (1980). Constructive processes in prose comprehension and recall. In R.J. Spiro, B.C. Bruce and W.F. Brewer (Eds.) *Theoretical Issues in Reading Comprehension.* Hillsdale, N.J.: Erlbaum.

Stein, N.L., and Glenn, C.G. (1979). An analysis of story comprehension in elementary school children. In R.O. Freedle (Ed.) *New Directions in Discourse Processing.* Norwood, N.J.: Ablex.

Thorndyke, P.W. (1977). Cognitive structures in comprehension and memory of narrative discourse. *Cognitive Psychology,* **9,** 77-110.

Thorndyke, P.W. (1984). Applications of schema theory in cognitive research. In J.R. Anderson and S.M. Kosslyn (Eds.) *Tutorials in Learning and Memory.* New York: Freeman.

Trabasso, T., Secco, T., and van den Broek, P. (1984). Causal cohesion and story structure. In H. Mandl, N.L. Stein and T. Trabasso (Eds.) *Learning and Comprehension of Text.* Hillsdale, N.J.: Erlbaum.

Trabasso, T., and Sperry, L.L. (1985). Causal relatedness and importance of story events. *Journal of Memory and Language,* **24,** 595-611.

Trabasso, T., Stein, N.L., and Johnson, L.R. (1981). Children's knowledge of events: A causal analysis of story structure. In G.H. Bower (Ed.) *Learning and Motivation,* Vol. 15. New York: Academic Press.

Trabasso, T., and van den Broek, P. (1985). Causal thinking and the representation of narrative events. *Journal of Memory and Language,* **24,** 612-630.

Cognitive approaches to reading
Edited by J. R. Beech and A. M. Colley
© 1987 John Wiley & Sons Ltd

CHAPTER 6

Cerebral Hemisphere Differences and Reading

ANDREW W. YOUNG

Psychology Department, Lancaster University

INTRODUCTION

The cortex of the human brain is divided into left and right cerebral hemispheres, with each being primarily responsible for controlling movements and sensations involving the opposite side of the body. These cerebral hemispheres are themselves interconnected by extensive nerve tracts known as the cerebral commissures, the most important of which are the corpus callosum and anterior commissure (Selnes, 1974).

During the nineteenth century, the remarkable observation was made that disorders of language usually follow injury to the left rather than to the right cerebral hemisphere of the brain. Such observations have now been very extensively documented, and the importance of the left cerebral hemisphere to language abilities is no longer disputed. For right-handed people the extent of left cerebral control of language abilities is very marked, and cases of 'crossed aphasia', in which a severe language disturbance follows right cerebral injury, have been found to be extremely rare (Donoso, 1984). Left-handed people also tend to show left cerebral control of language, though it is usually found that they do not display this tendency as strongly as right-handers (Branch, Milner and Rasmussen, 1964; Goodglass and Quadfasel, 1954; Rasmussen and Milner, 1977).

The impairments that can follow left cerebral injury include problems affecting the production or the comprehension of both spoken and written forms of language. The present chapter is concerned with cerebral asymmetries for processes involved in reading. I will examine available evidence both from clinical investigations and from studies of normal subjects.

Had I been old enough to take on this task 30 years ago, it would have been a relatively easy one. At that time it was generally agreed that, like other language abilities, reading was more or less exclusively organized in the left cerebral hemisphere. This neat conclusion has now, however, to be qualified by a large number of subsequent studies that have shown that the topic is much less straightforward than was originally thought. Cerebral hemisphere differences in reading are now intensively investigated, usually in the context of a more general interest in cerebral hemisphere differences in language abilities (Lambert, 1982a,b; Moscovitch, 1981; Searleman, 1977, 1983). The literature has become so extensive that it would be impossible to make a comprehensive review in the space available. Instead I will approach the topic selectively, looking only at the reading of alphabetic scripts and concentrating on some of the key issues that have arisen.

One question that needs to be asked is why cerebral hemisphere differences in language abilities have attracted such a great deal of attention. Obviously the topic is one of fundamental scientific interest, but there are many other important aspects of brain organization that remain relatively unexplored. It is always difficult to account satisfactorily for scientific fashions, but there are probably at least four reasons. The first is the general increase in interest in all aspects of cerebral asymmetry created by the publication of the dramatic findings of the studies of split-brain patients carried out by Sperry and his colleagues. The second is the fact that several studies have suggested that the right cerebral hemisphere has more extensive language abilities than was previously thought, and it is often attractive to undermine orthodox opinions. Third, if we understood the nature of cerebral hemisphere differences in language organization we might be able to see more clearly what the special requirements of verbal communication are. Fourth, it has become clear that understanding the nature of cerebral hemisphere differences in language abilities may be of importance to the rehabilitation of people who experience disorders of language (including reading) caused by cerebral injuries (see, for example, Glass, Gazzaniga and Premack, 1973).

For the purposes of exposition, studies of cerebral hemisphere differences in reading abilities can be conveniently divided into those involving clinical and those involving normal subject populations. Each will be considered separately. Useful and important findings have been made from both types of study, but there have also been controversies and the work needs to be approached cautiously. In particular, it is necessary to give careful attention to the advantages and limitations of the different types of study, and to specification of the aspects of reading that are actually being investigated in each case.

STUDIES OF PEOPLE WITH CEREBRAL INJURIES

There are three principal types of study that provide relevant information. These are studies of the effects of unilateral cerebral injuries, studies of hemispherectomy patients and studies of commissurotomy (split-brain) patients.

Unilateral cerebral injuries

Unilateral cerebral injuries (i.e. injuries affecting only the left or right cerebral hemisphere) can arise from a number of causes including strokes, tumours, missile wounds, and as a consequence of certain surgical procedures. Investigation of the effects of unilateral injuries forms one of the oldest of neuropsychological techniques and has yielded much valuable information.

As far as reading is concerned, the principal finding of studies of people with unilateral cerebral injuries is quite unequivocal. Disorders affecting reading are, like other language disorders, typically linked to left cerebral injury. Patients with right hemisphere lesions can have problems in understanding emotional aspects of language (Ross, 1984) and may also show defective understanding of certain concepts, or make overliteral interpretations of idioms and metaphors (e.g. Eisenson, 1962; Gainotti, Caltagirone and Miceli, 1983; Gardner, 1981; Moscovitch, 1983a; Wapner, Hamby and Gardner, 1981; Weinstein and Keller, 1963). Such problems do not, however, involve reading *per se* (they are equally apparent in the comprehension of spoken material) and it is still uncertain how they relate to more general intellectual impairments (see Gainotti, Caltagirone and Miceli, 1983).

The only disorder that has been shown to affect the comprehension of written but not spoken material following right cerebral injury is neglect dyslexia (Ellis, Flude and Young, in press; Kinsbourne and Warrington, 1962). In neglect dyslexia the left side of a page of printed text is ignored, with the patient reading only the side of each line falling to her or his right. Often individual words are also misread, whether presented as part of a piece of connected text or in isolation. The errors in reading individual words typically involve the initial (leftmost) letters, which may be omitted or (more commonly) replaced by different letters. In these errors the misread word need not preserve the sound or the syntactic class of the original (e.g. *harden* misread as 'warden'; *tint* as 'pint'; *never* as 'lever'), so that it would seem likely that they arise at a fairly early stage in the reading process. Moreover, all of the neglect dyslexic patients studied to date show neglect of items on the left side in other visual tasks, such as marking the circles in a random array of circles and crosses. Neglect of the left side of space is a fairly common consequence of right hemisphere injury (Heilman, 1979), and it would seem that neglect dyslexia arises when a more general visual neglect compromises the reading process (Ellis, Flude and Young, in press).

All other acquired reading disorders are associated with lesions involving the left cerebral hemisphere (but see Ogden, 1984), and there have been several attempts to relate the observed patterns of reading impairment to the sites of the various lesions responsible (reviews can be found in Heilman and Rothi, 1982; Kremin, 1982; Varney and Damasio, 1982).

One of the conditions that has been most extensively studied by neurologists is what they call alexia without agraphia, or pure alexia. In this condition patients can write quite well (to dictation, for example) but show seriously impaired reading. They can, however, recognize without difficulty spoken words or words that are spelt aloud, and can usually also identify raised letters and words felt by touch or 'written' onto the palm of the hand. Seen objects can be recognized without difficulty by some patients (Damasio and Damasio, 1983).

The lesions responsible for alexia without agraphia are typically located in the left occipital lobe, and either extend into the splenium of the corpus callosum or disrupt nerve connections from the splenium. Since the publication of the papers by Geschwind (1965) and Geschwind and Fusillo (1966), many people have accepted the view that the condition arises when a left occipital lesion disconnects visual information from language centres located in the left hemisphere. Many of the patients have right hemianopia (blindness in the right half of the field of vision). For these patients visual information can still be registered by the visual cortex of the right hemisphere (to which information from the intact left visual field is projected). However, it is argued that because the splenium of the corpus callosum is also affected this visual information remains disconnected from left hemisphere language centres.

Some patients, however, do not have a right hemianopia (Greenblatt, 1973; and including, apparently, the classic case of Déjerine, 1892; see Damasio and Damasio, 1983, 1986). For these patients the inability to read words falling in the right half of the visual field would seem to be due to damage to intrahemispheric pathways in the left hemisphere itself. This possibility is supported by Castro-Caldas and Salgado's (1984) description of a patient with a left occipital lesion that did not involve the splenium of the corpus callosum. This patient was able to identify drawings but not words presented in the right visual field and thus projected to the visual cortex of the left cerebral hemisphere; he could identify both drawings and words presented in the left visual field (and thus to the right hemisphere).

Although neurologists often discuss alexia without agraphia as if it were a unitary condition, this is not really the case. As just discussed, there can be differences in the underlying neurological mechanisms, and there are also behavioural differences between the patients themselves. Hécaen and Kremin (1976) point out that some patients are unable to identify words or letters, whereas others are able to identify letters and can thus read words 'letter-by-letter' (see also Landis, Regard and Serrat, 1980). Even letter-by-letter reading can itself be divided into different variants (Patterson and Kay,

1982; Shallice and Saffran, 1986; Warrington and Shallice, 1980).

Because many of the patients have right hemianopias, letter-by-letter reading raises the possibility that the right hemisphere is capable of letter recognition. This is an example of the more general point that the effects of damage to a highly lateralized information-processing system may reflect not only the functioning of the damaged system itself, but also residual capacities of the uninjured cerebral hemisphere. This point has often been discussed with regard to the aphasias (see Searleman, 1977, 1983), but it is only comparatively recently that it has also been raised for reading (Heilman *et al.*, 1979; Landis *et al.*, 1983; Moore and Weidner, 1974; Shallice and Saffran, 1986). The most notable exponent of this approach has been Coltheart (1980, 1983), who has argued that the reading abilities of deep dyslexic patients may reflect the properties of a right hemisphere reading system rather than those of the damaged left hemisphere system. These views have not, however, gone unchallenged (see Besner, 1981, 1983; Marshall and Patterson, 1983; Patterson and Besner, 1984a,b; but also Rabinowicz and Moscovitch, 1984; Zaidel and Schweiger, 1984).

Commissurotomy and hemispherectomy

In the commissurotomy operation the tracts of nerve fibres that interconnect the cerebral hemispheres are severed, whilst in the very drastic hemispherectomy operation the cortex of an entire cerebral hemisphere is removed. At first sight these operations allow the almost ideal research opportunity of examining the abilities of each cerebral hemisphere in isolation from the other. In practice, however, there are several complicating factors and the evidence obtained faces a number of problems of interpretation.

The hemispherectomy operation is usually performed for one of two distinct reasons (Smith, 1972). The first is the alleviation of the effects of extensive lateralized brain damage in children, which include otherwise intractable epileptic seizures (Krynauw, 1950). The second is for the removal of brain tumours in adults (Burklund, 1972; Dandy, 1928).

There have been a number of reports of the effects of hemispherectomy following early lateralized brain damage (see, for example, Basser, 1962; Carlson *et al.*, 1968; McFie, 1961; Smith and Sugar, 1975) and it is generally agreed that a remarkable degree of recovery of language function can occur, even following left hemispherectomy. Thus it is clear that the right hemisphere is able to support a considerable degree of language development when this is essential. The extent to which this is possible is such that differences between the language abilities of people whose left or whose right cerebral hemisphere were removed early in life are often not noticeable on casual examination and can only be detected with relatively subtle tests

(Dennis, 1980a,b; Dennis and Kohn, 1975; Dennis and Whitaker, 1976; but see also Bishop, 1983). This is as true for written as for spoken language (Dennis, Lovett and Wiegel-Crump, 1981).

Cases of hemispherectomy involving adult patients are much less frequent, and this is especially so for left hemispherectomies. Whereas right hemispherectomy does not lead to easily detected changes in an adult's language abilities (Dandy, 1928; Smith, 1972), left hemispherectomy leaves the patient with only very limited language abilities in the immediate postoperative period. In addition, recurrence of the tumour is common, so the left hemispherectomy operation has only rarely been performed (Crockett and Estridge, 1951; French *et al.*, 1955; Smith, 1972; Zollinger, 1935). Usually only a limited amount of relatively automatic speech and some comprehension ability remained, and some of the patients died within a few months of the operation. There is, however, evidence that in those patients who survived for any appreciable period of time some recovery of language abilities did take place following left hemispherectomy (Burklund, 1972; Burklund and Smith, 1977; Smith, 1966; Smith, 1972; Smith and Burklund, 1966). Thus it is quite probable that the high degree of recovery of language abilities seen after left hemispherectomy in childhood may be as much due to the comparatively long survival periods as to any differences in the relative 'plasticity' of cerebral organization in childhood or adulthood (St James-Roberts, 1979, 1981).

For the most part, only relatively general examinations of language comprehension abilities have been reported for adult hemispherectomy cases. It is commonly observed that an appreciable degree of verbal comprehension remains even after left hemispherectomy and that this can undergo quite marked improvement in the months following the operation (Burkland and Smith, 1977; Smith and Burklund, 1966). Reading is not generally found to be as well preserved as spoken language comprehension, and was also noted to be deficient in at least one case of *right* hemispherectomy (Crockett and Estridge, 1951).

The most detailed studies of language abilities in a left hemispherectomy patient have been those of the patient RS, originally studied by Gott (1973). RS's reading was also studied by Zaidel, together with the reading abilities of the right hemispheres of split-brain patients; these studies will be described later. RS was a ten-year-old girl at the time of her left hemispherectomy, but she was already pubescent and is often considered in relation to adult (rather than childhood) cases (Zaidel, 1977). The operation was performed to remove a tumour that had recurred following its removal from the left lateral ventricle at age eight years.

A comparable previous study of removal of the left hemisphere for malignant tumour in a fourteen-year-old boy (Hillier, 1954) had noted that during the 27-month survival period his reading ability was limited to the recognition of individual letters. RS, however, showed a rather different pattern of abilities. She read aloud correctly five of 20 three- and four-letter concrete words shown to her (cat, hat, boy, dog, baby) and produced responses that could be considered to be semantically appropriate to a further four (*egg*→'eat'; *cup*→'coffee, tea'; *book*→'poem'; *cake*→'yum yum'). She also performed surprisingly well in deciding whether or not the members of a list of 20 visually presented words rhymed with 'son' (16/20 correct). The list included words that did or did not rhyme in which the same number of letters had been changed from the original (e.g. *sun* rhymes and has one letter changed, *sin* does not rhyme yet has the same letter changed). The high level of performance was attained despite the fact that RS could only read aloud two of the 20 words (sun and boy). She could not, in contrast, name individual letters, and was only 31 per cent correct at choosing a named letter from four alternatives (though Gott actually concluded that word recognition was more difficult for her than letter recognition).

In contrast to these rather impoverished reading skills, RS showed relatively good comprehension of spoken language. She could understand verbal instructions quite well, and could follow quite complex directions (such as 'find the boy with the cup and the girl with the bell and draw a line under each') if they were repeated a few times. On the Peabody picture vocabulary test, which measures a person's hearing vocabulary without requiring a verbal response, she obtained an IQ of 70. She was 100 per cent correct correct in deciding whether or not members of a list of 20 spoken words rhymed with 'mat', but did not perform above chance level in deciding whether or not pairs of words were antonyms or unrelated, or in deciding whether or not pairs of words were synonyms or unrelated.

Gott's (1973) study of RS's language abilities illustrates well some of the difficulties of interpretation that arise in hemispherectomy studies. The data are intriguing, but what exactly do they tell us? Do they indicate the comprehension abilities of the normal right hemisphere, or has some reorganization of function already taken place because of the gradual progression of the tumour? Gott herself considered that RS's right hemisphere may have begun to acquire control of certain linguistic functions as early as age seven or eight years. It is also likely that some of the abilities found by Gott had been developed during the two-year period that had elapsed since the hemispherectomy operation. The potential contribution of subcortical structures of the left hemisphere that are left intact by the operation is also difficult to assess. On the other hand, it is always hard to rule out the possibility that there has been some additional damage to the remaining right hemisphere, in which case the pattern of abilities seen might actually be an *underestimate* of its competence. The suspicion of right hemisphere damage is strengthened in RS's case by the observation (mentioned by Gott) that she had left as well as right-sided motor deficits.

The problems of interpretation that arise in hemispherectomy studies make it difficult to draw precise conclusions from them. None the less, certain general points have been established. I will single out three for special attention here. First, it is clear that in certain circumstances the right hemisphere can sustain a remarkably high level of language abilities. Precisely what these circumstances are remains to be determined, and factors such as age at the time of onset of the underlying condition, time since operation, and the removal of potential interference or inhibition arising from the left hemisphere itself have all been considered to be possibilities. Secondly, the ability of the isolated right hemisphere to read seems relatively poor in comparison to its ability to understand speech. Thirdly, in the few cases where these have been examined (e.g. Dennis, Lovett and Wiegel-Crump, 1981; Gott, 1973), the patterns of reading abilities seen after left hemispherectomy are not simply impoverished versions of the pattern seen in normal readers. Instead, there are hints that right hemisphere reading may be achieved in different ways to normal reading.

The studies of split-brain patients confirm and extend these conclusions. The commissurotomy operation is carried out to alleviate certain types of epileptic seizure. Descriptions of the operation and its effects can be found in Dimond (1972) and Gazzaniga (1970). In principle, investigations of split-brain patients allow direct comparisons of the abilities of the left and right cerebral hemispheres to carry out various tasks. For visual stimuli this is achieved by taking advantage of the anatomical arrangement of the optic nerve pathways. As already noted, the optic nerves project stimuli falling in the left visual field (LVF; i.e. to the left of the point that a person is fixating) to the visual cortex of the right cerebral hemisphere, and project stimuli falling in the right visual field (RVF) to the visual cortex of the left cerebral hemisphere. It is important to grasp that this is due to division of nerve fibres originating in the nasal and temporal fields of the retina of *each* eye; hence the same division of visual information occurs even if the person is only looking through one eye. Because interhemispheric nerve connections are severed by the commissurotomy operation, a stimulus presented entirely in the LVF will be 'seen' by the split-brain patient's right hemisphere and a stimulus presented in the RVF will be 'seen' by the patient's left hemisphere. Thus it is possible to test the respective visual abilities of the left and right cerebral hemispheres.

In practice, however, there are a number of limitations to split-brain studies, despite their undoubted interest. Unless special precautions are taken, the anatomical arrangement of the optic nerves can only be utilized provided that central fixation is maintained whilst stimuli are presented. This can be achieved by presenting stimuli for less than the time needed to make an eye movement (around 150 ms; see Young, 1982a), but such a requirement places serious constraints on the tasks and stimuli that can be used. To overcome this difficulty, systems have been devised to produce lateralized visual input with prolonged viewing (Gazzaniga and Smylie, 1984; Myers and Sperry, 1982; Zaidel, 1975). Zaidel's system, for instance, uses a specially made scleral contact lens and short-focus collimator to superimpose the image of an occluding screen onto the LVF or the RVF. Zaidel (1975) estimated that the maximum possible effect of slippage of the contact lens would be to introduce an error of approximately 1° of visual angle. Thus he positioned the occluding screen so that it was slightly overlapping the visual midline.

Unfortunately, however, split-brain patients become adept at making use of subcortical channels to communicate certain types of information (possibly often in the form of somewhat non-specific cues) from one cerebral hemisphere to the other, and the probability that this will happen can in some circumstances be increased by prolonged viewing of the stimuli (Myers and Sperry, 1985; Sergent, 1983a). It is also necessary to prevent the use of overt (i.e. behavioural) cross-cuing of information (Gazzaniga, 1970). Such adeptness can be seen in Gazzaniga and Hillyard's (1971) demonstration that the split-brain patient LB was able to name numbers presented to his right hemisphere by adopting a strategy of counting subvocally with his left hemisphere until his right hemisphere signalled that the correct number had been reached. In his own words: 'What I do is to count up until I hit a number that "sticks out". Then I stop and tell you what it is.'

Further problems with the split-brain studies include the limited number of patients who have been investigated. This is problematic because there are marked individual differences between the patients themselves. Some of these individual differences are due to differences in the operations carried out. In particular, patients in the series operated on by Bogen and Vogel in California usually have both the corpus callosum and the anterior commissure severed, whereas for patients in the series operated on by Wilson in New York the anterior commissure is often left intact. Sometimes the operation is carried out in stages (McKeever *et al.*, 1981; Sidtis *et al.*, 1981a), and there are also cases in which only parts of the corpus callosum itself are sectioned (e.g. Gordon, Bogen and Sperry, 1971). Other causes of individual differences include differences in age of onset of epileptic symptoms, age at operation and time since the operation was performed. Above all, it needs to be borne in mind that the operation is intended to relieve otherwise intractable epileptic seizures, and that all of the patients have longstanding lesions of one or both cerebral hemispheres which may be focal or diffuse in nature. This seriously complicates the interpretation of the split-brain studies. Descriptions of the neurological status of a number of the patients are given by Bogen and Vogel (1975), Myers (1984) and Whitaker and Ojemann (1977).

The initial studies of split-brain patients carried out by Sperry and his associates established that the disconnected right hemisphere showed little ability to initiate speech (Gazzaniga and Hillyard, 1971; Gazzaniga and Sperry, 1967). This observation has usually been confirmed by subsequent studies, but a few split-brain patients have been found to develop some right hemisphere expressive language in the form of writing or speech (see Gazzaniga *et al.*, 1979; McKeever *et al.*, 1981b; but note that patient POV tested by McKeever and his colleagues is the same person as Gazzaniga's patient VP). These cases remain, however, exceptional among the split-brain patients. For the other patients the language abilities of the right hemisphere can only be properly demonstrated in tasks that do not require a verbal response. Some of the patients whose right hemispheres cannot initiate speech have nevertheless been shown to be able to point to the correct referent among distractor items for concrete words like *cup, knife* or *pen* presented in the LVF (Gazzaniga and Sperry, 1967) or to be able to choose the correct word (using the left hand) to correspond to a picture shown in the LVF (Gazzaniga and Hillyard, 1971; Gazzaniga and Sperry, 1967).

Levy and Trevarthen (1977) also confirmed that split-brain patients could match a word seen in the LVF to a picture of its referent, but found that the patients they tested performed poorly at matching a picture of an object presented in the LVF to a picture of another object with a rhyming name (they presented pictures of a rose, eye or bee, and used as the response choices pictures of toes, pie and key). Similarly, the patients could not determine whether or not a spoken word rhymed with the name of a picture presented in the LVF. This apparent inability of the right hemisphere to derive the sound of a seen object's name contrasts with Gott's (1973) report of relatively preserved rhyme judgments in her left hemispherectomy patient, though Gott used printed words instead of pictures as stimuli.

The findings of these studies of split-brain patients are certainly consistent with the findings of hemispherectomy studies in demonstrating that the right hemisphere can show a degree of language comprehension ability that outstrips its ability to initiate speech or writing. However, as Gazzaniga and Sperry (1967) remarked, it is difficult to see where the upper limits of this language comprehension lie because of the restrictions imposed by the need for brief lateral (LVF or RVF) stimulus presentations. In order to overcome this problem, Zaidel (1975) introduced the scleral contact lens system already described, which permits free eye movements whilst the image of a blank screen is superimposed on the LVF or on the RVF.

Using this technique Zaidel has carried out a number of detailed investigations of right hemisphere language comprehension abilities that have been reported and discussed in an extensive series of papers (Zaidel, 1976, 1977, 1978, 1979, 1982, 1983a,b, 1985; Zaidel and Peters, 1981). These studies have largely concentrated on the patients LB and NG, for whom the special contact lenses were made. LB and NG were chosen from the California split-brain series because they were thought to have relatively little extracallosal cerebral damage in comparison to the rest of the patients, and because they did not have the extensive left cerebral damage that might have led to the reorganization of language abilities in favour of the right hemisphere (Zaidel, 1977, 1983c, 1985). Against this it must be pointed out that the patients were seen several years after their operations (NG was operated on in 1963; LB in 1965), so that the possibility of postoperative reorganization cannot be ruled out. However, LB and NG had featured prominently in the original studies of right hemisphere language abilities in split-brain patients (e.g., Gazzaniga and Sperry, 1967) and the pattern of findings reported by Zaidel remains broadly consistent with the earlier reports of these patients' abilities. Tests using presentation of visual stimuli to the left hemispherectomy patient RS (previously studied by Gott, 1973) and the right hemispherectomy patients GE and DW have also been reported by Zaidel in the same series of papers (the need to 'lateralize' the visual input by means of the contact lens procedure does not, of course, arise for the hemispherectomy patients).

Zaidel (1976, 1977, 1979) gave standardized clinical and developmental tests of language comprehension to these patients. On tests involving the comprehension of single spoken words a remarkably rich auditory vocabulary was revealed, although performance was always poorer for the right hemisphere than for the left hemisphere for both LB and NG. This auditory vocabulary included not only concrete nouns but also abstract nouns and verbs. The level of performance shown by the right hemispheres of LB and NG was always equivalent to or better than that of a normal ten-year-old. Zaidel (1976) gives the mean right hemisphere performance for all tests for LB, NG and the left hemispherectomy patient RS as being equivalent to eleven years seven months.

With the token test, however, a much poorer level of performance was found (Zaidel, 1977). This test, originally developed by De Renzi and Vignolo (1962), involves complex and non-redundant spoken instructions such as 'touch the large yellow circle' or 'put the white rectangle behind the yellow circle'. Despite their relatively good ability to understand the words used when these were presented in isolation, the patients' right hemispheres only performed at a level comparable on average to that of a normal four-year-old on this test. Zaidel (1977) argued that the deficit reflects a limitation of short-term sequential verbal memory, which he presumed to be linked to the right hemisphere's inability to generate much in the way of spontaneous speech.

Zaidel (1978) used a reading version of the Peabody picture vocabulary test to investigate the extent to which LB and NG were able to read single words presented to their right hemispheres. In this test a seen word has to be matched to the appropriate one of four pictures. In addition, Zaidel also used the spelling subtest of the Peabody individual achievement test, in which the correct spelling of a spoken word must be chosen from four printed alternatives. On both tests LB's right hemisphere performed at a level roughly equivalent to that of a normal ten-year-old and NG's right hemisphere performed at a level roughly equivalent to that of a normal seven-year-old.

Thus for both LB and NG the right hemisphere's reading vocabulary, whilst appreciable in itself, fell short of its auditory vocabulary. In fact the reading vocabulary was itself a subset of the auditory vocabulary, and Zaidel (1978) could not find any words that were in the right hemisphere's reading vocabulary but not in its auditory vocabulary. He did, however, point out that the reading vocabulary of the right hemisphere may be organized in a different way to its auditory vocabulary, since it shows somewhat different patterns of deficits as a function of the part of speech to which the test word belongs (Zaidel, 1978, 1983a, 1985).

When printed words are combined to form phrases or sentences, all of the constituent words are continuously present. This contrasts with speech, where each word only occurs instantaneously. For this reason, it might be expected that the right hemisphere would not show the same deficit in reading phrases as was found for its auditory comprehension. Zaidel's (1978) work shows that, appealing as this speculation may be, it is incorrect. He used a test in which the subject had to choose which of an array of pictures presented in the LVF corresponded to a spoken phrase or to the same phrase presented in printed form in the LVF. The performances of LB's and NG's right hemispheres were consistently poorer for visual than for auditory presentation, and declined at the same rate for both visual and auditory stimuli as the number of words in the phrases increased. The simplest way of accounting for this pattern of findings is to argue (as Zaidel does) that short-term verbal memory is as important in understanding printed as in understanding spoken phrases. This account in not entirely satisfactory because Gott (1973) had observed that RS *could* follow relatively complex spoken instructions if they were repeated a few times, and visual presentation should also give ample opportunity for repetition. However, RS may be untypical in this respect because she did show some right hemisphere expressive speech ability.

Although the right hemisphere's comprehension of phrases and sentences was poor in comparison to its comprehension of spoken words, Zaidel (1973, 1985) found that it did show some ability to interpret basic syntactic structures, with NG's right hemisphere performing at around the five-year-old level on one of the tests used (test of auditory comprehension of language) and LB's right hemisphere performance at the test's ceiling (mental age > seven years).

Taken together, Zaidel's findings reveal an intriguing pattern of right hemisphere language abilities. It is clear that although it is convenient to compare the level of performance achieved by the right hemisphere on any particular test to the average performance of people of a given age on the same test, there is no sense in which the right hemisphere's performance is in general typical of any age. Instead it shows relative strengths in some areas, such as single-word comprehension, and considerable weaknesses in others. It is not simply the case that the right hemisphere shows an arrested or slowed development of language in comparison to the left hemisphere (Young, 1983; Zaidel, 1978, 1982). Zaidel's hypothesis that right hemisphere language abilities are qualitatively different to those of the left hemisphere is more plausible.

Much of this qualitative difference can, according to Zaidel, be attributed to the right hemisphere's impoverished ability to evoke the 'sound equivalent' of words. In the case of reading, he argues that seen words are decoded purely as visual patterns by the right hemisphere. This he calls 'ideographic reading', though it is important to realize that his conception of what ideographic reading involves is that it depends on what he calls 'fairly abstract' processes which would not necessarily be affected by case, typeface, handwriting style or vertical or horizontal orientation (Zaidel and Peters, 1981). It thus encompasses Coltheart's (1981) idea of abstract letter identities.

The view that the right hemisphere has difficulty in generating or accessing a sound equivalent of the words it understands is consistent with Levy and Trevarthen's (1977) finding of split-brain patients' inability to match pictures presented in the LVF to words with a rhyming name, but it does not square so well with Gott's (1973) report that RS could make some rhyme judgments accurately. The issue is complicated by the fact that Gott's patient did show some (albeit limited) expressive speech ability, and by Sidtis *et al.*'s (1981b) demonstration of ability to make rhyme judgments by the right hemisphere of VP, a split-brain patient who also showed some right hemisphere language expression ability. Moreover, the evidence from Zaidel's own studies (Zaidel, 1978; Zaidel and Peters, 1981) is a little mixed. He was able to show that the right hemispheres of both LB and NG could point to a picture of the referent of a printed word but could not point to another printed word that rhymed with the original. However, LB's right hemisphere *could* determine the equivalence of homonymic pictures presented in the LVF (such as a picture of a baseball *bat* and a picture of a flying *bat*) and could also match pictures on the basis of rhyme (such as a picture of a *bat* and a picture of a *hat*). Thus LB's right hemisphere seemed to have some ability to derive a sound equivalent to pictures but its performance tailed off on comparable tasks involving printed words (NG's right hemisphere was more or less at chance level with both types of stimuli).

Clearly, then, both LB and NG found difficulty in deriving the sound equivalents of visual stimuli presented in the LVF. This is consistent with

Zaidel's view. However, LB was not completely unable to do this, especially with picture stimuli. How his right hemisphere derived the sound equivalent of pictures remains uncertain, but there was little evidence of this being possible for reading. In particular, neither LB nor NG could match pronounceable non-words presented in the LVF for rhyme (Zaidel and Peters, 1981). Thus their right hemispheres did not seem to be able to make any use of spelling–sound correspondences.

Zaidel's detailed studies provide a rich source of information concerning the right hemisphere's language comprehension abilities. However, because they have involved the investigation of such a small number of patients it becomes essential to understand the extent to which language development in these patients' right hemispheres can be seen as typical of that of the normal population. At present this is difficult to assess. As already noted, Zaidel has given good reasons for his choice of these patients. Gazzaniga (1983a), however, has argued that most split-brain patients do not possess right hemisphere language of any kind. This claim has led to much discussion of the extent to which right hemisphere language abilities have been adequately assessed for most of the split-brain patients, and the extent to which right hemisphere damage may have interfered with language abilities that should otherwise have been present (Gazzaniga, 1983a,b; Levy, 1983; Myers, 1984; Zaidel, 1983c).

Subsequently, Gazzaniga and Smylie (1984) have developed this idea along lines previously sketched out by Sidtis *et al.* (1981b). They maintain that the split-brain patients can be divided into three types. These are those without right hemisphere language of any kind, those (such as LB and NG) who show right hemisphere lexical knowledge but no speech, and those (such as VP some time after her operation) with right hemisphere lexical knowledge, syntax and speech. It is clear, however, that the right hemisphere language abilities shown by the third type of patient (those with lexical knowledge, syntax and speech) do not reflect abilities present in the normal right hemisphere, since they are in large part acquired after the commissurotomy operation itself.

STUDIES OF NORMAL SUBJECTS

A lot of research effort has gone into studies of cerebral hemisphere differences for visually presented material in normal subjects. There are three principal reasons why this has happened. First, the argument that if you want to understand cerebral organization in the normal brain you should study it in the normal (as opposed to the injured) brain is an attractive one. Secondly, studies of normal subjects do not encounter many of the problems of interpretation inherent in studies of people with cerebral injuries, though this is not to deny that studies of normal subjects introduce a different set of interpretative problems of their own. Thirdly, most studies of normal subjects are, in comparison to studies of the effects of cerebral injuries, remarkably easy to carry out.

The basic anatomical principle on which studies of cerebral asymmetries in the processing of visually presented material by normal subjects depend is the same as that exploited for the split-brain studies, namely that the optic nerves project LVF stimuli to the visual cortex of the right cerebral hemisphere and RVF stimuli to the visual cortex of the left cerebral hemisphere. In most studies of normal people LVF and RVF positioning is achieved by presenting stimuli tachistoscopically for less than the time needed to make an eye movement (around 150 ms) whilst the subject fixates centrally (see Young, 1982a). This, of course, involves all of the limitations on the choice of stimuli and tasks that were also in the early split-brain studies. Consequently, attention has begun to be given to methods for achieving continuously lateralized input. The scleral contact lens technique introduced by Zaidel (1975) is generally thought to be too costly and demanding for work with more than a few subjects, so that other techniques have been developed (see Dimond and Beaumont, 1971; Dimond *et al.*, 1975; Myers and Sperry, 1982; Nettleton *et al.*, 1983; Sivak, Sivak and Mackenzie, 1985). Such methods, however, have not yet achieved widespread use in studies of normal subjects.

The main problem of interpretation that arises in studies of normal subjects is that the optic nerves are only responsible for the initial projection of LVF and RVF stimuli to the contralateral (right or left) cerebral hemisphere. What happens after that is something of a mystery at present. Clearly if ability to perform a particular task is asymmetrically organized in the cerebral hemispheres then information concerning stimuli presented to the non-specialized hemisphere will at some point have to be communicated to the specialized hemisphere for further processing. Unfortunately we know very little concerning how or at what stages of information processing such interhemispheric communication is achieved. Most of the studies that are informative about the possibilities for interhemispheric communication involve investigations of the effects of partial commissurotomy (e.g. Gordon, Bogen and Sperry, 1971; McKeever *et al.*, 1982; Risse *et al.*, 1978; Sidtis *et al.*, 1981a); these have not yet achieved the level of detailed knowledge necessary to determine precisely what types of interhemispheric communication will be available to normal subjects. Instead, investigators have had to rely on ingenious use of techniques of experimental psychology to narrow down the possibilities in studies of normal subjects (see, for example, Bertelson, 1982; Cohen, 1982; Hardyck *et al.*, 1985; Moscovitch, 1973, 1979, 1983b, 1986; Sergent, 1984; Umilta *et al.*, 1985; Zaidel, 1983b).

When words are briefly presented in the LVF or RVF to right-handed people, it is usual to find superior performance for the RVF. This phenomenon first received widespread attention following the investigation of Mishkin and Forgays (1952). At that time it was not generally considered to be due to cerebral asymmetry but to directional 'scanning' strategies arising from habits acquired in learning to read (see White, 1969). A number of variants of this scanning hypothesis were proposed. It is important to grasp that the hypothesis does not relate to overt scanning movements of the eyes, since the LVF and RVF stimuli are presented for less than the latency of a single eye movement. Instead it is claimed that the scanning is 'internal' and relates to the readout of items from some kind of exact memory trace of the stimulus display.

This hypothesized postexposural trace-scanning mechanism has always seemed to me a most unlikely way for a perceptual system to work, and I know of no direct evidence to support it. In fact, several reasons combine to suggest that it is inadequate as an explanation of RVF superiority for word recognition, which is now widely accepted as arising from factors related to cerebral asymmetry. The scanning hypothesis cannot for instance account for the fact that RVF advantages are found with right-handed subjects for vertically as well as horizontally arranged words (Barton, Goodglass and Shai, 1965; Boles, 1985; Bradshaw, Nettleton and Taylor, 1981a; Ellis and Young, 1977; Mackavey, Curcio and Rosen, 1975; McKeever and Gill, 1972; Young and Ellis, 1985) and for words in the Hebrew language, which is read from right to left (Babkoff and Ben-Uriah, 1983; Barton *et al.*, 1965; Carmon, Nachshon and Starinsky, 1976; Orbach, 1967; Silverberg *et al.*, 1980). Further support for an explanation in terms of cerebral asymmetry is provided by the fact that the RVF superiority for word recognition is reduced or absent in left-handed people (see Annett, 1982; Bradshaw, 1980; Hardyck and Petrinovich, 1977; Orbach, 1967; Schmuller and Goodman, 1979) and by findings of LVF superiorities in 'non-verbal' tasks such as face recognition (Ellis, 1983; Hilliard, 1973; Rizzolatti, Umiltà and Berlucchi, 1971).

The RVF superiority for word recognition has been extensively studied; an almost complete review of published studies up to about 1980 can be found in Beaumont (1982). It is clear that RVF superiorities occur across a wide variety of viewing conditions (Chiarello, Senehi and Soulier, in press) and that they are found to both unilateral (a single word falling in the LVF or in the RVF) or bilateral (one word in the LVF and another word simultaneously in the RVF) stimulus presentations, though bilateral presentation may increase the size of the RVF advantage (Boles, 1983a; McKeever, 1971; McKeever and Huling, 1971). In addition, RVF superiority is found not only for naming tasks but also for lexical decision (Babkoff and Ben-Uriah, 1983; Barry, 1981; Chiarello, Dronkers and Hardyck, 1984; Hardyck *et al.*, 1985; Leiber, 1976; McKeever and Hoff, 1982).

An approach to understanding cerebral hemisphere differences to visually presented words that has achieved some progress involves trying to identify which of the functional components involved in word processing are linked to the RVF superiority. This has been advocated by several authors, including Allen (1983), Chiarello (in press) and Moscovitch (1986). In terms of this approach the RVF superiority for lexical decision must reflect processes involved in the recognition of seen words and cannot be attributed to the superior expressive language abilities of the left hemisphere, since lexical decision tasks (in which subjects decide whether or not a string of letters is a familiar word) usually involve only a binary classification with a manual response.

Although the most prosaic way to account for visual hemifield differences in the processing of linguistic stimuli would be to claim that the right cerebral hemisphere is incapable of recognizing the constituent letters, this does not appear to be the case. The findings of studies of visual hemifield asymmetries for the identification of letters in unpronounceable strings have included all possibilities, ranging from LVF superiority (Scheerer, 1974) through to visual hemifield differences (Coltheart and Arthur, 1971; Smith and Ramunas, 1971) to RVF superiority (Bryden, 1966, 1970; Fudin and Kenny, 1972; Hirata and Bryden, 1976; Scheerer, 1974). Visual hemifield differences for single-letter identification have proved particularly labile, and several people have shown that they are readily affected by task and procedural factors (Bryden and Allard, 1976; Hellige and Webster, 1979; Jonides, 1979; Polich, 1978; but see Miller and Butler, 1980; Sergent, 1983b). It thus seems that both cerebral hemispheres are able to identify letters, so that the precise outcome of any given study rests on the relative contributions of a number of procedural factors. This view would be consistent with the clinical evidence, and it is also supported by Sullivan and McKeever's (1985) demonstration that stimulus repetition effects of the form identified for letter recognition by Miller and Butler (1980) only arise when both cerebral hemispheres can contribute substantially to the task involved.

In contrast to the identification of letters and unpronounceable letter strings, the use of pronounceable non-words has always led to findings of RVF superiority for right-handed subjects (Axelrod, Haryadi and Leiber, 1977; Bryden, 1970; Dornbush and Winnick, 1965; Levy and Reid, 1978; Levy *et al.*, 1983; Young and Ellis, 1985; Young, Bion and Ellis, 1980; Young, Ellis and Bion, 1984). This suggests that although both cerebral hemispheres can recognize letters, the left hemisphere is more sensitive to the orthographic properties of pronounceable non-words; a conclusion that is again compatible with the clinical evidence.

A factor that can have a marked effect on the size of visual hemifield asymmetries for word recognition is word length (i.e. the number of letters in the stimulus word). Studies by Bouma (1973), Gill and McKeever (1974), Melville (1957), Schiepers (1980) and Turner and Miller (1975) have all shown that for words in the conventional horizontal format the size of the RVF superiority increases as the number of letters in the words increases. Young and Ellis

(1985) showed that this is due to a decline in LVF performance with increasing word length whilst RVF performance remains relatively unaffected by the length of words in conventional format. RVF performance is, however, as sensitive as LVF performance to the length of non-words and to the length of words in unusual formats. Hence Young and Ellis (1985) argued that there is a qualitative difference in the method of lexical access used for normally formatted words presented in the LVF or in the RVF. Brand *et al.* (1983) reached a similar conclusion using a very different line of reasoning.

A qualitative difference in the methods of lexical access used for LVF and RVF stimuli might help in understanding a number of effects found in studies of visual hemifield differences for word recognition. The idea does not, however, address the issue as to whether the normal right cerebral hemisphere has a lexicon of its own or whether lexical access for LVF stimuli is achieved using the left hemisphere's lexicon. Two principal types of study are, however, relevant to this issue (but see also Hardyck *et al.*, 1985); these involve word-class effects and priming effects.

Word-class effects on LVF and RVF performance have been studied in normal subjects for some time. If it could be established that these differ reliably between LVF and RVF stimuli then the conclusion that the left and right hemispheres each have their own separate lexicon would seem to follow, and the structure of each lexicon could be mapped out. I have used word class as a generic term to cover several different factors that have been investigated, including grammatical class (Bradley and Garrett, 1983; Caplan, Holmes and Marshall, 1974; Goodall, 1984; Jackman, 1985), age of acquisition (Boles, Rogers and Wymer, 1982; Ellis and Young, 1977; Young and Bion, 1980; Young, Bion and Ellis, 1982), emotionality (Graves, Landis and Goodglass, 1981) and abbreviations (Besner, 1983). By far the most extensively investigated variables, however, have been concreteness and imageability (Boles, 1983b; Bradshaw and Gates, 1978; Bradshaw, Nettleton and Taylor, 1981b; Day, 1977, 1979; Ellis and Shepherd, 1974; Hines, 1976, 1977, 1978; Jackman, 1985; Lambert and Beaumont, 1983; Marcel and Patterson, 1978; Moscovitch, 1981; Orenstein and Meighan, 1976; Saffran *et al.*, 1980; Schmuller and Goodman, 1979; Shanon, 1979a,b; Young and Ellis, 1985).

The findings of the numerous studies of concreteness and imageability are fairly typical of this enterprise. Around half of the studies carried out have managed to replicate Ellis and Shepherd's (1974) finding of greater RVF superiority for abstract than for concrete words; the rest find no difference in the size of the RVF superiority to abstract and concrete words. No one really understands why the finding is not more consistently present or absent. It is possible to draw attention to methodological problems with studies that did not find a word-class × visual hemifield interaction (Coltheart, 1983) or with those that did find one (Lambert and Beaumont, 1983; Patterson and

Besner, 1984a). However, the fact that there are no reports in which the word-class × visual hemifield interaction is reversed (i.e. no reports of smaller RVF superiority to abstract than to concrete words) suggests that it is not simply a chance finding. It is more likely either that the finding arises artifactually (Lambert and Beaumont, 1983) or that it reflects the influence of some as yet unidentified procedural or stimulus variable. Until this has been clarified the word-class findings cannot offer strong support to the idea that the normal right hemisphere has a lexicon of its own.

The findings of priming experiments look more promising. A number of studies have recently reported different patterns of priming effects for words presented in the LVF and words presented in the RVF (priming refers to the facilitation of performance with a particular stimulus item caused by a previous or an accompanying item). Priming between orthographically (BEAK and BEAR), phonologically (JUICE and MOOSE), and semantically (INCH and YARD) related words has been investigated under conditions likely to produce automatic and controlled priming effects (Chiarello, 1985; Chiarello, Senehi and Nuding, in press; Klein and Smith, 1985; Rodel, Dudley and Bourdeau, 1983; Urcuioli, Klein and Day, 1981; Walker and Ceci, 1985). The findings of these studies are complex, but the existence of different patterns of LVF and RVF priming effects does point towards the view that LVF words can be looked up in a right hemisphere lexicon (though this is not to deny that this lexicon may itself be extensively interconnected with the left hemisphere's lexicon in the normal brain; see Chiarello, 1985).

OVERVIEW

Although a great deal of research has been carried out that is relevant to understanding cerebral hemisphere differences and reading, some aspects of the topic remain poorly understood. There is no disagreement concerning the main conclusion that the cerebral mechanisms involved in reading are, as other language skills, primarily dependent upon the left cerebral hemisphere in the brains of most people. Neither is there any disagreement with the view that the right hemisphere can support a considerable degree of language development when this is necessitated by childhood injury to the left hemisphere. The extent to which it is usual for the right cerebral hemisphere to possess reading abilities remains, however, less clearly established.

The reason why this issue has not been resolved despite such extensive investigation is simply that none of the available methods is free from substantial difficulties of interpretation. However, despite these limitations all of the methods used have provided indications that the right hemisphere does have some reading abilities. These right hemisphere reading abilities would seem to be limited in scope and would probably not have attracted such widespread interest were it not for the previously prevailing opinion that the right hemisphere had no language abilities at all.

The nature of right hemisphere reading abilities remains uncertain. On balance, the evidence available favours the view that the right hemisphere can deal with some of the constituent skills involved in reading more successfully than others. Thus, for instance, its letter and word recognition abilities would appear to considerably outstrip its ability to handle spelling–sound correspondences. The pattern of abilities observed is inconsistent with the intuitively plausible idea that right hemisphere language abilities are developed with relative ease early in life and then gradually fall behind those of the left hemisphere. This touches on the question as to the role that right hemisphere abilities play in normal reading. The limited capabilities thus far revealed suggest that any possible role would be restricted to the earliest steps in the reading process. It is possible, however, to doubt even this level of involvement and speculate that some word and letter recognition abilities might have developed merely from repeated exposure to stimuli in appropriate contexts.

An issue that deserves more serious consideration than it has generally received concerns why reading should be so highly lateralized. It seems most unlikely that a specific neural substrate has evolved for this purpose, given the fact that literacy has only recently become widespread in certain parts of the world. In evolutionary terms even the invention of writing itself is not very distant. Moreover, given its importance to other visual skills (Davidoff, 1982; Young and Ratcliff, 1983), the right hemisphere might have been expected to show a more sophisticated reading ability. That it does not is likely due to the ontogenetic organization of reading skills in close association with other language abilities for which structural predispositions that favour the left hemisphere certainly exist (see Witelson, 1977, 1983; Young, 1982b), but it would be useful to understand how and why this needs to be achieved.

REFERENCES

Allen, M. (1983). Models of hemispheric specialization. *Psychological Bulletin*, **93**, 73-104.

Annett, M. (1982). Handedness. In J.G. Beaumont (Ed.) *Divided Visual Field Studies of Cerebral Organisation*. London: Academic Press, pp. 195-215.

Axelrod, S., Haryadi, T., and Leiber, L. (1977). Oral report of words and word approximations presented to the left or right visual field. *Brain and Language*, **4**, 550-557.

Babkoff, H., and Ben-Uriah, Y. (1983). Lexical decision time as a function of visual field and stimulus probability. *Cortex*, **19**, 13-30.

Barry, C. (1981). Hemispheric asymmetry in lexical access and phonological encoding. *Neuropsychologia*, **19**, 473-478.

Barton, M.I., Goodglass, H., and Shai, A. (1965). Differential recognition of tachistoscopically presented English and Hebrew words in right and left visual fields. *Perceptual and Motor Skills*, **21**, 431-437.

Basser, L.S. (1962). Hemiplegia of early onset and the faculty of speech with special reference to the effects of hemispherectomy. *Brain*, **85**, 427-460.

Beaumont, J.G. (1982). Studies with verbal stimuli. In J.G. Beaumont (Ed.) *Divided Visual Field Studies of Cerebral Organisation*. London: Academic Press.

Bertelson, P. (1982). Lateral differences in normal man and lateralization of brain function. *International Journal of Psychology*, **17**, 173-210.

Besner, D. (1981). Deep dyslexia and the right-hemisphere hypothesis: what's left. *Bulletin of the Psychonomic Society*, **18**, 176-178.

Besner, D. (1983). Deep dyslexia and the right-hemisphere hypothesis: evidence from the U.S.A. and the U.S.S.R. *Canadian Journal of Psychology*, **37**, 565-571.

Bishop, D.V.M. (1983). Linguistic impairment after left hemidecortication for infantile hemiplegia? A reappraisal. *Quarterly Journal of Experimental Psychology*, **35A**, 199-207.

Bogen, J.E., and Vogel, P.J. (1975). Neurologic status in the long term following complete cerebral commissurotomy. In F. Michel and B. Schott (Eds.) *Les Syndromes de Disconnexion Calleuse Chez l'Homme*. Lyon: Hôpital Neurologique.

Boles, D.B. (1983a). Hemispheric interaction in visual field asymmetry. *Cortex*, **19**, 99-114.

Boles, D.B. (1983b). Dissociated imageability, concreteness, and familiarity in lateralized word recognition. *Memory and Cognition*, **11**, 511-519.

Boles, D.B. (1985). The effects of display and report order asymmetries on lateralized word recognition. *Brain and Language*, **26**, 106-116.

Boles, D.B., Rogers, S., and Wymer, W. (1982). Age of acquisition and visual field asymmetry in word recognition. *Perception and Psychophysics*, **32**, 486-490.

Bouma, H. (1973). Visual interference in the parafoveal recognition of initial and final letters of words. *Vision Research*, **13**, 767-782.

Bradley, D.C., and Garrett, M.F. (1983). Hemisphere differences in the recognition of closed and open class words. *Neuropsychologia*, **21**, 155-159.

Bradshaw, J.L. (1980). Right hemisphere language: familial and nonfamilial sinistrals, cognitive deficits and writing hand position in sinistrals, and the concrete–abstract, imageable–nonimageable dimensions in word recognition. A review of interrelated issues. *Brain and Language*, **10**, 172-188.

Bradshaw, J.L., and Gates, E.A. (1978). Visual field differences in verbal tasks: effects of task familiarity and sex of subject. *Brain and Language*, **5**, 166-187.

Bradshaw, J.L., Nettleton, N.C., and Taylor, M.J. (1981a). The use of laterally presented words in research into cerebral asymmetry: is directional scanning likely to be a source of artifact? *Brain and Language*, **14**, 1-14.

Bradshaw, J.L., Nettleton, N.C., and Taylor, M.J. (1981b). Right hemisphere language and cognitive deficit in sinistrals? *Neuropsychologia*, **19**, 113-132.

Branch, C., Milner, B., and Rasmussen, T. (1964). Intracarotid sodium amytal for the lateralization of cerebral speech dominance. *Journal of Neurosurgery*, **21**, 399-405.

Brand, N., Van Bekkum, I., Stumpel, M., and Kroeze, J.H.A. (1983). Word matching and lexical decisions: a visual half-field study. *Brain and Language*, **18**, 199-211.

Bryden, M.P. (1966). Left–right differences in tachistoscopic recognition: directional scanning or cerebral dominance? *Perceptual and Motor Skills*, **23**, 1127-1134.

Bryden, M.P. (1970). Left–right differences in tachistoscopic recognition as a function of familiarity and pattern orientation. *Journal of Experimental Psychology* **84**, 120-122.

Bryden, M.P., and Allard, F. (1976). Visual hemifield differences depend on typeface. *Brain and Language,* **3,** 191-200.

Burklund, C.W. (1972). Cerebral hemisphere function in the human: fact versus tradition. In W.L. Smith (Ed.) *Drugs, Development, and Cerebral Function.* Springfield, Illinois: Thomas.

Burklund, C.W., and Smith, A. (1977). Language and the cerebral hemispheres: observations of verbal and nonverbal responses during 18 months following left ('dominant') hemispherectomy. *Neurology,* **27,** 627-633.

Caplan, D., Holmes, J.M., and Marshall, J.C. (1974). Word classes and hemispheric specialization. *Neuropsychologia,* **12,** 331-337.

Carlson, J., Netley, C., Hendrick, E.B., and Prichard, J.S. (1968). A reexamination of intellectual disabilities in hemispherectomized patients. *Transactions of the American Neurological Association,* **93,** 198-201.

Carmon, A., Nachshon, I., and Starinsky, R. (1976). Developmental aspects of visual hemifield differences in perception of verbal material. *Brain and Language,* **3,** 463-469.

Castro-Caldas, A., and Salgado, V. (1984). Right hemifield alexia without hemaniopia. *Archives of Neurology,* **41,** 84-87.

Chiarello, C. (1985). Hemisphere dynamics in lexical access: automatic and controlled priming. *Brain and Language,* **26,** 146-172.

Chiarello, C. (in press). Lateralization of lexical processes in the normal brain: a review of visual half-field research. In H.A. Whitaker and A. Caramazza (Eds.) *Studies in Neuropsychology.* New Jersey: Erlbaum.

Chiarello, C., Dronkers, N.F., and Hardyck, C. (1984). Choosing sides: on the variability of language lateralization in normal subjects. *Neuropsychologia,* **22,** 363-373.

Chiarello, C., Senehi, J., and Nuding, S. (in press). Semantic priming with abstract and concrete words: differential asymmetry may be post-lexical. *Brain and Language.*

Chiarello, C., Senehi, J., and Soulier, M. (in press). Viewing conditions and hemisphere asymmetry for the lexical decision. *Neuropsychologia.*

Cohen, G. (1982). Theoretical interpretations of lateral asymmetries. In J.G. Beaumont (Ed.) *Divided Visual Field Studies of Cerebral Organisation.* London: Academic Press.

Coltheart, M. (1980). Deep dyslexia: a right hemisphere hypothesis. In M. Coltheart, K. Patterson and J. Marshall (Eds.) *Deep Dyslexia.* London: Routledge & Kegan Paul.

Coltheart, M. (1981). Disorders of reading and their implications for models of normal reading. *Visible Language,* **15,** 245-286.

Coltheart, M. (1983). The right hemisphere and disorders of reading. In A.W. Young (Ed.) *Functions of the Right Cerebral Hemisphere.* London: Academic Press.

Coltheart, M., and Arther, B. (1971). Tachistoscopic hemifield effects with hemifield report. *American Journal of Psychology,* **84,** 355-364.

Crockett, H.G., and Estridge, N.M. (1951). Cerebral hemispherectomy: a clinical, surgical and pathologic study of four cases. *Bulletin of the Los Angeles Neurological Society,* **16,** 71-87.

Damasio, A.R., and Damasio, H. (1983). The anatomic basis of pure alexia. *Neurology,* **33,** 1573-1583.

Damasio, A.R., and Damasio, H. (1986). Hemianopia, hemiachromatopsia and the mechanisms of alexia. *Cortex,* **22,** 161-169.

Dandy, W.E. (1928). Removal of right cerebral hemisphere for certain tumors with hemiplegia. *Journal of the American Medical Association,* **90,** 823-825.

Davidoff, J. (1982). Studies with non-verbal stimuli. In J.G. Beaumont (Ed.) *Divided Visual Field Studies of Cerebral Organisation*. London: Academic Press.

Day, J. (1977). Right-hemisphere language processing in normal right-handers. *Journal of Experimental Psychology: Human Perception and Performance*, **3**, 518-528.

Day, J. (1979). Visual half-field word recognition as a function of syntactic class and imageability. *Neuropsychologia*, **17**, 515-519.

De Renzi, E., and Vignolo, L.A. (1962). The Token Test: a sensitive test to detect receptive disturbances in aphasics. *Brain*, **85**, 665-678.

Déjerine, J. (1892). Contribution a l'étude anatomo-pathologique et clinique des différentes variétés de cécité verbale. *Comptes Rendues des Séances de la Société de Biologie*, **44**, 61-90.

Dennis, M. (1980a). Capacity and strategy for syntactic comprehension after left or right hemidecortication. *Brain and Language*, **10**, 287-317.

Dennis, M. (1980b). Language acquisition in a single hemisphere: semantic organization. In D. Caplan (Ed.) *Biological Studies of Mental Processes*. Cambridge, Mass: MIT Press.

Dennis, M., and Kohn, B. (1975). Comprehension of syntax in infantile hemiplegics after cerebral hemidecortication: left-hemisphere superiority. *Brain and Language*, **2**, 472-482.

Dennis, M., Lovett, M., and Wiegel-Crump, C.A. (1981). Written language acquisition after left or right hemidecortication in infancy. *Brain and Language*, **12**, 54-91.

Dennis, M., and Whitaker, H.A. (1976). Language acquisition following hemidecortication: linguistic superiority of the left over the right hemisphere. *Brain and Language*, **3**, 404-433.

Dimond, S.J. (1972). *The Double Brain*. Edinburgh: Churchill Livingstone.

Dimond, S.J., and Beaumont, J.G. (1971). Hemisphere function and vigilance. *Quarterly Journal of Experimental Psychology*, **23**, 443-448.

Dimond, S.J., Bures, J., Farrington, L.J., and Brouwers, E.Y.M. (1975). The use of contact lenses for the lateralisation of visual input in man. *Acta Psychologica*, **39**, 341-349.

Donoso, A. (1984). Crossed aphasia in dextrals. In A. Ardila and F. Ostrosky-Solis (Eds.) *The Right Hemisphere: Neurology and Neuropsychology*. New York: Gordon and Breach.

Dornbush, R.L., and Winnick, W.A. (1965). Right–left differences in tachistoscopic identification of paralogs as a function of order of approximation to English letter sequences. *Perceptual and Motor Skills*, **20**, 1222-1224.

Eisenson, J. (1962). Language and intellectual modifications associated with right cerebral damage. *Language and Speech*, **5**, 49-53.

Ellis, A.W., Flude, B.M., and Young, A.W. (in press). 'Neglect dyslexia' and the early visual processing of letters in words and nonwords. *Cognitive Neuropsychology*.

Ellis, H.D. (1983). The role of the right hemisphere in face perception. In A.W. Young (Ed.) *Functions of the Right Cerebral Hemisphere*. London: Academic Press.

Ellis, H.D., and Shepherd, J.W. (1974). Recognition of abstract and concrete words presented in left and right visual fields. *Journal of Experimental Psychology*, **103**, 1035-1036.

Ellis, H.D., and Young, A.W. (1977). Age-of-acquisition and recognition of nouns presented in the left and right visual fields: a failed hypothesis. *Neuropsychologia*, **15**, 825-828.

French, L.A., Johnson, D.R., Brown, I.A., and Van Bergen, F.B. (1955). Cerebral hemispherectomy for control of intractable convulsive seizures. *Journal of Neurosurgery*, **12**, 154-164.

Fudin, R., and Kenny, J.T. (1972). Some factors in the recognition of tachistoscopically presented alphabetical arrays. *Perceptual and Motor Skills*, **35**, 951-959.

Gainotti, G., Caltagirone, L., and Miceli, G. (1983). Selective impairment of semantic–lexical discrimination in right-brain-damaged patients. In E. Perecman (Ed.) *Cognitive Processing in the Right Hemisphere*. New York: Academic Press.

Gazzaniga, M.S. (1970). *The Bisected Brain*. New York: Appleton-Century-Crofts.

Gazzaniga, M.S. (1983a). Right hemisphere language following brain bisection: a 20-year perspective. *American Psychologist*, **38**, 525-537.

Gazzaniga, M.S. (1983b). Reply to Levy and to Zaidel. *American Psychologist*, **38**, 547-549.

Gazzaniga, M.S., and Hillyard, S.A. (1971). Language and speech capacity of the right hemisphere. *Neuropsychologia*, **9**, 273-280.

Gazzaniga, M.S., and Smylie, C.S. (1984). What does language do for a right hemisphere? In M.S. Gazzaniga (Ed.) *Handbook of Cognitive Neuroscience*. New York: Plenum.

Gazzaniga, M.S., and Sperry, R.W. (1967). Language after section of the cerebral commissures. *Brain*, **90**, 131-148.

Gazzaniga, M.S., Volpe, B.T., Smylie, C.S., Wilson, D.H., and LeDoux, J.E. (1979). Plasticity in speech organisation following commissurotomy. *Brain*, **102**, 805-815.

Geschwind, N. (1965). Disconnexion syndromes in animals and man. *Brain*, **88**, 237-294, 585-644.

Geschwind, N., and Fusillo, M. (1966). Color-naming defects in association with alexia. *Archives of Neurology*, **15**, 137-146.

Gill, K.M., and McKeever, W.F. (1974). Word length and exposure time effects on the recognition of bilaterally presented words. *Bulletin of the Psychonomic Society*, **4**, 173-175.

Glass, A.V., Gazzaniga, M.S., and Premack, D. (1973). Artificial language training in global aphasics. *Neuropsychologia*, **11**, 95-103.

Goodall, G. (1984). Morphological complexity and cerebral lateralization. *Neuropsychologia*, **22**, 375-380.

Goodglass, H., and Quadfasel, F.A. (1954). Language laterality in left-handed aphasics. *Brain*, **77**, 521-548.

Gordon, H.W., Bogen, J.E., and Sperry, R.W. (1971). Absence of deconnexion syndrome in two patients with partial section of the neocommissures. *Brain*, **94**, 327-336.

Gott, P.S. (1973). Language after dominant hemispherectomy. *Journal of Neurology, Neurosurgery and Psychiatry*, **36**, 1082-1088.

Graves, R., Landis, T., and Goodglass, H. (1981). Laterality and sex differences for visual recognition of emotional and non-emotional words. *Neuropsychologia*, **19**, 95-102.

Greenblatt, S.H. (1973). Alexia without agraphia or hemianopsia: anatomical analysis of an autopsied case. *Brain*, **96**, 307-316.

Hardyck, C., Chiarello, C., Dronkers, N.F., and Simpson, G.W. (1985). Orienting attention within visual fields: how efficient is interhemispheric transfer? *Journal of Experimental Psychology: Human Perception and Performance*, **11**, 650-666.

Hardyck, C., and Petrinovich, L.F. (1977). Left-handedness. *Psychological Bulletin*, **84**, 385-404.

Hécaen, H, and Kremin, H. (1976). Neurolinguistic research on reading disorders resulting from left hemisphere lesions: aphasic and 'pure' alexias. In H. Whitaker and H.A. Whitaker (Eds.) *Studies in Neurolinguistics*, Vol. 2. New York: Academic Press.

Heilman, K.M. (1979). Neglect and related disorders. In K.M. Heilman and

E. Valenstein (Eds.) *Clinical Neuropsychology*. New York: Oxford University Press.

Heilman, K.M., and Rothi, L.J. (1982). Acquired reading disorders: a diagrammatic model. In R.N. Malatesha and P.G. Aaron (Eds.) *Reading Disorders: Varieties and Treatments*. New York: Academic Press.

Heilman, K.M., Rothi, L., Campanella, D., and Wolfson, S. (1979). Wernicke's and global aphasia without alexia. *Archives of Neurology*, **36**, 129-133.

Hellige, J.B., and Webster, R. (1979). Right hemisphere superiority for initial stages of letter processing. *Neuropsychologia*, **17**, 653-660.

Hilliard, R.D. (1973). Hemispheric laterality effects on a facial recognition task in normal subjects. *Cortex*, **9**, 246-258.

Hillier, W.F. (1954). Total left cerebral hemispherectomy for malignant glioma. *Neurology*, **4**, 718-721.

Hines, D. (1976). Recognition of verbs, abstract nouns and concrete nouns from the left and right visual half-fields. *Neuropsychologia*, **14**, 211-216.

Hines, D. (1977). Differences in tachistoscopic recognition between abstract and concrete words as a function of visual half-field and frequency. *Cortex*, **13**, 66-73.

Hines, D. (1978). Visual information processing in the left and right hemispheres. *Neuropsychologia*, **16**, 593-600.

Hirata, K., and Bryden, M.P. (1976). Right visual field superiority for letter recognition with partial report. *Canadian Journal of Psychology*, **30**, 134-139.

Jackman, M.K. (1985). The recognition of tachistoscopically presented words, varying in imagery, part of speech and word frequency, in the left and right visual fields. *British Journal of Psychology*, **76**, 59-74.

Jonides, J. (1979). Left and right visual field superiority for letter classification. *Quarterly Journal of Experimental Psychology*, **31**, 423-439.

Kinsbourne, M., and Warrington, E.K. (1962). A variety of reading disability associated with right hemisphere lesions. *Journal of Neurology, Neurosurgery and Psychiatry*, **25**, 339-344.

Klein, R.M., and Smith, L.C. (1985). Is the emergence of a right visual field advantage in the category matching task dependent upon category constancy? *Canadian Journal of Psychology*, **39**, 88-99.

Kremin, H. (1982). Alexia: theory and research. In R.N. Malatesha and P.G. Aaron (Eds.) *Reading Disorders: Varieties and Treatments*. New York: Academic Press.

Krynauw, R.A. (1950). Infantile hemiplegia treated by removing one cerebral hemisphere. *Journal of Neurology, Neurosurgery and Psychiatry*, **13**, 243-267.

Lambert, A.J. (1982a). Right hemisphere language ability: 1. Clinical evidence. *Current Psychological Reviews*, **2**, 77-94.

Lambert, A.J. (1982b). Right hemisphere language ability: 2. Evidence from normal subjects. *Current Psychological Reviews*, **2**, 139-152.

Lambert, A.J., and Beaumont, J.G. (1983). Imageability does not interact with visual field in lateral word recognition with oral report. *Brain and Language*, **20**, 115-142.

Landis, T., Regard, M., Graves, R., and Goodglass, H. (1983). Semantic paralexia: a release of right hemispheric function from left hemispheric control? *Neuropsychologia*, **21**, 359-364.

Landis, R., Regard, M., and Serrat, A. (1980). Iconic reading in a case of alexia without agraphia caused by a brain tumour: a tachistoscopic study. *Brain and Language*, **11**, 45-53.

Leiber, L. (1976). Lexical decisions in the right and left cerebral hemispheres. *Brain and Language*, **3**, 443-450.

Levy, J. (1983). Language, cognition and the right hemisphere: a response to Gazzaniga. *American Psychologist*, **38**, 538-541.

Levy, J., Heller, W., Banich, M.T., and Burton, L.A. (1983). Are variations among right-handed individuals in perceptual asymmetries caused by characteristic arousal differences between hemispheres? *Journal of Experimental Psychology: Human Perception and Performance*, **9**, 329-359.

Levy, J., and Reid, M. (1978). Variations in cerebral organization as a function of handedness, hand posture in writing, and sex. *Journal of Experimental Psychology: General*, **107**, 119-144.

Levy, J., and Trevarthen, C. (1977). Perceptual, semantic and phonetic aspects of elementary language processes in split-brain patients. *Brain*, **100**, 105-118.

McFie, J. (1961). The effects of hemispherectomy on intellectual functioning in cases of infantile hemiplegia. *Journal of Neurology, Neurosurgery and Psychiatry*, **24**, 240-249.

Mackavey, W., Curcio, F., and Rosen, J. (1975). Tachistoscopic word recognition performance under conditions of simultaneous bilateral presentation. *Neuropsychologia*, **13**, 27-33.

McKeever, W.F. (1971). Lateral word recognition: effects of unilateral and bilateral presentation, asynchrony of bilateral presentation, and forced order of report. *Quarterly Journal of Experimental Psychology*, **23**, 410-416.

McKeever, W.F., and Gill, K.M. (1972). Visual half-field differences in the recognition of bilaterally presented single letters and vertically spelled words. *Perceptual and Motor Skills*, **34**, 815-818.

McKeever, W.F., and Hoff, A.L. (1982). Familial sinistrality, sex and laterality differences in naming and lexical decision latencies of right-handers. *Brain and Language*, **17**, 225-239.

McKeever, W.F., and Huling, M.D. (1971). Lateral dominance in tachistoscopic word recognition performances obtained with simultaneous bilateral input. *Neuropsychologia*, **9**, 15-20.

McKeever, W.F., Sullivan, K.F., Ferguson, S.M., and Rayport, M. (1981). Typical cerebral hemisphere disconnection effects following corpus callosum section despite sparing of the anterior commissure. *Neuropsychologia*, **19**, 745-755.

McKeever, W.F., Sullivan, K.F., Ferguson, S.M., and Rayport, M. (1982). Right hemisphere speech development in the anterior commissure-spared commissurotomy patient: a second case. *Clinical Neuropsychology*, **4**, 17-22.

Marcel, A.J., and Patterson, K.E. (1978). Word recognition and production: reciprocity in clinical and normal studies. In J. Requin (Ed.) *Attention and Performance, VII*. New Jersey: Erlbaum.

Marshall, J.C., and Patterson, K.E. (1983). Semantic paralexia and the wrong hemisphere: a note on Landis, Regard, Graves and Goodglass (1983). *Neuropsychologia*, **21**, 425-427.

Melville, J.P. (1957). Word-length as a factor in differential recognition. *American Journal of Psychology*, **70**, 316-318.

Miller, L.K., and Butler, D. (1980). The effect of set size on hemifield asymmetries in letter recognition. *Brain and Language*, **9**, 307-314.

Mishkin, M., and Forgays, D.G. (1952). Word recognition as a function of retinal locus. *Journal of Experimental Psychology*, **43**, 43-48.

Moore, W.H. Jn, and Weidner, W.E. (1974). Bilateral tachistoscopic word perception in aphasic and normal subjects. *Perceptual and Motor Skills*, **39**, 1003-1011.

Moscovitch, M. (1973). Language and the cerebral hemispheres: reaction-time studies and their implications for models of cerebral dominance. In P. Pliner, L. Krames and T. Alloway (Eds.) *Communication and Affect: Language and Thought*. New York: Academic Press.

Moscovitch, M. (1979). Information processing and the cerebral hemispheres. In

M.S. Gazzaniga (Ed.) *Handbook of Behavioral Neurobiology, Vol. 2: Neuropsychology.* New York: Plenum.

Moscovitch, M. (1981). Right-hemisphere language. *Topics in Language Disorders, 1,* 41-61.

Moscovitch, M. (1983a). The linguistic and emotional functions of the normal right hemisphere. In E. Perecman (Ed.) *Cognitive Processing in the Right Hemisphere.* New York: Academic Press.

Moscovitch, M. (1983b). Laterality and visual masking: interhemispheric communication and the locus of perceptual asymmetries for words. *Canadian Journal of Psychology, 37,* 85-106.

Moscovitch, M. (1986). Afferent and efferent models of visual perceptual asymmetries: Theoretical and empirical implications. *Neuropsychologia, 24,* 91-114.

Myers, J.J. (1984). Right hemisphere language: fact or fiction? *American Psychologist, 39,* 315-320.

Myers, J.J., and Sperry, R.W. (1982). A simple technique for lateralizing visual input that allows prolonged viewing. *Behavior Research Methods and Instrumentation, 14,* 305-308.

Myers, J.J., and Sperry, R.W. (1985). Interhemispheric communication after section of the forebrain commissures. *Cortex, 21,* 249-260.

Nettleton, N.C., Wood, R.G., Bradshaw, J.L., Thomas, C.D.L., and Donahoo, K.B. (1983). A moving video window or mask yoked to eye movements: a system to permit free ocular scanning within delimited areas of the visual field. *Behavior Research Methods and Instrumentation, 15,* 487-496.

Ogden, J.A. (1984). Dyslexia in a right-handed patient with a posterior lesion of the right cerebral hemisphere. *Neuropsychologia, 22,* 265-280.

Orbach, J. (1967). Differential recognition of Hebrew and English words in left and right visual fields as a function of cerebral dominance and reading habits. *Neuropsychologia, 5,* 127-134.

Orenstein, H.B., and Meighan, W.B. (1976). Recognition of bilaterally presented words varying in concreteness and frequency: lateral dominance or sequential processing? *Bulletin of the Psychonomic Society, 7,* 179-180.

Patterson, K., and Besner, D. (1984a). Is the right hemisphere literate? *Cognitive Neuropsychology, 1,* 315-341.

Patterson, K., and Besner, D. (1984b). Reading from the left: a reply to Rabinowicz and Moscovitch and to Zaidel and Schweiger. *Cognitive Neuropsychology, 1,* 365-380.

Patterson, K., and Kay, J. (1982). Letter-by-letter reading: psychological descriptions of a neurological syndrome. *Quarterly Journal of Experimental Psychology, 34A,* 411-441.

Polich, J. (1978). Hemisphere differences in stimulus identification. *Perception and Psychophysics, 24,* 49-57.

Rabinowicz, B., and Moscovitch, M. (1984). Right hemisphere literacy: a critique of some recent approaches. *Cognitive Neuropsychology, 1,* 343-350.

Rasmussen, T., and Milner, B. (1977). The role of early left-brain injury in determining lateralization of cerebral speech functions. In S.J. Dimond and D.A. Blizard (Eds.) *Evolution and Lateralization of the Brain. Annals of the New York Academy of Sciences, 299,* 355-369.

Risse, G.L., LeDoux, J.E., Springer, S.P., Wilson, D.H., and Gazzaniga, M.S. (1978). The anterior commissure in man: functional variation in a multisensory system. *Neuropsychologia, 16,* 23-31.

Rizzolatti, G., Umiltà, C., and Berlucchi, G. (1971). Opposite superiorities of the right and left cerebral hemispheres in discriminative reaction time to physiognomical and alphabetical material. *Brain*, **94**, 431-442.

Rodel, M., Dudley, J.G., and Bourdeau, M. (1983). Hemispheric differences for semantically and phonologically primed nouns: a tachistoscopic study in normals. *Perception and Psychophysics*, **34**, 523-531.

Ross, E. (1984). Disturbances of emotional language with right hemisphere lesions. In A. Ardila and F. Ostrosky-Solis (Eds.) *The Right Hemisphere: Neurology and Neuropsychology*. New York: Gordon and Breach.

Saffran, E.M., Bogyo, L.C., Schwartz, M.F., and Marin, O.S.M. (1980). Does deep dyslexia reflect right hemisphere reading? In M. Coltheart, K. Patterson and J.C. Marshall (Eds.) *Deep Dyslexia*. London: Routledge & Kegan Paul.

St James-Roberts, I. (1979). Neurological plasticity, recovery from brain insult, and child development. *Advances in Child Development and Behavior*, **14**, 253-319.

St James-Roberts, I. (1981). A reinterpretation of hemispherectomy data without functional plasticity of the brain. *Brain and Language*, **13**, 31-53.

Scheerer, E. (1974). Task requirement and hemifield asymmetry in tachistoscopic partial report performance. *Acta Psychologica*, **38**, 131-147.

Schiepers, C. (1980). Response latency and accuracy in visual word recognition. *Perception and Psychophysics*, **27**, 71-81.

Schmuller, J., and Goodman, R. (1979). Bilateral tachistoscopic perception, handedness, and laterality. *Brain and Language*, **8**, 81-91.

Searleman, A. (1977). A review of right hemisphere linguistic capabilities. *Psychological Bulletin*, **84**, 503-528.

Searleman, A. (1983). Language capabilities of the right hemisphere. In A.W. Young (Ed.) *Functions of the Right Cerebral Hemisphere*. London: Academic Press.

Selnes, O.A. (1974). The corpus callosum: some anatomical and functional considerations with special reference to language. *Brain and Language*, **1**, 111-139.

Sergent, J. (1983a). Unified response to bilateral hemispheric stimulation by a split-brain patient. *Nature*, **305**, 800-802.

Sergent, J. (1983b). Hemispheric competence and perceptual confusability. *Quarterly Journal of Experimental Psychology*, **35A**, 589-596.

Sergent, J. (1984). Role of contrast, lettercase, and viewing conditions in a lateralized word-naming task. *Perception and Psychophysics*, **35**, 489-498.

Shallice, T., and Saffran, E. (1986). Lexical processing in the absence of explicit word identification: evidence from a letter-by-letter reader. *Cognitive Neuropsychology*, **3**, 429-458.

Shanon, B. (1979a). Lateralization effects in lexical decision tasks. *Brain and Language*, **8**, 380-387.

Shanon, B. (1979b). Lateralization effects in response to words and non-words. *Cortex*, **15**, 541-549.

Sidtis, J.J., Volpe, B.T., Holtzman, J.D., Wilson, D.H., and Gazzaniga, M.S. (1981a). Cognitive interaction after staged callosal section: evidence for transfer of semantic activation. *Science*, **212**, 344-346.

Sidtis, J.J., Volpe, B.T., Wilson, D.H., Rayport, M., and Gazzaniga, M.S. (1981b). Variability in right hemisphere language function after callosal section: evidence for a continuum of generative capacity. *Journal of Neuroscience*, **1**, 323-331.

Silverberg, R., Gordon, H.W., Pollack, S. and Bentin, S. (1980). Shift of visual field preference for Hebrew words in native speakers learning to read. *Brain and Language*, **11**, 99-105.

Sivak, B., Sivak, J.G., and Mackenzie, C.L. (1985). Contact lens design for lateralizing visual input. *Neuropsychologia*, **23**, 801-803.

Smith, A. (1966). Speech and other functions after left (dominant) hemispherectomy. *Journal of Neurology, Neurosurgery and Psychiatry*, **29**, 467-471.

Smith, A. (1972). Dominant and nondominant hemispherectomy. In W.L. Smith (Ed.) *Drugs, Development and Cerebral Function*. Springfield, Illinois: Thomas.

Smith, A., and Burklund, C.W. (1966). Dominant hemispherectomy: preliminary report on neuropsychological sequelae. *Science*, **153**, 1280-1282.

Smith, A., and Sugar, O. (1975). Development of above normal language and intelligence 21 years after left hemispherectomy. *Neurology*, **25**, 813-818.

Smith, M.C., and Ramunas, S. (1971). Elimination of visual field effects by use of a single report technique: evidence for order-of-report artifact. *Journal of Experimental Psychology*, **87**, 23-28.

Sullivan, K.F., and McKeever, W.F. (1985). The roles of stimulus repetition and hemispheric activation in visual half-field asymmetries. *Brain and Cognition*, **4**, 413-429.

Turner, S., and Miller, L.K. (1975). Some boundary conditions for laterality effects in children. *Developmental Psychology*, **11**, 342-352.

Umiltà, C., Rizzolatti, G., Anzola, G.P., Luppino, G., and Porro, C. (1985). Evidence of interhemispheric transmission in laterality effects. *Neuropsychologia*, **23**, 203-213.

Urcuioli, P.J., Klein, R.M., and Day, J. (1981). Hemispheric differences in semantic processing: category matching is not the same as category membership. *Perception and Psychophysics*, **29**, 343-351.

Varney, N.R., and Damasio, A.R. (1982). Acquired alexia. In R.N. Malatesha and P.G. Aaron (Eds.) *Reading Disorders: Varieties and Treatments*. New York: Academic Press.

Walker, E., and Ceci, S.J. (1985). Semantic priming effects for stimuli presented to the right and left visual fields. *Brain and Language*, **25**, 144-159.

Wapner, W., Hamby, S., and Gardner, H. (1981). The role of the right hemisphere in the apprehension of complex linguistic materials. *Brain and Language*, **14**, 15-33.

Warrington, E.K., and Shallice, T. (1980). Word-form dyslexia. *Brain*, **103**, 99-112.

Weinstein, E.A., and Keller, N.J.A. (1963). Linguistic patterns of misnaming in brain injury. *Neuropsychologia*, **1**, 79-90.

Whitaker, H.A., and Ojemann, G.A. (1977). Lateralization of higher cortical functions: a critique. In S.J. Dimond and D.A. Blizard (Eds.) *Evolution and Lateralization of the Brain. Annals of the New York Academy of Sciences*, **299**, 459-473.

White, M.J. (1969). Laterality differences in perception: a review. *Psychological Bulletin*, **72**, 387-405.

Witelson, S.F. (1977). Early hemisphere specialization and interhemisphere plasticity: an empirical and theoretical review. In S.J. Segalowitz and F.A. Gruber (Eds.) *Language Development and Neurological Theory*. New York: Academic Press.

Witelson, S.F. (1983). Bumps on the brain: right–left anatomic asymmetry as a key to functional lateralization. In S.J. Segalowitz (Ed.) *Language Functions and Brain Organization*. New York: Academic Press.

Young, A.W. (1982a). Methodological and theoretical bases of visual hemifield studies. In J.G. Beaumont (Ed.) *Divided Visual Field Studies of Cerebral Organization*. London: Academic Press.

Young, A.W. (1982b). Asymmetry of cerebral hemispheric function during development. In J.W.T. Dickerson and H. McGurk (Eds.) *Brain and Behavioural Development*. Glasgow: Blackie.

Young, A.W. (1983). The development of right hemisphere abilities. In A.W. Young (Ed.) *Functions of the Right Cerebral Hemisphere*. London: Academic Press.

Young, A.W., and Bion, P.J. (1980). Hemifield differences for naming bilaterally presented nouns varying on age of acquisition. *Perceptual and Motor Skills*, **50**, 366.

Young, A.W., Bion, P.J., and Ellis, A.W. (1980). Studies toward a model of laterality effects for picture and word naming. *Brain and Language*, **11**, 54-65.

Young, A.W., Bion, P.J., and Ellis, A.W. (1982). Age of reading acquisition does not affect visual hemifield asymmetries for naming imageable nouns. *Cortex*, **18**, 477-482.

Young, A.W., and Ellis, A.W. (1985). Different methods of lexical access for words presented in the left and right visual hemifields. *Brain and Language*, **24**, 326-358.

Young, A.W., Ellis, A.W., and Bion, P.J. (1984). Left hemisphere superiority for pronounceable nonwords, but not for unpronounceable letter strings. *Brain and Language*, **22**, 14-25.

Young, A.W., and Ratcliff, G. (1983). Visuospatial abilities of the right hemisphere. In A.W. Young (Ed.) *Functions of the Right Cerebral Hemisphere*. London: Academic Press.

Zaidel, E. (1975). A technique for presenting lateralized visual input with prolonged exposure. *Vision Research*, **15**, 283-289.

Zaidel, E. (1976). Auditory vocabulary of the right hemisphere following brain bisection or hemidecortication. *Cortex*, **12**, 191-211.

Zaidel, E. (1977). Unilateral auditory language comprehension on the Token Test following cerebral commissurotomy and hemispherectomy. *Neuropsychologia*, **15**, 1-18.

Zaidel, E. (1978). Lexical organization in the right hemisphere. In P.A. Buser and A. Rougeul-Buser (Eds.) *Cerebral Correlates of Conscious Experience*. Amsterdam: North-Holland.

Zaidel, E. (1979). Performance on the ITPA following cerebral commissurotomy and hemispherectomy. *Neuropsychologia*, **17**, 259-280.

Zaidel, E. (1982). Reading by the disconnected right hemisphere: an aphasiological perspective. In Y. Zotterman (Ed.) *Dyslexia: Neuronal, Cognitive and Linguistic Aspects*. Oxford: Pergamon Press.

Zaidel, E. (1983a). On multiple representations of the lexicon in the brain: the case of two hemispheres. In M. Studdert-Kennedy and D. Caplan (Eds.) *The Psychobiology of Language*. Cambridge, Mass: MIT Press.

Zaidel, E. (1983b). Disconnection syndrome as a model for laterality effects in the normal brain. In J.B. Hellige (Ed.) *Cerebral Hemisphere Asymmetry: Method, Theory and Applications*. New York: Praeger.

Zaidel, E. (1983c). A response to Gazzaniga: language in the right hemisphere, convergent perspectives. *American Psychologist*, **38**, 543-546.

Zaidel, E. (1985). Language in the right hemisphere. In D.F. Benson and E. Zaidel (Eds.) *The Dual Brain: Hemispheric Specialization in Humans*. New York: Guilford.

Zaidel, E., and Peters, A.M. (1981). Phonological encoding and ideographic reading by the disconnected right hemisphere: two case studies. *Brain and Language*, **14**, 205-234.

Zaidel, E., and Schweiger, A. (1984). On wrong hypotheses about the right hemisphere: commentary on K. Patterson and D. Besner, 'Is the right hemisphere literate?' *Cognitive Neuropsychology*, **1**, 351-364.

Zollinger, R. (1935). Removal of left cerebral hemisphere: report of a case. *Archives of Neurology and Psychiatry*, **34**, 1055-1064.

Cognitive approaches to reading
Edited by J. R. Beech and A. M. Colley
© 1987 John Wiley & Sons Ltd

CHAPTER 7

Eye Movements, Reading Skill and the Spatial Code

ALAN KENNEDY

Department of Psychology, University of Dundee

INTRODUCTION

There have been three periods this century characterized by intense research interest in the reader's eye movements. Huey's text *The Psychology and Pedagogy of Reading* (1908) served to introduce the topic to a wide audience. Eye movements were directly recorded for the first time, using an effective, if primitive, contact lens system. From these early kymographic records the distinction between fixations and saccades was evident, as was their distribution across lines of presented text. However, it was not possible to conduct systematic experimental studies of reading because of the complexity of the recording technique and the demands it placed on the reader. Some thirty years later, following the development of accurate photographic techniques, eye movement recording and interpretation again became a fashionable issue in both psychological and educational circles. Publications by Buswell in particular (1920, 1935) led to renewed interest in the use of eye movement records as an index of reading skill and raised the possibility that reading disability might be treated in part by the training of appropriate scanning methods. Tinker's reviews of the relevant literature over this period moved from cautious optimism to extreme scepticism. His final judgment (Tinker, 1958) that research had reached a point of diminishing returns effectively closed the issue for 20 years. It appeared that saccadic eye movements were autonomous (that is, effectively decoupled from higher cognitive processes), highly regular and of little relevance to either the development or practice of reading.

In the 1970s, research by Carpenter and Just (1972, 1975), Levy-Schoen (1974), O'Regan (1975) and McConkie and Rayner (1975) reintroduced eye movement measurement to cognitive psychologists. The climate at that time was receptive for a variety of reasons. First, attempts to fractionate cognitive skills were yielding useful data. The work of Sternberg (1975) and Posner (1978) suggested an approach to word identification in terms of logically independent processing stages. To extend this profitably to the skill of reading continuous prose a suitable on-line measure was called for. Total reading time served to some extent (Garrod and Sanford, 1977; Haviland and Clark, 1974) but had the disadvantage of being indirect. In contrast, eye movement measurement was relatively unobtrusive and provided a continuous data stream amenable to fine-grain analysis. Secondly, the development of the discipline of psycholinguistics armed cognitive psychologists with more subtle questions to direct at the reading process. Tinker's pessimistic dismissal of eye movement measurement as an index was seen to be incorrect. The reader's patterns of inspection in fact relate in surprisingly complex ways to lexical, syntactic and semantic properties of text (Rayner, 1978). It is true, of course, that processing demand could be inferred from performance on secondary tasks such as phoneme-monitoring, click detection, mispronunciation detection and perception in noise; but all these measures induce task-specific strategies. The demand for an 'ecologically valid' measure found an answer in the analysis of the eye movements of normal readers processing normal text in relatively normal situations. Once it had been satisfactorily established that the duration and distribution of the reader's fixations could be sensibly related to cognitive processes, psychology was provided with an admirably direct means of attacking a number of theoretical questions. Finally, the development of efficient computer algorithms to deal with the data reduction problems, coupled with developments in recording techniques, made eye movement measurement a relatively routine laboratory task. In particular, the use of computer-generated text displays allowed for *contingent* eye movement measurement, in which the reader's line of regard itself determined what was read. This technique allows for rapid display changes and on-line masking, both of which may be used to address the question of when (and where) the reader's processing decisions are taken.

This third wave of research activity is now almost ten years on and the present chapter is an attempt to take stock, to summarize some of the stable findings which have emerged; to identify some controversial issues; and to relate what is known about eye movement control to the development of reading skill. In the space available, however, it is not possible to provide a comprehensive review of the literature. The reader is referred to Rayner (1978), Levy-Schoen and O'Regan (1979) and McConkie (1983).

FIRST-PASS EYE MOVEMENTS

It is useful to distinguish those fixations which represent the reader's first encounter with the words in a text from subsequent reinspections. When words are inspected for the first time, two important questions are at issue: the sources of control and the way in which the reader integrates or combines information from successive fixations. We shall consider each in turn.

Sources of control

Few people would now claim that the reader's eye movements are subject to no systematic control. The question is, how much and from what physical and linguistic variables? A range of possibilities can be considered. For example, Just and Carpenter (1980) in support of their 'immediacy hypothesis' claim that each and every eye movement is tightly coupled to the reader's concurrent cognitive processes. The eye comes to rest; the meaning of a fixated word is extracted; the location of the next fixation is computed; and then an eye movement is executed. At the other extreme, Kolers (1976) is inclined to doubt whether eye and mind are so closely in concert (Gonzalez and Kolers, 1985; Kolers, 1976). Subjects may *look*, but do they *attend*? If the existence of a 'cognitive lag' in processing (an eye–mind span) is difficult to discount, what might be termed 'cognitive overlap' is virtually impossible to discount. That is, the influence on a current fixation may be not only from properties of the word fixated, but also from prior words and from words to come.

Undoubtedly, the most potent source of control over the location of first-pass fixations is the physical length of words in the text. The reader is aware of the location of spaces between words and uses this information to determine the extent of a saccade. There is, for any word, what O'Regan (1981) calls a 'convenient viewing position'. This is slightly to the left of centre of the word to be fixated and is, within limits, where the eye will fall after a forward saccade. It follows that saccades out of long words are longer than average and that longer saccades are made into long words. Control is quite finely tuned: for example, if a word about to be fixated is moved during a saccade (at which time no visual input will be available) small corrective saccades occur, although the reader is unaware of them. Length is not the only determining influence, however. The frequency, syntactic function and meaning of individual words all influence fixation duration and the extent of saccades. Uncommon words may receive longer than average fixations whereas some short words may be skipped altogether, although whether this occurs depends in part on the syntactic function of the word in question (O'Regan, 1975). One strong conclusion stemming from the 'immediacy hypothesis' is that words which are skipped are not in fact processed at all. This proposition has been tested in an ingenious experiment by Fisher and Shebilske (1985). Subjects read a passage of text and their patterns of inspection were used to determine which words would be visible when the same text was presented to another, 'yoked', group of subjects. This latter group saw *only* those words which had been fixated by the other group. They did not see words which their yoked counterparts did not fixate (and hence, if the immediacy hypothesis is correct, did not process). Thus, if 'non-fixated' means 'unprocessed' no particular disadvantage should accrue. The crucial measure related to subjects' recall of *skipped* words. For the experimental group this was 59 per cent, whereas for the yoked controls it was only 26 per cent. It would appear, therefore, that words not fixated are none the less processed to some degree and consequently the 'immediacy hypothesis' must be challenged.

In summary, first-pass fixations and saccades are under tightly coupled control from local physical, structural and semantic properties of the text being read. The region of text in which such influences can be found for a particular fixation is quite large, spanning at least fifteen character spaces to the right and much less to the left. In addition, since contextual constraints influence fixation duration and location (McConkie and Rayner, 1975), eye movement control must involve some central, message-level, component. It will be evident from these observations that certain strategic options are, at least in principle, open to the reader on the first encounter with words in text. In particular, the number of fixations made may be traded off against their duration. The costs and benefits involved here are quite complex. A saccade takes time, shifts the field of view, and involves reestablishing a perceptual framework or coordinate system. On the other hand, extending a fixation in order to increase the probability of successful parafoveal processing involves operating on a stimulus which is in part perceptually indistinct. The reader must constantly pit *where* and *when* decisions against each other (Jacobs, 1986). In other words, the quality of information to determine the next ballistic saccade (the *where* signal) will increase to some extent as a function of the time available to make the decision (although the decision cannot be deferred indefinitely: there is an irresistible tendency to move on after a given interval). One way of examining these conflicting decisions is to be found in the correlation for a given reader between the number of fixations made and their duration. Here the data reveal an intriguing contrast, with a strong positive correlation in poor readers and an equally strong negative correlation in skilled readers (Heller and Heinisch, 1985). We shall return to this topic later.

Integration

Each time the eyes come to rest, a new region of the text is brought to the centre of the reader's field of view. The saccadic movement between each fixation acts to segment the stream of visual input since, while the eye is in flight, little or no visual processing takes place (Matin, 1976). As we have seen, control of first-pass eye movements is usually discussed in terms of 'push' or 'pull' models, the eyes being directed towards informative regions either through the detection of some salient physical or linguistic feature or because some central command has directed them to a particular location. It must be said, however, that to argue in this way begs a number of important questions regarding the integration of information from one fixation to the next. There is a striking discrepancy between our experience of a stable, spatially extended, page which is continually available for inspection and the highly discontinuous manner in which successive fixations deliver information to the visual system. This sequence of 'snapshots' must be glued together through a process of integration, but it is very much a matter for debate how this is achieved. When first raised in the context of reading, the question of trans-saccadic integration seemed relatively straightforward. For example, Rayner (1975) and McConkie and Rayner (1976) proposed an 'integrative visual buffer' acting to combine visual features from one fixation to the next. Following each saccade, as the eyes come to rest, a different stimulus pattern is brought into central vision. Putting it another way, during successive fixations the same physical stimulus falls on different parts of the retina. McConkie and Rayner proposed that the integrative visual buffer matched visual properties across saccades and derived a form of spatial code in which words were mapped onto an inner representation of the external page. Sadly, this attractive idea has proved difficult to substantiate and there are several pieces of evidence which appear to argue against it (Underwood, 1985). The most damaging is the fact that when case-alternated text is changed in phase *during* a saccade readers are quite unaware of the fact (McConkie and Zola, 1979). For example, a reader making an eye movement from the word *fat* to *drove* would experience the change in text format illustrated in (1) and (2):

(1)   ThE fAt MaN dRoVe A mErCeDes
(2)   tHe FaT mAn DrOvE a MeRcEdEs

Obviously in this case the purely visual properties of the text are changed very greatly from one fixation to the next. Thus, whatever mechanism is used to match successive views, it cannot depend on matching common visual properties. This is a grave embarrassment for the notion of an integrative visual buffer, but its difficulties do not end here. Direct attempts to produce evidence of fusion across fixations have yielded conflicting results (Breitmeyer, 1984; O'Regan and Levy-Schoen, 1983). In general, it would appear that displaying parts of a word at the same physical location before and after a saccade (where, of course, they fall on different retinal locations) does not result in the experience of percept localized in a single spatial location.

It is beyond doubt that our coding of pictures and of the visual world generally results in the experience of a spatially extended visual field. This page of text is, for example, obviously allocated a distinct location in space. But need we conclude that the text itself is spatially coded? There may well be significant differences in the way objects or representations of objects (pictures) are scanned and the way an alphabetic script is processed. There is no canonical scan path for the former—the same percept will arise from innumerable different patterns of inspection. In the latter case, however, letters within words or words within sentences do have a 'necessary order' which relates to their phonology. The advantage of preserving this in the pattern of inspection is obvious: in such circumstances the principal reason for a process of spatial integration would vanish. Each fixation would merely demand that the reader compute the visual world afresh (or at least that part of it relating to the printed surface of the page). Word identification would take place on the basis of the visual information coded in each fixation; coded, that is, in retinal coordinates. Once local foveal and parafoveal processing was completed the eyes would move on. At no time need the reader compute *where* words are (i.e. their relative position on the page).

The hypothesis that words may not be coded in spatial terms at all and hence that visual integration simply need not occur, although radical, is not inconsistent with what has been discussed concerning control over first-pass fixations. Although visual acuity falls off sharply away from the central foveal region, it is possible to identify some elements in parafoveal vision and to resolve spaces between words many character spaces to the right (or left) of a fixation. One direct test of the hypothesis is to examine reading in a situation where the eyes are stationary and the text is presented, one segment at a time, in a fixed location. This 'stepped-text' mode of presentation was first used by Bouma and deVoogd (1974) but has been explored in great detail more recently by Juola, Ward and McNamara (1982) and by Monk (1985a,b). The crucial point is, of course, that in this task readers cannot derive differential spatial coordinates, since all the words fall in the same location. If we make certain simplifying assumptions, the situation is directly analogous to that which would obtain in normal reading if no trans-saccadic integration of visual information took place. The results from a number of studies are both surprising and impressive. Text can apparently be processed and understood with equal facility whether presented as a whole page or word by word. Juola *et al*. conclude: '. . . there is apparently only a minor contribution to comprehension from the highly variable and somewhat erratic pattern of eye movements and fixation durations in normal reading' (Juola, Ward and McNamara, 1982, p. 224). Monk arrives at an even stronger conclusion, arguing that the evidence from stepped-text studies casts doubt on the necessity of postulating any representation with spatial coordinates playing a part in eye movement control (Monk, 1985a).

If these researchers are correct, the 'problem' of first-pass control is settled.

Fixations and saccades will be subject only to those sources of influence which can be computed on the basis of a series of 'visually disconnected', retinally coded images. This is not to suggest, of course,that saccades are not, at times, launched to targets outside the immediate span of attention, but the control of such eye movements will be central and based on the reader's knowledge of the temporal order of inspected words. It is this mapping between a spatially extended stimulus, which may in principle be freely inspected, and the fact that an alphabetic script involves a representation of a temporally coded event (speech) which makes reading such a complex endeavour. Stepped-text studies lead to the tempting conclusion that it is best for the reader to inspect all words and to inspect them in their correct (temporal) order since, if the spatial location of words is not derived, the price to be paid for scanning words in an inappropriate sequence could be a failure of comprehension. There is, in fact, ample evidence that it is poor readers whose pattern of eye movements involves frequent violations of the strict temporal order of words in text (e.g. they make many more regressive saccades). Thus, the possibility arises that reading failure might, in part, result from an inability to solve the problem of mapping a temporally coded to a spatially coded representation. Before turning to this question, however, it may be helpful to set out the alternative interpretations of reading failure which are suggested. It is possible, as Monk suggests, that spatial coordinates are not computed at all. Thus, irregularities in the temporal sequence of fixations will present a processing demand which may only be solved by deriving the appropriate message representation using operations in memory. As if, for example, one were asked to understand the sequence of words: 'grass' 'eat' 'sheep'. Often, lexical, syntactic or pragmatic information may solve this problem; but not always. On the other hand, there is the less extreme hypothesis that spatial coordinates are sometimes computed. That is, either always by some readers or sometimes by all readers. To examine this proposition it is necessary to consider the control and function of second-pass eye movements in reading.

SECOND-PASS EYE MOVEMENTS

It has long been known that a proportion of all eye movements are 'regressive', comprising saccades in a right–left direction. These occur both within and between words and typically involve the reinspection of words or parts of words already read. There are at least two sources of control over these second-pass eye movements. In the first place, as we have seen, the reader is sensitive to small changes in the location of a target which occurs during a saccade and may make a corrective eye movement if such changes occur. This suggests that the control system is intolerant of a mismatch between the intended position and that actually achieved. For relatively small saccades (including regressions), the evidence suggests that physical length (i.e. 'the convenient viewing position') is a primary determinant of the target location. Secondly, there have been a number of claims that second-pass eye movements are used in the service of the high-level processing of text: for example, to determine the antecedents of anaphoric expressions or to check points of cross reference. It will be immediately obvious, however, that such a claim is in conflict with the proposition that readers do not have access to information as to the spatial location of particular words. For example, a pronoun and its antecedent may be widely separated physically and second-pass eye movements spanning such a large number of character spaces will be highly inaccurate if their only source of control is an estimate of the number (and approximate length) of words which have intervened between the target and the present fixation. It follows that a measure of the accuracy of such large regressive saccades provides a test of the reader's ability to code spatial location. Fortunately, this is a relatively easy proposition to examine and Wayne Murray and I have recently carried out experiments to assess the accuracy of long accurate regressions directly (Kennedy and Murray, in press). Subjects were asked to read sentences presented on a single line of a video display. After a short interval a target word appeared to the right of the sentence, producing a display like (3):

(3)   When the girl strums her guitar the room falls quiet.   strums

Subjects' eye movements were monitored as they read each sentence and then decided, by pressing appropriate buttons, whether the target word was present in it or not. There were 60 sentences, half of which demanded a 'no' response, in which case the target was a synonym of a word in the sentence. The physical distance between the target and its match in the sentence was varied systematically from ten to 70 character positions. Thus, if a subject had occasion to make a reinspection from the target to its matched word, this would frequently call for a very large saccade.

The experimental procedure succeeded in eliciting a total of 44 regressions from a group of twelve subjects. The overall results were very straightforward. The accuracy of saccades (measured in character spaces from the centre of the fixated word) did not diminish as a function of their size. In fact, the correlation between accuracy and distance was effectively zero. Furthermore, the average error of location was only 2.55 character spaces, that is within the word. The conclusion to be drawn from this study is fairly obvious. Our sample of (adult) readers appear to have computed an accurate representation of the spatial location of previously read words. But if readers *normally* do this it is very surprising that studies of stepped-text presentations appear to show little or no decrement in performance. It is perhaps necessary to evaluate the conclusions drawn from these studies more carefully.

Presenting the words of a sentence one at a time in a single location solves an important problem for the reader: namely, the question of their exact temporal order. Spatially distributed text, freely inspected, demands that the reader assign the correct, sentence-specific, temporal order to the component words. This must be achieved on the basis of a series of fixations which may violate the temporal sequence—either by omitting the inspection of some words or by executing a train of fixations in an irregular fashion. In fact, this is not just a theoretical possibility, it represents the norm for most fluent readers. Words are often skipped and sentences are frequently not scanned rigidly from left to right. With stepped-text presentation temporal order is imposed: by definition words arrive in their correct sequence and one important processing problem is solved for the reader. However, another problem now looms. Some texts, for various reasons, may *demand* rereading: for example, those containing an initially ambiguous reference or some local syntactic ambiguity. In cases like this, single-word presentation should exact a penalty, since the reader will be denied the opportunity to reinspect what has gone before. This conclusion is clearly testable. A decrement in comprehension should be found with stepped-text presentation if sufficiently complex materials are employed: complex enough, that is, to demand careful reading and some reanalysis. We have examined this proposition in a study which looked at the way locally ambiguous sentences like (4) and (5) are processed (Kennedy and Murray, 1984):

(4)   While Julie was cleaning the kitchen stove it caught fire.
(5)   While Julie was cleaning the kitchen stove caught fire.

The ambiguity of these sentences is not resolved until the word *it* in (4) or *caught* in (5) is encountered. Typically subjects deal with sentences of this kind by treating the second noun phrase as if it were the object of the verb. The strategy fails with sentences like (5) in which the reader is 'garden pathed' and some reanalysis is called for. Our study used three distinct presentation conditions: (a) central—in which each word appeared in the same location; (b) sequential—in which each word appeared on its own in an appropriate spatial location across the display; and (c) cumulative—a condition identical to sequential but in which previously presented text remained on view. A measure was taken of subjects' inter-response times in a word-by-word self-paced presentation. Two contrasts are evident in this design. First, the comparison between cumulative and sequential presentation comments on the influence of visible prior text. Second, the comparison between sequential and central indicates the extent to which the availability of differential spatial information for words in the sentence aids the reader.

The results were clear-cut. A processing advantage is found in the conditions where readers have access to prior text. Sensitivity to the local structural ambiguity was *only* evident in the cumulative presentation condition. Thus, with suitable materials, it is possible to demonstrate a processing disadvantage in the single-word, single-location, presentation task. Direct eye movement recording in the cumulative and sequential conditions confirmed the results of Frazier and Rayner (1982): readers in the cumulative mode frequently made long regressive saccades which were launched from the point of disambiguation and directed to earlier parts of the sentence. It should be noted, however, that regressive eye movements were also apparent in the sequential presentation mode. On reaching the final word of a sentence presented in this way, subjects sometimes executed regressive saccades towards parts of the display which had previously contained informative text (although, of course, at this point the display was blank). This finding parallels that of Kennedy (1983), which also showed evidence of eye movements directed towards regions of a blank display which had previously contained text.

Although sentences like (5) are hard to process, they are quite short. In one sense, therefore, there is something odd about the fact that subjects, presented with such materials, should reinspect a word within a few seconds of reading it. It is difficult to imagine that the reader might have forgotten *what* a word was and yet remember *where* it was. We must ask, therefore, what function these second-pass fixations serve? In particular, what is the function of those which involve large saccades which can only be controlled by means of an accurate representation of the spatial location of at least some words? Part of the answer is provided by an analysis of the circumstances in which they occur. Two situations in particular can be identified: (1) structural ambiguity; and (2) anaphoric reference.

Structural ambiguity

This topic has already been touched on. Subjects, on encountering a word which does not fit the current syntactic analysis, will at times regress to an earlier part of a sentence. Frazier and Rayner (1982) identify three different possible forms these regressions might take: (1) forward reanalysis, which involves returning to the beginning of the sentence and reading it again; (2) backward reanalysis, which involves 'backing-up' through the sentence inspecting each word in turn in a right-to-left direction; and (3) selective reanalysis, in which the reader launches a saccade to just that part of the sentence which may have been incorrectly parsed. Of these three possible strategies the most costly, in processing terms, is backwards reanalysis since, although it does not involve a complete rereading, it does impose the penalty of a sequence of fixations (each 200–250 ms in duration) in which lexical identification is demanded in reverse order. It should be noted, however, that this may be the best strategy available to the reader who does not know where the target is (i.e. has no access to the spatial coordinates of previously read text). The most efficient strategy is that of selective reanalysis, in which only that part of a structure necessary to repair a faulty analysis is reread. In all cases, however, the same conclusion is suggested regarding the function of second-pass eye movements. On the first pass words are assigned a specific syntactic role and, if this must be revised, a word or words must be 'reentered' into the reader's (visual) lexicon. It would appear that for the reader, as distinct from the listener, a single syntactic analysis is performed (possibly on the basis of the most likely or most frequently encountered structure) rather than several alternatives being entertained simultaneously (Marslen-Wilson and Tyler, 1980). The 'single preferred analysis' option is, of course, open to the reader precisely because the text remains continuously visible and available for reinspection (Kennedy, 1986).

Anaphoric reference

A characteristic of written English is the extent to which structural coherence is achieved by the use of various forms of anaphoric expression. Thus, in (6) the words 'she' and 'aunt' refer to the same conceptual entity and the competent reader may be expected to arrive at this conclusion.

(6) My aunt hates travelling by car. After a few miles she becomes quite sick.

Quite frequently, however, anaphoric reference is incorrigibly ambiguous as in (7) or can only be resolved by use of pragmatic rules as in (8):

(7) Peter visited John on Friday. He always felt tired at the end of the week.
(8) Sally sold Jennifer her car because she failed her test.

It can be seen that anaphor imposes processing demands on the reader which, in some circumstances, may demand selective reanalysis. This will arise, for example, when a pronoun has two or more potential antecedents or when the reader discovers that an incorrect initial assignment has been made. Unfortunately, eye movement studies of anaphoric reference present a somewhat confused picture. Sometimes a pronoun can be shown to trigger a regressive saccade to a possible antecedent (Just and Carpenter, 1978; Kennedy, 1978). Other studies, using very similar materials (e.g. Ehrlich, 1983), show no such effects. There appear to be at least three possible reasons for this conflict of evidence. First, whether or not a regressive saccade occurs may be a function of the difficulty of the materials. Secondly, there are large individual differences in the frequency with which large regressive saccades are made (Kennedy and Murray, 1985; Kliegl, 1982). Finally, regressions may simply be more common in experimental situations restricted to single-line displays which are typically used in eye movement research (Just and Carpenter, 1978 is an exception). When multiple lines are displayed the critical target may be on an earlier line as in (9) and may, indeed, require a saccade in a left-to-right direction (e.g. from 'it' to 'car').

(9)   The policeman stood in the rain near the car.
      Seconds later it exploded causing great damage.

In those situations where second-pass inspections do occur, the same puzzling paradox is evident. Why should the reader reinspect a word which has been looked at no more than a few seconds earlier?

The spatial coding hypothesis

In a series of papers (Kennedy, 1982, 1983, 1984; Kennedy and Murray, 1984, 1985; Kennedy and Pidcock, 1981) my colleagues and I have addressed the question as to the function of second-pass eye movements and suggested an answer in terms of a spatial coding hypothesis. This proposes that fluent readers develop 'place-keeping' skills which allow for the selective reanalysis of text. Ambiguity—at a lexical, syntactic or semantic level—poses serious problem for the reader, since once a potential ambiguity has been detected the choice lies between constructing two or more parallel representations of structure or meaning, or adopting a single analysis and risking the penalty of error. It is precisely this penalty which availability of a selective reanalysis strategy minimizes. Selectivity of this kind, however, implies that the reader has access to previously read text, i.e. that points of potential ambiguity are coded in terms of their spatial coordinates. In this way, parts of previously read text can rapidly be made available for reprocessing. In the case of anaphoric reference it is frequently the case that the antecedent (for example of a pronoun) is initially unknown. Later access to potential candidates can, in such circumstances, only be achieved fluently if the reader knows where they lie (Kennedy, 1983, 1986). It is proposed that one mark of a successful reading style is this ability to code for place. The reader who can achieve this is able to use the printed page itself as an adjunct to memory. It comes to function like a 'stable map' in the sense used by Mackay (1973): that is, as a memory addressed through spatial coordinates. From this point of view, reinspections (or regressions) do not, as is frequently claimed, signal poor reading technique. On the contrary, they may play an important role in allowing the reader to arrive at a coherent representation of meaning. Regressive saccades are often precisely located: they lead to fixations on particular selected words, and are not directed randomly. The spatial coding hypothesis suggests that readers retain information, for some period of time, as to the location of words read (see also Christie and Just, 1976). This spatial code allows two essential 'place-keeping' operations to be carried out: (1) the location of items to be reinspected can be used by the eye movement control system; and (2) the location of the point of return can similarly be used to initiate a saccade. The use of this code reduces overall demands on working memory, maintaining what is essentially a verbatim record, addressed spatially, over a brief period of time (Hall, 1974; Kahneman and Lass, 1973; Kennedy, 1982). Thus, the reader may adopt an efficient, if risky, strategy of a 'single preferred analysis' both in terms of parsing and of cementing together the propositions of a text. The risk is, in fact, slight since if an analysis fails the fault can readily be mended by a process of reanalysis in which crucial items can be recovered rapidly.

The reader who does not adopt this coding strategy, for one reason or another, has more limited processing options. For example, faced with ambiguity, parallel representations of structure or meaning may be computed. The load placed on working memory by this activity is obviously very great. As an alternative, more costly reanalysis strategies must come into play involving either *ab initio* rereading or some kind of backward scan. This contrast between the fluent reader, capable of executing selective saccades in the service of reanalysis, and the more restricted strategies of the poorer reader is similar to the contrast Kliegl (1982) makes between 'explorers' and 'plodders'. It may also help explain the reversal in the sign of the correlation between the number of fixations and their duration discussed earlier. Heller and Heinisch (1985) argue that, as reading skill increases, this correlation develops from a positive into a negative relationship as a reflection of the increased ability to identify words. However, it also suggests a developing trade-off between the number of fixations and their duration, as if the better reader were more free to explore the text. Obviously, this issue can only be properly examined if first- and second-pass eye movements are distinguished in analysis.

The development of the spatial code

It can be seen that several predictions flow from the line of argument advanced so far: (1) the relationship between the number of fixations and their duration should differ for good and poor readers; (2) if complex materials are employed (i.e. calling for reanalysis) good readers should show more selective regressions than poor readers; (3) the incidence of large regressive saccades should be greater in good readers than in poor; (4) the process of reanalysis in poor readers should be characterized by non-selective reinspection (i.e. rereading *ab initio* or backward reanalysis).

It is possible to make some preliminary statements on all of these predictions. Wayne Murray and I have begun work on a series of cross-sectional developmental studies, looking at the reading style of children of otherwise normal intelligence who are either doing well at reading or failing.

We have examined the eye movements of a sample of over eighty schoolchildren aged 10–11 years. These have been designated as 'good' or 'poor' readers on the basis of standard reading tests. At the same time, non-verbal IQ has been carefully matched. We have also tested a control group of younger children, also matched for IQ, whose reading level in absolute terms matched the 'poor' group and in relative (standard score) terms was equivalent to the 'good' readers. This control is essential if group differences are to be discussed in terms of potential *causes* of reading failure (Bryant and Bradley, 1985).

This sample of subjects has been asked to read large numbers of sentence–question pairs. Typically, a sentence 10–12 words in length is read and then a question (usually 4–5 words) presented. Subjects respond to questions by button presses. The materials all fall on a single line and subjects' horizontal eye movements are measured as the sentence is read and the question answered. We have concentrated on the processing of pronominal and noun-phrase anaphors in the questions. Although the materials are all unambiguous and relatively easy to understand, these young readers quite often process anaphoric expressions by making regressive eye movements in the direction of possible antecedents. The data provided, therefore, are well suited to the examination of the various hypotheses outlined above.

The detailed results are presented elsewhere (Kennedy and Murray, 1985) but can be briefly summarized here. Taking the data from sentences and questions together, the results are consistent with the interpretation that number and duration of fixations can be traded off against each other and that 'good' readers can do this more effectively than 'poor'. There are very marked strategic differences in the way good and poor readers process anaphoric expressions. Good readers tend to locate a remote antecedent by executing a single (and long) regressive saccade. These large eye movements are located accurately and quite often associated with equally large return sweeps, recovering the initial point of departure. By contrast, poor readers process remote antecedents less efficiently, either by rereading the sentence *ab initio* or (and this is the more common strategy) by 'backtracking' through the text executing a series of fixations in a right-to-left direction. In addition, the initial response of poor readers to a question was much more likely (by a factor of ten) to be eye closure—taking the form of short blinks or quite sustained periods of time with the eyes closed. With regard to all the measures the control group of younger, matched readers behaved more like the good readers than the poor. The relevant statistical contrasts were all significant, suggesting that the obtained differences do not arise as a *result* of limited exposure to printed text but may be a possible *cause* of reading failure.

How can this pattern of results be explained? The literature on reading failure correctly places emphasis on the difficulties poor readers have with speech-based aspects of the reading skill (Bryant and Bradley, 1985) and their relatively low level of 'phonological awareness'. This emphasis is, at times, pressed to the point of denying the existence of significant (or interesting) differences in the visual skills of good and poor readers (Mitchell, 1982). The data reported here suggest that this conclusion may be unwarranted. Although our studies are not yet complete, the results point to the possibility of fundamental differences in the visual processing skills of normal and failing readers. Whether or not a reader 'codes for place' clearly influences the speed and fluency with which anaphor can be resolved. This is not a marginal phenomenon, since anaphoric reference is a crucial linguistic device determining coherence in text. Taken as a whole, our data raise the possibility that poor readers, quite literally, may not always know *where* crucial information is located. There is a natural reluctance to consider the processing of speech and writing to be fundamentally different. There are, however, some indications in the psycholinguistic literature which lead in this direction. Most obvious is the fact that contextual effects play such a large role in speech perception and yet are so relatively weak (or, as some would argue, non-existent) in reading. The traditional account of this difference (Forster, 1981) is that context is of help when the stimulus is impoverished, and whereas this is usually so when dealing with speech it is rarely the case with printed text. Eye movement studies provide an important gloss on this interpretation. It is not the clarity of text which bestows a processing advantage, but its permanence. For the reader who knows where critical elements lie, there is virtually no price to pay for adopting a single preferred analysis which may, if necessary, be revised. The possibility remains open, however, that not all readers code for place and it will be one goal for research over the next few years to chart the development of this important skill.

ACKNOWLEDGMENTS

The research reported here is supported by a grant from the Economic and Social Research Council to Alan Kennedy and Wayne S. Murray. Thanks are due to the pupils and staff of Blackness Primary School, Park Place Primary School and St Joseph's Primary School, Dundee.

Dorothy Lemon and Teresa O'Neill helped with testing and analysis.

REFERENCES

Bouma, H., and deVoogd, A.H. (1974). On the control of eye saccades in reading. *Vision Research*, **14**, 273-284.
Breitmeyer, B.G. (1984). *Visual Masking: An Integrative Approach*. New York: Oxford University Press.
Bryant, P.E., and Bradley, L. (1985). *Children's Reading Problems*. Oxford: Blackwell.

Buswell, G.T. (1920). An experimental study of the eye–voice span in reading. *Supplementary Educational Monographs*, 17.

Buswell, G.T. (1935). *How People Look at Pictures*. Chicago: University of Chicago Press.

Carpenter, P.A., and Just M.A. (1972). Semantic control of eye movements during picture scanning in a sentence–picture verification task. *Perception and Psychophysics*, **12**, 61-64.

Carpenter, P.A., and Just, M.A. (1975). Sentence comprehension: A psycholinguistic processing model of verification. *Psychological Review*, **82**, 45-73.

Christie, J., and Just M.A. (1976). Remembering the location and content of sentences in a prose passage. *Journal of Educational Psychology*, **68**, 702-710.

Ehrlich, K. (1983). Eye movements in pronoun assignment: A study of sentence integration. In K. Rayner (Ed.) *Eye Movements in Reading: Perceptual and Language Processes*. New York: Academic Press.

Fisher, D.F., and Shebilske, W.L. (1985). There is more than meets the eye in the Eyemind Assumption. In R. Groner, G. McConkie and C. Menz (Eds.) *Eye Movements and Human Information Processing*. Amsterdam: North-Holland.

Forster, K.I. (1981). Priming and the effects of sentence and lexical context on naming time: evidence for autonomous lexical processing. *Quarterly Journal of Experimental Psychology*, **33A**, 465-495.

Frazier, L., and Rayner, K. (1982). Making and correcting errors during sentence comprehension: Eye movements in the analysis of structurally ambiguous sentences. *Cognitive Psychology*, **14**, 178-210.

Garrod, S., and Sanford, A.J. (1977). Interpreting anaphoric relations: The integration of semantic information while reading. *Journal of Verbal Learning and Verbal Behavior*, **16**, 77-90.

Gonzalez, E.G., and Kolers, P.A. (1985). On the interpretation of eye fixation. In R. Groner, G. McConkie and C. Menz (Eds.) *Eye Movements and Information Processing*. Amsterdam: North-Holland.

Hall, D.C. (1974). Eye movements in scanning iconic imagery. *Journal of Experimental Psychology*, **103**, 825-830.

Haviland, S.E., and Clark, H.H. (1974). What's new? Acquiring new information as a process in comprehension. *Journal of Verbal Learning and Verbal Behavior*, **13**, 515-521.

Heller, D., and Heinisch, A. (1985). Eye movement parameters in reading: effects of letter size and letter spacing. In R. Groner, G. McConkie and C. Menz (Eds.) *Eye Movements and Human Information Processing*. Amsterdam: North-Holland.

Huey, E.B. (1908). *The Psychology and Pedagogy of Reading*. New York: MacMillan.

Jacobs, A.M. (1986). Eye movement control by independent, parallel processes. Paper to International Conference on Cognitive Approaches to Reading, Leicester, April.

Juola, J.F., Ward, N.J., and McNamara, T. (1982). Visual search and reading of rapid serial presentation of letter strings, words, and text. *Journal of Experimental Psychology: General*, **111**, 208-227.

Just, M.A., and Carpenter, P.A. (1978). Inference processes during reading: Reflections from eye fixations. In J.W. Senders, D.F. Fisher and R.A. Monty (Eds.) *Eye Movements and the Higher Psychological Functions*. Hillsdale, N.J.: Erlbaum.

Just, M.A., and Carpenter, P.A. (1980). A theory of reading: From eye fixations to comprehension. *Psychological Review*, **87**, 329-354.

Kahneman, D., and Lass, N. (1973). Eye position in tasks of association and memory. Unpublished manuscript, Hebrew University, Jerusalem. (Cited in D. Kahneman,

Attention and Effort. Englewood Cliffs: Prentice-Hall.)

Kennedy, A. (1978). Eye movements and the integration of semantic information during reading. In M.M. Gruneberg, R.N. Sykes and P.E. Morris (Eds.) *Practical Aspects of Memory*. London: Academic Press.

Kennedy, A. (1982). Eye movements and spatial coding in reading. *Psychological Research*, **44**, 313-322.

Kennedy, A. (1983). On looking into space. In K. Rayner (Ed.) *Eye Movements in Reading: Perceptual and Language Processes*. New York: Academic Press.

Kennedy, A. (1984). *The Psychology of Reading*. London: Methuen.

Kennedy, A. (1986). The case for place-text arrangement and reading skill: A review. *Current Psychological Research and Reviews*, **5**, 94-104.

Kennedy, A., and Murray, W.S. (1984). Inspection times for words in syntactically ambiguous sentences under three presentation conditions. *Journal of Experimental Psychology: Human Perception and Performance*, **10**, 833-847.

Kennedy, A., and Murray, W.S. (1985). The components of reading time: Eye movement patterns of good and poor readers. Paper presented to Third European Conference on Eye Movements, Dourdan, September 1985.

Kennedy, A., and Murray, W.S. (in press). Spacial coordinates and reading: comments on Monk (1985). *Quarterly Journal of Experimental Psychology*.

Kennedy, A., and Pidcock, B. (1981). Eye movements and variations in reading time. *Psychological Research*, **43**, 69-79.

Kliegl, R.M. (1982). On relations between cognition and reading styles: individual differences and developmental trends. Unpublished PhD thesis, University of Colorado.

Kolers, P.A. (1976). Buswell's discoveries. In R.A. Monty and J.W. Senders (Eds.) *Eye Movements and Psychological Processes*. Hillsdale, N.J.: Erlbaum.

Levy-Schoen, A. (1974). Le champ d'activité du regard; données experimentales. *L' année Psychologique*, **74**, 543-66.

Levy-Schoen, A., and O'Regan, K. (1979). The control of eye movements in reading. In P.A. Kolers, M.E. Wrolstad and H. Bouma (Eds.) *Processing of Visible Language*, Vol. 1. New York: Plenum Press.

Mackay, D.M. (1973). Visual stability and voluntary eye movements. In R. Jung (Ed.) *Handbook of Sensory Physiology*, Vol. 7. Springer: Berlin.

Marslen-Wilson, W., and Tyler, L.K. (1980). The temporal structure of spoken language understanding. *Cognition*, **8**, 1-17.

Matin, E. (1976). Saccadic suppression and the stable world. In R.A. Monty and J.W. Senders (Eds.) *Eye Movements and Psychological Processes*. Hillsdale, N.J.: Erlbaum.

McConkie, G.W. (1983). Eye movements and perception during reading. In K. Rayner (Ed.) *Eye Movements in Reading: Perceptual and Language Processes*. New York: Academic Press.

McConkie, G.W., and Rayner, K. (1975). The span of the effective stimulus during a fixation in reading. *Perception and Psychophysics*, **17**, 578-586.

McConkie, G.W., and Rayner, K. (1976). Identifying the span of the effective stimulus in reading. In H. Singer and R.B. Rudell (Eds.) *Theoretical Models and Processes of Reading*. Newark Del: International Reading Association.

McConkie, G.W., and Zola, D. (1979). Is visual information integrated across successive fixations in reading? *Perception and Psychophysics*, **25**, 221-224.

Mitchell, D.C. (1982). *The Process of Reading*. London: Wiley.

Monk, A.P. (1985a). Theoretical note: Co-ordinate systems in visual word recognition. *Quarterly Journal of Experimental Psychology*, **37A**, 613-626.

Monk, A.P. (1985b). Reading character-stepped text. *Acta Psychologia,* **58,** 173-189.

O'Regan, J.K. (1975). Structural and contextual constraints on eye movements in reading. Unpublished PhD thesis, University of Cambridge.

O'Regan, J.K. (1981). The convenient viewing position hypothesis. In D.F. Fisher, R.A. Monty and J.W. Senders (Eds.) *Eye Movements: Cognition and Visual Perception.* Hillsdale: Erlbaum.

O'Regan, J.K., and Levy-Schoen, A. (1983). Integrating visual information from successive fixations: does trans-saccadic fusion exist? *Vision Research,* **23,** 765-768.

Posner, M.I. (1978) *Chronometic Explorations of Mind.* Hillsdale, N.J.: Erlbaum.

Rayner, K. (1975). The perceptual span and peripheral cues in reading. *Cognitive Psychology,* **7,** 65-81.

Rayner, K. (1978). Eye movements in reading and information processing. *Psychological Bulletin,* **85,** 618-660.

Sternberg, S. (1975). Memory scanning: New findings and current controversies. *Quarterly Journal of Experimental Psychology,* **27,** 1-32.

Tinker, M.A. (1958). Recent studies of eye movements in reading. *Psychological Bulletin,* **55,** 215-231.

Underwood, G. (1985). Eye movements during the comprehension of written language. In A.W. Ellis (Ed.) *Progress in the Psychology of Language,* Vol. 2. London: Erlbaum.

Cognitive approaches to reading
Edited by J. R. Beech and A. M. Colley
© 1987 John Wiley & Sons Ltd

CHAPTER 8

Early Reading Development

JOHN R. BEECH

Department of Psychology, University of Leicester

EARLY READING SKILL DEVELOPMENT

So far in this volume there has been a concentration on the cognitive processes involved in the reading of skilled readers. We now turn to an examination of how children progress during the early stages of reading development. The present chapter will outline, among other things, the development of lexical identification, the identification of letter sounds, phonemic processing (an extended review is presented in Chapter 9) and the use of contextual information. The intention will be to suggest that reading does not develop in neat sequential stages and that supposedly contrasting modes of processing, involving phonics, coding lexically or analogical processing, could share processes in common, at least in the early phase of reading. Finally, the model of LaBerge and Samuels (1974) will be examined, which attempts to explain the kind of processes involved in acquiring knowledge about reading and which includes the features of hierarchical organization and automaticity. This model was originally devised by LaBerge (1973) as a hierarchical network with a central mechanism supervising a distributed intelligence throughout the network. This means that at nodes throughout this network there is a certain degree of sophistication in processing information independent of the central mechanism. The first section discusses the likely level of cognitive development of the child just as reading begins.

PRELIMINARIES TO LEARNING TO READ

At what point in the development of a child is he or she ready to read? Coltheart (1979) has criticized such a question on several grounds. The concept of reading readiness was initially developed by drawing an analogy between reading development and the acquisition of a physical skill such as learning to walk. However, walking is dependent on the maturation of the appropriate muscles whereas reading is not a skill which spontaneously develops. It is an artificially acquired skill probably influenced by considerable individual differences and differences in teaching environments. Coltheart also suggested that there is, as yet, no evidence concerning the nature of supposed reading readiness skills and, further-more, the reading concept is tautological in that the indication of a lack of readiness is the actual failure to learn to read.

Nevertheless, what is the level of cognitive development, in broad terms, by the time that the child starts to read and presumably starts to develop a hierarchy of reading skills? According to Ellis (1984), by the time the child begins formal education a large repertoire of words has developed both in listening and spoken vocabulary. The child mainly encounters printed words within this set of vocabulary. Also, processes necessary for the pars-ing of speech have already developed and will continue to develop. Palermo and Molfese (1972) believe that children continue to demonstrate substantial improvements in their understanding of syntactic structures up to about thirteen years of age. A problem which arises is that syntactic processing is different once a child begins to read strings of words compared with listen-ing to text, and Adams (1980) has described how such differences arise. Prosodic cues in speech (such as pauses) facilitate the syntactic processing of the incoming information, but in reading there is not the same richness of analogue information; instead syntactic boundaries are marked only by punctuation. Thus the acquisition of syntactic information during reading requires the development of a new skill as reading progresses.

There should be other processes and structures which have already developed that are important for the initial reading phase. According to Mitchell (1982) there are various obvious prerequisite structures to word recognition, for instance one such prerequisite should be an internal representation of a word. However, such a representation need not be a verbal one since Steinberg and Steinberg (1975), experimenting on their own child from an early age, demonstrated that he could identify a printed version of a word from alternatives even though unable to label a word verbally. Thus at ten months of age Kimio indicated that he knew that certain speech sounds referred to pictures of certain objects, even though he could not reproduce these sounds himself. For a time a picture and its correspon-ding word were fixed on the wall (the first words were *baby, car, boy* and *girl*) and he learned to point to the word and picture when it was verbally labelled. Gradually the pictures were removed leaving only the words, and then more words were added. By about the age of twelve months he had about nine words available and he could read the first four words but could not say them. By Kimio's thirtieth month he could read 181 different items. If one makes a distinction between input and output logogens (Morton, 1980; Morton and Patterson, 1980), in the initial phase this child had input logogens for these words but no output logogens (in other words, he could identify the referents of the words but not say them) and also had encoded some visual features of the words sufficient to identify them from others in the available set.

There are certain processes which are obviously essential to normal development in reading. The child needs to understand that the printed word actually symbolizes a word; there needs to be the facility of recognizing various visual features as part of the process of recognizing words; and so on. But there are other processes whose role as a prerequisite for the reading process are more debatable, such as whether it is necessary to be aware of the phonological constituents of individual words, even though the exemplars of most of the sound units can be rather variable. This will be discussed later.

BEGINNING TO READ

Teaching methods

Two main approaches to the teaching of reading are the phonics and the whole-word methods. In phonics teaching the units of analysis are the individual letters constituting the words and their corresponding phonemic representation. These units are systematically built up, mainly in the context of orthographically regular words, until the child is reading a fairly large range of words. In the phonics approach some teachers might begin with a limited set of letters and use these in various combinations to build different words. Others will use words with common initial letters to teach the beginning sounds of words. Gradually the number of letters is increased in a systematic manner so that previously acquired letters are also revised. In the whole-word method the unit of analysis is the word itself. Therefore, the child experiences highly frequent words which may or may not be regular in spelling. This lexical route for reading can potentially take place at a very early stage, for instance, as mentioned before, important reading skills can be learned during the prespeech period. In practice most teachers use an eclectic approach, because after a period of using the phonics approach the whole-word method has to be introduced so that the child experiences more irregularly spelled and often highly frequent words. Similarly, the whole-word approach benefits from phonics training in order for the child to be able to read new words on the basis of decoding individual letters, although this is not absolutely necessary as the child may function by using the pronunciation of analogously spelled words already within reading vocabulary.

The phonics and whole-word approaches have contrasting advantages and disadvantages, which is why it may be advantageous to use them in a complementary manner. It is quite a useful exercise to consider the kinds of processes which might be involved if the child employs each method of learning to read in its pure form. Of course, children may tackle reading in their individual ways, irrespective of the nature of the teaching style. However, there is evidence that the beginning reader's approach to reading can be substantially influenced by these contrasting teaching styles (Barr, 1974). Seymour and Elder (1986) studied children in their first year of reading taught primarily by the whole-word method and noted that these children appeared to be able only to read words already taught, and could not translate letters into sounds to read novel words. The various developments which take place during early reading will now be examined.

Developing logographic structures

The demonstration that a child can read a word correctly at the beginning of reading may be no more than an indication that the child recognizes one aspect of that word and is capable of uttering the sequence of sounds signified by the symbols representing that word. This does not mean that there has been any substantial analysis of the symbols nor of the individual sounds constituting the word. According to Marsh *et al*. (1981) the first stage in reading is 'glance-and-guess', whereby the child will identify the word because it is in the small set of sight vocabulary or else will make a guess at it. Leaving aside for the moment the problem of even proposing a first stage in reading, what exactly is being learned? It is very doubtful that the entire pattern comprising the word has been associated with a logogen (or word unit). Frith (1985) proposes that the child has memorized the salient graphic features but that the letter order has mainly been ignored. There is a stored semantic representation but no direct route to a phonological code. The child has probably stored, on the basis of a visual analysis, sets of featural representations corresponding to words and consequently will not have too much difficulty discriminating a word in that set from other words until a new word similar in appearance to one already in the set is encountered (e.g. *house* and *horse*). In terms of the development of a system that can recognize graphemes or graphemic clusters (or 'graphic units', see Henderson, 1985a) by analysing salient features, this will encourage the conscious discrimination of the symbols constituting the two words in order not to confuse them in the future. Marsh *et al*. (1981) called this process 'discrimination net guessing' and viewed it as a second stage in reading acquisition. Thus the child is seen as producing a discrimination net mechanism so that the extent of processing of graphemic processing is only sufficient to discriminate words similar in appearance. However, this kind of mechanism may not result in the discrimination of graphemes, in the sense of processing a limited set of letters of the alphabet. Instead, it may operate on the whole pattern of the word and concentrate on discriminating only a particular area of difference between the two words. Seymour and Elder (1986) presented evidence from children taught entirely by the whole-word method that they do not encode unanalysed *gestalts*. This was demonstrated by presenting the words vertically arranged or zigzagged, which produced considerably less disruption than predicted by a *gestalt* hypothesis although there were some readers who experienced substantial disruption. Instead, Seymour and Elder proposed that a number of features are analysed along the dimensions of information on word length, the shape of pertinent letters (perhaps limited to a set of about a dozen) and the position of such letters. These three dimensions would be sufficient to discriminate a reasonably large beginning sight vocabulary of words.

Developing a knowledge of graphemes inevitably includes knowledge concerning common combinations between graphemes, which leads on to a knowledge of orthographic structure. For instance, Massaro and Hestand (1983) had children in the first three grades choose, out of pairs of letter strings, the strings which 'looked more like a word'. The target items differed from their counterparts in terms of their rule-like orthographic structure. In the first grade (for six-year-olds on average) 58 per cent of the targets were correctly chosen (this is at chance level) and by grade 3 it was almost 80 per cent. As might be expected, this developing orthographic knowledge correlated with reading ability. Henderson and Chard (1980) found that both grade 2 and grade 4 children in a reaction-time lexical-decision task were sensitive to the positional letter frequency in non-words as well as to the presence or absence of vowels. For example, *shrnld* has a high positional frequency whereas *dtscfk* has a low frequency. Thus in contrast to the finding of Massaro and Hestand, this study suggests that even six-year-old readers have some awareness of some aspects of the orthographic structure of words.

The problem in understanding such processes and structures from the viewpoint of logographic representation lies in their fuzziness and overlap with those involved in analysing graphemes or graphic units in order to generate a phonological code. Suppose that before long the child becomes adept at extracting certain graphemic features from a word. One strategy might be to code the order and spatial distance between the words. For instance, if presented with *balloon* and *blank*, perhaps the child only codes the letters *b*, *a* and *n*, so that the featural representation will be a representation of *ba****n* and *b*an**. In this case the order is the same but discrimination is in terms of the spacing between the letters. What is important to the issue of whether processing is logographic during this process is the involvement of phonological coding, because this analysis could be logographic in the sense that a graphemic analysis is undergone in the absence of a phonological one, with the next stage being the retrieval of the representation of the word. Another way would be to translate graphemes into their corresponding phonological codes and *then* retrieve the word. This will be a problem examined in the discussion section.

When children progress in reading they improve at different rates for different kinds of subskills. When these smooth progressions are viewed together they give the impression of a series of transitions in skill over the course of reading development, even though the changes might only have been in the interrelationships between the components. Consequently most theorists have described reading development as progressing through several phases. But this will not be a view taken here because of the difficulty of defining the boundary of such phases, and because the variability in teaching methods makes it difficult to offer generalizations about the sequencing of these phases for all children.

To take just one example of the stages viewpoint, based on the stages of Marsh *et al.*, Frith has proposed three stages of reading development: logographic skills, alphabetic skills and orthographic skills. These are hypothesized to '. . .follow each other in strict sequential order' (p. 307). Although it might be conceded that the majority of schoolchildren pass through this sequence, it is more pragmatic to conceptualize these as overlapping processes with considerable individual variation, even across children within the same teaching environment. It is likely, however, that one could operationally define the transition into a particular phase, but this would give the erroneous impression of the beginning of a discrete phase. Furthermore, the sequence of phases would be different for different teaching environments (e.g. Barr, 1974). This returns us to the first point, that there are problems with describing the first stage of reading as being logographic as children can begin at the alphabetic stage; it may even be possible to start at the orthographic stage. It is unlikely that postulating such stages would stimulate fruitful research.

Development of graphemic processing and grapheme–phoneme connections

It is important, but not essential, early in reading that there should be a development in rudimentary analysis of the symbols constituting words as well as the establishment of the connections between symbols and the sounds they represent. This kind of analysis might develop as a by-product of the whole-word approach. During the course of early reading development there is a gradual improvement in graphemic knowledge. Biemiller (1970), adopting the stages approach, proposed three phases of reading during the course of the year for first-graders. The second phase was characterized by an increase in oral reading errors which were visually similar to the mistaken printed word. This second phase was operationally defined in terms of the number of refusals to say a word. An interpretation of these first two phases is that initially the child was processing the words, as described earlier, by developing a reading vocabulary and, if uncertain about the word, using context in order to guess intelligently what the word was likely to be. In the second phase, the increasing use of graphical information provided contradictory information about the word which caused difficulty in making a response. The child preferred not to make a response, thus producing the increase in refusals, as already mentioned; furthermore, there was a doubling of graphophonic errors (errors similar graphically and phonologically, Goodman, 1969), but contextual errors remained at the same high level. In the third phase, there were fewer refusals and evidence of increased use of graphophonic and contextual information. Consequently by the third phase processing graphemes had assumed even greater importance.

Further support for increasing grapheme-to-phoneme knowledge comes from Harding, Beech and Sneddon (1985), who examined the oral reading errors British children made from five to eleven years of age in a cross-sectional design. Independent raters judged the syntactic, semantic, graphophonic and phonemic similarity of each reading error to the original text. Between the ages of five and seven years there was an increase in the ratings of similarity in terms of both graphophonic and phonemic similarity. Unfortunately it is difficult to determine if this demonstrates increasing graphemic or phonemic awareness or both in the Biemiller and Harding *et al*. studies. Other evidence comes from Shankweiler and Liberman (1972), who found that oral errors in second-grade readers of a CVC (consonant vowel consonant) syllable were much more frequent on the final consonant than on the initial consonant; errors were greatest on the middle vowel. In fact, Liberman and Shankweiler (1976), interpreting this evidence, argue that this pattern of errors indicates problems in phonemic segmentation rather than in visual pattern recognition. But this could also be evidence that at least the first letter is being processed, which must entail a feature analysis of this grapheme and also a production of its sound.

A useful requirement for reading is that the child has some means of knowing the identity of a word other than just utilizing reading vocabulary knowledge (e.g. Jorm and Share, 1983). This can be a simple case of having someone available to say what the word is or providing the skills for self-help, often referred to as word-attack skills. These require the ability to analyse each grapheme, convert it into a phoneme and then synthesize the collection of phonemes into a word. Alternatively, groups of graphemes might be recognized as analogous to other words within reading vocabulary. Mitchell (1982) believes that the development of a reading vocabulary will depend on the development of such skills. In support of this, Williams (1976), monitoring individual children over a three-year period, found that when a child had mastered phonic skills this was followed by a substantial improvement in word recognition. Also, Farmer, Nixon and White (1976) had two matched groups undergo either sound-blending training or a control condition training in naming pictures. Afterwards the sound-blending group was better at reading than the picture-naming group, thus supporting the argument that training in word-attack skills helps the development of sight vocabulary. Presumably the improvement would have been even greater if the children had been trained in a fuller range of word-attack skills. However, there is evidence suggesting that dyslexic children do not have the necessary knowledge to carry out grapheme–phoneme conversion but develop their reading vocabulary despite this problem (Snowling, 1980; Kochnower, Richardson and DiBenedetto, 1983). Snowling compared dyslexics with younger children matched on reading and showed how the word-attack skills on a non-word visual–auditory matching task were much worse for the dyslexics, indicating that word-attack skills are not absolutely necessary for improving reading vocabulary but that they can be a substantial help. However, contradictory evidence has been produced by Beech and Harding (1984) and Treiman and Hirsh-Pasek (1985) (see Chapters 9 and 10).

Case-study evidence that grapheme–phoneme conversion may not be necessary in the adult has come recently from Campbell and Butterworth (1985). They tested a developmental phonological dyslexic and demonstrated that this student had learned to read to a sophisticated level presumably without grapheme–phoneme conversion as she could not read even the simplest non-words. She had deficiencies in phonemic processing which could have impaired the development of grapheme–phoneme conversion or else phonemic processing and grapheme–phoneme conversion did not develop in conjunction with each other.

Development of phonemic processing

There have been many experiments showing how the ability to divide words into their constituent phonological parts is related to the level of reading ability. An example of a study showing such a relationship between phonemic awareness and reading level is by Liberman *et al.* (1974), who tested children between prekindergarten and grade 1 (a range between four and six years old) on a task requiring tapping according to the number of segments within a list of utterances. They found that none of the children was able to do the task at prekindergarten level, but on average phonemic segmentation ability improved so that by first grade 70 per cent of the children could do the task. Also, first-grade phonemic segmentation ability was closely related to reading ability. Similarly, Fox and Routh (1980) found that first-grade children of average reading ability could decompose syllables into their phonemic constituent parts but those with severe reading problems were unable to do so. One might infer from such work that learning to segment words into their phonemic constituents could facilitate reading.

One way to demonstrate that improving phonemic awareness is instrumental in improving reading is to train children in phonemic awareness and produce an improvement in their reading performance compared with an appropriate control group. Bradley and Bryant (1983, see also Bryant and Bradley, 1985) selected 65 children out of 400 who were poor at phonemic awareness at the age of 4–5 years. In the following year they were divided randomly into four groups and over the next two years three groups were given a non-intensive training programme of 40 sessions at fifteen minutes each and the fourth group were given no training. One programme was a control training programme giving them training in a semantic categorization task. The other two groups had phonemic awareness training and one of these also had training with plastic letters in order to make the connection between letters and sounds more explicit. At the end of the longitudinal study, 3–4 years after the initial testing, those given phonemic awareness training alone were ahead of the semantic categorization control group in reading but not significantly so. The group who also had training with plastic letters were significantly better than the conceptual categorization control group, being over eight months ahead in reading. We can conclude that training children in both the individual sounds in words and the grapheme–phoneme connections can significantly help reading (and spelling as well, according to this study), but a causal connection between training in individual sounds and reading *per se* is not demonstrated according to this study. It could be argued that the plastic letters condition was equivalent to giving the children extra, if not better, phonics training than they received in class. The training of individual sounds, from this view, would be the administration of an isolated component of phonics training which did not work. Perhaps if there had been more training sessions the improvement in reading might have achieved significance.

Perfetti, Beck and Hughes (1981) (described in Perfetti, 1985) examined another aspect of phonemic processing and looked at causal connections in both directions between different types of phonemic processing and reading ability. They studied 99 first-grade children taught by an explicitly phonics method or by a popular basal reader. The children were tested before they received formal reading instruction and on three other occasions throughout the course of the year. Perfetti *et al.* used two contrasting phonemic tasks which they proposed tested implicit and explicit speech segmentation ability by means of a sound-blending and phoneme-deletion task (e.g. 'Say dog without the /d/'), respectively. In their analysis they examined time-lag correlations with same-time correlations partialled out, and found that, for both the phonics and basal readers, there was a point at which the preceding ability in sound-blending successfully predicted performance in reading pseudowords. Even more interesting was that they found, again for both groups, that on the third time of testing the preceding ability in pseudoword reading successfully predicted performance in the phoneme-deletion tasks. The picture is slightly more complicated than this because for the basal readers there was also a point at which performance on phoneme deletion predicted performance on pseudoword reading. However, passing over this slight complication, this is an experiment indicating that the experience in reading was helping the reader to advance to a more difficult level of phonemic analysis. This more difficult level, the phoneme-deletion task, requires that the child analyses the constituents of the word in order to remove one of those constituents. Furthermore, the remaining phonemes have then to be uttered. It seems that one or both of these abilities are facilitated by the reading process. The effect of learning to read on developing phonemic awareness was studied by Morais *et al.* (1979), who found that Portuguese subjects of peasant origin who had learned to read as adults demonstrated phonological awareness, whereas illiterate adults of the same background had no such awareness. Returning to what was stated at the beginning of this section, finding a correlation between phonemic processing and reading ability is only a first step to determining the precise nature of a causal connection. It is likely that the process of learning to read facilitates an awareness that speech can be broken into phonemic units, but it is more debatable whether phonemic awareness *per se* has an effect on learning to read.

Using contextual information

An implication of the rather rudimentary early whole-word strategy which has been described, according to Marsh *et al.* (1981), is that unknown words presented within a context will elicit a guess based not on any symbol-to-sound knowledge but rather on expectancies of what would be syntactically and semantically plausible in that location. The child might say 'the dog sat in his basket' when presented with *the dog sat in his glunk*. This is partially supported by Harding, Beech and Sneddon (1985), who found that across the age range of 5–11 years there was a steady decline in the syntactic similarity of such errors. The ratings of semantic similarity were reduced compared to syntactic similarity and there was also a less substantial decline in such semantic similarity from the age of six onwards. Such a pattern demonstrates that syntactic information is analysed at an early age in reading. Other research supports this conclusion; for instance, Pring and

Snowling (1986) demonstrated that young readers were much more facilitated in word recognition by a prior semantic context compared with older readers. Similarly, such semantic facilitation has been shown in several studies to be greater for poor readers compared with good readers (Schvaneveldt, Ackerman and Semlear, 1977; Perfetti and Roth, 1981; Underwood and Briggs, 1984).

If the reader were using an entirely lexical strategy for a particular word in the Harding *et al.* study, the source of semantically similar errors that did occur could come from two different modes of processing. In one, the reader recognizes the word as having been seen before and it evokes a semantic representation, but the word that is used to label that representation is not the same (e.g. 'tigers' might be said instead of 'lions', see Seymour and Elder, 1986, for further examples). The surrounding context is not actually useful in this case. In the other, the reader has understood the previous context, and might indeed understand the words following the unknown word, and makes a guess. This is a case in which there is no evocation of the meaning of the word; however, the context might be sufficiently restricted as to increase the probability that that particular semantic representation will be evoked. But the reader selects a word, on some of these occasions, which is not the perceived word but one similar in meaning. At other times (and probably more frequently according to this explanation) it is not similar in meaning but, due to the influence of context, it is syntactically similar.

Stanovich (1986) has pointed out that because of the slow rate of reading for less skilled readers, the use of contextual information is attentuated. However, this does not mean that they are incapable of using context to help to identify words in other situations. Corroborative evidence comes from Stanovich, Cunningham and Feeman (1984) in a longitudinal study of first-graders dividing them into skilled and poor readers (as they were middle-class, the reading performance of the poor readers was actually commensurate with their age). When the poor readers had reached the same reading level as the skilled readers were at when they were younger, it was found that they used contextual facilitation to the same, if not to a greater, extent. The method used was to compare performance reading a normal paragraph and the same paragraph with the words scrambled; thus the coherent paragraph contained contextual information whereas the other did not. When compared at the same chronological age (cross-sectionally) with the better readers, much smaller contextual effects were observed in the poorer readers. Thus as reading skill increases contextual information seems to serve an increasing role in contributing to reading performance. This seems to be somewhat contrary to the previous conclusion that younger readers might make relatively more use of contextual information than older readers, as shown by decreasing syntactic similarity scores as the children advanced in reading. However, perhaps syntactic contextual information may be relatively more important in the early stages, whereas other types of contextual information may play even more of a role within a wider context of comprehending the sense of what is being read. Nevertheless, a scrambled passage will contain very little propositional information which would otherwise normally interact with concurrent basic reading processes. Thus, another interpretation of the Stanovich *et al.* experiment might be in terms of the randomization of a passage having a greater disruptive effect on more automatic reading processes which may rely on the preceding gist of the passage. In the younger readers automaticity has not been developed to the same extent so that randomization does not produce the same degree of interference.

Goodman (1967) has been a strong advocate of the use of reading errors to give an indication of the kind of reading that a child may be using. He even goes so far as to suggest that contextual information is providing a substantial proportion of the information the child uses in order to identify an individual word. This means that the visual analysis which is taking place is only sufficient to verify these predictions. Ellis (1984) criticizes this viewpoint on the grounds that it is unlikely that familiar words are usually analysed in this way even though context may be otherwise used to generate a guess; furthermore, it would require considerable computational effort to generate sets of likely words each time a word is encountered.

To a certain extent recent work by Adams and Huggins (1985) has supported Ellis and has thrown more light on the matter. They gave frequency-graded irregularly spelled words to above- and below-average readers in the second through to the fifth grades. These words either had no preceding context or else were the last content word in a meaningful sentence (e.g. 'If you drop a cup, it might *break*'). They found that the effect of context depended on the prior familiarity of the word. Context was most potent in assisting recognition of words of intermediate familiarity. Words of greater familiarity did not need context and the least familiar were not facilitated by context. Moreover, this finding held for every age range and ability group. This relationship between familiarity and the effects of context may help to explain previous apparently contradictory findings. Where a differential contextual effect has been found across age groups, this could have been produced by the older group encountering material which is increasingly familiar.

DISCUSSION

The LaBerge and Samuels (1974) model

This model represents the most ambitious attempt to explain the processes

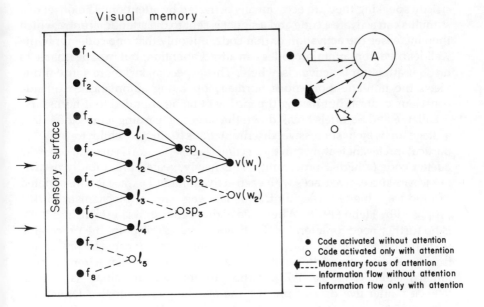

Figure 8.1 Model of visual memory showing two states of perceptual coding of visual patterns. Arrows from the attention centre (A) to solid-dot codes denote a two-way flow of excitation: attention can activate these codes and be activated (attracted) by them. Attention can activate open-dot codes but cannot be activated (attracted) by them. f, feature detector; l, letter code; sp, spelling pattern code; v(w), visual word code. From LaBerge and Samuels (1974) (*Reproduced by permission of Academic Press*).

involved when children learn to read. The first level of the LaBerge and Samuels model involves feature detectors processing lines, angles, curvature, closedness, etc. As reading progresses, succeeding stages develop so that the features are transformed into graphemes and these in turn into orthographic patterns. Eventually word codes are activated and occasionally word-group codes. There are other linkages which start at the featural level, bypass several stages and directly activate orthographic and word patterns. Figure 8.1 illustrates how visual memory (as described in their paper) might be arranged at one particular 'snapshot' of development. This part of the model is derived from many sources suggesting a similar organization (e.g. Bower, 1972; Gibson, 1971; Morton, 1969; Selfridge, 1959). However, the theoretical contribution of LaBerge and Samuels was to suggest a central mechanism, called an 'attention centre', which is necessary for the activation of certain codes (these will be called *attention codes* here and are illustrated by open circles in Figure 8.1), whereas others which are well learned can be activated without such assistance (these will be called *non-attention codes* and are illustrated by solid circles in the figure), although strictly speaking they are occasionally activated by attention. The onset of a stimulus can activate a code and a signal is sent to the attention centre which then increases the activation of that code, but only that one code. Only the well-learned non-attention codes can attract attention, but may be unable to do so if attention is active elsewhere. This aspect makes more sense if one views the non-attention codes normally operating automatically, outside conscious control, but having the facility of being attended to if necessary.

LaBerge and Samuels break down the stages of learning letters into, first, a stage in which successive discriminations train the child to look for particular relevant features; in the second stage, attention is used to construe a letter code (a higher-order unit). This newly created unit rapidly decays, but leaves successive traces with each activation until a trace is consolidated to produce a higher-order unit. This is a very similar mechanism to that proposed by Hebb (1949). When this higher-order unit is established there is no further need for attentional activation and at this point the processing up to the letter code is automatic. Experimental support came by presenting fluent readers with a letter-matching task involving familiar letters or non-familiar letters (LaBerge, 1973). Although there was an initial disparity in latencies, after five days of practice the matching of unfamiliar letters was just as fast as the matching of familiar letters. The initial disparity was attributed to the additional time necessary to process the features of the unfamiliar letters which required attentional resources. The convergence of latencies after five days suggested the gradual removal of attentional resources as processing of the unfamiliar letters achieved automaticity.

At a deeper level in the hierarchy of the visual-processing system there are codes representing the visual appearance of spelling patterns (e.g. -tion). At the next level, visual representations of whole words would be formed based on combinations of the previous spelling patterns. Again, the codes are either attentional or not depending on the extent to which they are learned. In phonological memory there are codes directly evoked from corresponding codes within visual memory. Thus the phonological system would operate in a highly similar manner. This means that the blending of the elements of a word may take place in either or both of the visual and phonological systems. Similarly, either or both systems can evoke the meaning of the word within semantic memory. As an illustration of how the visual system might do this, the homonyms *bread* and *bred* generate identical phonological codes but nevertheless evoke different meanings for the fluent reader, indicating a route from letter-processing to semantic coding bypassing phonological coding.

To summarize the model, LaBerge and Samuels suggest the development of a hierarchy of skills in learning to read. At the current level of development of the hierarchy, attentional resources are required in order to process information. As soon as these processes become automatic this releases resources for concentrating on processes at the next level in the hierarchy. They further suggest separating these individual skills for the purposes of coaching them in the appropriate sequence. However, Taylor and Taylor (1983) believe it more appropriate to train subskills together because of the difficulties in defining the boundary of each subskill, the possible effects of boredom in concentrating on only one skill and the problem of reintegrating the subskills afterwards. LaBerge and Samuels' model of reading seems to provide a plausible description of how reading processes might develop using a phonics strategy (that is, concentrating on translating letters into individual sounds). However, not all aspects might be directly testable. The model has components and operations which seem to cover most eventualities, but this leaves it with a restricted ability to make specific predictions. The model offers an explanation of the underlying developing processes during initial reading and can explain aspects not known when their paper was written. For instance, why should children who have problems in phonemic processing be helped by training in phonemic processing and in the connections between phonemes and graphemes? According to LaBerge and Samuels, connections may take place between the visual codes and their phonological associates or between spelling patterns and their corresponding phonological units (e.g. /bas/ and /ket/ are two phonological units which combine to produce 'basket'). Presumably if there is an absence of the necessary phonological units, this would slow down reading. Similarly, the reading process could also facilitate the development of phonological units. Thus we have a picture of a hierarchical organization of skills which, if there is an area of dysfunction, will not continue to develop normally unless there is remedial training given to that particular area.

What the model does not seem to predict is that there are areas of cognition (such as in visual processing) which are relevant to the reading process where training does not seem to lead to a corresponding improvement in reading performance (see, for instance, Beech, 1985; Hulme, 1981; Vellutino, 1979). For instance, Bieger (1974) selected 54 children with poor perceptual abilities and divided them into equivalent experimental and control groups. The experimental group was given regular training in visual and spatial processing and seven months later had improved in perceptual processing, but there was no significant improvement in reading relative to the controls. However, this kind of finding may be because the training has not been of those visual aspects most relevant to the reading task. A less serious problem in the LaBerge and Samuels model is the almost implicit assumption that reading develops mainly by learning graphemic information before lexical information. Some, but not enough, allowance is made for the possibility of direct lexical coding. Another aspect of the reading process in which the model is inadequate is in explaining the modular structure of reading processes when the reader becomes skilled (see Chapter 11 and

Seidenberg, 1985). For instance, there is no real distinction between word identification via the grapheme–phoneme route, via reading vocabulary or by the use of analogy. Pathways are specified which can access graphemes or directly to visual codes of words, but this is not sufficient to specify the kinds of operational distinctions which have emerged between different modules. This will now be attempted.

The development of two modules

It could be argued that adult readers have a module (a 'semi-independent subsystem . . . performing a unique, specialist role' Allport, 1985, p.34) for grapheme–phoneme translation and another for the identification of whole words or morphemes on the basis of a lexicon (e.g. Coltheart, 1978; Morton and Patterson, 1980). Although this view has its critics (e.g. Humphries and Evett, 1985), how would dual-route processing evolve in a developing reader? It seems that the child could develop either mode of processing in the relative absence of the other, at least *prima facie*. However, what exactly do we mean by these two types of processing? Closer examination will demonstrate some similarity, sufficient to suggest the development of both types of processing mostly within the same structure, even if functional disparities might emerge later. In the case of the processing involved in iden-tifying words lexically, at one level this involves processes which store a representation of a visual pattern and representations of the collection of semantic codes associated with the word. What is interesting is the sugges-tion by Seymour and Elder (1986), studying lexical processors, that the visual representation is not some form of template of the pattern but a rudimentary analysis of some crude features of it.

The strategy of the child within a pure phonics teaching environment may be to break words down into smaller units corresponding to phonemes; consequently, a visual representation of each letter is stored along with a representation of each associated phoneme or phonemes. The phonemic representations need to be stored in the short term until they can be matched to a stored representation already in the child's lexicon. Nevertheless, the operations which are required by both types of process could be very similar, if not identical.

Visual analysis

In the case of graphemic coding, the unit of analysis, obviously, is each sin-gle grapheme constituting a word. The various features of the grapheme are analysed and the appropriate one from the set of stored graphemic represen-tations is retrieved. Logographic (feature-based) recognition (see Seymour, Chapter 2) by contrast involves a greater variety of visual information for analysis. First, the word itself forms a rough outline shape. In this sense, it is difficult to speculate on the exact nature of this representation; for instance, salient patterns within the word shape might also be coded. Secondly, salient graphemes are coded within the word. This would be done by a rapid analysis of the graphemes, identifying those with which the reader is familiar. Finally, spatial and order information of the constituent graphemes might be noted as described in detail earlier. It is likely that this particular information is subordinate to constituent information, as a distortion of this by Seymour and Elder did not seriously disrupt processing by children using an exclusively whole-word approach. Thus at the stage of visual analysis there is the greatest similarity between individual letter coding and lexical analysis. The unit being processed in both cases undergoes an analysis of its visual features. Then, or concurrently, the collection of features may be sufficient to access a stored representation corresponding to these features. This might be achieved via processes described in the LaBerge and Samuels model.

Retrieving a phonemic code

This is the point of disparity between the two modes of processing, as in the case of lexical processing there is probably an intervening stage before a phonological code is accessed. By contrast, in individual-letter coding the initial letter is processed and a phonological representation should be retrieved. Sometimes no phonological representation will be retrieved; either way, the sequence of letters will be processed in serial. Perhaps as greater automaticity is achieved there will be an increasing overlap in generating the phonological representation of the nth grapheme and generating the phonological representation of the $(n + 1)$th grapheme to become a cascade-like process (McClelland, 1979). Suppose the phonemic representations are stored in the short term in a sequence of slots corresponding with the number of sounds in the words. Some slots may have a representation signifying that the particular phoneme is unidentified whereas others may contain one or more putative phonemes which are acoustically similar (e.g. /t/ and /d/). These representations, as they are assembled, would then form the basis for initiating a search for the appropriate word in the lexicon.

Henderson (1985b) has considered the problems posed by such an analysis. Problems arise because a grapheme or graphic unit can represent one or more phonemes (e.g. *sh*, *ch* represent one phoneme normally and *th* represents two as in *there* and *thesis*) and, even worse, most vowel digraphs need not consistently represent one or more phonemes (e.g. consider how *ie* is represented in *diet*, *lenient* and *thief*). Henderson goes on to outline problems in relying solely on grapheme–phoneme translation. However, in the beginning phase of reading the words encountered are usually reasonably regular, even though the vowels in particular will always potentially generate alternative phonemes. The value of Henderson's arguments is to appreciate that reading at a more advanced level must involve much more than grapheme–phoneme translation. Nevertheless, assembling putative phonemes and matching with a known representation in the lexicon is not an implausible strategy for the beginning reader, especially one taught explicitly by the phonics method.

Lexical coding, or logographic feature-based processing, produces a rich collection of features which are matched with stored semantic representations of words. This can induce several possible states when encountering a word. The child may be completely unable to match the word to any stored representation and concludes that the word is not within reading vocabulary. Secondly, the word may elicit several semantic representations and the preceding context may help to disambiguate the precise semantic form (cf Adams and Huggins). Finally, the subject may know the word very well and retrieve the precise response. In the other cases, knowing the meaning of the word may not evoke the precise phonemic code. There is not such an obvious similarity between the graphemic and lexical strategies at this juncture; certainly, they both require a combination of features in order to retrieve information. However, the information in one case is phonological and in the other it is semantic, leading on later, if successful or necessary, to a phonological representation.

In most school systems children learn by a combination of the two methods. How might these two approaches to processing coexist, if at all, within the same processing system? It follows from the preceding discussion that this would present no problem for the initial analysis of visual features. There would be parallel processing of the overall shape and pattern, the individual graphemes and their spatial order. During the course of this processing there would be access to semantic and phonological information. One possibility is that there is a rapid scan of the graphemes (in the absence of phonemic translation), identifying those which are familiar. This would be sufficient, along with processing the overall shape of the word, to initiate a search for a semantic representation; but meanwhile (or afterwards) a slower scan, converting each grapheme or graphic unit into a phonemic representation, would produce some form of sequence of phonemes or phonemic possibilities. The effect of the build-up of information over time would be to increase the probability of identification. The interesting question is how the two systems might eventually emerge as being distinctive from one another. Over the course of development, the rapid scanning of the graphemes will more frequently trigger the word before the generation of the phonological code is complete. The slower phonemic generation system, which was exceedingly useful during the early stages of reading, may at the mature stage only be needed for reading nonsense sequences of letters or low-frequency words whose spoken form may be known to the reader (e.g. McCusker, Hillinger and Bias, 1981). The process of rapidly scanning the graphemes may eventually become very fast to the point of being an apparently automatic process. A similar possibility is that the overall visual configuration is learned so that eventually the wholistic representation of the word enables the immediate access of a semantic representation. An implication of this explanation is that the early reader develops a structure to assist processing which gradually changes its function with maturity. Nevertheless, there is evidence that assisting the development of this grapheme-to-phoneme structure facilitates reading in the early stages, even though it may not be absolutely necessary for later development.

In adult reading it is possible that the prefix is identified and removed and then the stem morpheme is used as a basis for lexical access (e.g. Taft, 1981, 1985; Taft and Forster, 1975). Once the prefix is stripped, serial processing, as previously described, might then take place on the morpheme. This would have the virtue of economy of processing as the number of necessary lexical entries would reduce substantially. It is likely that prefix stripping would be a process that develops at some later phase in reading, but research is needed to look into the question of how the processing of the prefix changes over the course of development. However, Carr and Pollatsek (1985) raise some problems with the prefix-stripping hypothesis: in particular, it would be possible to explain current findings on adults in terms of postlexical prefix-stripping with initial lexical processing depending on the entire graphemic pattern.

Learning to read by other means

One major alternative way of reading is by retrieving an analogous orthographic pattern from reading vocabulary to facilitate the identification of a word (e.g. Baron, 1977; Glushko, 1979; Henderson, 1982; Kay and Marcel, 1981; Marcel, 1980). As pointed out by Glushko, if the adult reader is presented with a non-word such as *vate* a response may well be produced which rhymes with *rate*. Such a production could be the result of using grapheme–phoneme rules, but it could also be produced by matching with the familiar orthographic pattern *-ate* or by the use of an analogy with a real word such as *late*. The implication of analogy theory, according to Patterson and Morton (1985), is that decoding is based only on phonological and orthographic representations of known words. This means that no abstract rules are used which connect orthographic segments to their corresponding phonological representations. This entails locating the word or words which possess the relevant orthographic sequence, retrieving the corresponding phonological representation and assembling a pronunciation.

If a beginning reader were to use such a strategy, the strategy could not begin until a set of words had already been learned. Furthermore, if the child used a lexical strategy there could conceivably be confusion between words of similar orthographic appearance rather than a facilitatory effect. Suppose the child encounters a word similar in appearance to an already learned word. It has previously been suggested that a discrimination net mechanism is used to differentiate the words by taking special note of the graphemic features constituting the difference. By contrast, analogy would work by identifying similarity between the two printed words, segmenting the common orthographic pattern and attempting to generate a phonological code. Perhaps in many cases this could be facilitated by generating the phonological codes for both words and identifying commonality across the two acoustic sequences. This would be where phonemic awareness would be an asset (see Chapter 9 for an elaboration). However, difficulties might be encountered when trying to tag a graphemic difference onto a particular word while assigning a common orthographic pattern onto both the words.

It is interesting to speculate on the changing information which is stored about any particular word over time. Using an analogical strategy, the phonological representation of the word might have connected with it part of the orthographic pattern of another word (call it x) and perhaps two separated graphemes. On the next occasion another orthographic pattern from word y might be connected and perhaps a different grapheme. As this continues, with the accumulated knowledge of further words, or the same words, there will be an increasing strength in certain graphemic combinations; furthermore, other words (and perhaps their semantic associations) might gain stronger connections. Eventually the printed word might evoke the phonological representation without recourse to generating an analogy, or at least by retrieving appropriate orthographic units (this last process could be non-analogical using the definition of Patterson and Morton). In fact, the word may itself be used as the basis for generating an analogy with new words.

Goswami (1986) (see also Chapter 9 in this volume) presents evidence that this process of reading by analogy might occur from the beginning of learning to read. Such a mode of processing is less efficient than a grapheme–phoneme mode but could be more efficient than a whole-word mode because there would be an eventual economy in storing a common orthographic pattern assigned to several words. Given that it has been suggested that the lexical and grapheme–phoneme modes share common processes, it is plausible that reading by analogy would also share such processes. The main difference from the other two modes would be that the unit of analysis would be more complicated. In the case of the first two modes, the units of analysis consisting of identifying individual letters or whole words should be fairly easy. However, when using analogy, the decision that has to be made about the boundary or boundaries within the word is a more difficult one. For instance, identification of *shepherd* would become very difficult if this were broken into *she* and *pherd*, as might be likely if the reader is familiar with the word *she* and aware that *ph* is normally pronounced /f/. Another problem is that although Patterson and Morton have distinguished analogical analysis from orthographic analysis, in practice this might be difficult to define operationally. In one sense reading by analogy might involve retrieving a familiar orthographic segment which is a constituent of several words (e.g. *-ful*), rather than retrieving a particular word which contains this segment. Perhaps in the beginning the child uses whole-word analogies but passes through a continuum until orthographic segments are used without reference to any particular instance of a word or words.

CONCLUSION

An attempt has been made to examine some of the likely developing mechanisms during the course of early reading development. Reading develops like any other skill in terms of the development of a hierarchy of subskills because this is the most efficient form of organization. The LaBerge and Samuels model was examined in detail as an example, in particular, of how featural information could be organized and processed. It was seen that, in addition to the necessity for visual processing, it was important to establish a knowledge of individual sounds in words and to learn the correspondences between phonemes and graphemes. A discussion of the use of contextual information concluded that the use of such information depended on the level of concordance with existing knowledge. Thus if a word were either very familiar or unfamiliar, contextual information would not be useful but would be useful for words of intermediate familiarity. There are three possible distinctive ways of processing words in adults, namely lexical, grapheme–phoneme translation and by the use of analogy. Examining the processes involved it was concluded that these modes are in part sufficiently similar to suggest a sharing of processing mechanisms during the early phase of reading. However, eventually the whole-word (or lexical) strategy probably becomes most dominant as it gradually becomes the most efficient way of rapidly processing text. Finally, although there has been much discussion about the development of the processes and structures in reading, no attempt was made to suggest the sequence of development of these operations. Such a description would have to be confined to populations taught in a highly specific manner, and even then it is not likely that there would be a sequence of discrete stages through which all the children progressed. It is most likely that the majority of readers develop a combination of strategies in order to acquire meaning from print, rather than develop them in a set sequence.

ACKNOWLEDGMENTS

I am grateful to A.M. Colley, A.W. Ellis, L. Henderson and P.H.K. Seymour for their comments on a first draft of this chapter.

REFERENCES

Adams, M.J. (1980). Failures to comprehend and levels of processing in reading. In R.J. Spiro, B.C. Bruce and W.F. Brewer (Eds.) *Theoretical Issues in Reading Comprehension*. Hillsdale, N.J.: Erlbaum.

Adams, M.J., and Huggins, A.W.F. (1985). The growth of children's sight vocabulary: A quick test with educational and theoretical implications. *Reading Research Quarterly*, **20**, 262-281.

Allport, D.A. (1985). Distributed memory, modular subsystems and dysphasia. In S. Newman and R. Epstein (Eds.) *Current Perspectives in Dysphasia*. Edinburgh: Churchill Livingstone.

Baron, J. (1977). Mechanisms for pronouncing printed words: Use and acquisition. In D. LaBerge and S.J. Samuels (Eds.) *Basic Processes in Reading: Perception and Comprehension*. Hillsdale, N.J.: Erlbaum.

Barr, R. (1974). The effect of instruction on pupils' reading strategies. *Reading Research Quarterly*, **10**, 555-582.

Beech, J.R. (1985). *Learning to Read: A Cognitive Approach to Reading and Poor Reading*. London: Croom Helm.

Beech, J.R., and Harding, L.M. (1984). Phonemic processing and the poor reader from the developmental lag point of view. *Reading Research Quarterly*, **19**, 357-366.

Bieger, E. (1974). Effectiveness of visual perceptual training on reading skills of non-readers: An experimental study. *Perceptual and Motor Skills*, **38**, 1147-53.

Biemiller, A. (1970). The development of the use of graphic and contextual information as children learn to read. *Reading Research Quarterly*, **6**, 75-96.

Bower, G.H. (1972). A selective review of organizational factors in memory. In E. Tulving and W. Donaldson (Eds.) *Organization in Memory*. New York: Academic Press.

Bradley, L., and Bryant, P.E. (1983). Categorizing sounds and learning to read: A causal connection. *Nature*, **301**, 419-421.

Bryant, P.E., and Bradley, L. (1985). *Children's Reading Problems*. Oxford: Blackwell.

Campbell, R., and Butterworth, B. (1985). Phonological dyslexia and dysgraphia in a highly literate subject: a developmental case and associated deficits of phonemic awareness. *Quarterly Journal of Experimental Psychology*, **37A**, 435-475.

Carr, T.H., and Pollatsek, A. (1985). Recognizing printed words: A look at current models. In D. Besner, T.G. Waller and G.E. Mackinnon (Eds.) *Reading Research: Advances in Theory and Practice*, Vol. 5. Orlando, Fl.: Academic Press.

Coltheart, M. (1978). Lexical access in simple reading tasks. In G. Underwood (Ed.) *Strategies of Information Processing*. London: Academic Press.

Coltheart, M. (1979). When can children learn to read—and when should they be taught? In T.G. Waller and G.E. MacKinnon (Eds.) *Reading Research: Advances in Theory and Practice*, Vol. 1. New York: Academic Press.

Ellis, A.W. (1984). *Reading, Writing and Dyslexia: A Cognitive Analysis*. Hillsdale, N.J.: Erlbaum.

Farmer, A.R., Nixon, M., and White, R.T. (1976). Sound blending and learning to read: An experimental investigation. *British Journal of Educational Psychology*, **46**, 155-163.

Fox, B., and Routh, D.K. (1980). Phonemic analysis and severe reading disability in children. *Journal of Psycholinguistic Research*, **9**, 115-120.

Frith, U. (1985). Beneath the surface of developmental dyslexia. In K.E. Patterson, J.C. Marshall and M. Coltheart (Eds.) *Surface Dyslexia: Neuropsychological and Cognitive Studies of Phonological Reading*. London: Erlbaum.

Gibson, E.J. (1971). Perceptual learning and the theory of word perception. *Cognitive Psychology*, **2**, 351-368.

Glushko, R.J. (1979). The organization and activation of orthographic knowledge in reading aloud. *Journal of Experimental Psychology: Human Perception and Performance*, **5**, 674-691.

Goodman, K.S. (1967). Reading: A psycholinguistic guessing game. *Journal of the Reading Specialist*, **6**, 126-135.

Goodman, K.S. (1969). Analysis of oral reading miscues: Applied psycholinguistics. *Reading Research Quarterly*, **5**, 9-30.

Goswami, U. (1986). Children's use of analogy in learning to read: A developmental study. *Journal of Experimental Child Psychology*, **42**, 73-83.

Harding, L.M., Beech, J.R., and Sneddon, W. (1985). The changing pattern of reading errors and reading style from 5 to 11 years of age. *British Journal of Educational Psychology*, **55**, 45-52.

Hebb, D.O. (1949). *The Organization of Behavior*. New York: Wiley.

Henderson, L. (1982). *Orthography and Word Recognition in Reading*. London: Academic Press.

Henderson, L. (1985a). On the use of the term 'grapheme'. *Language and Cognitive Processes*, **1**, 135-148.

Henderson, L. (1985b). Issues in the modelling of pronunciation assembly in normal reading. In K.E. Patterson, J.C. Marshall and M. Coltheart (Eds.) *Surface Dyslexia: Neuropsychological and Cognitive Studies of Phonological Reading*. London: Erlbaum.

Henderson, L., and Chard, J. (1980). The reader's implicit knowledge of orthographic structure. In U. Frith (Ed.) *Cognitive Approaches to Spelling*. London: Academic Press.

Hulme, C. (1981). *Reading Retardation and Multi-sensory Teaching*. London: Routledge & Kegan Paul.

Humphries, G.W., and Evett, L.J. (1985). Are there independent lexical and nonlexical routes in word processing? An evaluation of the dual-route theory of reading. *The Behavioral and Brain Sciences*, **8**, 689-740.

Jorm, A.F., and Share, D.L. (1983). Phonological recoding and reading acquisition. *Applied Psycholinguistics*, **4**, 103-147.

Kay, J., and Marcel, T. (1981). One process, not two, in reading aloud: lexical analogies do the work of non-lexical rules. *Quarterly Journal of Experimental Psychology*, **33A**, 397-413.

Kochnower, J., Richardson, E., and DiBenedetto, B. (1983). A comparison of the phonic decoding ability of normal and learning disabled children. *Journal of Learning Disabilities*, **16**, 348-351.

LaBerge, D. (1973). Attention and the measurement of perceptual learning. *Memory and Cognition*, **1**, 268-276.

LaBerge, D., and Samuels, S.J. (1974). Toward a theory of automatic information processing in reading. *Cognitive Psychology,* **6**, 293-323.

Liberman, I.Y., and Shankweiler, D. (1976). Speech, the alphabet, and teaching to read. In L. Resnick and P. Weaver (Eds.) *Theory and Practice of Early Reading.* Vol. 2. Hillsdale, N.J.: Erlbaum.

Liberman, I.Y., Shankweiler, D., Fischer, F. W., and Carter, B. (1974). Explicit syllable and phoneme segmentation in the young child. *Journal of Experimental Child Psychology,* **18**, 201-212.

Marcel, T. (1980). Surface dyslexia and beginning reading: a revised hypothesis of the pronunciation of print and its impairments. In M. Coltheart, K. Patterson and J.C. Marshall (Eds.) *Deep Dyslexia.* London: Routledge & Kegan Paul.

Marsh, G., Friedman, M., Welch, V., and Desberg, P. (1981). A cognitive-developmental theory of reading acquisition. In G.E. MacKinnon and T.G. Waller (Eds.) *Reading Research: Advances in Theory and Practice,* Vol. 3. New York: Academic Press.

Massaro, D.W., and Hestand, J. (1983). Developmental relations between reading ability and knowledge of orthographic structure. *Contemporary Educational Psychology,* **8**, 174-180.

McClelland, J.L. (1979). On the time relations of mental processes: An examination of processes in cascade. *Psychological Review,* **86**, 287-330.

McCusker, L.X., Hillinger, M.L., and Bias, R.G. (1981). Phonological recoding and reading. *Psychological Bulletin,* **89**, 217-245.

Mitchell, D.C. (1982). *The Process of Reading: A Cognitive Analysis of Fluent Reading and Learning to Read.* Chichester: Wiley.

Morais, J., Cary, L., Alegria, J., and Bertelson, P. (1979). Does awareness of speech as a sequence of phones arise spontaneously? *Cognition,* **7**, 323-331.

Morton, J. (1969). The interaction of information of information in word recognition. *Psychological Review,* **76**, 165-178.

Morton, J. (1980). The logogen model and orthographic structure. In U. Frith (Ed.) *Cognitive Processes in Spelling.* London: Academic Press.

Morton, J., and Patterson, K.E. (1980). A new attempt at an interpretation, or, an attempt at a new interpretation. In M. Coltheart, K.E. Patterson and J.C. Marshall (Eds.) *Deep Dyslexia.* London: Routledge & Kegan Paul.

Palermo, D.S., and Molfese, D.L. (1972). Language acquisition from age five onward. *Psychological Bulletin,* **78**, 409-427.

Patterson, K.E., and Morton, J. (1985). From orthography to phonology: an attempt at an old interpretation. In K.E. Patterson, J.C. Marshall and M. Coltheart (Eds.). *Surface Dyslexia: Neuropsychological and Cognitive Studies of Phonological Reading.* London: Erlbaum.

Perfetti, C.A. (1985). *Reading Ability.* New York: Oxford University Press.

Perfetti, C.A., Beck, I.L., and Hughes, C. (1981). *Phonemic Knowledge and Learning to Read.* Paper presented at the Society for Research in Child Development, Boston, MA.

Perfetti, C.A., and Roth, S.F. (1981). Some of the interactive processes in reading and their role in reading skill. In A. Lesgold and C.A. Perfetti (Eds.) *Interactive Processes in Reading.* Hillsdale, N.J.: Erlbaum.

Pring, L., and Snowling, M. (1986). Developmental changes in word recognition: An information-processing account. *Quarterly Journal of Experimental Psychology,* **38A**, 395-418.

Schvaneveldt, R., Ackerman, B.P., and Semlear, T. (1977). The effect of semantic context on children's word recognition. *Child Development,* **48**, 612-616.

Seidenberg, M.S. (1985). The time course of information activation and utilization in visual word recognition. In D. Besner, T.G. Waller and G.E. MacKinnon (Eds.) *Reading Research: Advances in Theory and Practice*, Vol. 5. Orlando, Fl.: Academic Press.

Selfridge, O.G. (1959). Pandemonium: a paradigm for learning. In *Mechanisation of Thought Processes*, Vol. 1. London: HMSO.

Seymour, P.H.K., and Elder, L. (1986). Beginning reading without phonology. *Cognitive Neuropsychology*, **3**, 1-36.

Schankweiler, D., and Liberman, I.Y. (1972). Misreading: A search for causes. In J.F. Kavanagh and I.G. Mattingly (Eds.) *Language by Ear and by Eye*. Cambridge, Mass.: MIT.

Snowling, M. (1980). The development of grapheme–phoneme correspondence in normal and dyslexic readers. *Journal of Experimental Child Psychology*, **29**, 294-305.

Stanovich, K.E. (1986). Cognitive processes and the reading problems of learning disabled children: Evaluating the assumption of specificity. In J.K. Torgesen and B.Y.L. Wong (Eds.) *Psychological and Educational Perspectives on Learning Disabilities*. New York: Academic Press.

Stanovich, K.E., Cunningham, P.E., and Feeman, D.J. (1984). Relation between early reading acquisition and word decoding with and without context: A longitudinal study of first-grade children. *Journal of Educational Psychology*, **76**, 668-677.

Steinberg, D.D., and Steinberg, M.T. (1975). Reading before speaking. *Visible Language*, **9**, 197-224.

Taft, M. (1981). Prefix stripping revisited. *Journal of Verbal Learning and Verbal Behavior*, **20**, 289-297.

Taft, M. (1985). The decoding of words in lexical access: A review of the morphographic approach. In D. Besner, T.G. Waller and G.E. Mackinnon (Eds.) *Reading Research: Advances in Theory and Practice*, Vol. 5. Orlando, Fl.: Academic Press.

Taft, M., and Forster, K.I. (1975). Lexical storage and retrieval of prefixed words. *Journal of Verbal Learning and Verbal Behavior*, **14**, 638-647.

Taylor, I., and Taylor, M.M. (1983). *The Psychology of Reading*. New York: Academic Press.

Treiman, R., and Hirsh-Pasek, K. (1985). Are there qualitative differences between dyslexic and normal readers? *Memory and Cognition*, **13**, 357-364.

Underwood, G., and Briggs, P. (1984). The development of word recognition processes. *British Journal of Psychology*, **75**, 243-255.

Vellutino, F.R. (1979). *Dyslexia: Theory and Research*. Cambridge, Mass: MIT Press.

Williams, P. (1976). Early reading: Some unexplained aspects. In J.E. Merritt (Ed.) *New Horizons in Reading: Proceedings of the Fifth IRA Conference on Reading*. Newark, Del.: International Reading Association.

Cognitive approaches to reading
Edited by J. R. Beech and A. M. Colley

CHAPTER 9

Phonological Awareness and Learning to Read

PETER BRYANT AND USHA GOSWAMI

Department of Experimental Psychology, University of Oxford

INTRODUCTION

One of the most plausible ideas about learning to read is that it must depend to some extent on an awareness that words can be broken up into constituent sounds. Reading English (and most other orthographies) involves learning about the relations between sounds and alphabetic letters. It is hard to see how children could learn to decode print or to spell words without understanding that individual letters often represent the sounds in words.

The idea that phonological awareness plays an important role in learning is a causal hypothesis. The idea is that one of the two skills (phonological awareness) affects and partly determines the course of the other (reading and spelling), and thus that the extent of a child's phonological prowess decides (or at least partly decides) how well he or she learns to read. Causal hypotheses are never easy to settle, and we should not be surprised that people trying to answer this one have met problems. These problems are the main subject of our chapter.

TRAINING STUDIES

Rationale

This causal hypothesis predicts that successful training in phonological awareness should improve reading. Such training experiments have to fulfil several essential requirements. One is that they should include adequate control groups. Training in phonological awareness inevitably involves experiences with factors which have nothing to do with the hypothesis *per se*, such as one-to-one contact with an adult and experience with pictures and books. Control groups are needed to rule out the influence of these extra factors. Unseen control groups are quite inadequate.

The second requirement is a sharp separation between the independent variable, phonological awareness, and the dependent variable, the child's progress in reading. The training should be in phonological awareness (the independent variable) and should not involve reading directly. Several training experiments have involved experience with written material. This is an unsatisfactory test. If you think that A causes B, you test this by training A and measuring the effect on B, and not by training A and B together and looking at the effect on B.

The third requirement is that the outcome measures should be a genuine test of reading. Tasks which are merely analogous to reading, such as deciphering nonsense words or associating abstract symbols and sounds, are inadequate. They may have nothing to do with real reading.

Training studies with unseen control groups

One of the best-known training studies is a project by Wallach and Wallach (1976), who trained low-SES first-graders in various skills including alphabet sound training, awareness of initial sounds and oral segmentation. The children were also taught to connect written and spoken sounds and words. Wallach and Wallach found that the trained group were significantly better than their (unseen) controls in measures of reading, which included single-word reading, comprehension and consonant-sound tests. This looks like strong evidence that phonological training helps in learning to read. But Wallach and Wallach relied on an unseen control group and used written material in the training. So the gains made by the experimental group could have been the result of extraneous experiences in the training programme.

Much the same strengths and weaknesses characterize another well-known training study. Williams (1980) studied children between the ages of seven and twelve. Some were taught to identify the beginning, middle and end sounds in words, but this training was linked to written letters and words. The remaining children were given no training at all. The training group did much better than the control group in a reading test, but the results are hard to interpret because the control group received no attention and because there was no control for the extra experience with written material.

Training studies with inadequate outcome measures

Unrealistic material has been used in the final-outcome measures in several well-known training studies. An example is the study by Fox and Routh

(1976), who trained four-year-olds to blend sounds and compared their reading task to that of a group of untrained children. Half the children in each group were already proficient at segmentation (dividing words into either syllables or phonemes) and the rest were not. The reading task required the children to associate letter-like forms with spoken sounds and then to read two lists of words made up from pairs of these forms—tests which may or may not be related to genuine reading. Fox and Routh found some training effects, but only among the children who were already good segmenters.

Later Fox and Routh (1984) compared the effects of training some six-year-olds in segmentation, and some in segmentation and blending (forming words from either syllables or phonemes). There were two unseen control groups, one of which was already proficient in segmentation. Fox and Routh compared all four groups on their reading analogue task and found training effects, but only among the children who were taught both to segment and to blend. Only they, and the proficiently segmenting control group, were able to cope with the reading task. It is hard to form a definite conclusion from these two studies. Put together, they could suggest that training on the two skills together does lead to improvement, but it is impossible to say what skills were measured in the reading analogue task.

Skjelfjord (1985), a Norwegian psychologist, added some weight to the idea that training in segmentation helps children to learn to read. His hypothesis was that children can segment before they can blend and that segmenting is based on the use of articulatory cues while blending is a consequence of experiences derived from segmenting. His method for training children to segment was to concentrate on one sound at a time and to encourage the children to attend to articulatory cues. He reports the results of a training study by Carlsten (1984), who trained six-year-old children for 20 weeks by this method and compared their performance in tasks which involved segmenting, blending and reading nonsense words to that of controls who had received the normal run of teaching during the same period. The experimental group surpassed the controls in all three measures. However, the outcome measures were inadequate: we cannot tell whether the children would also have been better at reading real words.

We must make the same comment about work by Haddock (1976). She took five-year-olds and divided them into three groups. One received auditory training in blending, another auditory–visual training and the third group (the controls) learned letter–sound correspondences. The children were tested before and after the training on reading nonsense words. The auditory–visual group read more of them than the auditory group, who read more words than the control group. However, one cannot be sure about the effects of Haddock's blending training until we know what would have happened with real words.

The same criticism can be made about an attempt by Treiman and Baron (1983) to show a connection between phonological training and reading single words. They gave five- and six-year-old children two conditions. One involved training in segmenting nonsense syllables orally, the other in repeating such syllables. In each condition there was a second phase: the children had to read the same syllables in written form. Thus they might be taught 'hig', 'lem', 'hem' and 'lig' and then be tested on their reading of 'h', 'em', 'hem' and 'lig'. In the experimental condition, experience with segments of a syllable ('h', 'em' and 'hem') helped the children to some extent to read the full syllable (in this example the children were better at reading 'hem' than 'lig') although the effect was not significant. The opposite pattern was found in the control condition, where the children were better at reading the unrelated items ('lig' in this example). There is a clear effect here but there is no guarantee that it is related to reading real words.

Studies in which training involves the dependent as well as the independent variable

In some training studies elements of reading are involved in the actual intervention. For example, Goldstein (1976), in an otherwise admirable study, gave an experimental and a control group of four-year-olds a blending and a segmentation test. Then he gave the experimental group reading instruction, which involved learning about letter–sound correspondences and blending. The other group was taught letter names. After this training the children in the first of these groups were able to read more words than the other children. The controls in this study were impressive, but we still need to know whether training in phonological awareness on its own improves reading. Goldstein's results do not establish whether the experimental group's phonological experiences *per se* or the combination of these experiences with written material produced the effects.

Attempts to train phonological awareness on its own and to use realistic reading measures

We known of only two such studies. One was carried out by Olofsson and Lundberg (1985) with a follow-up by Olofsson (1985). Ninety-five children (mean age 6:11) were divided into experimental and control groups. The experimental groups were given training in rhyming, segmentation and blending, while the control groups either participated in a 'non-verbal auditory training programme' or were given 'normal Swedish preschool experiences'. A year later, 83 of these children were given tests of spelling, of silent reading and of reading irregular words. The results were disappointing. 'Great variances, ceiling effects and group heterogeneity created many difficulties' (p.21). Another problem was that the control group started at a higher reading level than the experimental group children. The two groups reached much the same level in the post-tests, and in fact the control children did rather better than the others at silent reading. However, after adjustments were made for initial reading level, the experimental group was significantly better at spelling and reading irregular words but there were no differences between the groups in silent reading. The result with irregular words must be discounted because there was a serious ceiling effect in this test.

Olofsson's follow-up (1985) a year later showed continuing qualitative effects but no lasting improvement in reading and spelling. He found that most of the experimental group's spelling errors tended to be 'rule-governed'. Even when they made mistakes, they followed phonological rules. In contrast, the controls produced more non-phonological spellings.

The second study dealt with the categorization of words by sounds (rhyme and alliteration). Bradley and Bryant (1983) took 65 six-year-old children and split them into four matched groups. One was trained over a period of two years in sound categorization. A second was trained for one year in sound categorization and for the second year both in sound categorization and in relationships between the sounds and alphabetic letters. A third (control) group was taught to categorize the same words semantically and the final group was an unseen control. A year or more later the children were given standardized tests of reading, spelling and mathematics.

The most important comparison was between the group trained just in sound categorization and the group trained in semantic categorization. A difference between these two groups would be strong evidence for a causal link between phonological awareness and reading. In fact the first group was ahead by three to four months on all the standardized tests of reading and spelling, but there was a fair amount of error variance and the difference was not significant. The group trained in sounds and letters was significantly better than the two control groups. Although this result has some practical significance, it does not take us any further forward with the question about the effects of phonological awareness. This study included no controls for the extra experience which the successful group had with alphabetic letters.

Conclusion

There is little to conclude from these studies, beset as they are by problems of unseen control groups (Fox and Routh, Wallach, Williams), unbalanced designs (Fox and Routh), narrow and unrealistic post-tests (Fox and Routh, Treiman and Baron) and insignificant effects (Bradley and Bryant, Fox and Routh, Goldstein, Olofsson and Lundberg). We cannot yet conclude that training in phonological skills has an effect on reading, although combining such training with experience with alphabetic letters does lead to considerable improvements. Training studies are an essential link in the chain of any argument about cause and effect. As far as the role of phonological awareness is concerned, that link is a weak one.

CORRELATIONAL EVIDENCE

A minimum requirement for any hypothesis that children's phonological awareness influences their progress in reading is that these two skills should be strongly related. The correlation should remain significant after controls have been put in for other variables, such as IQ or verbal ability, which might influence both skills. The most that correlational studies can do is to establish a connection between the two skills. On their own, they cannot be used to test a causal hypothesis. It is often impossible to work out whether the phonological skill being tested is a cause or a result of learning to read, and there is also a third possibility which no correlational study can exclude: it is that neither of the skills in question affects the other but that both are determined by some third factor.

One-to-one correspondence tasks

One commonly adopted way of testing children's awareness of the phonemes in words is to ask them to represent the number of phonemes in words which they hear. For example, Calfee, Lindamood and Lindamood (1973) asked children aged from six to eighteen to arrange coloured blocks to represent sounds which were either discrete units, like s-s-n, or integrated units, like 'ips'. This was more difficult to do with integrated units than with discrete units. There was also a strong relationship between segmentation, and reading and spelling. However, this relationship could simply be the product of the children's different intelligence levels: IQ was not partialled out.

   Liberman *et al.*, (1974) asked children aged four, five and six years to segment words by tapping with a wooden dowel. They had to tap once either for each syllable in a word ('popsicle' = three taps) or for each phoneme ('toy' = three taps). All the children were able to segment the words into syllables. The phonemic segmentation task was far more difficult: only 17 per cent of the five- and 70 per cent of the six-year-olds reached criterion and the four-year-olds could not manage the task. Later many of the children were given a standardized test of reading which showed that those who had had most difficulty with the phoneme task had also made least progress in reading. The authors concluded that there was a connection between phonological awareness and reading. However, there is nothing here to establish the direction of cause and effect.

Tunmer and Nesdale (1985) also established a relationship between scores in the phoneme-tapping task and reading. Six-year-old children had to tap out the sounds in words which either contained digraphs or did not. Their success with the latter group of words was strongly related to their reading scores—a relationship which was significant even after their verbal skills (as measured by a vocabulary test) were partialled out. This could either mean that the children's experiences in reading determined their performance in the tapping task or *vice versa*. We shall see later that another result in this study does suggest a considerable influence of knowledge gained from reading on the phonological task.

One problem with the tapping method is that it is a rhythmic test, and, since the rhythm of a word is captured in its syllables and not in its phonemes, that fact alone could account for the superiority of syllables over phonemes. Treiman and Baron (1981) showed that this objection is not a pertinent one. The children in their study had to put down a counter for each phoneme or syllable in nonsense stimuli spoken by the experimenter. The results were similar to those of Liberman *et al.* with their tapping test: phonemes were harder to count than syllables and between six and seven there was a sharp improvement in the phoneme, task. However, reading scores did not correlate with performance in the phoneme-counting task but did correlate with performance in the syllable-counting task.

This lack of a consistent relationship with reading is worrying. Further cause for alarm comes from two other projects, both of which suggest that the ability to count phonemes is largely a product of learning to read. Ehri and Wilce (1980) argue that children should hear the same number of phonemes in a word like 'pitch' as in a word like 'rich', unless they use spelling knowledge, in which case they should judge that 'pitch' contains one more phoneme than 'rich'. Ehri and Wilce asked nine-to ten-year-old children to segment pairs of such words ('pitch', 'rich', 'new' and 'do') into phonemes using counters and then to spell the words. The children heard an extra phoneme in 13.7/24 of the words with extra letters compared to 0.6/24 of the words without extra letters. Ehri and Wilce then showed that children taught nonsense words such as 'banyu' and 'tadge' put out more counters in a phoneme segmentation task than children taught 'banu' and 'taj'. These results imply that children rely on the spelling of words in phonemic segmentation tasks.

In the study just mentioned, Tunmer and Nesdale (1985) compared the segmentation of words and nonsense words which either contained single-phoneme vowel sounds normally represented by digraphs (e.g. '-ee', '-oo') or did not. If children use spelling knowledge to help them in the phonemic segmentation task, they should make 'overshoot errors' (i.e. extra taps) on the vowel digraph words. This prediction was confirmed. Again, this result fits the hypothesis that phonemic segmentation skills arise only after reading has begun, and are largely dependent on spelling knowledge.

Our conclusion about work on one-to-one correspondence is that there is some connection between performance in the tasks used in these studies and success in learning to read, but that the direction of cause and effect is unclear. Furthermore, one of the best ways of shedding light on the causal issue does not seem possible with tests of this kind, since it would involve giving the test to children before they learn to read and relating scores thus obtained to their later progress in reading. The problem is that the tasks are too difficult for prereaders as Calfee, Lindamood and Lindamood (1973) found in their blocks task, and nobody has yet found a suitable phoneme-tapping task for children who have not learned to read. Mann and Liberman (1984) did carry out a longitudinal study in which the prereading test was a syllable-tapping task and showed that scores on this test were related to later reading. However, this does not solve the question of the causal effects of analysing phonemes on learning to read.

Deletion and elision

One of the reasons for thinking that performance on the phoneme-counting tasks might be the product rather than the cause of learning to read is that children cannot manage these tasks well until they are quite old and have already begun to learn to read. The same is true of the commonly used deletion and elision tasks, in which children have to work out how a word would sound without a particular phoneme. Bruce (1964) was the first to introduce such a task. He gave children with mental ages ranging from five to nine years three tasks. In one ('jam–am') they had to work out the effects of removing the first sound, in another ('snail–sail') the middle sound, and in the third ('fork–for') the last sound. These were difficult tasks. The mean scores out of 30 for the five- and six-year-old groups were 0.0 and 1.8 (out of 20), respectively. Even the seven-year-olds only managed 8.75. Later each child was asked to spell some of the words, but no relation was found between spelling and Bruce's tasks. Very little can be concluded from this study about the connections between reading and phonological awareness.

Rosner and Simon (1971) independently devised a similar test of phonological awareness. Children aged from five to eleven were asked to delete either the initial, medial or final consonants or the initial or media syllables from words (e.g. 'man–an', 'desk–deck', 'belt–bell', 'carpet–pet', 'reproduce–reduce', 'location–lotion'). The task is difficult and nearly impossible for the youngest group. Among the older children there was a distinct relationship with reading, even when IQ was controlled. Here we do have evidence for a connection between phonological awareness and reading, although again the direction of cause and effect remains unsettled.

The possibility that performance in this sort of task is the product of learning to read came up in an explicit way in a study by Morais *et al* (1979), who compared a group of Portuguese illiterates to other adults who had been illiterate but had learned to read in adult literacy programmes. There were two tasks. One was to add a sound to a word ('alhaco'–'palhaco') and the other to subtract a sound from a word ('purso'–'urso'). The added and deleted sound was the same throughout the session but differed between subjects. The main result was that the illiterate group was very much worse at this task than the literate group, although they were able to manage some of the words (46 per cent success in the addition task with real words). The illiterates were particularly poor at both tasks when nonsense words were involved. The authors concluded that the ability to analyse sounds depends to a great extent on the experience of learning to read.

However, one cannot be at all sure that the two groups were equivalent in every way apart from reading. It is unlikely that pure chance determined which adults took the literacy courses. There could have been self-selection which might have been influenced by the people's different abilities. The second worry is that the real difficulty for the illiterate people was not so much with the business of adding and deleting phonemes but with nonsense words *per se*. We need control conditions which involve nonsense words but no phonological analysis. According to the Morais *et al.* hypothesis, the illiterates would have no particular difficulty in such tasks.

The thesis advanced by Morais *et al.* has received strong support from Read *et al.* (1987), who compared a group of people taught an alphabetic version of written Chinese (pinyin) with another group who had learned only the traditional Chinese orthography on tasks which were the exact equivalents of the Morais *et al.* test. The results were strikingly similar to those of Morais *et al.* The pinyin group were better in both tasks and the difference was more pronounced with nonsense words than with real words. The non-pinyin group reached roughly the same level with real words as the Portugese illiterate group. The authors' conclusion was that 'while the ability to recognise sameness and difference between phonemes within words appears to be a precondition for alphabetic literacy. . . the ability to manipulate (add and delete) phonemes within words appears to be a consequence of it'.

Some caution is needed over this conclusion. Again there is no control to ensure that the pronounced difficulty with nonsense words is a genuinely phonological one. Also the two groups may not have been comparable. Pinyin was introduced in Chinese schools in the late forties, and thus the non-pinyin subjects were on the whole older people who had been to school before this time. The discrepancy in the two groups' ages was quite considerable (mean ages of 49 years and 33 years). The non-pinyin people also had received three years less schooling than the others.

However, some variants of these tasks can be managed by younger children at very early stages of reading, which throws some doubt on the Morais *et al.*, hypothesis. Calfee (1977) devised a deletion test which differed in two major ways from those of Bruce and of Rosner and Simon. The sound to be deleted was not named; instead the experimenter said 'If I say "pies", you say "eyes", if I say "cake", you say "ache". (The deleted sound was always the first in the word.) Secondly, pictures were used, so that in the example just given the child would choose from a number of pictures, one of which was of pies and another of eyes. The children (kindergarteners) were given a small amount of training and then transfer tests involving both the same and new pictures. Their performance was extremely high and was related to their reading ability a year later. However, it is not clear whether there was any control for IQ in the multiple regression which showed this relationship.

The results of the deletion and elision tasks, therefore, give us few grounds for claiming that phonological awareness plays a role in reading, and some interesting but not completely convincing reasons for believing that the cause–effect relations might go the other way round. It would be most unlikely that the skills tested in these tasks could be a cause of reading because they come so late in development. Children cannot manage these tasks at all well until some years after they begin to read. This particular phonological skill is definitely not a precursor of reading.

Reversal and transposition of sounds

Children must be aware of a word's constituent sounds if they can reorder its phonemes. Lundberg, Olofsson and Wall (1980) gave six-year-old children a task in which they were asked to say words backwards. They were given other phonological and linguistic tests at the same time. The study was a longitudinal one, and the children's reading was tested one year later. The reversal task proved to be a powerful predictor of reading. This is an important result. For the first time we have evidence of a precursor which could be causal. The fact that the measures were taken before the children began to read rules out the possibility that the correlation is due to the effects of reading. However, one cannot be sure. There is the possiblitiy of the *tertium quid*—of both skills being controlled by some unknown third factor which accounts for the relation between them.

Alegria, Pignot and Morais (1982) used this kind of task to examine the possiblity that learning to read plays a role in determining the child's phonological awareness. They saw schoolchildren aged six to seven years, half of whom were at a school where reading was taught by a phonic method while the other half were at a school using a whole-word method of teaching reading. The children had to reverse the order of two words in one task, of two syllables in another and of two phonemes in the third. The children taught by the whole-word method performed extremely poorly in the phoneme-reversal task and were significantly worse than those taught by phonics. No such difference was found in the syllable-reversal task. There was a high correlation between the phoneme-reversal task and the teachers' evaluation of reading in the phonics group but not in the whole-word group.

The authors conclude that the difference between the two groups supports the notion of a 'reciprocal relation between reading instruction and awareness of phones', (p. 454). This is different from a simple hypothesis that reading *per se* causes phonological awareness. Both groups were learning to read, and presumably with equal success. So reading on its own cannot account for the difference between the two groups.

It has been suggested that the ability to reverse or transpose phonemes is related to spelling more than to reading. The Lundberg *et al.*, study mentioned above showed a strong relationship between phoneme reversal and spelling as well as reading and recently Perin (1983) has argued that the link with spelling is the stronger one. She gave fourteen- and fifteen-year-old children a transposition task in which they had to produce Spoonerisms by exchanging the initial phonemes of the names of well-known pop stars ('Chuck Berry' to 'Buck Cherry'). There were three groups. One group could read and spell normally, the second read normally but were poor spellers and the third were poor readers and spellers. The task was difficult for the latter two groups, and Perin concluded that the child's spelling skill is the important factor in transposition tasks.

This conclusion can be challenged. One needs a group of poor readers but good spellers to disentangle the different effects on reading and spelling. The missing group would be hard (and probably impossible) to find, but according to the hypothesis should find the task an easy one. Also, nothing can be said about cause and effect from this study. The poor performance of the two groups with reading and spelling difficulties could have been the result, and not the cause, of their slow progress in reading and spelling.

Segmentation and blending

One can directly ask children either to break words into their constituent sounds ('cat' to 'c-a-t') or to form whole words out of those sounds ('c-a-t' to 'cat'). This is quite a difficult task for young children, but one version— partial segmentation—is feasible for preschoolers. This was introduced by Fox and Routh (1975) in a study of three- to seven-year-olds who had to iden- tify the first word in a sentence ('Peter' out of 'Peter jumps'), then the first syllable in a word ('Pete' in 'Peter'), and finally the first phoneme in a syllable ('Pe in 'Pete'). The first two of these tasks were quite easy. The phoneme task was much harder, but even the three-year-old children managed to be right 25 per cent of the time and by the age of six the children were at ceiling. The syllable and phoneme segmentation measures were significantly correlated with reading. However, the paper does not make it clear how many of the children were given reading tests. The three- and four-year-olds probably were not. In any case the correlation tells us nothing about what is causing what.

The success of the preschool children in Fox and Routh's segmentation task can be explained by the fact that they only had to identify the first phoneme. We turn now to studies which involve all the sounds in a word.

Helfgott (1976) gave five-year-olds three kinds of segmentation and blending tasks, all of which involved CVC syllables. In one, the units were C-VC, in another CV-C, and in the third C-V-C. The C-V-C task was the hardest of the three, both in the segmentation and in the blending version. Even so, the children managed to segment nearly half of the words and to blend over half of the words correctly. Helfgott also found that the best predictor of reading was the children's segmentation ability. In a multiple regression the segmentation score accounted for 52 per cent of the variance. She also reports a correlation of 0.49 between blending and segmentation. However, because of the shared variance between these two variables blending did not even enter the equation in the multiple regression, and so we cannot gauge its effects. Mental age did not enter the prediction equation either, and thus one cannot say how much overlap there was between mental age and segmenting. Helfgott should have done a fixed-order multiple regression, entering mental age (and perhaps blending) before segmentation.

A large-scale study by Share *et al.*, (1984) adds considerable weight to Helfgott's claim. It involved 543 children who were initially seen at five and who were seen again when they were six and seven years. At five they were given a number of tasks, one of which was a version of Helfgott's test. In it the children had to divide words into either two segments (c-at) or three (c-a-t). This test turned out to be the strongest predictor of reading skills over the following two years, and stronger even than vocabulary scores. However, again, we are not told whether the relationship between segmentation and reading was still significant after verbal skills (IQ scores were not available) were partialled out.

Lundberg, Olofsson and Wall (1980) also looked at segmenting and blending in preschool children and later tested reading and spelling in their first and second years at school. Using path analysis, the authors found that the two most powerful predictors of reading were the tasks involving segmenting phonemes and reversing their order. This was true even when measures of non-verbal intelligence and of language skills were partialled out. In the second year, the reading scores were best predicted by the children's previous success at reversing phonemes, and rhyme. Thus by the second year the segmentation measure had lost its power. Nevertheless, this careful and comprehensive study is one of the best pieces of evidence for a relationship between preschool children's phonological skills and their success in reading.

Segmentation and blending skills have also been studied in older children already at school. Perfetti, Beck and Hughes (1981) (in an unpublished study, which is summarized by Perfetti, 1985, examined the relationship between these skills and reading when different methods of teaching reading were employed (the whole-word method of teaching or phonics). The children's blending and segmentation skills were measured before they began to learn to read, blending by the synthesis of isolated sounds into a word (e.g. 'c-a-t': 'cat') and segmentation by Liberman *et al.*'s tapping task and a phoneme-deletion task (e.g. 'Cat without the /t/ leaves ?'). The children were given these tests on four different occasions at two-monthly intervals and their progress in reading was assessed at the same time.

Perfetti *et al.* found that blending was an important predictor of later reading regardless of the way in which the child was taught to read. However, the method of instruction did seem to play a role with segmentation. For children taught by whole-word methods, early segmentation skill did not predict reading ability, while for the phonic group early reading predicted later segmentation skill, which in turn predicted later reading ability. Perfetti *et al.* concluded that blending skills are necessary for reading: 'success at reading depends on it' (p. 45). Segmentation skills, however, are mediated by reading experience: 'It is reading itself. . .that enables the children to be able to analyse words and to manipulate their segments' (p. 46). The discovery that blending scores predict reading cannot be used to conclude anything about causes. We still cannot be sure that all potential *tertium quids* have been excluded. Perfetti *et al.*'s striking data on differences between children taught in different ways, combined with the earlier results of Alegria *et al.*, are a useful reminder that we should take into account not only the child's abilities but also the ways in which he or she is being taught to use them.

All in all, the results of research on segmentation and blending demonstrate a strong relationship between a phonological skill and reading. The skill predicts, and to a certain extent precedes, reading. But we cannot be sure that it causes reading.

Rhyming

Detection and production of rhyme

To judge that 'hat' and 'cat' rhyme or that 'sun' and 'sock' begin in the same way is to analyse sounds in words. There is considerable evidence that many children conquer this skill long before they read. So, children's preschool experiences with rhyme might have a direct effect much later on their reading.

We have seen that in Lundberg *et al.'s* study preschool scores on a rhyme test were strongly related to silent reading two years later. Bradley and Bryant (1983) showed much the same thing in a three- to four-year longitudinal study of 368 children who were seen initially at four or five years and given tests of rhyme and alliteration detection. These rhyme and alliteration scores strongly predicted reading and spelling when the children were eight or nine, even after age, IQ and memory were partialled out. The effect was specific to reading: the same scores did not predict the children's mathematical skills.

Recently Ellis and Large (1986a) (also Ellis and Large, 1986b) examined the relationship between a number of metalinguistic tasks, including the Bradley and Bryant tests, and the reading and spelling of 40 children over three years. The children were first seen at age five, and then at yearly intervals until age eight. At age eight three groups of five children were selected, who were respectively of high IQ but poor reading (group A), of high IQ and good reading (group B) and of low IQ and poor reading (group C) and their performance on the different metalinguistic tasks over the three years of the study was compared. The largest difference between groups A and B was in Bradley and Bryant's rhyme test. Group B children were significantly better than group A children, in spite of the fact that the two groups were matched on intelligence. The second most important discriminator was a test of rhyme production. Thus the most striking difference between good and poor readers was in rhyme. The same two tests were most strongly related to reading in groups A and C (both groups equally poor at reading, but different IQ levels). Performance on Bradley and Bryant's rhyme test was the most important discriminator between groups B and C (good reading, high IQ, and poor reading, low IQ).

The only study which does not show a particularly strong relationship between rhyming and reading was done by Stanovich, Cunningham and Cramer (1984). They gave six-year-olds ten phonological awareness tasks, two of which involved rhyme. In one the children had to supply a rhyme and in the second they had to choose rhymes. The other tasks all involved detecting single consonants. Most of the correlations between the tasks were strong, but those between rhyme and the other tasks, though positive, were relatively low. The correlations between rhyme and a test of reading were not significant. However, as the authors note, there was a ceiling effect in the rhyme scores, and this was probably the reason for the lack of a connection. The important rhyme scores are probably those taken before children go to school.

Rhyme is another example of a skill which precedes and predicts reading. The strong relationship between early scores on rhyming and later success in reading is especially interesting because this particular phonological skill might well reflect the informal experience children have at home, before they go to school, with nursery rhymes and word games. However, impressive though the longitudinal predictions are, we cannot be sure that the relationship is a genuinely causal one. We still have to worry about the *tertium quid*.

Rhyme confusions in short-term memory tasks

Rhyme can be a source of confusion in tests of short-term memory and this kind of confusion actually increases with age. Conrad (1971) originally showed that children make more errors in recognizing pictures whose names rhyme than when the names of the pictures sound quite different from each other. The effect grew in strength from the age of five onwards. Liberman *et al.* (1977) argued that this development meant a growing phonentic representation which might affect success in learning to read. They gave eight-year-olds strings of five letters which were either composed of rhyming consonants (B,C,D,G,P,T,V,Z) or of non-rhyming consonants (H,K,L,R,Q,S,W,Y). The children were divided into superior, marginal and poor readers, and it was found that the words in the confusable (rhyming) list were harder for the superior readers to remember than the non-confusable list. No such effect was found in the other two groups. Liberman *et al.* concluded that they had shown a connection between a phonetic representation and reading. However, the direction of cause and effect is not established by these results.

Although the result has been repeated in at least one study (Siegel and Linder, 1984), other people have not found it. A second part of the Alegria, Pignot and Morais (1982) study mentioned above consisted of the Liberman *et al.* test. No difference was found between good and poor readers. There are several other failures to repeat the Liberman *et al.* result (Byrne and Ledez, 1983; Bisanz, Das and Mancini, 1984; Hall *et al.*, 1981; Johnston, 1982; Morais *et al.*, 1986).

Another attempt to relate memory for rhyming words to reading was made by Jorm *et al.* (1983) in a longitudinal study of 477 children. In kindergarten the children were given a short-term memory test, orginally devised by Mann, Liberman and Shankweiler (1980) with two sets of sentences, one of which contained rhyming words ('She ate a plate of date cake'). The rhyming sentences were harder to remember than the non-rhyming ones but there was no relationship between the rhyming–non-rhyming difference and progress in reading over the following year.

These memory studies confirm that rhyming plays a significant role in spoken language but do not establish a connection with reading. In contrast, studies in which children have to make explicit judgments about rhyme and alliteration have established this link.

Conclusions

Our survey shows a connection between reading and phonological awareness. However, the nature of the connection is unclear. The most pressing question is about causes. In many instances it seems quite possible that the child's experience with reading has determined his or her performance in the phonological tests. This was the case with measures of counting phonemes, elision of phonemes and reversal of syllables. These tasks are often impossible for children before they begin to read. However, some segmentation and blending measures and rhyming tasks are within the grasp of preschool children and the fact that scores on these tasks are related to later success in reading suggests that phonological awareness does to some extent determine reading. How plausible is this suggestion?

CAUSE AND EFFECT

The strengths and weaknesses of the available methods

Most of the causal claims that have been made about phonological awareness and reading are questionable. Each of the traditional methods for establishing causes in developmental psychology is beset by weaknesses. There are bound to be difficulties if only one method is used, and yet virtually all of the studies concerned have limited themselves to only one.

Longitudinal and intervention studies

The two methods most commonly used to tease out causal relationships are the longitudinal prediction and the training study. Both have strengths and weaknesses. The strength of a longitudinal study is that it can establish a definite relationship between a preschool measure and reading, but its weakness is that it cannot ensure that the relationship is a causal one. Both variables could be affected by some unknown, unmeasured *tertium quid*. However hard one tries one can never be sure that this possibility has been ruled out. In contrast, training studies do establish causes. However, their weakness is that they can be artificial. You can get an effect which has no relationship with what happens in real life.

The solution is to use both methods in combination with each other. The strengths of each cancel out the weaknesses of the other (Bryant and Bradley, 1985a). Sensitive longitudinal predictions establish relationships that do exist in real life, which the training study fails to do, and the training study shows that a relationship is definitely causal, thus filling the main gap left by any longitudinal study. Combined, the two methods give a convincing answer to a causal question.

Comparisons between poor and normal readers

There is a third method. It is to compare poor readers with good readers and to claim that any differences are factors which determine success in reading. We have already described several studies which have involved comparisons between good and poor readers of the same age (the age match). It is now generally recognized (Backman, Mamen and Ferguson, 1984; Bryant and Goswami, 1986) that one cannot conclude anything definite about causes from age match studies. Since the two groups are at different reading levels, any other differences between them could as well be a product as a cause of this reading difference.

The solution is to compare poor readers with younger normal readers who are at the same reading level (the reading age match). Any difference between the two groups cannot then be caused by a difference in reading achievement, since that is the same for both groups. Positive results in a reading age match experiment are extremely powerful, but there are not many of them. On the whole reading age matches have produced negative results (no difference between the two groups) or even positive results in the reverse direction (older poor readers better than the younger normal controls).

Our argument (Bryant and Goswami, 1986) is that some results in these two kinds of match are interpretable but that others can only be ambiguous. A positive result in a reading age match tells us something. If poor readers are worse in some task even though they are at the same reading level as the normal group and are actually the more intellectually advanced of the two (since their age and mental age is higher), then they must be at a grave disadvantage in the task in question. However, negative results in reading age match experiments are uninterpretable. The higher mental age of the poor readers may conceal a deep and genuine deficit, or on the other hand there may be no deficit at all. A 'no difference' result in a reading age match could either mean that there is no genuine deficit among the poor readers or that they are worse at the task being studied but have made up for this by being better at coping with some of the extraneous demands of the test.

We find the opposite pattern with the age match. Positive results do not distinguish cause from effect, but negative results can be important, albeit in a negative way. If, despite their considerably lower reading level, poor readers are as good as their age controls on some task, that task probably has nothing whatever to do with the business of learning to read.

Thus, a positive result in a reading age match can tell us something about the causes of reading and a negative result in an age match can help us to rule out some variables as causes. The other two possible results can tell us nothing. The combination of positive results in an age match and negative ones in a reading age match is the worst of both worlds and yet it is the most frequent pattern in comparisons between poor and normal readers. Anyone who plans to use data about poor readers to get at the causes of reading should beware.

THE EVIDENCE

Longitudinal and training studies combined

We know of one study only which has combined longitudinal prediction with intervention. This is Bradley and Bryant's 1983 study; we have already described both the longitudinal and the training parts of it. There were strong longitudinal connections between rhyme and reading, but the training effects, though positive, did not reach significance.

As we have seen, the other intervention studies are all beset by problems, and anyway were not combined with longitudinal predictions. The longitudinal studies also seem ambiguous to us since they do not rule out the possibility of the *tertium quid*. We have to conclude that work with normal readers has not yet established a strong causal link between phonological awareness and reading.

Comparisons between poor and normal readers

Comparisons between poor and normal readers matched on age give us no grounds for ruling out phonological awareness as a cause of reading. Positive results in age match studies have been found consistently in segmentation tasks (Perin, 1983) and in tests of rhyme (Bradley and Bryant, 1978). The only studies that we know of which found no difference between poor readers and age match controls were the failures to replicate the Liberman *et al.* (1977) effect which we described before.

The reading age match has produced two negative results. Bisanz, Das and Mancini (1984) and Johnston (1982) found no difference between poor readers and reading age matched controls in a Liberman *et al.* rhyming memory task. This puts this effect into the uninterpretable limbo which we warned against earlier.

Two tests have met with more success in the reading age match. One is rhyming. Bradley and Bryant (1978) compared a group of poor readers with reading age controls on the task used in the longitudinal study described earlier. The poor readers were considerably worse than the younger reading age controls. This is evidence that difficulties with rhyming and alliteration could lead to reading problems. However, the result may not be reliable. Beech and Harding (1984) were not able to replicate it. They compared poor readers to a group of normal children of the same reading age and another control group of the same chronological age in a rhyme production and a rhyme recognition task which was similar to the Bradley/Bryant oddity task. The poor readers managed these tasks as well as the reading age control group. We cannot explain the difference with the earlier Bradley/Bryant experiment.

The second example concerns the reading of non-words like 'wef' or 'molsmit'. These must be deciphered by using knowledge of letter–sound relationships as they cannot be recognized as familiar visual configurations. To read a word on the basis of its letter–sound relationships is to analyse and blend individual sounds, and so poor non-word reading may be caused by a phonological difficulty. But some caution is needed here. It is not certain that everyone reads non-words in this way: analogies from real words about letter strings in non-words are also possible (Glushko, 1979; Marcel, 1980).

Studies by Frith and Snowling (1983) and by Baddeley *et al.* (1982) showed that children with reading difficulties read lists of real words as well as their controls, as one would expect, but were worse with non-words. There is more evidence of this difficulty in a study by Snowling (1980); she presented two non-words at a time to poor readers and normal readers of the same absolute reading level and asked the children to judge whether they were the same or not. The non-words were given either visually (in written form) or auditorily (spoken). In two conditions both were visual or both auditory, but in another Snowling presented one visually and spoke the other (in effect a reading task). The poor readers were much worse than the normal readers in this third condition only. This shows that the difficulties of the poor readers were with reading non-words and not with non-words in general; it is worth knowing this given the special difficulties with non-words found in the studies of adult illiterates.

These three studies, combined with the evidence about rhyming, are compelling evidence that an insensitivity to the sounds in words is one cause of the difficulties of poor readers. However, here too there is some inconsistency. Recently Treiman and Hirsh-Pasek (1985) gave a non-word reading task to a group of eleven-year-old dyslexic readers at an eight-year reading level and a matched group of eight-year-old normal readers. They found virtually no difference in the two groups' ability to perform this task. Beech and Harding (1984) in the study mentioned above also found that poor readers read non-words as well as reading age controls.

It is not surprising that we can report few positive results in reading age match comparisons. These are extremely tough comparisons: it is worth noting that, scarce as these positive results are in work on phonological awareness, they are even scarcer elsewhere. As far as we know, the only other studies to have produced positive results concern children's syntactic and contextual understanding (Guthrie, 1973; Tunmer, Nesdale and Wright, 1987). One of the main results of the introduction of the reading age match design has been the realization that phonological difficulties probably play a crucial role in the problems of poor readers.

Conclusion—is phonological awareness a cause?

To decide that children's phonological skills affect reading is not to rule out the opposite possibility, that learning to read changes a child's phonological awareness. Both claims could be true. The hypothesis that reading affects the way in which children analyse sounds has received some impressive empirical support from studies of illiterates and from work on the effects of different methods of teaching. Furthermore, the fact that most of the tests of phonological awareness are too difficult for young children until after they have begun to learn to read suggests that these tests tap skills which are not the cause but the product of reading. Nevertheless, there are some impressive reasons for thinking that the effects go in the other direction as well.

Tests of rhyming give us a powerful reason for thinking that phonological skills affect reading. To varying extents children are aware of rhyme and can manage well in such tests before they begin to read (Chukovsky, 1974; Knafle 1973, 1974; Lenel and Cantor, 1981; Bradley and Bryant 1983, 1985; Lundberg, Oloffson and Wall, 1980). These tests predict success in reading well over several years. Training in rhyming has also led to some modest improvement in reading. Finally, tests of rhyme have sometimes though not always passed the stringent reading age test. The fact that studies of reading non-words have also passed that same test supports the idea that phonological awareness is a powerful determinant of progress in reading. The evidence has its inconsistencies but in the end suggests that phonological skills are a precursor and a cause of reading. No other possible causal factor has received nearly such strong empirical support.

DATA ON INDIVIDUAL DIFFERENCES

Normal readers

Although no one suggests that phonological processes are unimportant, it has been claimed that they are less important for some than for others. Baron (1979), Treiman and Baron (1981) and Treiman (1984) made the bold claim that children, as readers, can be divided into 'Phoenicians' and 'Chinese'. By this they meant that some depend on phonological processes when reading while others do not. These other children treat each word as an ideogram— hence their sobriquet.

Treiman and Baron's evidence involves an ingenious use of correlations. They gave children three closely matched lists of words to read. One consisted of regular words ('cut') which could easily be deciphered letter by letter using letter–sound relationships, another was made up of irregular words ('put') which could not be read in such a way and the third was a list of non-words ('lut'). The non-word list was assumed to measure dependence on phonological rules. The authors then correlated the children's performance on all three tests. They claimed that if there is a 'Phoenician' strategy, then there ought to be a higher correlation between performance on the regular words and the non-words than between irregular words and non-words. Non-words must be read phonologically and irregular words visually, and so if regular words are read on a phonological basis there should be a high correlation between success in reading them and in reading non-words. This correlation should be higher than the one between irregular words and non-words, because the irregular words cannot be read phonologically and the non-words can only be read phonologically. This difference has been found consistently (Treiman and Baron, 1981; Treiman, 1984).

In a similar fashion they argued that a higher correlation between performance in the regular and the irregular word list than between the irregular list and the non-words would be good evidence for the Chinese (visual) strategy. Irregular words, according to Treiman and Baron, can only be read visually and non-words only phonologically; therefore if children read words visually there should be a high correlation between their success on irregular and regular words because both can in principle be read on a visual basis. There should be a relatively low correlation between irregular words and non-words, because the former can be read on the basis of visual familiarity while the latter cannot. Again they consistently found this pattern.

These patterns do more than simply establish the existence of a Phoenician and a Chinese strategy. Treiman and Baron's argument also concerns individual differences between children. Their position (Baron and Treiman, 1980) is that if all children used these two strategies to the same degree then there would be no unevenness in the pattern of correlations. All three lists would correlate with each other to the same extent. The better children would simply do better on all three lists. The correlation between performance on irregular words and on non-words would not be relatively low, as it always has been in Treiman and Baron's work.

Thus Treiman and Baron's analysis does suggest a consistent pattern of individual differences in children's reading. However, there are several problems. One is that, though the experimenters' use of correlations is certainly novel, it is difficult to see why they did not also test their hypothesis with multiple regressions. They would surely, for example, predict a relationship between reading regular words and non-words when scores in the irregular word test (and perhaps reading level also) have been partialled out in a fixed-order multiple regression. Another difficulty is that Treiman and Baron's analysis leaves one in the curiously frustrating position of believing that there are Phoenician–Chinese differences without being able to pinpoint which individual children belong to which group.

A third problem stems from their assumption that non-words can only be decoded by phonological rules. As we have already noted, a non-word can be read by analogy with a familiar real (regular or irregular) word which shares the same spelling pattern. Thus we cannot be sure that the correlation between regular and non-words is due to children using phonological strategies to read both types of word. When reading non-words, children are probably more likely to make analogies with regular words than with irregular words, as generally groups of regular words with common spelling patterns are larger than corresponding groups of irregular words. This would account for the relatively high correlation between regular and non-words.

The final difficulty concerns the Treiman and Baron assumption that irregular words are the equivalent of ideograms, and thus can only be read visually. There is no independent evidence to support the assertion that such words are read as visual wholes, and anyway there is a plausible alternative, which is that children can recognize familiar orthographic sequences in regular and irregular words. It seems likely that children would use an orthographic sequences strategy with meaningful words more than with a list of non-words. Thus the Chinese–Phoenician question remains open.

Poor readers

The same distinction—between children who read visually and others who read phonologically—has been used with poor readers. Eleanor Boder (1973) claimed that some poor readers (dysphonetic group) are backward because of phonological difficulties, others (dyseidetic group) because of visual difficulties and still others (mixed group) through a combination of the two. The dysphonetic group is characterized by gross phonetic errors ('rember' for 'remember'), while the dyseidetic group cannot remember the appearance of irregular words like 'laugh'. The mixed group makes both kinds of mistake.

There are two reasons for caution about Boder's conclusions. First, one cannot be sure that difficulty with irregular words means a visual weakness. The problem could be in remembering orthographic sequences. The second difficulty is more serious. Boder's is a causal explanation. Each group has fallen behind because of a particular weakness. But she had no control group of normal readers. You can only argue that a pattern of individual differences among poor readers explains their difficulties if that pattern is atypical. If exactly the same pattern exists among normal readers whose progress has been and will go on being normal, it cannot be the cause of the poor readers' difficulties.

Recently Mitterer (1982) made similar claims, but on the basis of a comparison between dyslexic and normal readers. He claimed that he could divide a dyslexic group into two subgroups, the 'whole-word' group who read visually and the 'recoding' group who rely on phonological rules. He did not find this pattern among normal readers. However, the two groups were the same age and thus the reading level of the dyslexic group was a great deal lower than that of the normal children. The different patterns in the two groups may simply be a function of the different reading levels. Mitterer's subgrouping therefore might have nothing specifically to do with dyslexia.

Two other sets of researchers have shared Boder's reluctance to establish whether a pattern of individual differences is specific to dyslexics. Both applied some of the techniques used in research on adult acquired dyslexics to children with reading problems. Temple and Marshall (1983) described a seventeen-year-old girl with a ten-year reading level whose symptoms resembled those of a typical 'phonological dyslexic'. She could hardly read non-words, and long regular words like 'herpetology' also caused her a lot of difficulty. She made 'visual paralexic' errors (e.g. reading 'camp' for 'cape') which seemed to show that she depended on the appearance of words. She read irregular words as easily as regular ones and so was not helped by the fact that regular words can be decoded phonologically. Temple and Marshall (and Marshall, 1984) concluded that the girl's main weakness was phonological and that this was the cause of her problems.

The other case, also a girl of seventeen with a reading level of ten years studied by Coltheart *et al.* (1983), had different symptoms. She read regular words more easily than irregular ones. She made regularization errors (a rigid use of phonological rules, e.g. 'steek' for 'steak') and stress errors (reading words with stress on the wrong syllable). Coltheart *et al.* point out that these are the symptoms of an adult 'surface dyslexic'. They argued that the girl's problem was in visual or orthographic recognition of familiar words. However, they also found that she was rather poor at reading non-words—a result which is hard to reconcile with their view that her phonological system was intact.

Neither of these two studies included any data on equivalent normal children and so the causal hypotheses are obviously in doubt. It has now been shown (Bryant and Impey, 1987) that all but one of the 'symptoms' shown by these girls are found among children who read normally. So are the differences between the two girls. There are marked differences among normal children too, and they take the same form. The differences seem to reflect the Phoenician/Chinese distinction made by Treiman and Baron.

The one symptom which was more pronounced in both dyslexic girls than in equivalent normal readers was their striking difficulty with non-words.

This repeats the findings of Frith and Snowling and of Baddeley *et al.* which we have already mentioned.

Conclusion

There are differences in the ways children read. These differences occur in normal children and in poor readers, and so far it looks as though they take the same form in both groups. The study of these differences has been bedevilled by a naive belief that non-words can only be read 'phonologically' and irregular words only 'visually'. If this were the case, then there would be good grounds for the claim that some children read phonologically and others visually. But other possible strategies, like the use of analogies, cut across the phonological/visual distinction. We need tests which take other strategies into account. These strategies are the subject of the next section.

THE PATHWAY

This conclusion raises a question. What is the pathway between phonological awareness and reading? The most obvious answer is that the ability to analyse the sounds in words allows children to learn letter–sound relationships. Rozin and Gleitman (1977) argue that children who are beginning to read already possess an oral mental lexicon and simply need to associate the written letter strings representing these words with the sounds which they already know.

There is a great deal to be said for this claim, and the work on segmenting and blending certainly supports it. However, phonological awareness could work at other levels too. It could allow children to recognize and use *strings* of letters, and thus to decipher words which cannot be read letter-by-letter on the basis of letter–sound rules. A word like 'light' shares a sequence of letters and a common sound with many other words ('fight', 'night', 'tight'. . .). We know that children put rhyming words in categories before they begin to read, and that their skill at this is related to success in reading. It is possible that this skill works by allowing them to learn that there are sets of words with sounds in common which also share common orthographic sequences (*light, fight, night*). One advantage of this learning is that children could make inferences or analogies about new (to them) written words which have spelling patterns in common with words that they can already read. Thus they could read a new word like 'peak' if they could already read 'beak'.

This strategy has usually been thought too difficult for young children. For example, Marsh and his co-workers (Marsh and Desberg, 1983; Marsh, Desberg and Cooper, 1977; Marsh *et al.*, 1981; Marsh *et al.*, 1980) claim that an analogy strategy is used only in the final stage of learning to read. They asked children to read non-words which are analogues of real words (e.g. 'puscle' (muscle); 'tepherd' (shepherd); 'faugh' (laugh)). The words were chosen so that a pronunciation based on analogy (e.g. 'pussle') would differ from one based on rules ('puskle'). Marsh, Desberg and Cooper (1977) found that ten-year-olds made analogies 39 per cent of the time when given single non-words of this type to read while sixteen-year-olds made analogies 46 per cent of the time. In a second study involving prose passages seven-year-olds made analogical responses 14 per cent of the time, ten-year-olds 34 per cent and college students 38 per cent. However, the experimenters did not check whether the younger subjects knew the real words on which the analogies had to be based.

In contrast Baron (1977) suggested that younger children could make analogies. He taught kindergarteners words and sounds such as *b*, *at*, *bat*, *ed*, *red*; and tested transfer to reading new words such as *bed*, *rat*, *bad* and *bet*. Children's performance on words such as *bed* and *rat* was around 90 per cent, compared to 15 per cent for *bad* and *bet*. Baron argued that analogy is used to decode *bed* and *rat*, whereas *bad* and *bet* depend on knowledge of the correspondences between single letters and sounds. As the children performed so well on the analogical words at transfer, Baron argues that analogy strategies are more natural in the beginning stages of reading than correspondence strategies.

However, half of the 'correspondence' test words in Baron's study contained consonant−vowel units which could be extracted from the *beginn-ings* of the training words, and so an analogy could in principle be made between the segment *ba-* in *bat* and *bad*. If analogy strategies are more natural in the beginning stages of reading, children should also use analogies here. Furthermore, the children were trained on the subunits required to read *bed* and *rat* by analogy (the *-ed* and *-at* segments), but were not trained on the subunits of the correspondence words (e.g. *-ad* and *-et*). This means that the 'correspondence' words were more difficult to segment and blend than the analogous words.

Goswami (1986) recently carried out a study which avoided these problems. It involved no training on the analogous units and it did not rely solely on non-words. Children aged from five to eight played a word game in which they had to read words and non-words which were either analogous or non-analogous to 'clue' words which were present throughout each session. For example, if the clue word was *beak*, the test words might be *bean*, *bead*, *peak*, *weak*, *bask* and *lake*. The non-words would be *beal*, *beap*, *neak*, *feak*, *bawk* and *pake*. After the experiment, the children were given the Bradley/Bryant 'odd man out' test of auditory organization to assess whether analogical skill and rhyming skills were related.

Children at all reading levels could make analogies between both words and non-words. There were no differences at all between the two older groups (six and seven years), who made analogies irrespective of reading level. The children found analogies between the ends of words (beak–peak) easier than analogies between the beginnings of words (beak–bean). In fact the youngest group (five years) made almost no analogies of the latter type. However, even the non-readers were able to make analogies between the ends of words. This result means that the ability to make analogies in reading has nothing to do with reading level, but is available from the very beginning of learning to read. Analogies are also used to read non-words.

There were significant correlations between scores on the Bradley and Bryant auditory organization test and the number of analogies made between the beginnings and ends of words. In fixed-order multiple regressions, in which age and verbal IQ were entered as the first steps, there was a significant relationship between the ability to make analogies and the Bradley/Bryant rhyming tests for the two oldest groups, although the relationship between analogy use and alliteration just missed significance. This relationship between rhyme and analogy is important because it shows another way in which phonological awareness affects reading. It goes much further than the idea that phonological awareness works through letter–sound associations, and directs our attention to the possibility that children categorize words on the basis of orthographic sequences as well as sounds very early in reading and integrate these two kinds of category. This integration of rhyming and analogy will help in decoding irregular as well as regular words.

GENERAL CONCLUSIONS

In order to establish a cause of reading one has to show convincing relationships in a longitudinal predictive study and to demonstrate in an intervention study that improvements in the suggested causal factor lead directly to consequent improvements in reading. It also helps one's case (although it is not essential) to have found positive results in a reading age match.

If one applies these criteria strictly, the striking and surprising result is that the hypothesis of phonological awareness as a cause of reading has yet to be proved. Much of the evidence is consistent with this hypothesis. Phonological skills are related to reading even when IQ is held constant, and some measures of phonological awareness taken before children learn to read predict their success with written language, again even when IQ is controlled. Some tests of phonological awareness withstand the formidable test of the reading age match, though they do so inconsistently. However, there is no evidence yet that training phonological awareness has any effect on reading real words and sentences.

Training studies are a persistent problem. One possible solution is that the timing of the phonological training in most intervention studies might be wrong. The hypothesis, after all, is that phonological awareness is a precursor of reading, which implies that training the skill should be most effective in the preschool period. This idea is supported by the fact that the longitudinal predictive studies which have shown the strongest links between phonological awareness and reading have used measures of phonological skills taken in the preschool period. Yet only two of the training studies that we have reviewed dealt with preschool children, and one of these (Haddock, 1976) used an unrealistic outcome measure while the other (Goldstein, 1976) combined phonological training with experience with written material.

Another possibility is to exploit the obvious success of methods that combine phonological training with alphabetic experience. Thus far it is not clear whether it is the combination of the two things that is important or whether training with letters has an independent effect. More studies are needed in which some groups are given phonological and alphabetic training and others just alphabetic training in order to disentangle these effects.

The fact that the hypothesis of phonological awareness as a cause has been so difficult to establish does not of course mean that it is false. Nor does it mean that the opposite hypothesis, that reading causes phonological awareness, is true. The evidence for that hypothesis also has its problems. The studies with illiterates, though ingenious, are open to alternative explanations. The main differences between the two groups were with non-words, and also there are grounds for doubting that the literate and illiterate groups are comparable in every way apart from reading skill. Furthermore, the demonstration that phonic methods improve phonological awareness is not a proper test of the hypothesis, which is that reading in general (and not just one kind of reading) produces phonological awareness.

Nevertheless, the idea that children's experiences in reading affect their phonological skills has some plausibility, and anyway the two causal hypotheses are not in any way exclusive (Bertelson *et al.*, 1985; Bryant and Bradley, 1985b). The fact that some phonological tests are relatively easy, and can be managed (to some extent) by children who have not yet learned to read, while others are impossible for children until they have been at school for some time, suggests that some forms of phonological awareness are causes of reading and others caused by it.

The varying levels of difficulty in phonological tasks raise some interesting possibilities. Children seem to cope with rhyme and with the analysis of syllables at an early stage. Analysing a word into all its constituent sounds develops much later. Division of a word into beginning consonant/s and the remaining vowels and final consonant (onset and rime) seems to constitute an intermediate step (Treiman, 1986). This sequence may account for the relative ease with which children make analogies about spelling patterns in the beginning stages of reading. The idea of a link between early rhyming and the use of analogies in learning to read should be pursued in longitudinal studies.

Studies of this sort would tell us more about the nature of the pathway between phonological awareness and reading. It is no longer enough to say that the two are connected, or even that they are causally connected. We now need to know what form the connections take. When we know that, we will be able to devise the right kind of training experiment.

REFERENCES

Alegria, J., Pignot, E., and Morais, J. (1982). Phonetic analysis of speech and memory codes in beginning readers. *Memory and Cognition*, **10**, 451-456.

Backman, J.E., Mamen, M., and Ferguson, H.B. (1984). Reading level design: conceptual and methodological issues in reading research. *Psychological Bulletin*, **96**, 560-568.

Baddeley, A.D., Ellis, N.C., Miles, T.R., and Lewis, V.J. (1982). Developmental and acquired dyslexia: a comparison. *Cognition*, **11**, 185-199.

Baron, J. (1977). Mechanisms for pronouncing printed words: Use and acquistion. In D. LaBerge and S.J. Samuels (Eds.) *Basic Processes in Reading: Perception and Comprehension*. Hillsdale, N.J.: Erlbaum.

Baron, J. (1979). Orthographic and word-specific mechanisms in children's reading of words. *Child Development*, **50**, 60-72.

Baron, J., and Treiman, R. (1980). Some problems in the study of differences in cognitive processes. *Memory and Cognition*, **8**, 313-321.

Beech, J.R., and Harding, L.M. (1984). Phonemic processing and the poor reader from the developmental lag point of view. *Reading Research Quarterly*, **19**, 357-366.

Bertelson, P., Morais, J., Alegria, J., and Content, A. (1985). Phonetic analysis capacity and learning to read. *Nature*, **313**, 73-74.

Bisanz, G.L., Das, J.P., and Mancini, G. (1984). Children's memory for phonemically confusable and nonconfusable letters: Changes with age and reading ability. *Child Development*, **55**, 1845-1854.

Boder, E.M. (1973). Developmental dyslexia: A diagnostic approach based on three atypical reading–spelling patterns. *Developmental Medicine and Child Neurology*, **15**, 663-687.

Bradley, L., and Bryant, P.E. (1978). Difficulties in auditory organisation as a possible cause of reading backwardness. *Nature*, **271**, 746-747.

Bradley, L., and Bryant, P.E. (1983). Categorising sounds and learning to read—a causal connection. *Nature*, **301**, 419-421.

Bradley, L., and Bryant, P.E. (1985). *Rhyme and Reason in Reading and Spelling*, IRARLD Monographs No. 1. Ann Arbor: University of Michigan Press.

Bruce, D.J. (1964). The analysis of word sounds. *British Journal of Educational Psychology*, **34**, 158-170.

Bryant, P.E., and Bradley, L. (1985a). *Children's Reading Problems*. Oxford: Blackwell.

Bryant, P.E., and Bradley, L. (1985b). Phonetic analysis capacity and learning to read. *Nature*, **313**, 73-74.

Bryant, P.E., and Goswami, U. (1986). The strengths and weaknesses of the reading level design. *Psychological Bulletin*, **100**, 101-103.

Bryant, P.E., and Impey, L. (1987). The similarities between normal children and dyslexic adults and children. *Cognition*. **24**, 121–37.

Byrne, B., and Ledez, J. (1983). Phonological awareness in reading-disabled adults. *Australian Journal of Psychology*, **35**, 185-97.

Calfee, R. (1977). Assessment of individual reading skills: basic research and practical applications. In A.S. Reber and D.L. Scarborough (Eds.) *Toward a Psychology of Reading.* Hillsdale, N.J.: Erlbaum.

Calfee, R.C., Lindamood, P., and Lindamood, C. (1973) Acoustic–phonetic skills and reading—kindergarten through twelfth grade. *Journal of Educational Psychology*, **64**, 293-298.

Carlsten, C.T. (1984). Preventing reading difficulties. An experimental study of the effect of training articulatory sequential analysis on the acquistion of technical reading skill of first grade pupils considered to be in danger of developing reading difficulties. Report from The Norwegian Postgraduate College of Further Education (described in Skjelfjord, 1984).

Chukovsky, K. (1974). *From Two to Five.* Berkeley: University of California Press.

Coltheart, M., Masterson, J., Byng, S., Prior, M., and Riddoch, J. (1983). Surface dyslexia. *Quarterly Journal of Experimental Psychology*, **35**, 469-495.

Conrad, R. (1971). The chronology of the development of covert speech in children. *Developmental Psychology*, **5**, 398-405.

Ehri, L.C., and Wilce, L.S. (1980). The influence of orthography on readers' conceptualisation of the phonemic structure of words. *Applied Psycholinguistics*, **1**, 371-385.

Ellis, N., and Large, B. (1986a). A longitudinal study of reading. Paper to BPS Cognitive Psychology Section's International Conference on Cognitive Approaches to Reading at the University of Leicester, April.

Ellis, N., and Large, B. (1986b). The development of reading. What you find is what you look for. Unpublished manuscript.

Fox, B., and Routh, D.K. (1975). Analyzing spoken language into words, syllables and phonemes: A developmental study. *Journal of Psycholinguistic Research*, **4**, 331-342.

Fox, B., and Routh, D.K. (1976). Phonemic analysis and synthesis as word-attack skills. *Journal of Educational Psychology*, **68**, 70-74.

Fox, B., and Routh, D.K. (1984). Phonemic analysis and synthesis as word attack skills: Revisited. *Journal of Educational Psychology*, **76**, 1059-1064.

Frith, U., and Snowling, M. (1983). Reading for meaning and reading for sound in autistic and dyslexic children. *British Journal of Developmental Psychology*, **1**, 329-342.

Glushko, R.J. (1979). The organization and activation of orthographic knowledge in reading aloud. *Journal of Experimental Psychology: Human Perception and Performance*, **5**, 674-91.

Goldstein, D.M. (1976). Cognitive–linguistic functioning and learning to read in preschoolers. *Journal of Educational Psychology*, **68**, 680-688.

Goswami, U. (1986). Children's use of analogy in learning to read: A developmental study. *Journal of Experimental Child Psychology*, **42**, 73-83.

Guthrie, I.T. (1973). Reading comprehension and syntactic responses in good and poor readers. *Journal of Educational Psychology*, **65**, 294-299.

Haddock, M. (1976). Effects of an auditory and an auditory–visual method of blending instruction on the ability of pre-readers to decode synthetic words. *Journal of Educational Psychology*, **68**, 825-31.

Hall, J.W., Ewing, A., Tinzmann, M.B., and Wilson, K.P. (1981). Phonetic coding and dyslexic readers. *Bulletin of the Psychonomic Society*, **17**, 177-178.

Helfgott, J.A. (1976). Phonemic segmentation and blending skills of kindergarten children: Implications for beginning reading acquisition. *Contemporary Educational Psychology*, **1**, 157-69.

Johnston, R.S. (1982). Phonological coding in dyslexic readers. *British Journal of Psychology*, **73**, 455-460.

Jorm, A.F., Share, D.L., Maclean, R., and Matthews, R. (1983). Phonological confusability in short term memory for sentences as predictor of reading ability. *British Journal of Psychology*, **75**, 393-400.

Knafle, J.D. (1973). Auditory perception of rhyming in kindergarten children. *Journal of Speech and Hearing Research*, **16**, 482-487.

Knafle, J.D. (1974). Children's discrimination of rhyme. *Jornal of Speech and Hearing Research*, **17**, 367-372.

Lenel, J.C., and Cantor, J.H. (1981). Rhyme recognition and phonemic perception in young children. *Journal of Psycholinguistic Research*, **10**,57-68.

Liberman, I.Y., Shankweiler, D., Fisher, F.W., and Carter, B. (1974). Explicit syllable and phoneme segmentation in the young child. *Journal of Experimental Child Psychology*, **18**, 201-12.

Liberman, I.Y., Shankweiler, D., Liberman, A.M., Fowler, C., and Fischer, F.W. (1977). Phonetic segmentation and recoding in the beginning reader. In A.S. Reber and D.L. Scarborough (Eds.) *Toward a Psychology of Reading*. Hillsdale, N.J.: Erlbaum.

Lundberg, I., Olofsson, A., and Wall, S. (1980). Reading and spelling skills in the first school years predicted from phonemic awareness skills in kindergarten. *Scandinavian Journal of Psychology*, **21**, 159-173.

Mann, V.A., and Liberman, I.Y. (1984). Phonological awareness and verbal short term memory. *Journal of Learning Disabilities*, **17**, 592-599.

Mann, V.A., and Liberman, I.Y., and Shankweiler, D. (1980). Children's memory for words strings in relation to reading ability. *Memory and Cognition*, **8**, 329-335.

Marcel, A.J. (1980). Phonological awareness and phonological representation: Investigation of a specific spelling problem. In U. Frith (Ed.) *Cognitive Processes in Spelling*. London: Academic Press.

Marsh, G., and Desberg, P. (1983). The development of strategies in the acquisition of symbolic skills. In D.R. Rogers and J.A. Sloboda (Eds.) *The Acquisition of Symbolic Skills*. New York: Plenum.

Marsh, G., Desberg, P., and Cooper, J. (1977). Developmental strategies in reading. *Journal of Reading Behavior*, **9**, 391-394.

Marsh, G., Friedman, M.P., Desberg, P., and Saterdahl, K. (1981). Comparison of reading and spelling strategies in normal and reading disabled children. In M.P. Friedman, J.P. Das and N. O'Connor (Eds.) *Intelligence and Learning*. New York: Plenum.

Marsh, G., Friedman, M.P., Welch, V., and Desberg, P. (1980). A cognitive–developmental approach to reading acquisition. In G.E. MacKinnon and T.G. Waller (Eds.) *Reading Research: Advances in Theory and Practice*, Vol.3. New York: Academic Press.

Marshall, J.C. (1984). Towards a rational taxonomy of developmental dyslexia. In R.N. Malatesha and H.A. Whitaker (Eds.) *Dyslexia: A Global Issue*. The Hague: Nijhoff.

Mitterer, J.O. (1982). There are at least two kinds of poor readers: whole word poor readers and recoding poor readers. *Canadian Journal of Psychology*, **36**, 445-461.

Morais, J., Cary, L., Alergria, J., and Bertelson, P. (1979). Does awareness of speech as a sequence of phones arise spontaneously? *Cognition*, **7**, 323-331.

Morais, J., Cluytens, M., Alegria, J., and Content, A. (1986). Speech-mediated retention in syslexics. *Perceptual and Motor Skills*, **62**, 119-126.

Olofsson, A. (1985). Effects of phoneme awareness training in kindergarten on the use of spelling–sound rules in Grade 2. In Phonemic awareness and learning to read: a longitudinal and quasi-experimental study. Doctoral dissertation, Department of Psychology, University of Umea, Sweden.

Olofsson, A., and Lundberg, I. (1985). Evaluation of long term effects of phonemic awareness training in kindergarten: illustrations of some methodological problems in evaluation research. *Scandinavian Journal of Psychology*, **26**, 21-34.

Perfetti, C.A. (1985). *Reading Ability*. Oxford: University Press.

Perfetti, C., Beck, I., and Hughes, C. (1981). Phonemic knowledge and learning to read. Paper presented at the meeting of the Society for Research In Child Development, Boston, March 1981.

Perin, D. (1983). Phonemic segmentation and spelling. *British Journal of Psychology*, **74**, 129-144.

Read, C., Zhang, Y., Nie, H., and Ding, B. (1986). The ability to manipulate speech sounds depends on knowing alphabetic writing. *Cognition*, **24**, 31–44.

Rosner, J., and Simon, D.P. (1971). *The Auditory Analysis Test: An Initial Report*. Learning Research and Development Center, University of Pittsburgh.

Rozin, P., and Gleitman, L.R. (1977). *The Structure and Acquisition of Reading II. The Reading Process and the Acquisition of the Alphabetic Principle*. Hillsdale, N.J.: Erlbaum.

Share, D.L., Jorm, A.R., Maclean, R., and Matthews, R. (1984). Sources of individual differences in reading acquisition. *Journal of Educational Psychology*, **76**, 1309-1324.

Siegal, L., and Linder, B.A. (1984). Short term memory processes in children with reading and arithmetic learning disabilities. *Developmental Psychology*, **20**, 200-207.

Skjelfjord, V.J. (1985). *Phonemic Segmentation: An Important Subskill in Learning to Read*. Rapport nr. 1. 1985. Pedagogisk forskningistitutt: University of Oslo.

Snowling, M.J. (1980). The development of grapheme–phoneme correspondence in normal and dyslexic readers. *Journal of Experimental Child Psychology*, **29**, 294-305.

Stanovich, K.E., Cunningham, A.E., and Cramer, B.B. (1984). Assessing phonological awareness in kindergarten children: Issues of task comparability. *Journal of Experimental Child Psychology*, **38**, 175-190.

Temple, C., and Marshall, J.R. (1983). A case study of developmental phonological dyslexia. *British Journal of Psychology*, **74**, 517-533.

Treiman, R. (1984). Individual differences among children in reading and spelling styles. *Journal of Experimental Child Psychology*, **37**, 463-477.

Treiman, R. (1986). The role of intrasyllabic units in learning to read and spell. Unpublished manuscript prepared for The Conference on Early Reading Acquisition, University of Texas at Austin, March 1986.

Treiman, R., and Baron, J. (1981). Segmental analysis ability: Development and relation to reading ability. In G.E. MacKinnon and T. G. Waller (Eds.) *Reading Research: Advances in Theory and Practice*, Vol. III. New York: Academic Press.

Treiman R., and Baron, J. (1983). Phonemic analysis training helps children benefit from spelling rules. *Memory and Cognition*, **11**, 382-389.

Treiman, R., and Hirsh-Pasek, K. (1985). Are there qualitative differences between dyslexic and normal readers? *Memory and Cognition*, **13**, 357-364.

Tunmer, W.E., and Nesdale, A.R. (1985). Phonemic segmentation skill and beginning reading. *Journal of Educational Psychology*, **77**, 417-427.

Tunmer, W.E., Nesdale, A.R., and Wright, A.D. (1987). Syntactic awareness and reading acquisition. *British Journal of Developmental Psychology*, **5**, 25–34.

Wallach, M.A., and Wallach, L. (1976). *Teaching all Children to Read*. Chicago: University of Chicago Press.

Williams, J. (1980). Teaching decoding with an emphasis on phoneme analysis and phoneme blending. *Journal of Educational Psychology*, **72**, 1-15.

CHAPTER 10

Reading Retardation

CHARLES HULME

Department of Psychology, University of York

INTRODUCTION

Many children learn to read with remarkable alacrity. This should give us cause to marvel; reading is a highly complex cognitive skill that is also in some sense 'artificial'. We have evolved to walk upright and talk but we have not, presumably, evolved any specific mechanisms for reading. The conventions used for written language must dovetail well with our cognitive capacities that have been developed primarily for other purposes.

This brings us back to the old observation that reading is in some sense parasitic on speech. This is true both in developmental and evolutionary terms. Spoken language certainly evolved long before reading and writing began, and in the course of normal development children learn to talk before attempting to learn to read. Learning to read consists, in a very real sense, of learning to map spoken language onto a new written representation. In this light it is perhaps not surprising that various subtle impairments of language in children may have important effects on the process of learning to read. This is one of the major findings to emerge from research reviewed here dealing with a small group of children who have severe difficulties in learning to read.

DEFINITIONS OF READING RETARDATION

A substantial minority of children experience difficulties in learning to read. There may be a variety of reasons for this. Some children suffer from impairments of hearing or vision that may interfere with learning. Others may have general intellectual impairments which produce a low level of learning across the board. Our concern in the present chapter, however, is with a small group of children who experience severe problems of learning to read without any apparently sufficent cause. Reading retardation is defined by a process of exclusion. Retarded readers have severe problems in learning to read in the absence of general intellectual impairments, sensory impairments or emotional problems, and given adequate educational opportunities.

To establish whether a significant number of children experience difficulties in learning to read we need to conduct population surveys. Rutter, Tizard and Whitmore (1970) screened the entire population of nine-, ten- and eleven-year-olds resident on the Isle of Wight. In presenting the findings of this study the distinction between reading backwardness and reading retardation was stressed (Yule *et al.*, 1974). Backwardness refers to a difficulty with reading regardless of a child's intelligence. Retardation is a more precise term referring to a difficulty in learning to read that is not explicable in terms of a child's general intelligence. Because IQ is highly correlated with success in reading (to the extent of about 0.60 in the Isle of Wight study), if we are interested in factors specific to reading we need some way of excluding its influence. A neat way of doing this is by using regression techniques. In this study retardation was defined in terms of a regression formula in which expected reading level was predicted on the basis of a known relationship between reading, IQ and age in the total sample. (IQ was measured with a short form of the WISC and reading was measured with a prose reading test, the Neale Analysis of Reading Ability.) Retardation was defined as a reading accuracy or comprehension score two years four months below that expected on the basis of age and IQ.

Using this definition, which is clearly quite stringent, 3.7 per cent of the nine- to eleven-year-olds on the Isle of Wight were classed as retarded in reading. This figure, which was considered a slight underestimate because of imperfections in screening, is really quite large. In an area that is considered to be similar in social composition to the rest of England as a whole, as many as 4 per cent of children have severe and specific problems in learning to read.

One finding of this survey that has attracted a lot of attention is that reading retardation, as defined by regression techniques, exceeded the rate expected if reading ability is a normally distributed variable. This 'hump' at the lower end of the distribution of reading achievement appeared analogous to the existence of an equivalent hump in the IQ distribution due to various pathological causes of mental reatardation. The natural implication of this finding is that cases of reading retardation represent something more than the bottom of a continuum in reading skills. The existence of this hump, and the fact that certain correlates differentiated the retarded from the backward readers, was taken as support for the importance of the distinction between backwardness and retardation.

Recently the existence of this hump has been shown to be an artifact of a ceiling effect in the reading test used in this study. van der Wissel and Zegers (1985) showed by a computer simulation that the deviation from a normal distribution in the reading scores produced by this ceiling effect was quite sufficient to explain the excess of retarded readers obtained. More directly, in an analysis of the results from a sample of over 8000 ten-year-olds in the Child Health and Education Study, no evidence for an equivalent excess of retarded readers was found when the reading and IQ scores were normalized (Rodgers, 1983). The same was true in a large sample of nine-year-old boys in New Zealand (Silva, McGhee and Williams, 1985).

These studies show that the Isle of Wight study over estimated the number of children whose reading attainment falls far below that expected on the basis of their age and IQ. The question is whether these recent results invalidate the distinction drawn between retardation and backwardness by Yule *et al*. This depends upon the uses to which the distinction is put. For the purposes of research, it would seem perfectly legitimate to focus attention upon retarded readers in order to understand the impairments which may lead to reading difficulties. In this sense retarded readers simply represent a group of children whose reading is clearly incommensurate with their overall ability. They are, therefore, a useful group with which to try to isolate factors which may have a direct impact on the process of learning to read.

A further question, then, is whether retarded readers are in any qualitative sense different from backward readers. At the moment it seems quite possible that they will turn out not to be. There may be a variety of cognitive skills important for learning to read which show continuous variation amongst children. Some children may be very much superior in these skills and will tend to read well in relation to their peers of equal age and IQ, others may be inferior in these skills and so be retarded in reading. It remains for further research to establish whether the problems of retarded readers are clearly distinct from those found in backward readers.

This is an important question given the educational implications sometimes attributed to the distinction between backwardness and retardation. It may be that this distinction is not one which carries any direct implications for prognosis and treatment. The answer to this question also has an important bearing on research. If reading retardation is simply the lower end of a continuum of reading skills, then research with other groups which show less extreme variations in reading skill may also help to reveal the nature of the processes underlying these individual differences in performance. But if retarded readers really show qualitative differences from normal readers, then research with less extreme groups will not help to clarify the nature of their problem.

For the moment, suffice it to say that there exists a significant number of children who experience relatively severe and specific difficulties in learning to read. The present chapter will review some of what is known about the nature and causes of these children's reading problems.

METHODOLOGICAL ISSUES: TRYING TO ESTABLISH CAUSES

When children have reading difficulties, it may be comparatively straightforward to measure the extent of their reading problems and describe some associated difficulties. It is much more difficult, however, to try to show the underlying causes of their reading problems.

Most of the evidence we have about reading retardation comes from studies which compare retarded readers with normal readers of the same age. Studies of this sort reveal a number of differences between normal and retarded readers in, for example, language and memory tasks.These studies provide important clues as to the possible causes of the reading problem but they are in themselves logically incapable of demonstrating causes. Effectively, what they show is a correlation between performance on a given task and reading ability, with low reading ability being associated with poor performance and good reading ability with better performance.

Logically there are three possible explanations for correlations of this sort. It may be, as commonly suggested, that a task that is performed badly by retarded readers taps a cause of their reading difficulty. Alternatively, the causal connection could be of the opposite form; their poor performance on a task could be a consequence of not having learned to read. A third possibility is that some deficits may be irrelevant to the retarded readers' difficulties. An example of this might be the delays shown amongst retarded readers in various motor functions and reflexes (see Morrison, 1985, for a description of some examples of this sort). Such delays are in themselves unlikely to cause reading problems. On the other hand, reading problems may depend on some general delay in the maturation of the central nervous system which is indexed by these abnormalities of motor development. This particular line of reasoning is probably of great importance. If retarded readers show neurological immaturity (e.g. Rutter, Tizard and Whitmore, 1970), it seems likely that their performance on many psychological tasks will deviate from that of normal children; but many of these deviations may be quite irrelevant to the cause of their reading problems. This correlational problem has been neglected in many studies.

There are three ways of reducing the ambiguities of such correlational findings. First, one may add a further control group matched for reading achievement and IQ but whose reading is appropriate for their age, i.e. a younger control group (e.g. Bradley and Bryant, 1978). If the retarded readers are inferior on a given measure in comparison to such a group this difference cannot be attributed to their lack of reading experience or ability. The probability of it being related to the cause of the reading problem is therefore increased. Some studies of the spelling patterns of retarded readers have made use of this type of comparison in the past (e.g. Frank, 1936), but paradoxically its advantages have not been appreciated until recently.

The value of comparing groups matched for reading age and IQ but differing in chronological age depends on the kind of results obtained. Such a comparison involves pitting the effects of an inferred deficit amongst the retarded readers against developmental trends in the processes of interest, e.g. various aspects of language development. Negative results will be hard to interpret. Failure to domonstrate a difference on a task between such groups when there was a difference between groups matched for age and IQ but differing in reading age does not show that this arose from differences in reading experience or skill. The difference may reflect a developmental lag in some process which contributes to the retarded readers' difficulties. On the other hand, positive results in such comparisons are important, as they may tell us something about the causes of reading retardation.

The logic behind this type of comparison is in fact exactly the same as in longitudinal studies. In these studies, measurements of certain abilities are made in children before they have started to learn to read. Their progress in reading is then followed and related to these early measurements. If these measures are predictive of later reading failure at least one can be sure that they relate to the causes and not to the effects of such failure. One advantage of studies which match on reading age is that they are easier to conduct than longitudinal studies. On the other hand, longitudinal studies are probably more likely to produce positive results, because they do not involve comparisons of groups of different ages. One disadvantage of longitudinal studies that begin before children start learning to read, however, is that we are unlikely to find a substantial number of children severely retarded in reading in such studies. They are more suitable for exploring factors relating to individual differences in reading achievement than for studying severe reading retardation.

The results of longitudinal studies, or those in which subjects are matched for reading age, still have a major problem of interpretation because any deficits found which relate to reading retardation may be irrelevant to its cause. Interpretations here will be guided by the logical relationship between the task and the process of learning to read. A causal interpretation in such a case can be strengthened by forging explicit links between the observed deficit and the retarded readers' difficulties. This involves looking for evidence in the pattern of reading and writing errors made by these children which implicates the same type of difficulty. For example, if it could be shown that some retarded readers have poor visual memories, the causal status of this finding might be supported by showing that their spelling errors tended to be visually dissimilar to the correct form of the word but similar phonetically (cf Boder, 1973).

The third and most direct (and also the most difficult) way out of this correlational problem is to perform training studies aimed at correcting the inferred deficit and observe the effects of this on reading. Such studies also require careful controls to separate the specific and non-specific influences which may operate. Although difficult to conduct, studies of this type probably provide the most direct route for demonstrating the causes of reading retardation. A problem for these studies, however, is that some deficits which we find in retarded readers' and which seem likely candidates as causes of their reading problem, may not be amenable to improvement by training.

It will be clear from all this that the problems facing us in trying to establish the causes of reading retardation are formidable. Once we accept the idea that different causes may operate in different cases (see below) and that there may be multiple causes that interact in complex ways, the task becomes even more daunting. I will try, therefore, in what follows to assess the likelihood that various findings do tap a cause of the reading problem. The main criterion here will be the logical relationship between the tasks used and the processes involved in learning to read. In order to do this it is necessary to say a few words about the nature of the reading problems seen in retarded readers. Reading is clearly a complex skill and there are a variety of ways in which such a skill might break down. This has been amply demonstrated in recent neuropsychological research with adults whose reading impairments result from brain damage (see e.g. Ellis, 1984). Fortunately, in the case of children with reading retardation, all the evidence is that the problem occurs at an early stage of the process. The clearest difficulty they have is in developing adequate word recognition skills. As a result of this they naturally have difficulty in comprehending what they read, but this can easily be explained as a consequence of their poor word recognition skills. This is not to deny that some children have difficulties in the comprehension of prose that are out of line with their word recognition skills. However, such difficulties are not typical of retarded readers. In fact, Perfetti, Goldman and Hogaboam (1979) found that a story context helped retarded readers more than normal children. This is an important result that makes a lot of sense: if your word recognition skills are weak you should benefit greatly from clues to the identity of a word. This emphasizes the fact that it is the word recognition difficulties of retarded readers that we need to explain. (See Stanovitch, 1986, for further evidence and a discussion of this issue.)

POSSIBLE CAUSES OF READING RETARDATION

Visual problems

Historically, the predominant approach to explaining reading retardation was in terms of visual problems. Cases of reading problems were consistently interpreted in terms of problems of visual memory and perception by pioneers such as Hinshelwood (1895, 1917) and Orton (1937). For many years, theories about visual problems causing reading retardation had an almost hypnotic effect on research in this area.

The most prominent variant of this sort of theory was that retarded readers might have some generalized weakness in perceiving and remembering visual patterns such as words. It is clear that if such a problem existed it would provide a good explanation for difficulties in learning to read. There has been a large amount of research addressed to testing this idea. Most of this research provides a clear answer: for most retarded readers, problems of visual perception and memory are not the cause of their problems. Much of this research has been reviewed in detail before (see, for example, Hulme, 1981; Jorm, 1983; Vellutino, 1979); it will be sufficient here to summarize some of the more prominent findings of the older studies in this area.

Vellutino and his colleagues have demonstrated normal visual memory abilities in retarded readers in several studies. Vellutino *et al.*, (1973) showed Hebrew words to normal and retarded readers and asked them to draw them from memory. Both groups did this equally well, although children who were learning to read Hebrew, not surprisingly, did better than either group. This experiment looked at short-term memory. In a further study, long-term memory for Hebrew letters was assessed by recognition, either immediately or after 24-hour or six-month delays. Once again there were no differences between normal and retarded readers (Vellutino *et al.*, 1975). Retarded readers have also been found to perform normally on visual paired-associate tasks (Goyen and Lyle, 1971; Vellutino, Steger and Pruzek, 1973). The tasks in these studies are demonstrably similar in their visual requirements to learning to read, and yet retarded readers perform normally on them. Taken together, therefore, they argue persuasively against the idea that retarded readers typically have visual problems that cause their reading problems. Quite recently there have been attempts to revive the idea of a visual deficit as a cause of reading retardation using different tasks. We will consider three such attempts in some detail now.

Eye movements

Skilled reading involves the control of complex sequences of eye movements. Eye movements were one of the first aspects of reading to attract interest in the studies of experimental psychologists. It was soon noticed that people who read poorly showed abnormal eye movements (Tinker, 1958). This is a classic example of a correlation being misinterpreted. Unfortunately it was assumed by some that the peculiar eye movements of poor readers were a cause of their reading problems. Training programmes to correct these problems were devised but it soon became apparent that such training was not useful. As Tinker pointed out, however, the peculiar eye movements of the poor readers were a consequence and not a cause of their poor reading.

Recently this old idea about the cause of reading difficulties has resurfaced in a rather puzzling way. Pavlidis (1981) reported that a group of retarded readers showed erratic eye movements when asked to track a series of sequentially illuminated lights. He argued that these disordered eye movements might be a direct cause of the reading problem, or alternatively both the reading and eye movement problems might reflect some underlying 'general sequencing disability'. It is now clear that this alleged problem with the control of eye movements is not a reliable correlate of reading retardation. Three separate studies have failed to replicate Pavlidis's finds. Brown *et al.*, (1983) and Stanley, Smith and Howell (1983) found absolutely no difference in the eye movements of normal and retarded readers when tracking sequences of lights. Most convincingly Olson, Kliegl and Davidson (1983) set out to conduct an exact replication of Pavlidis's study and, as in the other two attempted replications, there was absolutely no difference between the retarded readers' ability to track a sequence of lights and that of normal control children. It seems an inescapable conclusion that, contrary to the original claims of Pavlidis, retarded readers do not have difficulty with such tasks. This is not, of course, to deny that they make peculiar eye movements when reading, but this is a consequence and not a cause of their reading problem. There may be very rare cases of individuals with neurological damage who show grossly abnormal eye movements which interfere with their ability to read (e.g. Pirrozolo and Rayner, 1978). There is absolutely no evidence, however, that a significant number of retarded readers suffer from some basic deficit in the control of eye movements that prevents them from learning to read.

Eye dominance

Since the pioneering work of Orton (1937), ideas about hemispheric dominance have figured large in work on reading retardation. One recent descendant of this tradition has focused on the development of what has been referred to as the dominant or reference eye. This idea concerning the link between the lateralization of visual function and reading retardation was first advanced by Dunlop, Dunlop and Fenelon (1973). To begin with it is necessary to describe their rather complicated 'reference eye test' in some detail.

In this test the child looks down two tubes in an apparatus called a synoptophore. Each eye then has a view of one of two similar slides. In both slides there is a picture of a house with a central front door and the subject is asked to fixate the centre of this door. In one slide there is a small tree to the left of the front door and in the other there is a larger tree to door's right. To begin with the tubes converge and the subject has the impression of a fused image of a single house with a tree on either side of the door in the central two or three degrees of binocular vision.

Following this the tubes are made to diverge, and if this occurs slowly and smoothly most subjects get a strong impression that one of the trees moves towards the door. Fusion then breaks down and two separate images are seen. Now in both slides the position of the tree and the door clearly remain fixed in relation to each other. However, as the tubes diverge the neural signals responsible for monitoring eye movements and eye position indicate that the eyes are no longer in a position consistent with looking at the same object; nevertheless the image on each fovea is still largely the same. There is thus a conflict between retinal and extraretinal signals. It is the resolution of this conflicting information which somehow leads to the perception of apparent movement. The eye whose image remains static is said to be the 'dominant' or 'reference' eye. The neurological basis of this effect is little understood.

Dunlop, Dunlop and Fenelon (1973) studied fifteen retarded readers and and fifteen controls using this procedure and reported that crossed reference, i.e. a reference eye on the opposite side to the preferred hand, was associated with reading retardation. The retarded readers also had a raised incidence of convergence deficiency, defective stereopsis and esophoria. They proposed a causal theory on the basis of these findings, the idea being that the failure to develop an appropriate reference eye leads to perceptual problems which interfere with learning to read. Just why crossed reference should be so crucial in this respect is not clear.

This idea has been pursued by Stein and Fowler (1982). They studied a large group of retarded readers and a matched group of normal children. All the children received ten trials on the Dunlop reference eye test. On the basis of their responses children were classified as showing 'fixed' dominance if the test located the dominant eye on the same side eight or more times out of ten, otherwise the child was said to have 'unfixed' dominance. The results obtained were striking, though different to those of Dunlop *et al*. Fifty (63 per cent) of the retarded readers, compared to only one normal reader, showed unfixed dominance. Contrary to Dunlop *et al*., crossed dominance was less common in the retarded readers than the normals.

Recently Stein and Fowler (1985) have reported an intervention study designed, by occluding one eye, to produce fixed ocular dominance in retarded readers. If such a procedure succeeds in producing stable ocular dominance and this has beneficial effects on the children's reading, this would be very strong evidence in support of a causal link between ocular dominance and reading problems. Unfortunately there are a number of problems with this paper which make such conclusions far from secure.

The basic design of the trial was that a large group of retarded readers were divided into those with fixed and those with unfixed reference. One hundred and one of the 148 retarded readers in the study were deemed to have unfixed reference. Next, some of the children in each of these groups were given plain glass spectacles with the left lens occluded with tape, the remaining children being given the same spectacles without an occluded lens. The children were told to wear the spectacles when reading or doing other close work for the next six months.

It would be desirable in a study of this sort to allocate children to receive the treatment or not at random. This was not done; of the unfixed group roughly 60 per cent received the occluded spectacles whilst in the fixed group only 28 per cent did so. It is hard to see how this happened given the claim that the allocation was done at random. A further very basic difficulty is that we are not informed of the characteristics of the children in these different groups: their ages, reading ages and IQs are not given.

After six months all the children were retested to assess their progress with reading and their ocular dominance. The crucial point is whether occlusion produced stable ocular dominace and whether this led to a significant improvement in reading ability in the children who started out with unfixed dominance. Of those children with unfixed reference whose reference became fixed, reading scores increased 11.6 months in six months. For the remaining children in the unfixed group who remained without a fixed reference (roughly 50 per cent of the group), reading scores increased by only 5.6 months over the same six-month period.

It is obvious that this difference cannot unambiguously be attributed to occlusion. Children have been selected for their improvement on one measure (responding consistently in the reference eye test) and found to increase more on another measure (reading). It is quite conceivable that this group simply learn better than the other children; it is also quite possible that they differed in pertinent ways such as in age, IQ and reading level before any treatment began.

Stein and Fowler try to counter this latter argument by presenting a further *ad hoc* analysis based on two groups of 20 children matched ('as far as possible'; details not given) on initial reading retardation and IQ: one group had received plain spectacles and remained unfixed the other had received occluded spectacles and become fixed. They claim greater increases in reading scores for those in the latter group. This analysis again suffers from the bias of selecting children for performing well on one test and then comparing their performance on another. It also ignores the possibility of age effects.

One final problem concerning this research is the failure of other studies to confirm the association between ocular dominance and reading problems. Bishop, Jancey and Steel (1979) examined the incidence of orthoptic problems, including eye dominance problems, in a large unselected group of eight-year-olds. They found no association between these measures and reading problems. In particular, performance on the reference eye test did not relate to differences in reading ability, although children giving inconsistent responses to this test (equivalent to Stein and Fowler's unfixed children) were of slightly lower IQ.

Essentially the same result has recently been reported in a larger unselected group of 323 eight-year-old children by Newman *et al.*, (1985): rates of unstable ocular dominance did not differ between those with reading and spelling problems and control children. Thus two studies with unselected samples of children do not find any evidence of an association between reading problems and the Dunlop test of ocular dominance.

If problems of ocular dominance do occur in retarded readers they are almost certainly quite rare. Just how rare will take more research to establish clearly. The further and more difficult question of whether such problems are ever a cause of reading retardation is an open one. If they are, it is probably only for a tiny minority of retarded readers.

Brief visual displays

Many studies show that retarded readers have difficulty in dealing with rapid visual displays. An early example of this is in the work of Lyle and Goyen (1975). They looked at the recognition of abstract shapes presented in a tachistoscope to normal and retarded readers. Retarded readers were less accurate in recognizing the forms but only at very brief exposures. There was no difference between the groups at longer exposure durations and both groups were similarly affected by making the discriminations required more difficult.

Two types of experiment have tried to examine this sort of difficulty in more detail. One technique that has been used is backward masking. In these studies a brief presentation of a stimulus that has to be identified is followed by an interfering stimulus (the mask). Typically, retarded readers require longer separations between the stimulus and the mask in order to identify the stimulus correctly than normal children (e.g. O'Neill and Stanley, 1976; Stanley and Hall, 1973). The second technique looks at the temporal integration of successive stimuli when the interval between them is varied. Usually the subject has to judge whether two separate stimuli occurred or just one. The interval required for separation to occur provides an index of visual persistence, i.e. the length of time the first stimulus remains visible. It is common to find that retarded readers show longer visual persistence than normals (Lovegrove, Billig and Slaghuis, 1978; O'Neill and Stanley, 1976; Stanley and Hall, 1973), but it has been suggested that this is only true when stimulation of the same retinal areas occurs (Badcock and Lovegrove, 1981).

In a recent, very careful study, DiLollo, Hanson and McIntyre (1983) investigated this possibility. They found that retarded readers needed longer intervals between the target and mask in two masking studies. They also needed a longer interval to detect separation between two successive straight lines presented in the same location. There was no significant difference, however, in the time interval over which the normal and retarded readers could maintain an image of a matrix formed by successively displayed dots which fell on different retinal locations.

These sorts of results have been taken as evidence of slow information processing by the visual system of retarded readers. This, it has been suggested, is a likely cause of their reading problems (see e.g. DiLollo, Hanson and McIntyre, 1983, pp. 930-1, for an admirably clear statement of this). Such a causal interpretation is clearly going far beyond the evidence presented. These studies involving brief visual displays have all compared retarded readers with normal children of the same age. It is quite possible, therefore, that their results are a product of differences in reading skill and experience. Another relevant point is that similar difficulties with rapid visual displays are also exhibited by mentally retarded children (Thor and Holden, 1969). Furthermore, visual persistence decreases with age in normal children (e.g. Gummerman and Gray, 1972). These observations make it seem likely that difficulties on these sorts of tasks are a sign of an immature or inefficient central nervous system. Retarded readers are more likely than normals to show signs of minor neurological damage or immaturity (Rutter, Tizard and Whitmore, 1970). These differences in visual information processing probably simply reflect this and may be quite unrelated to the cause of reading problems.

Finally, we must ask how plausible it is that these differences cause the reading problem. In many ways such an idea is distinctly implausible. When learning to read, children are not trying to catch fleeting glimpses of words in a tachistoscope; they can look at a word for as long as they need in order to recognize or memorize it. Lyle and Goyen (1975) found that at longer exposure durations retarded readers were indistinguishable from normal readers when asked to recognize forms. This is what we should expect given the findings reviewed above of normal performance in a whole host of other visual memory tasks that do not involve rapid exposures.

In conclusion, there is no evidence that these rapid visual tasks are tapping a cause of the reading problem. The differences revealed are most likely simply an irrelevant correlate of the problem.

Language problems

Impairments in language skills are common in retarded readers. Parental reports show that they often learn to talk later than normal, and in interviews they may show evidence of less complex language than normal children of the same age; it is also common for retarded readers to show higher performance, than verbal, IQ scores (Rutter, Tizard and Whitmore, 1970). The problem, as always, is to show that any particular deficit is causally related to the reading problem, and this problem is acute here. It is quite plausible that language skills may influence learning to read but it is also likely that learning to read in turn affects the development of language skills.

Verbal memory

This is one area of language function that has been investigated a great deal in retarded readers. This is not surprising: learning to read is a massive feat of verbal memory and it is clear that problems in this area are likely causes of reading problems.

Short-term memory

A common measure of short-term memory is digit span: the number of digits a child can repeat in correct serial order immediately after hearing them. As is usual in short-term memory tasks, the person has to remember a small amount of information for a relatively short time, and the order of recall is important. There is ample evidence that retarded readers typically do poorly on digit span tests and other measures of short-term memory (these studies have been reviewed by Hulme, 1981 and Jorm, 1983).

The question is how such memory problems might hinder learning to read. Short-term memory is often held to serve as a working memory system when reading (Baddeley and Hitch, 1974), the idea being that this system is used to keep track of the order of words in phrases and sentences (e.g. Kleiman, 1975). Impairments of short-term memory might, therefore, be expected to lead to problems in the comprehension of prose, particularly when word order is crucial to the meaning. However, as was mentioned earlier, there is no evidence that retarded readers have any particular difficulty with reading prose, over and above that attributable to their difficulties in identifying words.

It is less obvious how short-term memory problems could create difficulties in learning to identify individual words, which is where, it has been argued, the retarded reader's problems lie. One possibility is that these problems lead to difficulties with phonic blending. When decoding a word that is not known, the child must produce a set of possible pronunciations for the letters in the word. These separate sounds must then be blended to produce a possible pronunciation for the word as a whole. Beginning readers can often be heard to go through this process overtly. Short-term memory problems could make this procedure difficult for the retarded reader.

Torgeson *et al.*, (in press) tested this possibility. They compared a group of retarded readers selected for low digit span scores with normal readers and with a group of retarded readers with normal digit spans on a sound-blending test from the Illinois Test of Psycholinguistic Abilities. In this test a series of words and non-words is spoken to the child, one at a time, in segmented form (e.g.'b-a-g' : bag) and the child is asked to say the word. The retarded readers with low spans were very much worse on this task than the normal readers or the retarded readers with normal spans, who did not differ. Retarded readers often do have particular difficulty with phonics, as shown, for example, by their difficulty in reading non-words (e.g. Snowling, 1981, but see below for further discussion of this). It is likely from this evidence that, at least for some retarded readers, their short-term memory problems contribute to these difficulties with phonics.

An alternative explanation for the short-term memory problems of retarded readers is that they are a consequence, and not a cause, of the reading problem. Perhaps learning to read brings improvements in short-term memory. One approach to this is to compare retarded readers with normals of the same reading age. When this is done the groups do not differ on short-term memory tasks (Hulme, 1981; Johnston, 1982). But this may be because of the age differences between the groups.

A better approach is to conduct longitudinal studies, where memory is assessed before children start to learn to read. The evidence from this sort of study on the whole suggests that memory difficulties precede reading difficulties. Jorm *et al.*, (1984) gave a large group of five-year-olds a sentence memory task on entry to school. They tested all the children again on the memory test when they were almost seven and also gave them an IQ and a reading test. Memory scores at first testing correlated with later reading scores when the effects of age and IQ were partialled out. This indicates that good memory scores before learning to read are predictive of later success in reading and is consistent with the possibility of a causal influence of memory ability on reading ability. It is worth noting that the memory test used here, involving sentences, differs from conventional short-term memory tasks, which involve meaningless strings of items. This difference may be important. It could be argued that memory for sentences is a sensible thing to assess and might reasonably be expected to correlate with reading ability. The task is not directly comparable with conventional tests of short-term memory, however, and probably places a greater emphasis on long-term memory and language comprehension skills. However, Mann and Liberman (1984) assessed memory for unrelated strings of words in kindergarten children before they started reading and found that this did correlate with reading scores one year later.

A contrasting claim has been made by Bryant and Bradley (1985) on the basis of their longitudinal study. They assessed short-term memory before children started learning to read and then measured and spelling ability one and a half years later. They did not find a significant correlation between initial memory scores and later reading scores, but they did find that performance on a memory task at the end of the study, after four years in school, correlated with the reading scores at the middle point of their study. They argue that this favours the idea that short-term memory scores are influenced by success in reading, and not *vice versa*.This claim is difficult to assess because no details of the procedures used and the results obtained are given. The reasons for the differences between this study and the Jorm *et al.*, and Mann and Liberman study are not clear. It could be argued that the differences between the sentence task of Jorm *et al.*, and conventional measures of short-term memory are important. Mann and Liberman, however, did use a conventional measure of short-term memory and found that it was predictive of later success in reading.

In conclusion, it seems quite possible that the short-term memory problems commonly found in retarded readers do contribute to their difficulties in learning to read. The most obvious way in which this might come about is because of difficulties with phonic blending. In addition, short-term memory problems may lead to difficulties in holding partially decoded words in mind whilst they are compared with the pronunciations of words retrieved from long-term memory. The idea that short-term memory problems are causally related to reading problems is far from firmly established however. It is clear that there is an association between short-term memory problems and reading problems. The slight inconsistencies in the evidence on this probably reflect the fact, very nicely demonstrated by Torgeson *et al.*, that these problems are not characteristic of all retarded readers. The time would now seem ripe for studies designed to show that this association reflects a causal link between memory problems and reading problems. The natural way to do this would be to conduct training studies which attempt to improve the short-term memory abilities of retarded readers. If such training was effective and led to improvements in reading, this would be good evidence for a causal connection.

Long-term memory

Even if short-term memory problems were of no consequence as causes of reading difficulties, it might still be the case that problems with more durable forms of memory were important. Rather surprisingly, studies of long-term memory in retarded readers are less common that those of short-term memory.

One long-term memory task that has been studied a good deal is paired-associate learning. Here the child has to make an arbitrary association between a stimulus and a response. The most relevant task to learning to read is visual–verbal paired-associate learning. Here the child has to learn a name to go with some visual stimulus (often an abstract shape).The evidence from paired-associate tasks is very clear: when these tasks involve a verbal component, retarded readers almost invariably perform more poorly than normal children of the same age (for a review of these studies see Hulme, 1981).

It is plausible that difficulties of this sort could lead to problems in learning to read. In the early stages of learning to read, children may develop a considerable sight vocabulary simply by learning arbitrary associations between certain patterns of letters and their spoken couterparts. A child who has difficulty with paired-associate learning will have difficulty at this most elementary stage in learning to read. The other major way of learning to read is by phonics. Here the child learns rules relating the letters used to spell words to their constituent sounds. A necessary step for this to happen is that the child learns the sounds of the letters. This again is an example of paired-associate learning, and many retarded readers have profound difficulty in mastering the names and sounds of letters.

Although it is quite plausible that these difficulties could be a cause of reading problems, we do not have any direct evidence that they are. It would be a useful starting point to have some longitudinal studies that looked at the link between paired-associate learning in preschool children and subsequent success in reading. It seems a reasonable bet that variations in this skill would be predictive of subsequent success in reading. In line with this expectation Mann (1985) has found that knowledge of letter names in kindergarten children correlates with their reading scores a year later. A natural next step would be to investigate the possibility of improving such skills by training. However, it is not clear how feasible this would be.

Another task that probably taps a related process to the paired-associate tasks is known as rapid automatized naming (RAN). The classic study of this is by Denckla and Rudel (1976). They gave normal children and retarded readers random lists of objects, colours, letters and numbers to name as fast as possible. The retarded readers were very much slower here and, although the appropriate analysis is not reported, it looks as though the older retarded readers were actually slower than younger normal children of the same reading age. The retarded readers' difficulty here is probably not simply a consequence of their poor reading skill.

It is not clear what types of information-processing operations are responsible for this difference. Each stimulus must be encoded, its name retrieved from long-term memory and the response articulated. A likely candidate for the retarded readers' difficulty here is a problem in retrieving information from long-term memory. This task may therefore provide another index of the long-term verbal memory deficits in these children. Further research will be necessary to pinpoint the nature of this difficulty however.

In summary, long-term verbal memory problems appear quite likely as contributory causes to the reading problems of retarded readers. The case for such a view is far from established however. Further research on this issue is badly needed.

Phonological awareness

In an alphabetic language, sounds in the spoken word are mapped onto letters in the written word. So, in English, the forty or so phonemes are represented by just 26 letters. This is clearly a design of great economy; all the thousands of words in the language can be represented by combinations of just 26 symbols. This economy is only exacted at a price however: in order for this system to be mastered effectively the reader needs an explicit awareness of the sounds of spoken words. This analytic awareness of speech sounds seems much more crucial for learning to read than for learning to talk. There is now a good deal of evidence that awareness of speech sounds is closely related to learning to read.

One of the first studies of this was by Liberman *et al.*, (1977). They gave children a task involving segmenting words into either syllables or phonemes by tapping out the number present in words that they heard. Performance on the phoneme segmentation task before learning to read correlated with later reading ability. Subsequent studies by the Haskins group have confirmed that tests of syllable and phoneme segmentation before reading begins are predictive of later success in reading (Mann, 1985).

The strongest evidence for a link between phonological awareness and learning to read has been produced by Bradley and Bryant. In their first study they compared a large group of retarded readers with normal children of the same reading age and IQ (Bradley and Bryant, 1978). Their task involved asking the children to categorize words according to their sounds. On each trial the children heard four words and had to decide which was the odd one out. In one series the similar words had the same final phoneme (weed, peel, need, deed), in another they shared the same middle phoneme (nod, red, fed, bed) and in the last series they shared the opening phoneme (sun, see, sock, rag). The results were quite striking. The retarded readers were much worse on this auditory task than the normal children, who were some three and a half years younger but read at the same level. This established that retarded readers have difficulty in categorizing words on the basis of their sound and that this difficulty is not simply a consequence of their poor reading skills.

These two studies used different methods of assessing children's phonological awareness and both found a relationship between this skill and learning to read. This association is highly robust, having been obtained in a number of studies. Lundberg, Olofsson and Wall (1981) gave a large group of Swedish children a battery of measures of phonological awareness. They found that these tests were predictive of reading scores a year and a half later. A similar result to this has been obtained by Stanovich, Cunningham and Cramer (1984), who found that a battery of measures of phonological awareness administered before starting to learn to read predicted success in reading one year later. The different tests of phonological awareness were highly intercorrelated, suggesting that they were measuring some common underlying skill.

Bradley and Bryant (1983) set out to test whether difficulties with sound categorization were a cause of reading difficulties. This was a longitudinal study. At the beginning, the sound categorization ability of over 400 four- and five-year-old children was assessed before they started to learn to read. Over three years later their reading and spelling ability and verbal intelligence were assessed. Performance on the sound categorization task was predictive of later reading scores even when measures of intelligence and memory were taken into account.

To try to check that this correlation between early sound categorization skills and reading reflected a causal influence, Bradley and Bryant included a training study. In this study 65 children who initially were poor at sound categorization were split into four groups. One group was trained in sound categorization and a second was additionally taught letter–sound correspondences. There were also two control groups: one group was taught to group words according to semantic categories; the other received no training. After training spread over two years, the group that had been taught sound categorization and letter–sound correspondences was some eight to ten months ahead of the taught control group in reading scores. The group that had only been taught to categorize sounds was about four months ahead of the control group in reading but this difference was not statistically significant. These results fail to clinch the argument for the causal role of sound categorization in learning to read. To prove this would require that the group taught only to categorize words on the basis of their sound was significantly ahead of the group taught to categorize on the basis of meaning. There was a tendency for this to happen but not to a statistically reliable degree. The group taught to categorize sounds and to link letters to sounds did show very impressive improvements but it is difficult to be sure of the source of these gains. A sceptic might argue that this was entirely due to training in letter-sound correspondences. This after all is very directly a part of teaching people to read and spell. It might be that this group's success depends upon having both sound categorization and letter–sound training. But we cannot tell. To establish this would require another group given the letter–sound training alone.

Theoretically, it is easy to see how problems with phonological awareness could lead to problems in learning to read. Problems of this sort will block the development of phonic skills because the child will be unable to see the connection between the way words sound and the way they are spelt. There is a good deal of evidence that retarded readers have particular difficulty in mastering the phonic aspects of reading. There are two basic sorts of evidence here. In some studies retarded readers have been found to have a difficulty in reading non-words, which presumably depend upon the application of phonic rules for their correct decoding, even when they are compared with younger normal readers of the same reading age (Snowling, 1981; Olson *et al.*, 1985). Retarded readers have also been found to be less sensitive to the effects of spelling-to-sound regularity than normal readers of the same reading age (Frith and Snowling, 1983). These findings show that many retarded readers are reading by a different method than normal readers of equivalent reading skill, and this pattern is just what we should expect if their problem reflected an underlying weakness with phonological awareness. Recently some discrepant findings have called the generality of these effects into question. Beech and Harding (1984) and Treiman and Hirsch-Pasek (1985) found equivalent accuracy in reading regular and irregular words and non-words in groups of retarded and normal readers of the same reading age. The reasons for this conflict in results are not entirely clear. The most likely explanation is in terms of the different materials used. Snowling (1981) found that retarded readers were only significantly worse than normal readers at pronouncing complex non-words. Most of the words and non-words used in these other two studies were short and simple. Further research would be needed to test this interpretation.

In summary, the evidence for phonological skills being a cause of reading difficulties is stronger than for any other area we have considered. It remains true, however, that a definite causal connection remains to be established. Bradley and Bryant's work has shown in great detail just how such a connection could be established, and indeed the evidence to date points very strongly towards this connection.

DIFFERENT TYPES OF READING RETARDATION?

Reading is a complex skill and a variety of impairments might lead to delays in its acquistion. So far the discussion has focused on the possible causes of reading retardation that have been proposed and the evidence in favour of them. Implicit in these discussions has been the idea that there may be different causes of reading retardation in different cases. This issue is of immense importance. Different causes are likely to require different treatments. Further research would also be facilitated if more homogeneous groups of children could be reliably identified. However, given the difficulties in establishing causes it is no surprise that so far little can be said with certainty on this issue. We will consider here some of the more prominent suggestions about the possible different groups of retarded readers.

There is a fair degree of unanimity on the likely subgroups of retarded readers. Many different people have suggested that there are two main sources of reading difficulties: language problems and visual problems. One prominent exponent of this idea has been Boder (1973). On the basis of studying reading and spelling patterns she identified three groups: dysphonentic dyslexia, in which there is an inability to develop phonic skills; dyseidetic dyslexia, where there are visual problems with the recognition of words as visual patterns; and a third group of mixed cases who display both types of problem. Mattis, French and Rapin (1975) also drew a distinction between reading problems associated with language problems and those associated with visual problems. In both of these reports reading problems associated with visual problems are claimed to be quite rare.

These putative subgroups are consistent with the evidence that we have considered about the causes of reading retardation. It is usually argued that most cases of reading retardation reflect an impairment of various language skills. In studies which only consider retarded readers as a single group, differences in language skills between retarded and normal readers generally come through strongly. The research reviewed in this chapter has failed to provide any convincing evidence for visual problems being commonly associated with reading problems. This is just what we should expect, however, if such problems only account for a small minority of cases. The existence of a small group of retarded readers whose difficulties reflect some visual problem is quite plausible. The existence of such a group has certainly not been established firmly however.

The studies quoted above are typical of many other more recent studies (e.g. Rourke, 1985) which simply look for correlations amongst different symptoms in groups of retarded readers with varying degrees of statistical sophistication. Logically, such studies are obviously incapable of showing that different subgroups of retarded readers suffer from different underlying causes. We can do little more at the moment than sketch the sort of research strategy which ultimately may lead to firm evidence for different types of reading retardation with different causes.

A good starting point would be with large-scale studies which look in detail at the reading and spelling of retarded and normal readers matched on reading age. We would expect those with language problems to be particularly prone to make phonetically inaccurate spellings and to find it difficult to read non-words. They should also be relatively insensitive to the difference between regular and irregular words when reading words which are not in their sight vocabulary. The visual group might be expected to show complementary error patterns. Their spellings should be phonetically accurate but often visually inaccurate. They should not have any particular difficulty with reading non-words and be sensitive to the difference between regular and irregular words.

These different subgroups would be expected to show corresponding patterns of weaknesses on other measures. So, the language-impaired group might be expected to show poor phonological awareness and verbal memory but intact visual perceptual and memory skills. The visual group on the other hand would be expected to perform normally on measures of language skills but badly on measures of visual perception and memory. Ultimately, if such different subgroups could be reliably identified, it would require some combination of longitudinal and training studies to establish that they really reflected different underlying causes.

HELPING TO OVERCOME THE PROBLEM

One motivation for trying to understand the problems of retarded readers is so that we can help these children overcome their difficulties. If we endorse the conclusion that one source of difficulty for retarded readers is phonological awareness, a natural strategy would be to try to eradicate this deficit. There is now good evidence that such training is effective (e.g. Lewkowicz, 1980) and it probably can improve the reading skills of children who have poorly developed phonological awareness to begin with (Bradley and Bryant, 1983). This leads naturally to the recommendation that these procedures be incorporated into teaching. This evidence from research is consistent with the typical practices of remedial teachers, who make great use of structured phonic teaching which they find effective for retarded readers (e.g. Naidoo, 1981). There is some evidence from controlled studies that such teaching is effective. For example, Gittelman and Feingold (1983) gave a group of retarded readers a systematic programme of phonic teaching and another group an equal amount of extra teaching which was not relevant to learning to read. The group that received the phonic teaching made more progress with reading. The research on phonological awareness gives this approach a rather different emphasis, however, because it indicates that exercises to develop phonological awareness may be necessary for the child to benefit fully from phonic teaching.

One special set of teaching methods which have been particularly influential in the teaching of retarded readers are referred to as multisensory teaching techniques. These involve input of information from several sensory modalities simultaneously. For example, in teaching a child the name of a letter one would instruct them to trace manually around the outline of the letter while looking at the shape and saying the letter name. This involves input from the visual modality (seeing the shape of the letter), the auditory modality (hearing the letter name) and the kinaesthetic modality (the sensation of the finger moving around the letter outline and of the speech movements).

Much of the background to these techniques and evidence for their effectiveness has been reviewed by Hulme (1981). One of the first educators to advocate that tracing or writing movements should precede the learning of reading was Montessori (1915). She constructed a wooden three-dimensional alphabet which she encouraged her pupils to look at and touch 'in the manner of writing'. She also recommended that children trace around sandpaper cutouts of letters and practice writing movements in sand. The rationale behind these exercises was that 'touching the letters and looking at them at the same time fixes the image more quickly through the cooperation of the senses'. Essentially the same kind of suggestion was made by Fernald (1943), who claimed remarkable success in treating children with severe and specific reading difficulties. Fernald's technique involved the teacher writing out a word in large, cursive script. The pupil then traced it with finger contact, saying each syllable as it was traced. This was repeated as many times as necessary until the word could be written without looking at the original copy. Fernald did not have a well-developed theory as to how her method worked, although she did suggest that kinaesthetic cues produced by tracing helped the child to link the spoken and written forms of the word.

Orton (1928) also advocated tracing as an effective method of helping children with reading difficulties. He talked of reading in terms of an associative process between the visual symbol and the verbal label of the letter or word. In his view tracing provided a third sensory channel by which information from the visual and verbal channels could be linked. This theoretical framework was incorporated into a systematic teaching method, similar to that of Fernald but with a greater emphasis on phonics, by Gillingham and Stillman (1956).

Although these methods have a long and venerable history in education, it is only recently that attempts have been made to assess whether they are effective, and if so why. Hulme (1981) looked at the effects of the motor activity involved in tracing on memory for sequences of letters and letter-like forms in retarded and normal readers. He found that tracing improved visual recognition of forms in a short-term memory task. Retarded readers gained a selective benefit from tracing letters and this was attributed to their failure to employ a speech code to memorize the letters. Hulme also found that tracing around triplets of letter-like forms facilitated learning to associate a word with the forms in a paired-associate learning task. Hulme and Bradley (1984) found that simultaneously writing a word and saying the names of the component letters was particularly effective as a method of teaching retarded readers to spell.

It is clear, therefore, that multisensory techniques may be useful in teaching spelling and that the motor activity involved in them has demonstrable effects on memory. A well-developed theory of how such methods work is not yet available. It would appear, however, that the information derived from different sensory inputs leads to the establishment of multiple memory traces and that these help the retarded reader hold information about spelling patterns in memory.

ACKNOWLEDGMENTS

I should like to thank Maggie Snowling for her helpful comments on this chapter.

REFERENCES

Badcock, D., and Lovegrove, W. (1981).The effects of contrast, stimulus duration, and spatial frequency on visible persistence in normal and specifically disabled readers. *Journal of Experimental Psychology: Human Perception and Performance, 7,* 495-505.

Baddeley, A.D., and Hitch, G. (1974). Working memory. In G.H. Bower (Ed.) *The Psychology of Learning and Motivation,* Vol. 8. New York: Academic Press.

Beech, J.R., and Harding, L.M. (1984). Phonemic processing from a developmental lag viewpoint. *Reading Research Quarterly, 19,* 357-366.

Boder, E.M. (1973). Developmental dyslexia: a diagnostic approach based on three atypical reading–spelling patterns. *Developmental Medicine and Child Neurology, 15,* 663-687.

Bishop, D.V.M., Jancey, C., and Steel, A. McP. (1979). Orthoptic status and reading disability. *Cortex, 15* 659-666.

Bradley, L., and Bryant, P.E. (1978). Difficulties in auditory organisation as a possible cause of reading backwardness. *Nature, 271,* 746-747.

Bradley, L., and Bryant, P.E. (1983). Categorising sounds and learning to read: a causal connexion. *Nature, 301,* 419-421.

Brown, B., Haegerstrom-Portnoy, G., Adams, A.J., Yingling, C., Galin, D., Herron, J., and Marcus, M. (1983). Predictive eye movements do not discriminate between dyslexic and control children. *Neuropsychologia, 21,* 121-128.

Bryant, P.E., and Bradley, L. (1985). *Children's Reading Problems.* Oxford: Blackwell.

Denckla, M.B., and Rudel, R.G. (1976). Rapid automatised naming: Dyslexia differentiated from other learning disabilities. *Neuropsychologia, 14,* 471-479.

DiLollo, V., Hanson, D., and McIntyre, J.S. (1983). Initial stages of visual information processing in dyslexia. *Journal of Experimental Psychology: Human Perception and Performance, 9,* 923-935.

Dunlop, D.B., Dunlop, P., and Fenelon, B. (1973). Vision-laterality analysis in children with reading disability: The results of new techniques of examination. *Cortex, 9,* 227-236.

Ellis, A. (1984). *Reading, Writing and Dyslexia.* London: Erlbaum.

Fernald, G.M. (1943). *Remedial Techniques in Basic School Subjects.* New York: McGraw Hill.

Frank, H. (1936). 'Word-blindness' in school children. *Transactions of the Ophthamological Society of the U.K., 56,* 231-238.

Frith, U., and Snowling, M. (1983). Reading for sound in autistic and dyslexic children. *British Journal of Developmental Psychology, 1,* 329-42.

Gillingham, A.M., and Stillman, B.U. (1956). *Remedial Training for Children with Specific Disability in Reading, Spelling and Penmanship,* 5th edn. New York: Sackett & Wilhems.

Gittelman, R., and Feingold, I. (1983). Children with reading disorders I: Efficacy of remediation. *Journal of Child Psychology and Psychiatry,* **24,** 167-92.

Goyen, J.D., and Lyle, J.G. (1971). Effect of incentives on retarded and normal readers on a visual associate learning task. *Journal of Experimental Child Psychology,* **11,** 274-280.

Gummerman, K., and Gray, C.R. (1972). Age, iconic storage and visual information processing. *Journal of Experimental Child Psychology,* **13,** 165-70.

Hinshelwood, J. (1895). Word-blindness and visual memory. *Lancet,* **2,** 1564-1570.

Hinshelwood, J. (1917). *Congenital Word-Blindness.* London: Lewis.

Hulme, C. (1981). *Reading Retardation and Multi-sensory Teaching.* London: Routledge & Kegan Paul.

Hulme, C., and Bradley, L. (1984). An experimental study of multi-sensory teaching with normal and retarded readers. In R.N. Malatesha and H.A. Whitaker (Eds.) *Dyslexia: A Global Issue.* The Hague: Nijhoff.

Johnston, R.S. (1982). Phonological coding in dyslexic readers. *British Journal of Psychology,* **73,** 455-460.

Jorm, A.F. (1983). Specific reading retardation and working memory: a review. *British Journal of Psychology,* **74,** 311-342.

Jorm, A.F., Share D.L., MacLean, R., and Matthews, R. (1984). Phonological confusability in short-term memory for sentences as a predictor of reading ability. *British Journal of Psychology,* **75,** 393-400.

Kleiman, G.M. (1975). Speech recoding in reading. *Journal of Verbal Learning and Verbal Behavior,* **14,** 323-339.

Lewkowicz, N. (1980). Phonemic awareness training: What to teach and how to teach it. *Journal of Educational Psychology,* **72,** 686-700.

Liberman, I.Y., Shankweiler, D., Liberman, A.M., Fowler, C., and Fischer, F.W. (1977). Phonetic segmentation and recoding in the beginning reader. In A.S. Reber and D. Scarborough (Eds.) *Toward a Psychology of Reading.* Hillsdale, N.J.: Erlbaum.

Lovegrove, W., Billig, G., and Slaghuis, W. (1978). Processing of visual contour information in normal and disabled reading children. *Cortex,* **14,** 268-278.

Lundberg, I., Olofsson, A., and Wall, S. (1981). Reading and spelling skills in the first school years predicted from phonemic awareness skills in kindergarten. *Scandinavian Journal of Psychology,* **21,** 159-173.

Lyle, J.G., and Goyen, J.D. (1975). Effect of speed of exposure and difficulty of discrimination on visual recognition of retarded readers. *Journal of Abnormal Psychology,* **84,** 673-676.

Mann, V. (1985). Longitudinal prediction and prevention of early reading difficulty. *Haskins Laboratories: Status Report on Speech and Hearing,* **SR-81,** 105-120.

Mann, V., and Liberman, I.Y. (1984). Phonological awareness and verbal short-term memory: Can they presage early reading success? *Journal of Learning Disabilities,* **17,** 592-599.

Mattis, S., French, J.H., and Rapin, I. (1975). Dyslexia in children and young adults: three independent neuropsychological syndromes. *Developmental Medicine and Child Neurology,* **17,** 150-163.

Montessori, M. (1915). *The Montessori Method.* London: Heinemann.

Morrison, D.C. (1985). *Neurobehavioral and Perceptual Dysfunction in Learning Disabled Children.* Toronto: Hogrefe.

Naidoo, S. (1981). Teaching methods and their rationale. In G. Th. Pavlidis and T.R. Miles (Eds.) *Dyslexia Research and its Application to Education.* Chichester: Wiley.

Newman, S.P., Karle, H., Wadsworth, J.F., Archer, R., Hockly, R., and Rogers, P. (1985). Ocular dominance, reading and spelling: a reassessment of a measure associated with specific reading difficulties. *Journal of Research in Reading*, **8**, 127-138.

Olson, R.K., Kliegl, R., and Davidson, B.J. (1983). Dyslexic and normal readers' eye movements. *Journal of Experimental Psychology: Human Perception and Performance*, **9**, 816-25.

Olson, R.K., Kliegl, R., Davidson, B.J., and Foltz, G. (1985). Individual and developmental differences in reading disability. In T.G. Waller (Ed.) *Reading Research: Advances in Theory and Practice*, Vol. 4. New York: Academic Press.

O'Neill, G., and Stanley, G. (1976). Visual processing of straight lines in dyslexic and normal children. *British Journal of Educational Psychology*, **46**, 323-327.

Orton, S.T. (1928). Specific reading disability-strephosymbolia. *Journal of the American Medical Association*, **90**, 1095-9.

Orton, S.T. (1937). *Reading, Writing and Speech Problems in Children*. London: Chapman and Hall.

Pavlidis, G.Th. (1981). Do eye movements hold the key to dyslexia? *Neuropsychologia*, **19**, 57-64.

Perfetti, C., Goldman, S.R., and Hogaboam, T. (1979). Reading skill and the identification of words in discourse context. *Memory and Cognition*, **7**, 273-82.

Pirrozolo, F.J., and Rayner, K. (1978). The neural control of eye movements in acquired and developmental reading disorders. In H. Avakian-Whitaker and H.A. Whitaker (Eds.) *Advances in Neurolinguistics and Psycholinguistics*. New York: Academic Press.

Rodgers, B. (1983). The identification and prevalence of specific reading retardation. *British Journal of Educational Psychology*, **53**, 369-373.

Rourke, B.P. (Ed.) (1985). *Neuropsychology of Learning Disabilities: Essentials of Subtype Analysis*. New York: Guilford Press.

Rutter, M., Tizard, J., and Whitmore, K. (Eds.) (1970). *Education, Health and Behaviour*. London: Longmans.

Silva, P.A., McGhee, R., and Williams, S. (1985). Some characteristics of nine-year-old boys with general rading backwardness or specific reading retardation. *Journal of Child Psychology and Psychiatry*, **26**, 407-421.

Snowling, M. (1981). Phonemic deficits in developmental dyslexia. *Psychological Research*, **43**, 219-234.

Stanley, G., and Hall, R. (1973). Short-term visual information processing in dyslexics. *Child Development*, **44**, 841-844.

Stanley, G., Smith, G.A., and Howell, E.A. (1983). Eye movements and sequential tracking in dyslexic and control children. *British Journal of Psychology*, **74**, 181-187.

Stanovitch, K.E. (1986). Cognitive processes and the reading problems of learning-disabled children: Evaluating the assumption of specificity. In J. Torgeson and B. Wong (Eds.) *Psychological and Educational Perspectives on Learning Disabilities*. New York: Academic Press.

Stanovitch, K.E., Cunningham, A.E., and Cramer, B.B. (1984). Assessing phonological skills in kindergarten children: Issues of task comparability. *Journal of Experimental Child Psychology*, **38**, 175-190.

Stein, J.F., and Fowler, S. (1982). Diagnosis of dyslexia by means of a new indicator of eye dominance. *British Journal of Ophthalmology*, **66**, 332-336.

Stein, J.F., and Fowler, S. (1985). Effect of monocular occlusion on visuo motor perception and reading in dyslexic children. *Lancet*, July 13, 69-73.

Thor, D.H., and Holden, E.A. (1969). Visual perception of sequential numerosity by normals and retardates. *Journal of Abnormal Psychology*, **74**, 676-681.

Tinker, M. (1958). Recent studies of eye movements in reading. *Psychological Bulletin*, **55**, 215-231.

Torgeson, J.K., Rashotte, C., Greenstein, J., Houck, G., and Portes, P. (in press). Academic difficulties of learning disabled children who perform poorly on memory span tasks. In H.L. Swanson (Ed.) *Memory and Learning Disabilities: Advances in Learning and Behavioral Disabilities*. Greenwich, Conn.: JAI Press.

Treiman, R., and Hirsch-Pasek, K. (1985) Are there qualitative differences in reading behavior between dyslexics and normal readers? *Memory and Cognition*, **13**, 357-364.

van der Wissel, A., and Zegers, F.E. (1985). Reading retardation revisited. *British Journal of Developmental Psychology*, **3**, 3-9.

Vellutino, F.R. (1979). *Dyslexia: Theory and Research*. Cambridge: MIT Press.

Vellutino, F.R., Pruzek, R.M., Steger, J.A., and Meshoulham, U. (1973). Immediate visual recall in poor and normal readers as a function of orthographic–linguistic familiarity. *Cortex*, **9**, 368-384.

Vellutino, F.R., Steger, J.A., DeSetto, L., and Phillips, F. (1975). Immediate and delayed recognition of visual stimuli in poor and normal readers. *Journal of Experimental Child Psychology*, **19**, 223-232.

Vellutino, F.R., Steger, J.A., and Pruzek, J.M. (1973). Inter- versus intra-sensory deficit in paired-associate learning in poor and normal readers. *Canadian Journal of Behavioral Science*, **5**, 111-123.

Yule, W., Rutter, M., Berger, M., and Thompson, J. (1974). Over- and under-achievement in reading: distribution in the general population. *British Journal of Educational Psychology*, **44**, 1-12.

Cognitive approaches to reading
Edited by J. R. Beech and A. M. Colley
© 1987 John Wiley & Sons Ltd

CHAPTER 11

The Alexias

CHRISTINE M. TEMPLE

*Department of Psychology, Royal Holloway and Bedford New College,
University of London and Neuropsychology Unit, Radcliffe Infirmary,
Oxford*

INTRODUCTION

The alexias or acquired dyslexias are reading disorders which are
manifested in previously literate adults as a result of injury or disease.
Often reading is partially preserved and in some cases the disorders reflect
the selective disruption of specific components of the reading process. By
studying cases in detail one can determine the nature of the component
processes. Neuropsychological data can thus aid cognitive psychologists in
their development of normal models of reading. As Caramazza, Miceli and
Villa (1986) state: 'the approach that is used increasingly in the analysis of
cognitive disorders is to formulate a detailed model of the component structure of a particular cognitive system which, when "lesioned" appropriately,
functions in such a way as to generate the patterns of cognitive impairments
observed in brain-damaged patients'(p.37).

A variety of different dyslexic syndromes have been described but most
of the data which have been used in the development of reading models
have arisen from the study of three central dyslexias (Shallice and Warrington, 1980): deep dyslexia, surface dyslexia, and phonological dyslexia.
These three disorders and the theoretical explanations proposed for them
will be the focus of this chapter.

DEEP DYSLEXIA

New interest in studying the acquired dyslexias arose following the description in 1966 of an apparently novel case of acquired dyslexia consequent
upon a penetrating missile wound (Marshall and Newcombe, 1966). The
most striking feature of the performance of the patient, GR, was the

occurrence of semantic paralexias. These errors were found in the reading of sentences, but of more interest, when single words were presented out of context, over half of the reading errors were of this type. The errors ranged from synonyms, e.g. *sick* → 'ill', to responses sharing only one or two semantic features with the stimulus, e.g. *bad* → 'liar'. The reading syndrome exhibited by GR, has since been named deep dyslexia (Marshall and Newcombe, 1973).

Of all the acquired dyslexias, deep dyslexia seems to have captured the imagination of researchers the most. Undoubtedly the intriguing production of semantic errors is responsible. The incidence of this error type to individual words varies from about 5 per cent in some patients, e.g. KF (Shallice and Warrington, 1975), to almost 60 per cent in others, e.g. GR (Marshall and Newcombe 1966, 1973). Ellis and Marshall (1978) have argued that if pairs of English words are randomly selected, 10 per cent of these pairs are semantically related, and the label deep dyslexia should only be applied to patients whose semantic error rate is higher than this.

Most of the other errors made by deep dyslexics fall into one of the following categories: visual errors, where at least half of the letters in the stimulus are found in the response or *vice versa*, e.g. *cheat* → 'chest'; derivational errors (more precisely called morphological errors), where the base lexical item is read correctly and the bound morpheme is dropped, added or substituted, e.g. *children* → 'child'; function word substitutions, e.g. *them* → 'us'; visuo-semantic errors, where stimulus and response share both visual and semantic features, e.g. *question* → 'query'; visual + semantic errors, e.g. *their* → 'earl' (via heir); circumlocutions, e.g. *enemy* → 'I know it . . . something . . . different countries fighting together . . . spy'.

Deep dyslexics show effects of word frequency, word concreteness and word imageability (Richardson, 1975 a,b). Marcel and Patterson (1979) have shown that imageability is more crucial than concreteness. Deep dyslexics also appear to show an effect of part of speech, where nouns are read more easily than adjectives, which are read more easily than verbs. However, it has been shown that this effect is an artefact of imageability differences between verbs, adjectives and nouns (Allport and Funnel, 1981; Nolan and Caramazza, 1982). Whether the difference between the ease of reading content words and the ease of reading function words is also an artefact of imageability effects is unclear.

Patterson (1982) has distinguished between addressed and assembled phonology. Addressed phonology becomes available after a word is recognized. Assembled phonology has no representation in the internal phonological lexicon but is logically necessary to read non-words aloud. Assembling phonology from print is impossible in deep dyslexia. The patients are unable to read pronounceable non-words, e.g. *gip, plag*. Their responses to these stimuli tend to be omissions or lexicalizations, e.g.

plag → 'flag'. Although in lexical decision tasks normal readers take longer to reject non-words that are homophonic with real words, (e.g. *flore*), deep dyslexics do not show this effect (Patterson and Marcel, 1977). Addressing phonology from print is also impaired (Coltheart, 1980a). They are unable to judge, except on the basis of visual similarity, whether printed words rhyme (Marin, Saffran and Schwartz, 1975).

Deep dyslexics can understand more words than they can read aloud correctly. Although it has not been extensively investigated, whether a word can be read aloud may depend on its context (Andreewsky and Seron, 1975; Coltheart, 1980a, Low, 1931). Finally, deep dyslexics always have two associated deficits in addition to impairment of reading (Coltheart, 1980a). They have an impaired auditory−verbal short-term memory which can be detected by poor performance on digit span tests; they are also dysgraphic when writing either spontaneuously or to dictation.

Theoretical explanations

Cognitive process theories

A particularly significant model in cognitive psychology (from which many of the models decribed later have derived) is that of Morton (1969, 1979). In this model, he postulated the existence of so-called 'logogens', or abstract units of word recognition. Each unit corresponds to an individual word (or morpheme) and underlies the perception and production of this word. In reading, two sets of logogens are proposed. One set, called visual input logogens, recognizes the visual representations of words. The units of logogen system have thresholds of activation. When a logogen reaches threshold the word is recognized and transmitted to the cognitive system for assignment of lexico-semantic features, that is, to be assigned 'meaning'. The other logogen set follows the cognitive system and stores representations of the oral pronunciations of words. These are called output logogens. Responses from this system are held in a response buffer prior to output. In addition to this reading route through the semantic system, there is a direct reading route which proceeds directly from input logogens to output logogens, bypassing semantics. In this model, phonological recoding (analysis of the sound pattern of the word) is not essential to the attainment of meaning. In order to read non-words or unfamiliar words a distinct phonological reading route is employed.

In deep dyslexia (Morton and Patterson, 1980) a malfunction of the phonological reading route accounts for the inability to read non-words. The direct route is also broken. Words can only be read via the semantic system, so the patients can only read aloud words for which they understand the meaning. Restricted semantic representations of some words account for visual paralexias, omissions and some misses in lexical decision. Where the semantic code does not uniquely specify an entry in the output logogens, semantic errors result which are not detectable by the patient. Some logogens have heightened thresholds, accounting for other omissions and for those semantic paralexias which the patient can identify as errors. Linguistic ('syntactic') processing is impaired, giving rise to derivational paralexias and function word errors. Additionally there may be difficulty in accessing the response buffer, which is a store where responses are held prior to output. Morton and Patterson's model proposes the largest number of 'functional lesions' in deep dyslexia but it also attempts to account for the widest number of features in deep dyslexia.

A number of theories of meaning have assumed that the element representing the word in the semantic system is associated with a number of features, or predicates. Jones (1985) proposes that in deep dyslexia highly imageable words are read more easily because they have a higher 'ease of predication'. Semantic errors arise when predicates are sufficiently detailed to specify the stimulus word uniquely but nevertheless delimit the correct semantic domain. Ease of predication of words producing semantic errors is significantly less than that of those read correctly and significantly more than that of those not read (Barry, 1984). Visual paralexias arise from the excitation of an adjacent input logogen when the correct input logogen fails to summon a predicate.

Shallice and Warrington (1980) focused on the variability in the error patterns in deep dyslexia and to account for this they posit two subtypes. In each there is an impairment of a phonological reading route (accounting for the failure to read non-words) and one further impairment. The site of the second impairment differs.

In the first subtype, certain classes of visually presented words, for example abstract words, are unable to achieve adequate semantic representations. The semantic unit corresponding to a visually similar, more concrete word then becomes the most strongly activated unit. This unit dominates the semantic representation of the original stimulus thereby producing a visual error. Thus concrete words are read more accurately than abstract words. Furthermore, there are comprehension deficits for abstract words.

In the second subtype, there is an output difficulty from the verbal semantic system. Semantic processing is adequate but the appropriate verbal label cannot be obtained. Semantic errors are thus *nominal* errors. In many types of aphasia, nominal errors, as Shallice and Warrington point out, show only a loose semantic connection between stimulus and response (Lhermitte and Beauvois, 1973). Shallice and Warrington claim that patients with this second form of deep dyslexia make a larger number of semantic errors relative to visual errors than those with the previous form. They consider that one advantage of this subdivision of the deep dyslexias is that it can account for the variation in the incidence of semantic errors between patients. However, they do not explain why they think the patients with the first type of deep dyslexia should make fewer semantic errors than those with the second.

Shallice and Warrington also suggest that there may be a third form of deep dyslexia which results from damage to the verbal semantic memory itself. In addition to damage to the phonological route in reading, these patients would have associative agnosia. Friedman and Perlman's (1982) theoretical interpretation of deep dyslexia is in some ways similar to that of Shallice and Warrington (1980). Friedman and Perlman believe that semantic errors reflect two different underlying disorders. In one disorder, a related but incorrect concept is accessed from the perceptual input of a written word. Naming of this (incorrect) concept will result in paralexic error. The other disorder arises when the correct concept is aroused but an incorrect spoken word is retrieved.

Friedman and Perlman also believe that the disorder is not unique to reading but is part of a more general language-processing deficit. However, this notion can hardly account for the fact that deep dyslexia can occur even when speech is only mildy impaired or is impaired in ways that do not correspond to the reading impairment (e.g. Low, 1931; Sasanuma, 1974; Schwartz, Saffran aand Marin, 1977; Shallice and Warrington, 1975; Yamadori, 1985).

Newcombe and Marshall (1980) conjecture that the semantic system is intrinsically unstable and that peripheral devices (such as grapheme–phoneme conversion reading systems) act as stabilizing mechanisms to prevent errors. They suggest that, in reading, the product of the input logogen system activates not only the correct semantic entry but also a number of semantically related entries in the semantic system. Even minimal phonological recoding (as found in phonological dyslexia) will be sufficient to block semantic errors. In deep dyslexia, they suggest that the patients both are unable to use the grapheme-phoneme conversion system and have an exacerbated amount of instability in the semantic system. In addition, they propose that their patient, GR, is unable to use a phoneme–grapheme conversion (spelling) system, with consequent semantic errors arising in writing to dictation (deep dyslexia).

In their theory, the phoneme–grapheme system is nevertheless quite separate from the grapheme–phoneme system. The underlying orthographic lexical codes used in reading are functionally dissociable from those used in written and spoken spelling.

In contrast to the theory of Newcombe and Marshall (1980), Allport and Funnell (1981) have proposed that the same phonological and orthographic representations are used in grapheme–phoneme conversion and phoneme–grapheme conversion. Input and output phonology are both dependent upon the same underlying representations.

In their model three sets of codes are symmetrically and reversibly interconnected, i.e. cognitive, phonological and orthographic. Deep dyslexia is interpreted as resulting from a functional disconnection between orthographic and phonological codes. In some patients the impairment may be bidirectional. Similar semantic errors are then observed in writing to dictation.

Nolan and Caramazza (1982) also propose that there is one phonological processing system which is used for any process that requires phonological codes. Thus they argue that the deficits observed in deep dyslexia are not modality-specific but can be observed in repetition, writing and, for some aspects, in naming. Although it had been reported that some patients do not have such extensive deficits (e.g. Newcombe and Marshall, 1980), Nolan and Caramazza assume that testing was not stringent enough to reveal the impairment.

Right hemisphere theory

It has been suggested by Coltheart (1980b) and Saffran *et al.* (1980) that the right hemisphere is particularly involved in reading performance of deep dyslexics. In Coltheart's formulation, lexical access activates a set of semantic features corresponding to the word within the right hemisphere semantic system. The semantic information is then passed via the corpus callosum to an output system in the left hemisphere where an entry is selected from the lexicon and a pronunciation retrieved and articulated.

Sometimes there will be small differences between the semantic representation sent from the right hemisphere and the semantic representation of the selected response item in the left hemisphere lexicon. As a result, feature loss semantic errors and function word substitutions may be produced. As a result of the associative organization of the right hemisphere lexicon a number of associatively related words may be activated in response to a stimulus. Sometimes selection from this word set will be incorrect. Incorrect semantic representations will thus be transmitted to the left hemisphere and an associative semantic error will result.

If a word fails to activate sufficiently an entry in the right hemisphere, the subject may use approximate visual access and select an entry with orthographic similarity. A visual error will result. Words which lack semantic richness (poor semantic specification) in the right hemisphere such as abstract and function words will be less likely to be read correctly. Words with the same root morpheme may have the same entry in the semantic system. The right hemisphere is believed to have little or no syntactic processing ability (Zaidel, 1978) and may be unable to select the correct affix to attach to the root morpheme. Derivational errors will result.

Many of the features of deep dyslexia are consistent with the characteristics of the reading system of the right hemisphere. The evidence relating to the reading system of the right hemisphere comes from tachistoscopic studies of normal individuals, investigations of commissurotomy and hemispherectomy patients, and observations of the course of recovery in aphasic patients. This work is reviewed elsewhere (Coltheart, 1980b; Lambert, 1982a,b). In particular, there is evidence that the right hemisphere is unable to convert print to phonology (Zaidel, 1978) and also that the right hemisphere has selective difficulty in processing words of low imageability (Zaidel, 1981). The syntactic skills of the right hemisphere are very limited. There is also some evidence that the right hemisphere is particularly prone to make semantic errors (Zaidel, 1981).

The right hemisphere theory of deep dyslexia is consistent with the uniformity of the syndrome but a difficulty for the theory is the existence of pure alexia. This disorder is often interpreted as a disconnection syndrome with visual areas isolated from left hemisphere language areas. The patients have intact right hemisphere yet are unable to read. Recently, Patterson and Kay (1982) have investigated whether reading comprehension might be superior to oral reading in pure alexia, but they have been unable to reveal any significant degree of reading comprehension prior to the letter-naming strategy that the patients adopt.

Various suggestions have been put forward to account for the reading failure in pure alexia. Brown (1981) has suggested that pure alexias have disturbed function in right hemisphere visual areas. Alternatively, Coltheart (1980b) has proposed that the splenium is necessary for interhemispheric transmission of semantic representations of alphabetically printed words. Since the splenium is intact in deep dyslexia and severed in pure alexia, the reading of deep dyslexics is superior. This explanation is not applicable to all pure alexics, since in some the splenium is intact (Damasio, 1983).

Another criticism of the right hemisphere theory has been raised by Besner (1981, 1983). His experiments with normal subjects suggest that there is no representation in the right hemisphere for words that denote colour nor lexical entries for abbreviations that can be accessed by visual presentation. Deep dyslexics show considerable sparing of the ability to read both colour names and abbreviations. Besner concludes that the right hemisphere account of residual reading abilities seen in deep dyslexia is not a sufficient one.

However, in most cases of deep dyslexia the lesion to the left hemisphere is very large (Marin, 1980). For some patients there appears to be little healthy residual tissue apart from that which resides in the right hemisphere. Landis et al. (1983) present data which show that the larger the lesion to the left hemisphere in aphasia, the higher the incidence of semantic errors in reading performance. In support of the right hemisphere theory of reading in deep dyslexia they suggest that semantic paralexias represent a release of right hemisphere function from the control of the left hemisphere.

Marshall and Patterson (1983) argue that these data are also consistent with a theory of paralexia resulting from 'malfunctioning' as distinct from 'nonfunctioning' of the normal reading path in the left hemisphere. Greater damage simply leads to greater malfunction. The debate on this issue continues (Jones and Martin, 1985; Marshall and Patterson, 1985). It is to be hoped that new imaging techniques may resolve the question since cognitive psychologists seem to have reached stalemate.

It should be noted that not all deep dyslexics have large left hemisphere lesions. Hayashi, Ulatowska and Sasanuma (1985) report a case of deep dyslexia in Japanese in which the responsible lesion is subcortical. They suggest that the 'intact cortex does not function properly if there is an extensive and crucial lesion in the subcortical tissues which are connected to the intact cortex' (p.308).

Recently Seymour and Elder (1986) have described the reading performance of young beginning readers taught with emphasis on the formation of a 'sight vocabulary'. These children, termed logographic readers, had not yet developed phonic skills. They could not read new words and made visual, semantic, visual plus semantic, and derivational errors. Their performance thus paralleled that of deep dyslexia. Some of the children spontaneously began to develop phonic skills over the course of the year studied, others would receive specific instruction later. A small number of developmental dyslexics may never proceed to develop even minimal phonic skills. Johnston (1983) and Siegel (1985) report cases of dyslexic reading which resembles deep dyslexia, although semantic error rate is low. The children described in these studies have very low reading ages and restricted reading skills of any sort. They have no ability to assemble phonology. Thus in some teaching regimes the first words to be learnt rely upon a semantic reading system, with phonological reading being taught later or being spontaneously adopted. For some children this natural development to phonological use fails to be established. However, such children are very rare and probably have a multiplicity of deficits also leading to the failure to develop a large sight vocabulary. Certainly, other children with poor phonological skills attain much higher reading levels (e.g. Temple and Marshall, 1983).

Concluding comments

Deep dyslexic patients make semantic, visual, derivational, visuo-semantic and visual then sematic errors. Their reading is affected by word frequency and imageability and they are unable to read non-words. Theorists agree that they can no longer use a phonological reading system. Morton and Patterson (1980) posit at least five further impairments to account for the constellation of symptoms. Thus they account for many features but their theory is difficult to test. Shallice and Warrington (1980) suggest that there are different types of deep dyslexia: one in which there is difficulty accessing semantic representations and one in which semantic constructs are accessed but cannot be named. Newcombe and Marshall (1980) propose that semantic errors represent an exacerbation of an intrinsic instability in the semantic system which is normally stabilized by phonological recoding. Allport and Funnell (1981) focus on the symmetry of reading and spelling, proposing the same underlying codes in each. Coltheart (1980a) has pointed out that the features of deep dyslexic reading coincide with what is known about the reading capacity of the right hemisphere and suggests that this compensatory reading system is being employed. However, the reading failure of pure alexics who have intact right hemispheres is problematic for this view.

Deep dyslexia created more excitement than the other dyslexias. The syndrome has shown conclusively that much reading can proceed even if the ability to assemble phonology from print is completely abolished. It has stimulated investigation and raised many questions about other components of the reading process. Unfortunately its complicated constellation of features makes it less amenable to distinguishing between different cognitive models than the other dyslexias.

SURFACE DYSLEXIA

Surface dyslexia was first described by Marshall and Newcombe (1973). Many of its features contrast with those of deep dyslexia. Surface dyslexics read words with regular spelling-to-sound patterns more easily than those with irregular spelling-to-sound patterns. A number of errors look as if they have arisen from the logical application of a rule system, e.g. *sweat* → 'sweet; *gnome* → 'ginomy'/gɪnɔɔmeɪ/. These errors are called regularizations (e.g. Coltheart *et al.*, 1983) or valid errors (Temple, 1985a). In some cases the system seems to have failed or only been applied partially. These errors have been called invalid (Temple, 1985a), e.g. *sweat* → 'sweeg'. Visual paralexias are also made but semantic, derivational, visuo-semantic and visual + semantic paralexias are effectively absent. In addition there are often stress errors. Paralexic responses are usually smaller in number than neologistic responses.

Word length in letters or syllables affects ease of reading in surface dyslexia with longer words more prone to produce errors. The effects of rated imageability and frequency, if present, are not large, although both have been observed. In contrast to deep dyslexia, non-words are not harder to read than words. Similarly, function words are not harder to read than content words. Any difficulty reading function words arises from the irregularity of the spelling-to-sound patterns of some long function words, e.g. *enough, although*. Another distinctive characteristic of surface dyslexia is homophone confusion, e.g. *blue–blew*. These words may be read aloud correctly but descriptions of meaning reveal confusion between the pair (Coltheart, 1981).

Theoretical interpretations

Three broad groups of theories have been proposed to account for surface dyslexia. The difference between them is best exemplified by the mechanism which they invoke for the reading aloud of pronounceable non-words. One group of theories (e.g. Newcombe and Marshall, 1980) consider that non-words are read by an abstract process of grapheme–phoneme conversion. The second group of theories (e.g. Shallice and Warrington, 1980) consider that they are read by a conversion system based upon orthographic units which may be larger than the grapheme. (Some writers used the word grapheme to refer to a single letter, but it is used here as it is used by Coltheart (1978), who defines grapheme as the written representation of a single phoneme.) Both of these groups of theories assert that the process of reading non-words is clearly separate and dissociable from a semantically based mechanism of reading which may be used for reading real words. The third group of theories (e.g. Marcel, 1980) consider that this separation is artificial; that there are not *multiple* routes to reading aloud. For these theorists, non-words are read by analogy with the pronunciation of real words. To illustrate and clarify, one theory from each group will be outlined.

Newcombe and Marshall (1981)

Newcombe and Marshall's model of reading is very similar to other contemporary models and owes much to an original formulation of Coltheart (1978). It contains three routes by which a word may be read aloud: a phonological route, a semantic route and a direct route. In surface dyslexia the semantic and direct routes are impaired and reading proceeds predominantly by the phonological route. Words read by this phonological route are parsed into graphemes. These are translated via an abstract set of grapheme–phoneme correspondence rules into phonemes which are then blended together. The response is held in the output buffer and then may be spoken aloud. Surface dyslexics' overreliance on this reading method leads to erroneous reading of words with irregular spellings. However, reading of non-words and function words can be as good as reading content words. Since surface dyslexics do show instances of faulty grapheme–phoneme conversion it must be assumed that the grapheme–phoneme conversion system is itself damaged, unless one considers that such instances result from intrinsic instability.

How does the surface dyslexic who reads via the phonological route decide upon meaning? Marshall and Newcombe (1973) observed that their patient JC defined the words he read in terms of the erroneous response rather than in terms of the stimulus item. Therefore there must be a feedback mechanism from phonological output to the semantic system. The functional impairment in the semantic route must occur earlier than the semantic system itself.

Marshall and Newcombe's theoretical explanation has been criticized by Marcel(1980). He suggests that their explanation will not account for all the data of their first patient JC (Marshall and Newcombe, 1973). Marcel claims that there is evidence of lexical involvement in the reading of JC, with concreteness, part of speech and frequency effects and errors tending to be nouns and to be more frequent than the target. However, for JC, imageability or concreteness effects are fairly mild. With respect to part of speech, JC read 16/20 nouns, 10/20 adjectives and 9/20 verbs. A retest in 1980 (personal communication Freda Newcombe) indicates that 14/20 nouns, 10/20 adjectives and 13/20 verbs were read. There is thus little evidence for a part of speech effect. Marcel also notes that only about one quarter of the errors were neologisms. Thus there was a strong tendency to produce words as responses. The emphasis here may be misleading, since it is the production of a quarter of errors as neologisms which is unusual and requiring explanation, not the preservation of some word production skills. With more justification, Marcel notes that failed or misapplied grapheme–phoneme rules suggested by Newcombe and Marshall cannot fully account for the data of JC. For example, in the error *incense* → 'increase', an /r/ has appeared and an /n/ disappeared. In vowel digraphs often only one vowel is given a realization, e.g. *violent* → 'volent'. Whole syllables are sometimes deleted or added. Marcel's own theoretical account of surface dyslexia will be outlined later.

Shallice and Warrington (1980: Shallice, Warrington and McCarthy, 1983)

Shallice and Warrington assume the lexically stored orthographic-to-sound correspondences are not limited to graphemes, as in the theory of Newcombe and Marshall. They suggest that there are correspondences for various sizes of orthographic unit. These include graphemes, consonant clusters, subsyllabic units, syllables and morphemes. They postulate a *visual-word form* system which can detect letter groups of different sizes and then send information about them to corresponding units in the phonological system. Orthographic units could only exist in the word form system if the letter group corresponding to it actually existed in at least one English word. The units might be restricted to letter groups with functional phonological or semantic correspondence. Letter groups with more than one possible pronunciation would have each distinct pronunciation represented by a separate correspondence rule. These correspondences could differ in strength. Correspondences for different units are achieved serially from left to right.

Finally, Shallice and Warrington assume that, as a result of neurological pathology, when the route is impaired larger units are affected more severely than smaller units. Increasing impairment leads to increased reliance on smaller and smaller units. In surface dyslexia, reliance is on orthographic units which are too small to cope effectively with the notorious irregularity of English orthography. (Shallice and Warrington's model also differs from that of Newcombe and Marshall in that they abandon the direct route and incorporate it into their expanded phonological route.)

Marcel (1980)

Marcel's model differs from those just described in that lexical processes are not separated from the other reading systems. There is only *one* mechanism for converting print to sound. The visual input lexicon is specified for all known words and morphemes. They are coded in terms of a left-to-right description of letters in ordinal positions. This representation is not based on a whole-word *gestalt* description. Each address in the visual input lexicon has a connection to a semantic description and an entry or combination of entries in the output lexicon, or what Marcel calls the aural–oral lexicon. As each letter is encountered in a left-to-right scan it is marked as a possible segment for parsing. Then as each new letter is encountered it is added to the previous letters and a series of ever larger segments is marked, with the previous segments remaining. There are morpheme-sensitive specifications in the visual input lexicon. If the specification for a segment represented as a lexical address is met, then the criterial segment in the letter string is marked, but the grouping internal to that segment is not overriden. Lexical specifications can also override or delete candidate bracketings. In the case of *read*, the potential bracketing of (re) would be overriden since -ad is not a segment which exists as a lexical address and the most satisfactory lexical 'account' of the letter string is thus to treat it as (read).

When a non-word is encountered the same mechanism is employed. It will be segmented by the parser and input–lexical specifications will mark those segments which occur in known words. The segments which are marked will activate all their potential pronunciations and that which is found in the greater number of words will 'win'.

In surface dyslexia, orthographic specifications in the input lexicon for some words have been lost. In addition, it is assumed that a strategy is adopted by the reader such that since the printed letter string is a word, what is pronounced should be recognized by the reader; that is, there should be an entry in the aural–oral lexicon. The lack of specification for a whole word will have two effects. First, the pronunciation cannot be retrieved as a whole and must therefore rely on parsed *segments*. Secondly, primary bracketings in the parsing of the letter string will not be overriden by lexical knowledge, nor will later letters override previous bracketings. The eventual phonology will be affected by the most frequent phonology of the segments parsed in this way, with the constraint that the result is an entry in the aural–oral lexicon. Marcel does permit that, in some cases, the result need not be an entry in the aural–oral lexicon, but he does not specify the circumstances in which this overruling is absent.

By including the strategy that a response should be an entry in the aural–oral lexicon, Marcel can effectively account for all paralexic responses in which there is even moderate resemblance between target and response. What is then of interest is the extent to which Marcel's theory can account for the neologistic responses made by surface dyslexics. Lack of overriding of letter segmentations can account for the removal of the effect of *e* and *i* on *c* and *g*; the removal of the effect of final *e* on vowels preceding the consonant before the *e*; removal of the effect of vowels in digraphs for synthesis to make diphthongs; and the assignment of a phonentic value to silent letters. Since morphemic segments are not overriden one may also get errors of the sort *island* → 'izland' (is + land), *begin* → 'beggin' (beg + in). The retrieval of the most frequent pronunciation for a segment will account for a number of other neologistic responses, e.g. *recent* → /rɔkɛnt/.

Thus Marcel's theory can account for more of the error responses of surface dyslexics than the theory of Newcombe and Marshall (1980). It can account for all paralexic responses and all valid neologistic responses. But, all three groups of theories fail to account for many of the invalid neologistic responses found in the error corpora of surface dyslexics. In none of the above theories is a phonological mechanism specified which would account for the errors: *chair* → 'chaip/t∫eip/, *organisation* → 'organation' /ɔːgəneɪʃən/. Some researchers would explain these errors as emanating from a visual processing stage prior to phonological processing and would call them visual errors. Caramazza, Miceli and Villa (1986) argue that they emanate from a phonological buffer.

Patient variability

Since the original description by Marshall and Newcombe (1973), a number of surface dyslexics have been described whose pattern of deficit is crucially different from that of JC. This has led to the suggestion that surface dyslexia is not one syndrome but a group of syndromes.

Bub, Cancelliere and Kertesz (1985) have described a case of surface dyslexia in which virtually all errors made are valid. 'Reading of exception words is frequently incorrect with the overwhelming majority of errors dictated by inappropriate but valid application of spelling–sound principles' (p.25). Although MP is the 'purest' surface dyslexic reported in that her incidence of invalid errors is minimal, Shallice and Warrington (1980) have reported on cases who make fewer invalid errors than the originally reported case of JC. They have called these cases 'semantic dyslexias' (Shallice, Warrington and McCarthy, 1983.

MS (Newcombe and Marshall, 1985) made errors that were patently rule-bound to the extent that it was possible to predict the errors he would make. When reading individual words aloud MS tended to assign a phonetic value to each letter of the stimulus item, e.g. *shoe* pronounced /sə//h ɔ //e/.

In describing the patient JC, Marshall and Newcombe (1973) noted that comprehension of the printed word was based on the response rather than the original stimulus. It was considered that this pattern of comprehension was characteristic of all surface dyslexics, but recently two patients have been described who do not conform to this pattern. Both patients, BF (Goldblum, 1985) and EST (Kay and Patterson, 1985), sometimes give correct definitions for words that they have read aloud in error. To the word *gauge* EST said 'something about the railway. . . /g ɔ :dz/'. In both patients the incidence of these responses was small.

In order to account for this patient variability Temple (1985a) has proposed an expanded model of the phonological route in which there are three main stages: parser, translator and blender. The parser divides the letter sequence into a number of segments or chunks. The smallest chunk is the grapheme. Larger chunks are polygraphemic. The reader will initially parse into the largest chunks that the rest of the system can deal with. These will be larger in a fluent reader than a child. Kay and Lesser (1985) have provided evidence that normal adults do segment at levels above the grapheme.

If the translator has no representation to translate a chunk it has been sent, a feedback demand will be made for reparsing into smaller units. In the translator each chunk is assigned to one of several valid phonological segments which are graded in probability. The segments are combined in the blender but if the output is not a word a second feedback system may demand retranslation. Surface dyslexia can therefore arise from one or more disorders at any of the three stages and different error patterns will result.

Malfunction of the parser may lead to translation based upon inappropriately small segments, e.g. MS (Newcombe and Marshall, 1985), PT (Kay and Lesser, 1985). Malfunction in the translator may lead to inappropriate selection between alternative valid translations, leading to valid translation errors, e.g. *low* → /laɑ/, or it may lead to mismatches between chunks and segments resulting in invalid errors, e.g. *table* → 'pable'. Malfunctions of the blender may lead to omission or repetition of phonological segments. There are thus four dimensions upon which surface dyslexics may vary: their chunking skills; their ability to choose from multiple valid translations; their ability to use only valid translations; and their ability to blend. Temple (1985a) presents cases of surface dyslexia and explains their relative deficits in terms of malfunction at the different stages.

Marcel (1980) pointed out that a number of normal children who are learning to read display patterns of performance similar to surface dyslexia. These children are more advanced readers than those described by Seymour and Elder (1986) but they seem to overapply their phonic skills prior to the development of larger numbers of orthographic specifications in the input lexicon. Some developmental dyslexics never seem to develop the full range of these specifications in their input lexicon and continue to look like acquired surface dyslexics. The similarity was first pointed out by Holmes (1973) and further case reports have been described (Coltheart et al., 1983; Temple, 1984a, 1985a). The similarity between the data of developmental and acquired surface dyslexics is so great that given two sets of data and asked to determine which was which, it would not be possible. A parallel has also been reported to the pure case of surface dyslexia described by Bub, Cancelliere and Kertesz (1985) in which no valid errors were made. Temple (1984b) reports a case of surface dyslexia in a child with epilepsy where phonic skills were extremely well developed and only valid errors were made. This indicates that an abstract phonological reading route may develop efficiently in relative isolation from semantic systems.

Concluding comments

In surface dyslexia there is overreliance upon phonological reading systems leading to regularity effects and regularization errors. The theoretical explanations differ in the mechanism they propose for reading non-words. Early suggestions of grapheme–phoneme conversion systems (e.g. Coltheart, 1978; Newcombe and Marshall, 1980) were countered by proposals of reading based upon analogy with real words (e.g. Marcel, 1980). Recent theoretical developments have suggested a conversion system based upon larger and more variable graphemic and phonemic units (e.g. Shallice, Warrington and McCarthy, 1983; Temple, 1985a), thus incorporating aspects of both earlier theories. Whichever theory is preferred, surface dyslexia covers a range of reading disorders of varying severity and nature. The mechanisms involved in the phonological reading system have also been addressed with data from the third acquired dyslexia to be discussed: phonological dyslexia.

PHONOLOGICAL DYSLEXIA

Phonological dyslexia is the most recently described of the dyslexic syndromes and its existence was predicted before its appearance. It was argued that if deep dyslexia results from destruction of the phonological route and an additional impairment to the semantic route, then there should theoretically exist a disorder in which disturbance of the phonological route occurred but the semantic route was intact. In this disorder the reading of words should be relatively good but reading of non-words should be impaired. This was confirmed in the first description of phonological dyslexia by Beauvois and Dérouesné (1979). The variation in phonological dyslexia has been reviewed by Sartori, Barry and Job (1984). The salient feature of the disorder is that non-word reading is impaired in relation to word reading. However, there is variation in the extent of this discrepancy. Most phonological dyslexics can read some non-words. Errors to non-words include both visually similar words (lexicalizations) and incorrect non-words. Some phonological dyslexics have been reported to be more successful at reading non-words that are homophonic with real words than pronounceable but non-homophonic non-words. Thus, *floo* is easier than *ploo* (Beauvois and Dérouesné, 1979; Patterson, 1982). The validity of this claim has been questioned: in reported cases, visual similarity to real words has been a confounding factor (Martin, 1982; Patterson, 1982).

Patterson (1982) has suggested that the effect results from the strategy that is used. The patient may locate in his lexical system the word that is most visually similar to the non-word he is trying to read, and then retrieve the pronunciation of this visually similar word. Inadvertently this may result in a correct reading of the non-word. Dérouesné and Beauvois (1985) have shown with the patient LB that, although homophonic non-words are read better than non-homophonic non-words, the effect is significant only when the use of the homphonic strategy has been suggested to the patient. Visual similarity did not affect the patient's performance when the non-words were graphemically simple; if the words were graphemically complex and homophonic to a word, then visual similarity did significantly affect performance.

Just as non-word reading levels vary in phonological dyslexia, so word reading levels also vary. In the main, the level varies for an ability to read from 50 per cent to 100 per cent of test material. These comparisons have limitations since different stimuli for both words and non-words were employed for different patients, even within the same language.

When phonological dyslexics make reading errors they are generally one of two types: derivational (e.g. *weigh* → 'weight', *child* → 'children') or visual (e.g. *camp* → 'cape', *picture* → 'patter'). The incidence of visual and derivational errors in phonological dyslexia varies from case to case. Clearly, in a patient with over 90 per cent accuracy the incidence of either error type must be small. It has been argued that one or other of the error types (derivational or visual) may not be a crucial characteristic of phonological dyslexia

(Funnell, 1983, Patterson, 1982) and that one type (derivational or visual) may be assimilated to the other. Phonic regularization errors (*broad* → 'brode' /broͻd/) of the type characteristic of surface dyslexia (Marshall and Newcombe, 1973) are not found in these patients. In only one case of phonological dyslexia have semantic errors been reported (Funnell, 1983), and here the incidence was extremely small. An occasional error in phonological dyslexia may be classified as visuo-semantic, e.g. *satirical* → sarcastic (Patterson, 1982). The incidence of these errors is also small and they have not been reported for every patient.

Some phonological dyslexics have difficulty reading function words in isolation although in some cases these function word substitutions have a visual component, e.g. WB: *an* → 'and', 'many' (Funnell, 1983); AM: *neither* → 'either', *is* → 'his' (Patterson, 1982). Beatrice (Sartori, Barry and Job, 1984) made substitutions which did not have a visual component. Other phonological dyslexics have been reported to have no difficulty with function words. Since this feature is variable, it cannot be considered a defining characteristic of phonological dyslexia. However, it is possible that even those phonological dyslexics who do not have difficulty reading function words in isolation have extreme difficulty reading function words within text (Kremin, 1985; Shallice, personal communication).

The effects of imageability, frequency, length and regularity have not been thoroughly investigated in most cases of phonological dyslexia. The available data are contradictory. Sartori, Barry and Job (1984) conclude that 'no variables have been a consistent or general effect'. It is possible that for some patients, where effects of linguistic dimensions were not significant, a ceiling effect was operative. Some other specific tests have been carried out on selective patients so their universality cannot be assessed. For example, Beauvois and Dérouesné (1979) found that their phonological dyslexic patient RG was impaired at word reading when stimuli were presented with their letters typed in the reversed order, thus prohibiting global perception, but was not impaired in reading handwritten stimuli.

Finally, although dyslexia and dysgraphia almost always result from lesions to the left hemisphere of the brain, at least three patients with phonological dyslexia have right hemisphere lesions. One of these cases, Leonardo (Job and Sartori, 1984), is right-handed with no familial history of left-handedness. Given that some of these patients have unusual hemispheric organization, some caution may be required in generalizing from their performance.

Theoretical explanations

Dérouesné and Beauvois (1979) considered that the pattern of performance of their patient, RG reflected a disturbance of the lexical reading process, and therefore supported the existence of the postulated non-phonological reading route. Since their patient's speech was normal the phonological processes necessary for speech had to be separate from the phonemic representation used in reading, and as loss of grapheme–phoneme correspondence rules was found in reading without being found in writing, reading and writing were concluded not to be symmetrical activities.

Shallice and Warrington (1980) consider that whereas deep dyslexia is a multiple-component dyslexic syndrome, requiring more than one functional lesion for explanation, phonological dyslexia is a single-component syndrome. They argue that phonological dyslexics have a highly selective deficit involving the assembly of phonology.

Shallice and Warrington, and Beauvois and Dérouesné explain phonological dyslexia in terms of one functional impairment. But they do not address the issue of why phonological dyslexics not only have difficulty reading non-words but also make derivational errors and often have difficulty reading function words, even if only in text. Patterson (1982) has attempted to address the issue via the model of reading proposed by Shallice and Warrington (1980).

Patterson points out that in Shallice and Warrington's (1980) model (outlined in the section on surface dyslexia), short frequent words and frequently occurring subword segments are represented as whole units in the phonological route. She suggests that the most likely candidates for the two classes are function words and affixes. In Shallice and Warrington's model there is only one route in addition to the phonological route. This route involves orthographically based identification of the word which provides access to the word's semantic representation, which in turn addresses phonology in an output lexicon of known words. If this route is not suited to reading function words and bound morphemes (which have a laregely syntactic role) then the only alternative for dealing with these segments will be the phonological system. Patterson suggests that the phonological system is particularly well equipped to provide a code for those segments, a code that would support oral reading and could assist comprehension. Kolers (1966) has indicated that the reading of text, even aloud, appears to be guided by the semantic system, and an increased incidence of function word errors in text is noted even for normal readers, though not to the same degree as in cases of phonological dyslexia.

Patterson suggests that the variability between patients in the degree of function word difficulty (in contrast to their consistent difficulty with derivational endings) may result from the fact that minimal graphemic segmentation is required for reading function words whereas some segmentation is required for reading affixes and non-words. She predicts that patients with a deficit in assembling phonology from print (deep and phonological dyslexics) will invariably have difficulty in reading grammatical morphemes, and that patients with an impairment of reading *via* the semantic system, who therefore rely on the phonological system for reading (surface dyslexics), should never show a selective deficit on grammatical morphemes. Finally, Patterson considers that since phonological dyslexics read fairly well this adds further support to the view that the system for phonological recoding is used very little by normal adult readers. It may be used for items which are deficient in semantic information—function words, non-words, unfamiliar words and names.

Job and Sartori (1984) have discussed Patterson's model in relation to their patient, Leonardo, a phonological dyslexic with a severe inability to read non-words. Yet, he reads aloud and comprehends quite well affixes presented in isolation (even though these are non-words). When presented with non-words formed by a false root morpheme and a real affix he is more accurate in reading the affixes than the false roots. Yet derivational errors are made. Decomposable words are more likely to be wrongly classified in a lexical decision task and misread with decomposition errors. Job and Sartori consider that their results support models like Patterson's in which affix stripping (Taft, 1981) takes place prior to word recognition, but they propose that root morphemes and affixes have separate recognition devices which are both within the semantic route and interconnected. In this they agree with Marshall (1984). Affix substitution (derivational paralexias) and root morpheme substitution (visual paralexias) may both result from the activation of inappropriate logogens, because of inaccurate visual analysis. In order to account for deletion and addition of prefixes, Job and Sartori (1984) suggest that root morpheme recognizers carry greater weight than affix recognizers. Whilst Job and Sartori's model is perfectly valid and supported by several researchers one should note that the patient Leonardo, although right-handed, has dyslexia following injury to the right hemisphere not the left and therefore his reading system may differ from that of normal right-handers.

Newcombe and Marshall (1980) believe that the absence of semantic errors in phonological dyslexia results from the stabilizing effect of the residual, albeit restricted, phonological reading skills. Some support for this hypothesis is provided by the patient WB (Funnell, 1983). WB is the only phonological dyslexic reported who is unable to read any non-words and therefore seems to have no residual phonological reading skills. He is also the only phonological dyslexic who has been observed to make a small number of semantic errors which do not have a visual component.

De Bastiani, Barry and Carreras (in press) have tried to explain phonological dyslexia within the theory of lexical analogy Glushko, 1981, (Henderson, 1982; Marcel, 1980). The impairment is seen in terms of damage to the systems of orthographic segmentation and phonological assembly. De Bastiani described an Italian patient AMM. They argue that

AMM's performance reflected damage to the assembly of lexically activated phonology. This would explain her visual errors to non-words, e.g. *funvo* → 'fungo' (mushroom), and the production of strings of such responses, e.g. *ralgo* → 'salgo, salvo'. They speculate that such strings may include hesitatingly produced, incorrect non-words made of syllables that are derived/assembled from lexically activated phonology (e.g. *tampo* → 'tango, tanpo'). If impairment is also assumed in the process of orthographic segmentation, then the account may extend to the visual and derivational errors made in reading words.

One criticism of lexical analogy theories as explanations of phonological dyslexia has been raised by Funnell (1983). She claimed that orthographic segmentation was intact in her phonological dyslexic patient WB, since he was able to find and pronounce words embedded in non-words (e.g. *alforsut*). Funnell also argued that phonological assembly was intact since WB could repeat separately two syllables of an auditorally presented word, e.g. *forget* → 'for' + 'get'.

Sartori, Barry and Job (1984) also note that WB could orally repeat letter strings that he could not read. They therefore suggest that Funnell's phonological assembly tasks could be performed by an auditory 'arm' of a model of phonological recoding and not a component that is necessarily involved in the assembly of phonology from print.

Bradley and Thomson (1984) have studied non-word reading in their patient PM in more detail. Although only able to read 13 per cent of non-words, when presented with a familiar word (one letter of which was circled) and asked to pronounce the non-word produced by the deletion of the circled letter performance rose to at least 50 per cent. This was true even for items where some assembled phonology had to be constructed as phonemes needed to be changed, not just deleted, e.g. salt/saɒlt/ → sal /sæl/. Barry and De Bastiani (1985) believe that these results are explicable by lexical analogy theory if one proposes that a lexical analogy procedure operates on the basis of simply producing the most common correspondence of orthographic segments as they occur in words.

Developmental dyslexic analogues to acquired phonological dyslexia have also been described (Campbell and Butterworth, 1985; Seymour and MacGregor, 1984; Snowling, Stackhouse and Rack, 1986; 1985b; Temple and Marshall, 1983). Some of these children read individual words comparatively well but testing of phonic skills reveals severe deficits and reading of text exacerbates the production of derivational errors and function word substitutions. Nevertheless the children illustrate that competent levels of reading can be established despite restricted phonological skills.

Concluding comments

Phonological dyslexics are poorer at reading words than non-words. They make visual and derivational errors and some have function word difficulties. Their phonological reading system is impaired, though not completely as in the deep dyslexia. Patterson (1982) suggests that affixes and function words are subword segments processed in the phonological reading route. In contrast, Job and Sartori (1984) suggest that affixes have separate recognition devices within the semantic route. Lexical analogists discuss the data from phonological dyslexia in relation to systems of orthographic segmentation and phonological assembly.

FINAL REMARKS

The psycholinguistic analyses of the acquired dyslexias have given neuropsychologists a better understanding of their patients and have provided cognitive psychologists with evidence for the construction of information-processing models. A basic assumption of these studies is that, when damaged, the brain functions in a way that reflects at least part of its previous cognitive system and is not completely reorganized. Related to this assumption is the concept of modularity (Foder, 1983). A modular organization of brain processes makes evolutionary sense if one module may be modified without the need to reprogramme the full system. Different reading systems have been seen to be dissociable but the extent to which they are intimately interconnected in the normal brain is not yet known.

As Ellis (1985) points out, dyslexic categories contain heterogeneous sets of patients. It is not clear that these categories are discrete entities. Rather, they may represent corner points on a multidimensional array. This may also be true for the developmental dyslexias. Providing cognitive psychologists allow that there may be partial impairment of multiple modules within the system, then the existence of many patients with intermediate features is not problematic. For the neuropsychologist such a state of affairs renders the categories of less clinical utility. Developmental dyslexia provides us with the opportunity to study the dynamics of the changing nature of reading disorders with time. More studies of patients during recovery would provide similarly valuable information. For a full understanding of reading mechanisms cognitive neuropsychologists will need to move beyond static analyses.

REFERENCES

Allport, A., and Funnell, E. (1981). Components of the mental lexicon. *Philosophical Transactions of the Royal Society of London*, **B.295**, 399-410.

Andreewsky, E., and Seron, X. (1975). Implicit processing of grammatical rules in a case of agrammatism. *Cortex*, **11**, 379-90.

Barry, C. (1984). Consistency and types of errors in a deep dyslexic patient. In R.N. Malatesha and H.A. Whitaker (Eds.) *Dyslexia: A Global Issue*. The Hague: Nijhoff.

Barry, C. and De Bastiani, P. (1985). Phonological dyslexia, lexical analogy, and functional models of oral reading: A critique of Bradley and Thomson. *Brain and Language*, **26**, 173-180.

Beauvois, M.F., and Dérouesné, J. (1979). Phonological alexia: Three dissociations. *Journal of Neurology, Neurosurgery and Psychiatry*, **42**, 1115-1124.

Besner, D. (1981). Deep dyslexia and the right-hemisphere hypothesis: What's left? *Bulletin of the Psychonomic Society*, **18**, 176-178.

Besner, D. (1983). Deep dyslexia and the right-hemisphere hypothesis: evidence from the U.S.A and the U.S.S.R *Canadian Journal of Psychology*, **37**, 565-571.

Bradley, V.A., and Thomson, M.E. (1984). Residual ability to use grapheme–phoneme conversion rules in phonological dyslexia. *Brain and Language*, **22**, 292-302.

Brown, J.W. (1981). Review of deep dyslexia. *Brain and Language*, **14**, 383-92.

Bub, D.N., Cancelliere, A., and Kertesz, A. (1985). Whole-word and analytic translation of spelling to sound in a non-semantic reader. In K.E. Patterson, J. C. Marshall and M. Coltheart (Eds.) *Surface Dyslexia*. Hillsdale, N.J.: Erlbaum.

Campbell, E., and Butterworth, B. (1985). Phonological dyslexia and dysgraphia in a highly literate subject: A developmental case with associated deficits of phonemic processing. *Quarterly Journal of Experimental Psychology*, **37A**, 435-477.

Caramazza, A., Miceli, G., and Villa, G. (1986). The role of the (output) phonological buffer in reading, writing and repetition. *Cognitive Neuropsychology*, **3**, 37-76.

Coltheart, M. (1978). Lexical access in simple reading tasks. In G. Underwood (Ed.) *Strategies of Information Processing*. London: Academic Press.

Coltheart, M. (1980a). Deep dyslexia: A review of the syndrome. In M. Coltheart, K.E. Patterson and J.C. Marshall (Eds.) *Deep Dyslexia*. London: Routledge and Kegan Paul.

Coltheart, M. (1980b). Deep dyslexia: A right hemisphere hypothesis. In M. Coltheart, K.E. Patterson and J.C. Marshall (Eds.) *Deep Dyslexia*. London: Routledge and Kegan Paul.

Coltheart, M. (1981). Disorders of reading and their implications for models of normal reading. *Visual language*, **15**, 245-286.

Coltheart, M., Masterson, J., Byng, S., Prior, M., and Riddoch, J. (1983). Surface dyslexia. *Quarterly Journal of Experimental Psychology*, **35A**, 469-495.

Damasio, A.R. (1983). Pure alexia. *Trends in Neurosciences*, **6**, 93-96.

De Bastiani, P., Barry, G., and Carreras, M. (in press). Mechanisms for reading nonwords: Evidence from a case of phonological dyslexia in an Italian reader. In F. Denes, C. Semenza, O. Bisiacchi and E. Andreewsky (Eds.) *Perspectives on Cognitive Neuropsychology*. Hillsdale, N.J.: Erlbaum.

Dérouesné J., and Beauvois, M.F. (1979). Phonological processes in reading: data from alexia. *Journal of Neurology, Neurosurgery and Psychiatry*, **42**, 1125-1132.

Dérouesné, J., and Beauvois, M.F. (1985). The 'phonemic' stage in the non-lexical reading process: evidence from a case of phonological alexia. In K.E. Patterson, J.C. Marshall and M. Coltheart (Eds.) *Surface Dyslexia*. Hillsdale, N.J.: Erlbaum.

Ellis, A.W. (1985). The cognitive neuropsychology of developmental (and acquired) dyslexia: A critical survey. *Cognitive Neuropsychology*, **2**, 169-206.

Ellis, A.W., and Marshall, J.C. (1978). Semantic errors or statistical flukes? A note on Allport's 'On knowing the meaning of words we are unable to report'. *Quarterly Journal of Experimental Psychology*, **30**, 569-575.

Foder, J.A. (1983). *The Modularity of Mind*. Cambridge, Mass: MIT Press/Bradford

Friedman, R.B., and Perlman, M.B. (1982). On the underlying causes of semantic paralexias in a patient with deep dyslexia. *Neuropsychologia*, **20**, 559-568.

Funnell, E. (1983). Phonological processes in reading: new evidence from acquired dyslexia. *British Journal of Psychology*, **74**, 159-180.

Glushko, R.J. (1981). Principles for pronouncing print: The psychology of phonography. In A.M. Lesgold and C.A. Perfetti (Eds.) *Interactive Processes in Reading*. Hillsdale, N.J.: Erlbaum.

Goldblum, M.C. (1985). Word comprehension in surface dyslexia. In K.E. Patterson, J.C. Marshall and M. Coltheart (Eds.) *Surface Dyslexia*. Hillsdale, N.J.: Erlbaum.

Hayashi, M., Ulatowska, H., and Sasanuma, S. (1985). Subcortical aphasia with deep dyslexia: A case study of a Japanese patient. *Brain and Language*, **25**, 292-313.

Henderson, L. (1982). *Orthography and Word Recognition in Reading*. London: Academic Press.

Holmes, J. (1973). Dyslexia: A neurolinguistic study of traumatic and developmental disorders of reading. Unpublished PhD thesis, University of Edinburgh.

Job, R., and Sartori, G. (1984). Morphological decomposition: Evidence from crossed phonological dyslexia. *Quarterly Journal of Experimental Psychology*, **36A**, 433-458.

Johnston, R.S. (1983). Developmental deep dyslexia? *Cortex*, **19**, 133-140.

Jones, G.V. (1985). Deep dyslexia, imageability and ease of prediction. *Brain and Language*, **24**, 1-19.

Jones, G.V., and Martin, M. (1985). Deep dyslexia and the right-hemisphere hypothesis for semantic paralexia: A reply to Marshall and Patterson. *Neuropsychologia*, **23**, 685-688.

Kay, J., and Lesser, R. (1985). The nature of phonological processing in oral reading: Evidence from surface dyslexia. *Quarterly Journal of Experimental Psychology*, **37A**, 39-81.

Kay, N., and Patterson, K.E. (1985). Routes to meaning in surface dyslexia. In K.E. Patterson, J.C. Marshall and M. Coltheart (Eds.) *Surface Dyslexia*. London: Erlbaum.

Kolers, P.A. (1966). Reading and talking bilingually. *American Journal of Psychology*, **79**, 357-376.

Kremin, H. (1985). Routes and strategies in surface dyslexia and dysgraphia. In K.E. Patterson, J.C. Marshall and M. Coltheart (Eds.) *Surface Dyslexia*. London: Erlbaum.

Lambert, A.J. (1982a). Right hemisphere language ability: I Clinical evidence. *Current Psychological Reviews*, **2**, 77-94.

Lambert, A.J. (1982b). Right hemisphere language ability: II Evidence from normal subjects. *Current Psychological Reviews*, **2**, 139-152.

Landis, T., Regard, M., Graves, R., and Goodglass, H. (1983). Semantic paralexia: a release of right hemispheric function from left hemisphere control? *Neuropsychologia*, **21**, 359-364.

Lhermitte, F., and Beauvois, M.F. (1973). A visual–speech disconnection syndrome. Report of a case with optic aphasia, agnosic alexia and colour agnosia. *Brain*, **96**, 695-714.

Low, A.A. (1931). A case of agrammatism in the English language *Archives of Neurology and Psychiatry*, **25**, 556-597.

Marcel, T. (1980). Surface dyslexia and beginning reading: a revised hypothesis of the pronunciation of print and its impairments. In M. Coltheart, K.E. Patterson and J.C. Marshall (Eds.) *Deep Dyslexia*. London: Routledge & Kegan Paul.

Marcel, A., and Patterson, K. (1979). Word recognition and production in clinical and normal studies. In J. Requin (Ed.) *Attention and Performance VII*. Hillsdale, N.J.: Erlbaum.

Marin, O. (1980). CAT scans of five deep dyslexic patients. In M. Coltheart, K. Patterson and J.C. Marshall (Eds.) *Deep Dyslexia*. London: Routledge & Kegan Paul.

Marin, O.S.M., Saffran, E.M., and Schwartz, M.F. (1975). Dissociations of language in aphasia: Implications for normal function. *Annals of the New York Academy of Science*, **280**, 868-884.

Marshall, J.C. (1984). Toward a rational taxomy of the developmental dyslexias. In R. N. Malatesha and H.A. Whitaker (Eds.) *Dyslexia: A Global Issue*. The Hague: Nijhoff.

Marshall, J.C., and Newcombe, F. (1966). Syntactic and semantic errors in paralexia. *Neuropsychologia*, **4**, 169-176.

Marshall, J.C., and Newcombe, F. (1973). Patterns of paralexia: A psycholinguistic approach. *Journal of Psycholinguistic Research*, **2**, 175-199.

Marshall, J.C., and Patterson, K.E. (1983). Semantic paralexia and the wrong hemisphere: A note on Landis, Regard, Graves and Goodlass (1983). *Neuropsychologia*, **21**, 425-427.

Marshall, J.C., and Patterson, K.E. (1985). Left is still left for semantic paralexias: A reply to Jones and Martin (1985). *Neuropsychologia*, **23**, 689-690.

Martin, R.C. (1982). The pseudohomophone effect: the role of visual similarity in non-word decisions. *Quarterly Journal of Experimental Psychology*, **34A**, 395-409.

Morton, J. (1969). Interaction of information in word recognition. *Psychological Review*, **76**, 165-178.

Morton, J. (1979). Word recognition. In J. Morton and J.C. Marshall (Eds.) *Psycholinguistic Series 2*. Cabridge, Mass: MIT Press.

Morton, J., and Patterson, K. (1980). A new attempt at an interpretation, or an attempt at a new interpretation. In M. Coltheart, K.E. Patterson and J.C. Marshall (Eds.) *Deep Dyslexia*. London: Routledge & Kegan Paul.

Newcombe, F. and Marshall, J.C. (1980). Trascoding and lexical stabilization in deep dyslexia. In M. Coltheart, K.E. Patterson and J.C. Marshall (Eds.) *Deep Dyslexia*. London: Routledge & Kegan Paul.

Newcombe, F., and Marshall, J.C. (1981). On psycholinguistic classification of the acquired dyslexias. *Bulletin of the Orton Society*, **31**, 29-44.

Newcombe, F., and Marshall, J.C. (1985). Reading and writing by letter sounds. In K.E. Patterson, J.C. Marshall and M. Coltheart (Eds.) *Surface Dyslexia*. Hillsdale, N.J.: Erlbaum.

Nolan, K.A., and Caramazza, A. (1982). Modality-independent impairment in word processing in a deep dsylexic patient. *Brain and Language*, **16**, 237-264.

Patterson, K.E. (1982). The relation between reading and phonological coding: Further neuropsychological observations. In A. Ellis (Ed.) *Normality and Pathology in Cognitive Functions*. London: Academic Press.

Patterson, K.E., and Kay, J. (1982). Letter-by-letter reading: psychological description of a neurological syndrome, *Quarterly Journal of Experimental Psychology*, **34A**, 411-441.

Patterson, K.E., and Marcel, A.J. (1977). Aphasia, dyslexia and phonological coding of written words. *Quarterly Journal of Experimental Psychology*, **29**, 307-318.

Richardson, J.T.E. (1975a). The effect of word imageability in acquired dyslexia. *Neuropsychologia*, **13**, 281-288.

Richardson, J.T.E. (1975b). Further evidence of the effects of word imageability in dyslexia. *Quarterly Journal of Experimental Psychology*, **27**, 445-449.

Saffran, E.M., Bogyo, L.C., Schwartz, M.F., and Marin, O.S.M. (1980). Does deep dyslexia reflect right-hemisphere reading? In M. Coltheart, K.E. Patterson and J.C. Marshall (Eds.) *Deep Dyslexia*. London: Routledge & Kegan Paul.

Sartori, G., Barry, C., and Job, R. (1984). Phonological dyslexia: A review. In R.N. Malatesha and H.A. Whitaker (Eds.) *Dyslexia: A Global Issue*. The Hague: Nijhoff.

Sasanuma, S. (1974). Kanji versus Kana processing in alexia with transient agraphia: a case report. *Cortex*, **10**, 89-97.

Schwartz, M.F., Saffran, E.M., and Marin, O.S.M. (1977). An analysis of agrammatic reading in aphasia. Paper presented at the International Neuropsychological Society Meeting, Sante Fe.

Seymour, P., and Elder, L. (1986). Beginning reading without phonology. *Cognitive Neuropsychology*, **3**, 1-36.

Seymour, P., and MacGregor, C.J. (1984). Development dyslexia: A cognitive analysis of phonological, morphemic and visual impairments. *Cognitive Neuropsychology*, **1**, 43-82.

Shallice, T., and Warrington, E.K. (1975). Word recognition in a phonemic dyslexic patient. *Quarterly Journal of Experimental Psychology*, **27**, 187-199.

Shallice, T., and Warrington, E.K. (1980). Single and multiple component central dyslexic syndromes. In M. Coltheart, K.E. Patterson and J.C. Marshall (Eds.) *Deep Dyslexia*. London: Routledge & Kegan Paul.

Shallice, T., Warrington, E.K., and McCarthy, R. (1983). Reading without semantics. *Quarterly Journal of Experimental Psychology*, **35A**, 111-138.

Siegel, R. (1985). Deep dyslexia in childhood? *Brain and Language*, **26**, 16-17.

Snowling, M., Stackhouse, J., and Rack, J. (1986) Phonological dyslexia and dysgraphia: A developmental analysis. *Cognitive Neuropsychology*, **3**, 309–339.

Taft, M. (1981). Prefix stripping revisited. *Journal of Verbal Learning and Verbal Behaviour*, **20**, 289-297.

Temple, C.M. (1984a). New approaches to the developmental dyslexias. In Rose, C. (Ed.) *Progress in Aphasiology*. London: Plenum Press.

Temple, C.M. (1984b). Surface dyslexia in a child with epilepsy. *Neuropsychologia*, **22**, 569-576.

Temple, C.M. (1984c). Developmental analogues to acquired phonological dyslexia. In R.N. Malatesha and H.A. Whitaker (Eds.) *Dyslexia: A Global Issue* The Hague: Nijhoff.

Temple, C.M. (1985a). Surface dyslexia: Variation within a syndrome. In K. Patterson, J.C. Marshall and M. Coltheart (Eds.) *Surface Dyslexia*. Hillsdale, N.J.: Erlbaum.

Temple, C.M. (1985b). Reading with partial phonology. *Journal of Psycholinguistic Research*, **14**, 523-541.

Temple, C.M., and Marshall, J.C. (1983). A case study of developmental phonological dyslexia. *British Journal of Psychology*, **74**, 517-533.

Yamadori, A. (1975). Ideogram reading in alexia. *Brain*, **98**, 231-238.

Zaidel, E. (1978). Lexical organisation in the right hemisphere. In P.A. Buser and A. Rouguel-Buser (Eds.) *Cerebal Correlates of Conscious Experience*. INSERM. Symposium No.6. Elsevier, Amsterdam: North-Holland Biomedical Press.

Zaidel, E. (1981). Reading by the disconnected right hemisphere aphasiological perspective. In Y. Zotterman (Ed.) *Wenner-Gren Sympsium on Dyslexia*. London: Plenum Press.

Author Index

Page numbers in italics indicate the reference in full

Subject Index